CIT

From a Survey by I.H.Adams, Assist. U.S.Coast Survey,1858.
with additions from
Smith's Map of Henrico County, 1853.

Prepared at the U.S.Coast Survey Office
A.D.Bache Supt.
1864.

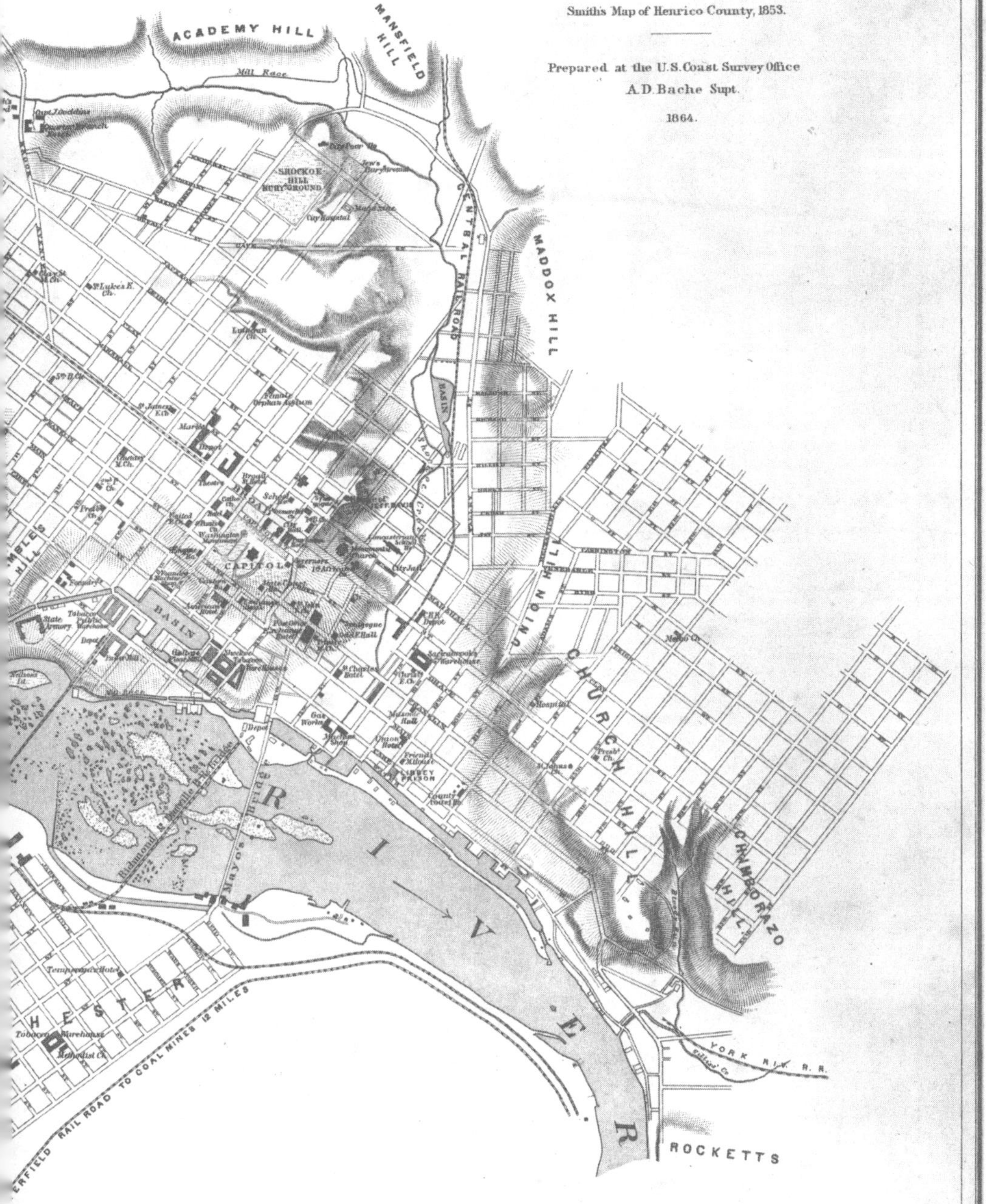

ACADEMY HILL
MANSFIELD HILL
Mill Race
SHOCKOE HILL BURY GROUND
CENTRAL RAIL ROAD
MADDOX HILL
BASIN
CAPITOL
UNION HILL
CHURCH HILL
CHIMBORAZO HILL
LIBBY PRISON
Mayos Bridge
R I V E R
YORK RIV. R. R.
ROCKETTS
HESTER
RAIL ROAD TO COAL MINES 12 MILES

1500 Yards
One Mile

H. Lindenkohl & Chas G. Krebs, Lith.

IRONMAKER TO THE CONFEDERACY

JOSEPH R. ANDERSON
AND THE TREDEGAR IRON WORKS

IRONMAKER TO THE CONFEDERACY

Joseph R. Anderson
and the Tredegar Iron Works

BY CHARLES B. DEW

with a new preface, maps, and illustrations

THE LIBRARY OF VIRGINIA
Richmond • 1999

Library of Congress Catalog Card Number: 99-65775
Standard Book Number: 0-88490-190-4

Library of Virginia, Richmond, Virginia

First edition 1966 by the Yale University Press.

This book is printed on acid-free paper meeting requirements of the American Standard for Permanence of Paper for Printed Library Materials.

Jacket illustration: *The Casting of a Brooke Gun*, by Jack Coggins. Oil on canvas. Courtesy of Ethyl Corporation, Richmond, Virginia.

Jacket design: Sara Daniels Bowersox, Graphic Designer, Library of Virginia.

For my father and my mother

Preface to the 1999 Edition

The republication of a book long out of print provides a welcome occasion for the author to revisit his or her own scholarship. In the case of my study of the Tredegar Iron Works, this process of reappraisal was given an extraordinary boost by the extensive research done by the Valentine Museum in the early 1990s in conjunction with its development of the Tredegar site as a historical park.

Thanks to the superb work done by the Valentine staff and outside consultants, we now have much more detailed and accurate information on the Tredegar property than I managed to piece together when I was doing my original research for *Ironmaker to the Confederacy* back in the 1960s. The discovery of additional photographic evidence and the creation of new maps showing the location and function of Tredegar buildings has brought the physical setting of J. R. Anderson & Company's sprawling industrial complex into much-sharper focus.[1] I am grateful to the staffs of the Valentine Museum and the Library of Virginia for bringing this material to my attention and for giving me full access to this research for the present edition.

Using fire insurance policies and some preliminary archaeological excavations, the Valentine researchers identified two areas of worker housing that I had not been able to locate. One set of buildings—two multiunit brick row-house tenements located along the James River and Kanawha Canal—were identified in fire insurance records as housing for rolling-mill workers and undoubtedly provided lodging for a number of Tredegar slaves. This area of the Tredegar Works is clearly visible in a photograph of the canal side of the property taken in May 1865. The photograph, along with a fuller, more accurate map of the entire Tredegar site, is included in this edition.

1. See Michael S. Raber, Patrick M. Malone, and Robert B. Gordon, "Historical and Archeological Assessment, Tredegar Iron Works Site, Richmond, Virginia," report prepared by Raber Associates, South Glastonbury, Conn., and submitted to the Valentine Museum and the Ethyl Corporation, 1992, and "Archeology at Tredegar Iron Works' Workers' Housing," grant application submitted by the Valentine Museum to the National Endowment for the Humanities, 1994. Copies of both documents are available at the Valentine Museum, Richmond, Virginia. See also Robert B. Gordon, *American Iron, 1607–1900* (Baltimore: Johns Hopkins University Press, 1996), 244–247.

The text of this reprinting is unchanged from the original version published by Yale University Press in 1966. If I had found significant materials containing new details of the Tredegar's history during the Civil War era, I certainly would have incorporated this information in a new edition. But the only substantial amount of new manuscript material that has come to my attention is a collection of Joseph R. Anderson's military papers housed at the Museum of the Confederacy in Richmond. The Eleanor S. Brockenbrough Library at the Museum has some 727 items covering the period from September 1861 to July 1862 when Anderson served as a brigadier general in the Confederate army. Correspondence, orders, circulars, reports, and telegrams relating to his military activities in North Carolina and Virginia are included in this valuable collection. Since Anderson's military service was largely outside the scope of my study, however, I have not used any of the Brockenbrough material in this edition; it was Anderson's *absence* from the Tredegar Works during 1861 and 1862 that largely concerned me. But certainly anyone undertaking a full-scale biography of Anderson would want to consult this collection.

One aspect of the Tredegar story that I found particularly interesting was Anderson's extensive use of slave labor, initially at the Tredegar Works and then during the war throughout his far-flung industrial empire. It was a fascinating but often frustrating subject to tackle. I caught occasional glimpses of the slaves' work in scattered sources such as the single extant payroll from the Civil War period, but the picture I was able to assemble was fragmentary at best. The Tredegar's experience with slave labor simply could not be recaptured in any depth from the surviving company records. And once Anderson broke the strike of his white workers in 1847 and introduced sizable numbers of slave artisans into his rolling mill, the subject of slavery at the Tredegar largely disappeared from the pages of Richmond's newspapers.[2]

There was so much more I wanted to know about industrial slave life and labor after I finished researching the Tredegar project that I subsequently undertook a broader investigation of the use of slave workers throughout the southern iron industry. This quest, in turn, took me to the Valley of Virginia and a Rockbridge County ironworks known as Buffalo Forge. Readers who would like to know more about industrial slavery than I was able to present in the Tredegar book might find of some interest my

2. For recent discussions of the 1847 strike and its aftermath, see Patricia A Schechter, "Free and Slave Labor in the Old South: The Tredegar Ironworkers' Strike of 1847," *Labor History* 35 (1994): 165–186, and Gregg D. Kimball, "Place and Perception: Richmond in Late-Antebellum America" (Ph.D. diss., University of Virginia, 1997), 237, 248–262. Kimball also provides a very perceptive discussion of Anderson's relations with his white labor force in the late antebellum years.

discussion of slave ironworkers and their families in *Bond of Iron: Master and Slave at Buffalo Forge.*[3] In addition, several other very informative books, articles, and dissertations on the use of slaves in southern industry have appeared during the three decades since *Ironmaker to the Confederacy* was originally published.[4]

Finally, I would like to thank Gregg Kimball, John Kneebone, Emily Salmon, Stacy Moore, Sara Bowersox, and the other members of the publications staff of the Library of Virginia for their interest in bringing this book back into print and their help in making this edition possible. I cannot imagine a better or more appropriate publisher for this book than the institution that has done so much to preserve the Tredegar record and to make the company's history accessible to historians. In addition, the Library of Virginia Foundation raised funds for the reprint and received generous support and assistance from Williams College and the Richmond National Battlefield Park, National Park Service, which will open their new visitor center at the Tredegar Iron Works in the year 2000. Soon visitors to Richmond will again be able to have access to both the records and the actual site of the *Ironmaker to the Confederacy.*

Charles B. Dew
Williamstown, Massachusetts
July 1999

3. W. W. Norton & Co., 1994; Norton also published a paperback edition in 1995.
4. See Robert S. Starobin, *Industrial Slavery in the Old South* (New York: Oxford University Press, 1970), Ronald L. Lewis, *Coal, Iron, and Slaves: Industrial Slavery in Maryland and Virginia, 1715–1865* (Westport, Conn.: Greenwood Press, 1979), Suzanne G. Schnittman, "Slavery in Virginia's Urban Tobacco Industry, 1840–1860" (Ph.D. diss., University of Rochester, 1987), T. Stephen Whitman, "Industrial Slavery at the Margin: The Maryland Chemical Works," *Journal of Southern History* 59 (1993): 31–62, John E. Stealey III, *The Antebellum Kanawha Salt Business and Western Markets* (Lexington: University Press of Kentucky, 1993), John Bezis-Selfa, "Forging a New Order: Slavery, Free Labor, and Sectional Differentiation in the Mid-Atlantic Charcoal Iron Industry, 1715–1840" (Ph.D. diss., University of Pennsylvania, 1995), Robert B. Outland III, "Slavery, Work, and the Geography of the North Carolina Naval Stores Industry, 1835–1860," *Journal of Southern History* 62 (1996): 27–56, and Midori Takagi, *"Rearing Wolves to Our Own Destruction": Slavery in Richmond, Virginia, 1782–1865* (Charlottesville: University Press of Virginia, 1999).

Preface to the 1966 Edition

An outstanding historian of the American Civil War was perhaps belaboring the obvious when he wrote almost thirty years ago that "not all the victories of the North . . . were achieved on the battlefield. Some were won in the industrial areas far behind the lines. And of all the industries which contributed to the war effort on both sides, the iron mills unquestionably deserve to be ranked first."[1] Charles W. Ramsdell, a leading authority on the Confederacy, agreed with this assessment and explained, in part, why the immense body of literature dealing with the Civil War contains so little on the industrial history of the Confederate South. "Everybody knows that one of the heaviest handicaps of the Confederates was their lack of mechanical industries to supply their own needs," he wrote. "We can only hope that sometime enough records may turn up to enable the historian to reconstruct their story in greater part than now seems possible."[2]

In 1952 and 1958, the kind of manuscripts sought by Ramsdell were finally made available to the public. In those two years, the Tredegar Company of Richmond, Virginia, deposited with the Virginia State Library probably the most complete set of nineteenth-century Southern business records still in existence. The records of the Tredegar Iron Works, unquestionably the South's most important antebellum and wartime manufacturing establishment, offer an unparalleled opportunity to investigate the industrial history of the region during the Civil War period. These voluminous manuscripts form the primary basis for this study.

The Tredegar records were not a completely untapped mine, however. Kathleen Bruce, a descendant of Joseph Reid Anderson, the Tredegar developer, gained access to the papers and used part of the holdings now at the Virginia State Library in writing *Virginia Iron Manufacture in the Slave Era* (New York, 1930). She devoted a considerable portion of her book to the origins and growth of the Tredegar works before the war and outlined the history of the company between 1860 and 1865 in two concluding chapters. She did not, however, have at her disposal all the records now housed at the State Library or any of the extensive collection of Confederate records in the National Archives. As a result, her pioneering

1. Allan Nevins, *Abram S. Hewitt, With Some Account of Peter Cooper* (New York, Harper & Brothers, 1935), p. 192.
2. Charles W. Ramsdell, "Some Problems Involved in Writing the History of the Confederacy," *Journal of Southern History*, 2 (1936), 138–39.

study into the industrial history of the Old South is in many ways incomplete. She was unable to deal with a number of problems which available manuscript sources now illuminate—the close connection between industrial production and military success or failure, pricing, profits, and the company's relationship with the government, for example. In the space she devoted to the wartime history of the Tredegar, she could do little more than sketch the outlines of the company's expanding activities and she did not carry her work beyond the war.

I believed, after examining the chief manuscript sources, that the major portion of the history of the company during the Civil War era was still untold. Subsequent research confirmed this initial impression. This study attempts to investigate the new avenues opened by these sources and concentrates on the crucial years between 1859 and 1867, when the partnership of J. R. Anderson and Company owned and operated the works. These dates permit an examination of the attitudes of Southern businessmen and the problems facing Southern industry before, during, and after the war. Even more important, these years encompass the period when Tredegar performance had a direct and significant impact on the history of the South and the nation.

I wish to express my deep debt of gratitude to Professor C. Vann Woodward of Yale University, under whose direction the study was undertaken at The Johns Hopkins University. Professor Woodward graciously consented to continue to act as the director of my dissertation after he left that institution, a courtesy for which I am extremely grateful. I have profited greatly from his advice, encouragement, and scholarly example throughout the course of this work. I also wish to thank Professor David Donald of Johns Hopkins and Professor T. Harry Williams of Louisiana State University for giving me the benefit of their detailed knowledge of the Civil War and Reconstruction periods. Their searching criticisms and invariably helpful suggestions have contributed much to whatever merit this study may possess.

Without the assistance of numerous archivists and librarians, this book could never have been written. I particularly want to thank the staffs of the archives and reference divisions of the Virginia State Library for their unfailing patience and good humor in the face of endless requests for aid. They helped make my many months in Richmond both pleasant and rewarding. My special thanks go also to the archivists of the Army and Air Corps Branch of the National Archives, who guided me into a fruitful examination of their magnificent resources. In addition, I wish to thank the staffs of the manuscript divisions of the following institutions for their generous help: the Duke University Library; the Huntington Library; the Library of Congress; the North Carolina Department of Archives and History; the South Carolina Archives Department; the University of North

Carolina Library; the University of Virginia Library; the Valentine Museum, Richmond, Virginia; the Virginia Historical Society; and the Washington and Lee University Library. The Richmond Civil War Centennial Committee and the National Park Service staff at the Richmond Battlefield extended me every courtesy during my stay in Richmond and I wish to thank them for their many kindnesses.

I am grateful to Mrs. John R. Weske of Sandy Spring, Maryland, for kindly allowing me to use a collection of Anderson family letters which were in her possession; these letters have since been deposited in the University of Virginia Library. Mrs. Maureen Carleton deserves a special vote of thanks for a superb typing job. Finally, I owe a particular debt of thanks to the Samuel S. Fels Fund of Philadelphia for a fellowship which enabled me to devote the academic year 1962–63 solely to research and writing.

C.B.D.
Baton Rouge, Louisiana
October 1965

Contents

Illustrations

Tables

Figures

Abbreviations

The following symbols are used in the footnotes to designate manuscript depositories:

DUL	Duke University Library
HL	Huntington Library
LC	Library of Congress
NA	National Archives
NCA	North Carolina Department of Archives and History
SCA	South Carolina Archives Department
UNC	University of North Carolina Library
UVA	University of Virginia Library
VHS	Virginia Historical Society
VSL	Virginia State Library
WLU	Washington and Lee University Library

IRONMAKER TO THE CONFEDERACY

JOSEPH R. ANDERSON AND THE TREDEGAR IRON WORKS

1

The Tredegar Matures

A Richmond newspaper reporter, sent by his editor to tour the Tredegar Iron Works in the fall of 1861, was amazed at what he saw. At the cannon foundry, artisans had charged two large furnaces with iron prior to casting a heavy naval gun while workmen in the adjoining gun mill were laboriously boring out six mammoth coast defense cannon. A crew of picked blacksmiths in a nearby shop was forging wrought-iron carriages for these guns. Artillery projectiles of all calibers, weights, and shapes occupied the lathes and crowded the floor of the machine shop. At the Tredegar rolling mill, the armor plate for the *Merrimack* was rapidly coming off the rolls. As he continued on through the sprawling works, the newspaperman noted over a dozen other separate shops, ranging in size from the massive blacksmith shop, ringing with the almost deafening din of forty active forges, to a small brass foundry where a handful of skilled founders were casting light field artillery. The thousand-man labor force producing iron and munitions for the Confederacy was supplemented by a swarm of carpenters and masons who were just beginning construction of a large new gun foundry and another rolling mill.

At the end of his inspection of the arsenal of the Confederacy, the reporter was impressed and more than a little puzzled. Of one thing he was certain. Without the Tredegar's facilities, it was "difficult to conceive how the South . . . could have successfully resisted the assaults of a neighboring, powerful, and well-appointed enemy." But how had a region so devoid of industrial development acquired such a "vast and magnificent establishment?" The location of the works within the borders of the Southern nation, he concluded, had to be "the result of a special direction, which the enthusiastic patriot may well be excused from regarding as providential." [1]

To answer his question, the enthusiastic newspaperman did not need to

1. Richmond *Enquirer*, Sept. 28, 1861.

look beyond the office of the Tredegar's senior partner, Joseph Reid Anderson. After assuming direction of the company's affairs in 1841, this talented and determined Virginia entrepreneur had transformed the small, debt-ridden foundry and rolling mill into the South's largest and best equipped ironworks. Largely because of Anderson's skilled and forceful leadership during the 1840s and '50s, the Confederacy possessed at the outbreak of the war a superb heavy industrial complex, capable of turning out large quantities of ordnance, munitions, armor plate, and a host of other desperately needed iron products. The Tredegar's performance in the bloody years that lay ahead would unquestionably be a major factor in the success or failure of Southern arms.

I

A growing demand for finished iron products, abundant water power, and ready access to raw materials combined to foster the growth of Richmond's antebellum iron industry. The development of Virginia's state supported system of railroads and canals was unquestionably the most important single factor in Richmond's emergence as a major iron manufacturing center. A railroad boom in Virginia during the 1830s provided the market needed to stimulate the original investment in foundries and rolling mills. Between 1830 and 1837, the state chartered over two dozen railway companies and six of these, representing some three hundred miles of track, began construction during that decade.[2] The James River and Kanawha Canal did not consume spikes or rails but this waterway was almost as important as the railroads to the city's industrial growth. Extended from Richmond to Lynchburg between 1835 and 1840 and opened to Buchanan in 1851, the canal penetrated the Blue Ridge Mountains and tapped the heart of the Virginia iron country. This artery united the blast furnaces of the Valley of Virginia with the coal pits of the Richmond basin at the city built just below the falls of the James. As Virginia's rail system grew, the iron horse joined canal boat teams in hauling pig metal to Richmond's booming factories.

From its inception in the 1830s to the outbreak of the Civil War, the Richmond iron industry underwent a remarkable growth. By 1860, the

2. Charles W. Turner, "The Early Railroad Movement in Virginia," *Virginia Magazine of History and Biography*, 55 (1947), 350–71; Turner, "The Louisa Railroad, 1836–1850," *North Carolina Historical Review*, 24 (1947), 34–57; Angus James Johnston, II, *Virginia Railroads in the Civil War* (Chapel Hill, 1961), p. 4.

Virginia capital had become the iron center of the South. Her foundries, machine shops, forges, and rolling mills, representing a capital investment of more than $800,000, employed over 1,500 free and slave laborers and produced approximately $1,500,000 worth of finished iron.[3]

The Tredegar Iron Works was far and away Richmond's largest and most important iron establishment. The nucleus of the extensive plant that ran day and night to supply the Confederacy in 1861 was a small foundry and a forge and rolling mill built in the mid-1830s on a narrow strip of land between the James River and the Kanawha Canal in southwest Richmond. Late in 1836, Francis B. Deane, Jr., an experienced Virginia blast furnace operator, interested a group of Richmond businessmen in financing construction of an iron works that could exploit the growing local market for railroad iron. Deane and his associates, organized as the Tredegar Iron Company, secured a charter from the state legislature on February 27, 1837, capitalizing the corporation at not less than $175,000 or more than $300,000 and authorizing the owners to manufacture iron and steel in the city of Richmond. On the same day, the legislature approved a charter requested by another group of Richmond businessmen organized as the Virginia Foundry Company. This corporation, also authorized to manufacture iron and steel within the city, was capitalized at a minimum of $50,000 and a maximum of $100,000.[4]

Neither company wasted any time getting into production. The Virginia Foundry Company had actually begun its casting operations in December 1836; the Tredegar forge and mill, built adjacent to the foundry, commenced rolling iron the following May. An engineer trained at the famous iron works at Tredegar, Wales, designed the new mill and it was named after the Welsh works in his honor.[5]

Less than a year after the completion of the Tredegar rolling mill, the directors of the two companies were considering uniting their establishments. Since both concentrated on the production of railroad iron and possessed complementary facilities, the discussions proceeded smoothly. Early in 1838, the Tredegar Iron Company absorbed the neighboring

3. Manuscript returns, Census of Manufactures, 1860, Virginia, VSL.

4. *Journal of the [Virginia] House of Delegates, 1836* (Richmond, 1836), pp. 20–21, 44; *Acts of the [Virginia] General Assembly, 1836–37* (Richmond, 1837), pp. 216–17; Richmond *Enquirer*, Feb. 6, 1838, May 31, 1847; Kathleen Bruce, *Virginia Iron Manufacture in the Slave Era* (New York, 1930), pp. 150–52.

5. Ibid., p. 151

foundry. The General Assembly legalized the merger in March and authorized the Tredegar Company to increase its capital stock to $500,000.[6]

The young company quickly fell on hard times. The panic of 1837 and the ensuing depression sent prices tumbling and brought an abrupt halt to Virginia's railroad boom. The Tredegar was suddenly left without a market. In an effort to sell off large stocks of finished iron and relieve the company of a rapidly mounting debt, the directors in September 1840 appointed one of the original organizers of the Virginia Foundry Company as the Tredegar's commercial agent, with full financial and business responsibility for the company's affairs. When he failed to extricate the corporation from its difficulties, the owners handed the job in March 1841 to a young, ambitious ex-army officer, Joseph Reid Anderson.[7]

II

The man who built the Tredegar works into the industrial giant of the antebellum South had just turned twenty-eight when he assumed control of the company's fortunes. Joseph, the youngest of nine children, was born on a modest farm near Fincastle in the Valley of Virginia on February 16, 1813. His father, William Anderson, the son of a Scotch-Irish immigrant, had moved to the Valley from his native Delaware in 1770 at the age of seven. He spent most of his adult life as a farmer in Botetourt County and built Walnut Hill, the pioneer home of stones and round logs where Joseph and the other Anderson children were born. William's public career included service in a number of positions—state legislator, presiding justice of the county magistrate's court, a state commissioner in charge of James River improvements, county surveyor, and tours of military duty in both the Revolution and the War of 1812. As a sixteen-year-old, he had enlisted in the Revolutionary forces and had fought at Cowpens and in the Shenandoah Valley; during the second war with Great Britain, he had served as a colonel in command of a regiment of Virginia militia at Norfolk. His military background and his strong Presbyterian faith led William to rear his large family with a stern hand. Joseph's Maryland-born mother, Anna Thomas, descended from Episcopalian planter stock, may have softened household discipline somewhat but the

6. Ibid., pp. 152–54; *Acts of the [Virginia] General Assembly, 1838* (Richmond, 1838), pp. 190–91.

7. Bruce, pp. 158–64; Turner, "Early Railroad Movement," pp. 369–70.

children learned the virtues of thrift, honor, and obedience at an early age.[8]

Thrift was acquired, in part, because there was no choice. Young Joseph grew up in circumstances which contributed greatly to the driving ambition he displayed later in life. In 1832, a family friend described William Anderson as being financially "barely in a condition of rural independence" and having "nothing to spare to his son, beyond a maintenance until he passes his minority." [9] Joseph knew he would have to make his own way in the world and he gave early evidence that he intended to do so.

By the time he reached his middle teens, the youngest of the Anderson children had grown into a handsome, intelligent, and quite serious young man. He was a dark-haired youth of erect carriage, almost six feet tall, with broad, slightly sloping shoulders. Intense dark eyes dominated his full face and he possessed prominent cheekbones, a strong jaw, and a wide forehead. Spending his boyhood on a farm in the Blue Ridge country had obviously contributed to his robust health and his love of the outdoors.[10]

With typical Scotch-Irish thoroughness, his father had seen to it that Joseph developed his mind as well as his body. After spending two sessions at the academy of Daniel Stephens in Fincastle, his teacher described him as "tolerably well versed in Geography, Euclid, Algebra, and Arithmetic," and as "a good classical scholar" who needed "only an *opportunity* to become a *very good scholar.*" He was, his mentor believed, "a young Gentleman . . . of good morals, a very good capacity, and of a generous and manly disposition." [11] Joseph's "capacity" was for learn-

8. Bruce, pp. 180–82; Ellen Glasgow, *The Woman Within* (London, 1955), p. 298; Anne Hobson Freeman, "A Cool Head in a Warm Climate," *Virginia Cavalcade, 12* (Winter 1962–63), 10; J. R. Anderson to Thomas Nelson Page, March 18, 1891, Thomas Nelson Page Papers, DUL; Allan Johnson and Dumas Malone, eds., *Dictionary of American Biography* (20 vols. New York, 1928–36), *1,* 268–69. Hereafter cited as *D.A.B.*

9. Robert Craig to Secretary of War [Lewis Cass], Feb. 13, 1832, filed under Joseph Reid Anderson, 121–1832, in Military Academy Applications, Adjutant General's Office, Record Group 94, NA. Hereafter cited as Mil. Acad. Applications, RG 94, NA.

10. James Breckenridge and others to John H. Eaton, Jan. 19, 1830, ibid.; portrait of Anderson by H. Bebie in the possession of Mrs. John R. Weske, Sandy Spring, Md.; photograph of Anderson, LC-B8172-2073, LC.

11. Certificate signed by Daniel Stephens, Jan. 18, 1830, Mil. Acad. Applications, RG 94, NA.

ing, not for strong drink. Following a stage trip in 1832, the young man wrote his brother that he found his fellow passengers "quite agreeable & gentlemanly and what is a little remarkable among all of us & there were 12, not one used ardent spirits." [12]

Although two of his older brothers had taken up the law and the other medicine, Joseph had his heart set on West Point and a military career. He first applied for an appointment to the military academy in 1830, just before his seventeenth birthday. His father enlisted the aid of his congressman, Robert Craig, Governor John Floyd, and nineteen of Botetourt's leading citizens, headed by General James Breckenridge, who signed a letter supporting Joseph's application. Despite this aid, he failed to gain admission to the academy in 1830. A second application the following year, endorsed by Senators John Tyler and Littleton W. Tazewell, was also unsuccessful. Young Anderson had given up hope when Congressman Craig informed him in January 1832 that he had again submitted his name to the Secretary of War. Two months later, Joseph learned that his appointment had gone through.[13]

"I feel desirous to penetrate the unexplored vista that lies before me," Anderson wrote home solemnly as he headed north to West Point in the spring of 1832.[14] He survived the rigorous first summer of drill and soon began building a fine academic record. A fellow cadet who kept a private journal describing the student body noted that Anderson was "one of the most popular men in his class," had "a warm heart and a frank disposition," a "firmness . . . of character," and possessed "a noble and worthy pride." "This Virginian," he thought, "truly merits all the praise that has ever [been] bestowed on the sons of the 'Old Dominion.' " [15] When he graduated in 1836, Anderson held the rank of cadet captain, the highest command in his class, and ranked fourth in a class of forty-nine, having taken a first in artillery and a second in infantry tactics.[16]

12. Anderson to Francis T. Anderson, May 12, 1832, Anderson Family Papers, UVA.

13. Anderson to Eaton, Feb. 1, 1830, to Craig, Jan. 13, 1832, and to Secretary of War [Cass], March 26, 1832; Craig to Eaton, Jan. 29, 1830, Jan. 11, 15, 1831, and to Secretary of War [Cass], Jan. 18, Feb. 13, 1832; J. Floyd to Secretary of War [Eaton], March 22, 1830; Breckenridge and others to Eaton, Jan. 19, 1830; and John Tyler and Littleton W. Tazewell to Eaton, Jan. 15, 1831, Mil. Acad. Applications, RG 94, NA.

14. Anderson to F. T. Anderson, May 12, 1832, Anderson Papers, UVA.

15. Extract from the Journal of Cadet Augustus Porter Allan, 1835, copy, Pegram-Johnson-McIntosh Family Papers, VHS.

16. George W. Cullum, *Biographical Register of the Officers and Graduates of the United States Military Academy* (3 vols. Boston and New York, 1891), *1*, 631; Anderson to

Despite his distinguished four years at West Point, Joseph's youthful enthusiasm for a soldier's life waned during his stay at the academy. The fellow cadet who had described Anderson's manly character in 1835 also thought he had "an ambition sufficiently grasping to ensure a due portion of the world's gifts & honors" and predicted that the Virginian would not stay in the army.[17] The diarist evidently knew Anderson well. Shortly before graduation, Joseph candidly informed his brother that he had no intention of following a military career if he could possibly avoid it. "If I remain in the army I can make out to live. But then I will be literally throwing away my life and here are 4 years of valuable time lost which could perhaps have been improved to much greater advantage in some other way," he wrote. "Those who are not born to fortunes should take every step with a view to its practical benefit." He would prefer a career as a civil engineer but he knew of no such position open anywhere in the country. "The prospect is dreary—clouds and darkness hang around it," he concluded gloomily. "I shall not determine positively till I graduate. I shall then see what I can do and if I can see a prospect of doing any thing I shall not remain in the army." [18]

Anderson failed to find any immediate alternative to military service. Perhaps because there were no openings in the Corps of Engineers, the young West Point graduate went on active duty in July 1836 as a second lieutenant of the Third Artillery. But despite his commission as an artillery officer, he was immediately assigned to engineering duties, first at the Washington office of the Corps of Engineers and then in August at Fort Monroe near Norfolk.[19] These two choice assignments failed to change Joseph's attitude toward an army career. "If I could get there as an engineer I believe I should go direct to the N. West of Indiana to speculate in lands," he wrote his family soon after he arrived at Fort Monroe. But such a move was hardly feasible. So he planned instead to keep "Bachelor's Hall" at Old Point Comfort and hoped that frequent family visits would relieve the boredom of peacetime army duty. "This sort of living

---

L. P. Walker, Aug. 21, 1861, in Field and Staff Officers File, War Department Collection of Confederate Records, Record Group 109, NA. Hereafter this collection, containing most of the extant Confederate archival material, will be cited as RG 109, NA. Anderson graduated one notch above Montgomery C. Meigs, the brilliant Union Quartermaster General during the Civil War.

17. Extract from Allan Journal, VHS.

18. Anderson to F. T. Anderson, March 19, 1836, Anderson Papers, UVA.

19. Cullum, *I*, 631; Bruce, p. 187.

has few charms for me," he admitted. "I sometimes think if I had a right pretty little wife (I mean by that clever in every respect) I should not be quite so lonesome." He jokingly authorized his brother to have a friend "court and if practicable marry one of the beauties in his neighborhood as my proxy and she can accompany him . . . when he comes on." [20] But a handsome bachelor officer certainly did not have to resort to such expedients to find a bride, as Joseph quickly discovered. The post surgeon, Dr. Robert Archer, had several pretty daughters and soon seventeen-year-old Sally and Lieutenant Anderson had begun a courtship.

Their romance was temporarily interrupted when Anderson received his official transfer to the Corps of Engineers and was ordered to Fort Pulaski near Savannah. On his way south, he stopped off in Charleston where friends gave the still rather shy and perhaps somewhat heartsick young officer a very hospitable welcome. "I had several acquaintances here but was resolved not to seek them out because I feel an aversion to company and would have preferred much to have remained in quiet retirement in my room whilst detained here," he wrote his brother in December 1836. But his friends had seen his name on the list of arrivals and had showered him with invitations. Several pleasant days in Charleston convinced him that the South Carolinians were "the most generous, warm hearted, enthusiastick people I have ever seen," but neither Charleston nor Savannah could make him forget Sally Archer back in Virginia. The following spring when he returned to Fort Monroe, he and Sally were married.[21]

The long-awaited chance to enter civilian life came soon after Joseph's marriage. Colonel Claude Crozet, the French engineer in charge of turnpike construction in Virginia, offered him a position as an assistant state engineer to supervise the building of the Valley Turnpike between Staunton and Winchester. Anderson promptly resigned his commission in September 1837 and accepted the post. That fall, he and his bride moved to Staunton where Joseph took up his new duties.[22]

Anderson found his new job attractive for a number of reasons. It got him out of the army, of course, and it took him back to his native Shenandoah Valley. But it also offered him the chance to do something tangible

20. Anderson to F. T. Anderson, Aug. 6, 1836, Anderson Papers, UVA.

21. Anderson to F. T. Anderson, Dec. 6, 1836, ibid.; *History of Virginia* (6 vols. Chicago and New York, 1924), *6,* 631.

22. Bruce, p. 188; Freeman, "Cool Head," p. 10.

to further the economic development of the state. While still at West Point, he had compared the bustling commerce of New York with the languid pace of economic activity in Virginia and decided that internal improvements lay behind Yankee prosperity. "The immense profits of the New York Canals are enriching the state," he noted in 1834. "Every day numberless vessels are seen wafting on the waters of the Hudson to the great city of New York the inexhaustible resources which these very improvements have increased or developed." It was time for Virginians to wake from their economic slumber, start digging canals and building turnpikes, and secure their share of trade and wealth.[23] After settling in Staunton, he supported various canal and railroad projects intended to improve transportation between the Valley and the Tidewater.[24] This interest in internal improvements led him first into the Whig party and then into the Southern commercial convention movement, which was just beginning in Virginia in the late 1830s.

Anderson's political and internal improvement activities soon brought him into contact with the industrialists who had recently inaugurated the Tredegar Iron Works. In November 1838, a meeting of prominent Staunton citizens chose Anderson as one of several delegates to represent the city at a commercial convention scheduled for Norfolk later that month. The Tredegar owners were among the leading participants in a similar local meeting held at Richmond the previous June and several of them also attended the sessions at Norfolk. There they doubtless met the energetic young engineer from the Valley.[25] Anderson's participation in Whig political gatherings, such as the state convention at Richmond in October 1840, again brought him together with the Richmond iron men. These contacts paved the way for his appointment as commercial agent of the Tredegar in March 1841.[26]

Despite the fact that his acquaintance with the iron business was at best casual, Anderson had actively sought the Tredegar post. A number of things prompted him to apply for the position. Certainly the gnawing awareness that he was one of "those who are not born to fortunes," as he had phrased it during his West Point years, was a major consideration. He wanted desperately to achieve material success, something he could

23. Anderson to F. T. Anderson, Dec. 30, 1834, Anderson Papers, UVA.

24. Anderson to F. T. Anderson, Feb. 4, 1838, March 21, 1839, ibid.

25. Bruce, p. 188; Richmond *Enquirer*, June 15, 19, Nov. 16, 20, 1838.

26. Anderson to F. T. Anderson, Oct. 11, 1840, Anderson Papers, UVA; Richmond *Enquirer*, Oct. 6, 9, 1840.

hardly accomplish on his state engineer's salary. The birth of his first child, a son, Archer, in 1838 only increased this desire. "I have made you all in Bot[etourt County] frequent visits," he informed his brother in 1840, "and altho I do not love my brothers and sisters the less, yet I will be obliged *in future* to make them less frequent as it behooves me to devote my time to making a support for my little family." [27] His new job would hold considerable risk but it also offered substantial rewards for success—a 5 per cent commission on sales and 2½ per cent of the company's debt if he settled it successfully. Two of his older brothers, Francis and John, had recently gone into the manufacture of pig iron in the Valley and they may well have advised Joseph to accept the job and given him some financial aid to facilitate the move. In addition, Anderson and his wife had a number of good friends in Richmond so their introduction to the city's social life would be smooth. All these factors pointed toward the Tredegar Iron Works and a new life in the Virginia capital.[28]

III

With railroad construction at a standstill in Virginia, Joseph's first move as commercial agent was to secure a market for Tredegar iron with the Federal government. He successfully negotiated a contract with the navy for chain cable, shot, and shell which gave the company some immediate financial relief. By the end of 1842, Anderson had sold the government almost $90,000 worth of iron and his success in developing this market encouraged him to embark on an ambitious new venture. Late in 1841, he asked the Tredegar owners for authorization to erect the furnaces, cranes, lathes, and other equipment necessary for casting heavy ordnance. The directors, impressed by their enterprising commercial agent's ability to secure military contracts, agreed and Anderson promptly obtained a naval order for one hundred cannon in 1842.[29]

While these pieces were being cast and bored, Anderson pressed for more government orders. "I have been in Washington nearly a fortnight," he informed his brother John in April 1843, but he had found that the ordnance bureaus had few guns to give out. The army would probably order fifty cannon from the Tredegar but an additional navy requisition

27. Anderson to F. T. Anderson, Jan. 24, 1840, Anderson Papers, UVA.

28. Anderson to F. T. Anderson, Nov. 24, 1837, July 22, 1841, Sept. 28, 1842, ibid.; Bruce, pp. 160–65, 188–89.

29. Ibid., pp. 190–91.

was doubtful. The young entrepreneur had therefore directed most of his attention to developing yet another area of manufacture. "I have been endeavoring to procure the building of Iron Steamers for the Govt.," he continued, "and there being four to be contracted for whilst I was there I proposed for the Tredegar Company to build one or more." When he learned that all four vessels had gone to Northern shipbuilders, Anderson made a hurried call on the White House. "I remonstrated with Mr. Tyler against it and still hope to get him to order one to be built here." "The President only wants a little persuasion to order one to be built here," Anderson went on, "and if he does not the north will have the start and greatly the advantage over us as they will have all the experience when the next parcel are put under contract." He urged his brothers "and every man interested in Iron" to write the President and urge Richmond's case. "I will either go back in a few days or send some one to Wash^{n} to push this matter and your letters w^{d} do much good," he concluded.[30]

Anderson soon had to rush back to Washington but for something much more urgent than lobbying for an iron steamer contract. In the summer of 1843, his attempts to establish a permanent government market for Tredegar ordnance received a major setback. The Navy Department, after accepting sixty of the one hundred cannon ordered in 1842, rejected the final forty when five pieces burst during test firings. Anderson tried strenuously but without success to persuade the navy to accept the undamaged tubes and also attempted to learn where his production methods had failed. Experiments with various brands of high quality Virginia charcoal pig iron and different types of coal soon revealed what seemed to be an ideal combination for cannon—Cloverdale and Grace iron, produced by two Botetourt County furnaces owned by his brother John, and Black Heath coal from pits near Richmond. Using this combination, Tredegar workmen cast test pieces which Anderson hoped would persuade government officials to give the Richmond firm another chance.[31]

This crisis also brought Anderson's difficulties with the Tredegar directors to a head. The ambitious young commercial agent had already evidenced some dissatisfaction with the specifications of his position. In February 1843, he had obtained a guarantee from the owners that he would be indemnified for any advances, engagements, or liabilities he made in behalf of the company. But this did not satisfy Anderson's major

30. Anderson to John T. Anderson, April 30, 1843, Anderson Papers, UVA.
31. Bruce, pp. 192–94.

complaint—undue interference by the directors in his handling of the company's technical as well as business affairs. The navy's rejection of the forty cannon prompted him to press for a major change in his arrangement with the stockholders. In November 1843, he leased the entire plant for five years at an annual rent of $8,000. His brother John, who owned the two Valley furnaces that provided Joseph with gun metal, loaned him enough money to complete the transaction. "Whatever may be the result of the change in my business to myself (and I have no fears of its being profitable) it will certainly be beneficial to you," Joseph informed his brother in late November, "as I shall always be disposed to give you the best price I can afford for the whole of your Iron." "Besides I will now have no restraint (fear of unkind thoughts or remarks of ignorant & censurous people) in doing justice to the Iron in guns, having to consult only my own judgment and no Board of Directors," he added in a postscript.[32]

Anderson's confidence in his own judgment and abilities and his high opinion of his brother's gun metal were soon confirmed. In December 1844, the Army Ordnance Bureau ordered 60 heavy guns from the Tredegar works and the navy followed with an order for 112 pieces the next year. By giving close attention to his casting methods and using only Cloverdale and Grace iron, Anderson reestablished and maintained a high reputation for his cannon. Between 1844 and 1860, the company cast and delivered a total of 881 pieces of ordnance to the Federal government and Anderson claimed that not one gun failed to pass proof firing tests after the 1843 failure.[33]

Shortly after Anderson leased the works, the pressure which he and other local iron men had been putting on their fellow Virginian, President Tyler, paid off in the form of a contract for an iron steamer. In 1844, the Treasury Department awarded the revenue cutter *Polk* to the Tredegar and Anderson set out immediately to equip a yard and hire skilled shipbuilders. He also attempted to obtain additional contracts by applying whatever political leverage he could exert on Washington. His shipyard super-

32. Anderson to John T. Anderson, Nov. 22, 1843, Anderson Papers, UVA; Richmond City Hustings Court, Deed Books No. 45, pp. 32–33, and No. 46, pp. 226–29, microfilm copy, VSL.

33. Bruce, p. 198; Statement of Contracts, Records of the Office, Chief of Ordnance, Record Group 156, NA; Record of Contracts ("Contract Ledger A"), Records of the Bureau of Ordnance, Department of the Navy, Record Group 74, NA. Hereafter cited as RG 156 and RG 74, NA.

intendent, for instance, who knew Representative Thomas Butler King, asked the Georgia Congressman to come to Richmond to examine the *Polk* and the Tredegar facilities. "Mr. Anderson is a Southern man," he emphasized, who "would give you as fine work and as good Iron as can be had in America." [34] When Tyler left the White House, however, Anderson found shipbuilding contracts considerably more difficult to come by. Although he did an excellent job on the *Polk,* the only other marine work executed for the Federal government prior to the war was done between 1855 and 1857, when the Tredegar constructed the engines and boilers for two Norfolk-built navy frigates.[35]

Anderson had the good fortune to bring the works more fully under his control just as a cyclical upturn brought the economy out of the severe depression and inaugurated a period of marked business expansion. The revival of railroad building in Virginia restored an important market and Anderson developed new customers for his rolling mill products in New England, New York, and Pennsylvania. He cultivated business south of Virginia as well, selling bar iron, spikes, and rail fastenings to Southern roads and steam engines and mills to Louisiana sugar planters.[36]

The Tredegar's ordnance business also remained brisk and included a major new customer. During the tension-filled months surrounding the Nashville Convention and the Compromise of 1850, the South Carolina legislature appropriated funds to purchase a substantial number of heavy siege and seacoast artillery. State officials soon approached Anderson about supplying such weapons and when he gave assurances that his works could execute a large order in a short time, he obtained the contract. The Tredegar cast a total of sixty-four pieces of ordnance for South Carolina in 1850 and 1851; a decade later, some of these weapons played key roles in the bombardment that opened the Civil War.[37]

IV

A few months before his five-year lease expired, Anderson moved to obtain permanent control of the Tredegar works. On April 4, 1848, he purchased the entire plant from the stockholders for $125,000. The own-

34. Henry Hunter to T. Butler King, Aug. 6, 1846, Thomas Butler King Papers, UNC.

35. Bruce, pp. 198–202, 282–83.

36. Ibid., pp. 203–11.

37. Ibid., p. 280; Maj. J. H. Trapier to the Board of Ordnance, Nov. 1, 1851, Nov. 11, 1852, filed under Military Affairs, Reports, 1851, 1852, SCA; Ashley Halsey, Jr., "South Carolina Began Preparing for War in 1851," *Civil War Times Illustrated, 1* (April 1962), 9–12.

ers agreed to stagger his payments over six years, with the first payment of $25,000 falling due on January 1, 1849; the remaining $100,000 was to be paid in five equal annual installments. With financial help from a prominent Richmond banker, William H. Macfarland, and with his past and future Tredegar profits, Anderson confidently expected to meet these sizable payments and assume absolute ownership of the business he had done so much to build up.[38]

Anderson had a number of things in his favor. Markets for Tredegar foundry products and merchant bar iron were already well established and ordnance sales to the Federal government brought in a steady cash income. The eight Virginia railroads chartered between 1846 and 1853 and under construction—a total of over nine hundred miles of track—offered a potentially lucrative market for rail chairs, spikes, locomotives, and rolling stock. And Anderson had always given the most scrupulous attention to his credit relationships, care which placed him on good terms with his Richmond bankers, Virginia pig iron producers, and Northern commission houses.[39]

He did not achieve his goal without a struggle, however. Rolling mill profits fell off sharply in the late '40s and early '50s. "No change in the times here for business like mine. The Foundry branch of my business is brisk—the other depressed," he wrote in 1851.[40] Much of the trouble came from low-cost British rails and bar iron which were crowding the American market following the end of the English railway boom of the 1840s. After attempting to compete with Northern and British rail manufacturers during the early 1850s, the Tredegar abandoned rail production and concentrated on rolling merchant bar iron and rail chairs.[41]

Faced with his large annual payments to the Tredegar stockholders, Anderson found the increasingly narrow profit margin on his rolling mill

38. Richmond City Hustings Court, Deed Book No. 54, pp. 111–13, microfilm copy, VSL; Bruce, pp. 216, 228. Miss Bruce mistakenly dates Anderson's purchase of the works as 1850.

39. Johnston, *Virginia Railroads*, p. 4; Anderson to J. T. Anderson, Nov. 22, 1843, and to F. T. Anderson, May 2, 1850, Feb. 1, 1855, Nov. 7, 1856, Anderson Papers, UVA; Anderson to Charles T. Wortham, March 6, 1853, Francis T. Anderson Papers, DUL.

40. Anderson to F. T. Anderson, Sept. 21, 1851, Anderson Papers, UVA.

41. Anderson to S. & W. Welsh, Jan. 31, 1854, Tredegar Letterbooks. These and all other Tredegar manuscripts referred to, unless otherwise indicated, are located in the Tredegar Company Records, VSL. For a discussion of the British invasion of the American iron market, see Peter Temin, *Iron and Steel in Nineteenth-Century America: An Economic Inquiry* (Cambridge, Mass., 1964), pp. 21–25, 115. Rail chairs were rolled iron plates used to support the rail and anchor it to the tie.

sales a matter for serious concern. He persuaded the owners to grant him more time to meet his installments and then set out to solve his financial problems. His solution was to form a series of partnerships which eventually removed him almost entirely from the rolling mill operation. In December 1853, Charles Y. Morriss, a Richmond financier, became a partner in the Tredegar mill for $25,000, the amount Anderson owed the stockholders on January first. Less than two years later, Anderson sold a three-fourths interest in his rolling mill to his plant superintendent, John F. Tanner, and to Morriss for $90,000 and used part of these funds to complete his payments to the Tredegar owners in February 1856.[42]

In the frequently trying years that followed, John Tanner held a position second only to Anderson in the management of the sprawling Tredegar establishment. Tanner, forty-five years old and a native Virginian, had been associated with the works since 1843. He was Anderson's first bookkeeper and later became superintendent of the rolling mill. The two men developed a close friendship and the Tredegar head had a high regard for Tanner's business acumen. "I doubt whether his superior in ability, business accomplishments and energy is to be found," Anderson wrote of his good friend in later years.[43] Under Tanner's skilled direction, the rolling mill branch of the business operated as Morriss, Tanner and Company until Anderson undertook to consolidate the entire plant in 1859.

Anderson also took partners into the foundry and machine shop branches of his business but he did this primarily to acquire skilled personnel. Two Boston locomotive builders joined him in 1852 and the engine and machine shops operated as Anderson, Souther and Pickering until the two machinists returned to New England in the fall of 1853. They left at a propitious moment. Just after their departure, the boilers of two Tredegar-built locomotives exploded on the Virginia and Tennessee Railroad. When railroad officials blamed the disasters on poor workmanship, Tredegar machine shop sales dropped precipitously. This branch of the

42. Anderson to Charles Morris[s], Nov. 8, 1853, Tredegar Letterbooks; Richmond City Hustings Court, Deed Books No. 68B, pp. 423–24, No. 69B, pp. 601–07, and No. 70B, pp. 86–87, microfilm copy, VSL. The rolling mill operated as Anderson, Morriss and Company in 1854.

43. Manuscript copy of speech given by Anderson to the American Society of Mechanical Engineers, Richmond, Nov. 12, 1890, in Special Summaries, Tredegar Company Records; Bruce, p. 173; manuscript population schedule, Henrico County, Va., Eighth Census, 1860, in "Federal Population Censuses, 1840–1880," *National Archives Microfilm Publications*, No. 55–7 (Washington, 1955).

business lost almost $30,000 during the first half of 1854 and Anderson had to take action to regain both his losses and the reputation of Tredegar locomotives. In July 1854, he sold a half interest in the foundry and machine shops to three men for $77,500. Matthew Delany, a skilled machinist, was to supervise construction, and Francis T. Glasgow, Anderson's nephew, and William Steptoe, another young Virginian, were to assist in managing the business and promoting sales. This partnership, known as Anderson, Delany and Company, successfully rebuilt the foundry and machine shop operations. Shortly after Anderson completed his payments to the Tredegar stockholders early in 1856, he bought out these three partners for the amount of their original investment.[44]

A healthy, growing family made these years of business activity even richer for the new owner of the Tredegar. By 1847, Joseph decided it was high time he moved his wife and children from their rented home on Fifth Street to a larger and more fashionable Richmond residence. His son Archer now had two sisters to get in his way, Kathleen, born in 1840, and Fannie, born six years later. Anderson purchased a columned stucco mansion at the corner of Franklin and Jefferson Streets and there Sally gave birth to two more girls, Ellen in 1849 and Mary in 1855, and another boy, Joseph, in 1851.[45]

V

The series of financial combinations which Anderson effected during the 1850s culminated with the formation of a partnership in 1859, merging control of the various Tredegar facilities and a neighboring rolling mill under the heading Joseph R. Anderson and Company. The adjacent plant, known as the Armory rolling mill, had been built as a rail mill in the mid-1840s on property leased from the Virginia State Armory. Anderson had taken a financial interest in this project at the beginning and had served briefly as president of the Armory Iron Company. But in 1848, he had relinquished this post to his father-in-law, Dr. Robert Archer, who had retired from the army and moved to Richmond. Dr. Archer and his son, Robert S. Archer, had converted the mill to merchant

44. Bruce, pp. 281–82; Anderson to John R. McDaniel, Nov. 23, 30, 1853, and to Henry D. Bird, Dec. 23, 1853, and John F. Tanner to John Souther, Dec. 23, 1853, Tredegar Letterbooks; agreement of partnership, Anderson, Delany, Glasgow, and Steptoe, July 1, 1854, Anderson Family Papers, VSL; Richmond City Hustings Court, Deed Books No. 68A, pp. 196–98, and No. 70A, pp. 231–32, microfilm copy, VSL.

45. Freeman, "Cool Head," pp. 13–15.

bar iron production in the 1850s and operated the property as R. Archer and Company during that decade.[46]

Under the terms of the partnership agreement signed on January 1, 1859, Anderson contributed his foundries and machine shops, his interest in the Tredegar rolling mill, and $60,000 in working capital. John Tanner resold his quarter interest in the Tredegar rolling mill to Anderson for $30,000 and put that sum toward the new company's working funds. The Archers brought the Armory mill and $10,000 in capital into the partnership. Anderson assumed overall direction of the affairs of the company and was to receive two thirds of future profits. Tanner, in addition to an annual salary of $2,000, was allocated one sixth of the profits while Dr. Archer and his son were to share the remaining one sixth of the profits and each receive a salary of $1,500 per year.[47]

Several months elapsed before the partners closed up the business of their old firms and Anderson completed negotiations with Morriss to buy the latter's half interest in the Tredegar rolling mill. Finally, on March 19, 1859, Morriss agreed to accept $60,250 for his share of the property, to be paid by Anderson personally in payments staggered over four years. Ten days after Anderson completed his repurchase of the rolling mill, dissolution notices for Morriss, Tanner and Company and Archer and Company were placed in the Richmond *Dispatch*, along with the announcement of the formation of the firm of Anderson and Company. The new partnership also introduced itself to old customers in a printed circular dated April 1, 1859, asking for continued orders for their wide range of rolling mill and foundry products.[48]

Anderson took on a heavy financial burden in launching the new partnership but the clearing financial horizon in late 1858 and past Tredegar profits seemed to justify the risk. Both personal factors and economic logic influenced his decision to form the partnership. Anderson had evidently found the arrangement with Morriss personally unsatisfactory and he was anxious to consolidate the foundry, machine shop, and rolling mill operations. The various partnerships of the 1850s fragmenting control of the works were largely makeshift arrangements to enable Anderson to solve temporary financial and technical difficulties. By 1859, these prob-

46. Bruce, pp. 214–23.

47. Agreement of copartnership, J. R. Anderson & Co., Jan. 1, 1859, Anderson Papers, VSL; Richmond City Hustings Court, Deed Book No. 74B, pp. 139–40, microfilm copy, VSL.

48. Ibid., No. 73A, pp. 523–25; Morriss to Anderson, March 19, 1859, Tredegar Contract Books; broadside in Anderson Papers, UVA.

lems had been met and he was financially able to reestablish control over the Tredegar. In announcing the new partnership to his brother, Anderson expressed his pleasure at being united in business with good friends, his satisfaction in owning the whole property again, and his expectation of bringing his sons into the new company when they became of age.[49]

Additional motives lay behind the formation of Anderson and Company. Following his retirement as president of the Armory mill, Anderson had given financial aid to his father-in-law during the 1850s to enable Archer and Company to ride out slack periods in the iron trade. In 1853, the Armory and Tredegar mills had joined forces to roll rails and after British competition had forced the owners to abandon this project, they frequently walked the short distance separating their works to confer on joint bids for furnishing large orders. The partnership agreement signed in January 1859 formalized this close association and gave the new company extensive facilities to meet an anticipated increase in trade.[50]

Before he moved to Richmond, there was little in Dr. Archer's background to indicate that he was a likely candidate to take charge of a rolling mill. Born in Norfolk in 1795, he had served twenty-five years as an army surgeon before retiring to a farm near Fort Monroe in 1839. Nine years later, at the urging of his son-in-law, he decided to enter the iron business. The doctor had, by his own admission, a marked mechanical ability and he demonstrated this skill in his successful operation of the Armory mill. He and his eldest son, Robert S. Archer, offered proven technical talent as well as plant and capital to the new partnership.[51]

VI

If the newspaper announcement of the formation of Anderson and Company brought any curious Richmonders out to see the plant, a climb up Gamble's Hill afforded an excellent view of the entire establishment. At the foot of the hill was the South's largest iron works, compactly built over some five acres between the James River and the Kanawha Canal.

49. Anderson to F. T. Anderson, March 24, April 4, 1859, ibid.

50. Bruce, pp. 216–22; R. Archer & Co., Current and Interest Account with J. R. Anderson, Jan. 1, 1853–Jan. 1, 1856, Watson-Archer Papers, VHS; Archer & Co. to Joseph J. White & Co., Dec. 15, 1858, and to Murray Hazelhurst, March 9, 1859, Tredegar Letterbooks.

51. B. Johnson Barbour, "Biographical Sketch of Dr. Robert Archer of Richmond, Va.," typescript in Watson-Archer Papers, VHS; Robert Archer, "History of the Archer and Silvester Families," manuscript in Joynes Family Papers, VHS; Richmond *Enquirer*, Sept. 28, 1861.

Down the canal at the east end of the plant stood the Armory rolling mill, with nine puddling furnaces and four heating furnaces for preparing pig and scrap iron for two trains of rolls, capable of producing 5,000 to 6,000 long tons of railroad and bar iron per year. The panic of 1857 had caused a sharp drop in sales and this mill operated at considerably less than full capacity in 1858, producing only 1,277 long tons of rolled iron which sold for slightly over $90,000. Spanning the gap between the Armory and Tredegar rolling mills on the canal were a large tenement and several smaller buildings which served as quarters for the slave labor force. West of these structures stood the more extensive Tredegar rolling mill, with its nine puddling and seven heating furnaces, three trains of rolls, and an annual productive capacity of 7,000 to 8,000 long tons of finished iron. Sales from February through December 1858 amounted to almost $220,000 on 2,578 tons. Business at both mills had picked up markedly in the last quarter of 1858, with monthly highs for the year recorded in October at the Tredegar and in November at the Armory. The air of optimism surrounding the formation of the partnership in January 1859 reflected this increased production late the previous year.[52]

Adjoining the Tredegar mill was the spike factory, a three-story structure containing spike machines, a cooper shop, and a pattern storage attic. This factory, fed by spike rods directly from the Tredegar rolling mill, could produce fifteen tons of railroad and ship spikes per day.

Stretching south of the Tredegar mill and spike factory to the banks of the James River stood a cluster of buildings comprising the foundry, machine, and forge departments. In the L-shaped gun foundry skilled workmen melted specially manufactured gun iron in two large furnaces, prepared the flasks, and cast cannon ranging in size from small mountain howitzers weighing several hundred pounds to great ten-ton coast defense cannon. In the neighboring gun mill, the cannons were cut, bored, turned, and finished. A foundry for general iron work, a new brick car wheel foundry, and a small brass foundry rounded out this department.

Connected to the gun mill was a fully equipped machine shop, where car wheels were bored, axles turned, and a multitude of similar tasks performed. West of the machine shops, forming the western boundary of the

52. Ibid., Nov. 16, 1858; J. P. Lesley, *The Iron Manufacturer's Guide to the Furnaces, Forges and Rolling Mills of the United States* (New York, 1859), p. 244; insurance policies dated Jan. 1, 1861, Tredegar Contract Books; entries for Jan.–Dec. 1858, Tredegar Rolling Mill Sales Books; Tanner to W. Bollman, Oct. 22, 1858, Tredegar Letterbooks.

works, stood the locomotive shop, a sprawling three-story building, 150 feet long and 45 feet wide. Here, and in the connecting and equally large finishing shop, locomotives and engines of all descriptions were built. In the adjoining carpenter shop, Tredegar workmen completed woodwork for saw mills, sugar mills, and freight cars.

Finally, several buildings running along the river bank comprising the forge department formed the southern boundary of the Tredegar plant. The boiler shop consisted of a building 160 feet long and the blacksmith shop, 180 feet in length, had 25 fires and a number of large tilt hammers.

The entire plant represented a capital investment of $435,000. Powered by water drawn from the canal, the furnaces and rolling mills consumed annually some 12,000 long tons of pig iron, over 16,000 tons of bituminous coal, and required 150,000 firebrick, as well as smaller amounts of copper, wood, and other raw materials. The works employed Richmond's largest industrial working force, approximately eight hundred free and slave laborers—a figure exceeded by only three other ironworks in the United States.[53] The facilities of Anderson and Company could produce almost every conceivable type of finished iron.

Under Anderson's knowledgeable hand, the Tredegar had grown from its inception in 1836 as a small foundry and rolling mill into one of the nation's largest and best equipped iron works. In the opinion of the historian who has given the closest study to the founders of the American iron industry, "Anderson was one of the great organizers of his generation" and "one of the great American entrepreneurs." [54] As the molder of this impressive industrial complex, the young Virginian had clearly demonstrated that he possessed the qualities of the "creative entrepreneur"—imagination, resourcefulness, and a strong will.[55] During the Tredegar's rise, he had displayed a marked ability to expand production, initiate the manufacture of new items, and enter previously untapped

53. Manuscript returns, Census of Manufactures, 1860, Virginia, VSL; Richmond *Dispatch*, April 29, 1859; Richmond *Enquirer*, Sept. 5, 1860, Sept. 28, 1861; map of the works dated Jan. 1880, Tredegar Company Records. In 1860, the Montour Iron Works at Danville, Pa., employed 3,000 workers, the Cambria Iron Works at Johnstown, Pa., 1,948, and the Phoenix Iron Company at Phoenixville, Pa., 1,230. Abram S. Hewitt's and Peter Cooper's Trenton Iron Company had a labor force of 786 men in 1860; see Temin, *Iron and Steel in Nineteenth-Century America*, p. 109.

54. Fritz Redlich, *History of American Business Leaders: A Series of Studies* (2 vols. Ann Arbor, Mich., Edwards Brothers, 1940), *1*, 84.

55. Ibid., pp. 12–18. See also Joseph A. Schumpeter, *The Theory of Economic Development* (reprint ed. New York, 1961), pp. 89–94.

markets. When a branch of his operation was threatened, he had invariably taken prompt and effective action to meet the challenge. By skillfully arranging partnerships at critical moments, he had secured enough capital to meet his obligations and had avoided most of the financial difficulties that plagued so many contemporary iron manufacturers.[56] The consolidation of the various Tredegar departments in 1859 represented the final victory in Anderson's sixteen-year campaign for control of the works.

It had been an impressive performance but the Richmond industrialist could not afford to rest on his laurels for very long. The new firm of J. R. Anderson and Company would soon need all the talent and experience the senior partner had at his command.

56. See Louis C. Hunter, "Financial Problems of the Early Pittsburgh Iron Manufacturers," *Journal of Economic and Business History*, 2 (1930), 520–21.

2

Slaves, Pig Iron, and Sales

In the 1840s and '50s, the Tredegar works, like all Southern iron establishments, labored under a number of competitive handicaps. The generally inadequate market for iron in the South forced local mills to operate at considerably less than full capacity and thus deprived them of the economies of large-scale operation. The most advanced technological innovations usually failed to penetrate the Mason and Dixon Line because of the limited demand for finished iron products. There were labor problems as well. Northern and European ironworkers were reluctant to settle in slave states and could only be lured south by premium wages. Lagging railway development also shackled Southern iron producers with high transportation costs and prevented them from tapping some of the region's best sources of raw materials—the great seams of coking coal in western Virginia and the richest of the Alabama coal and iron deposits, to name only two.

Because of these burdens, the iron men of the South were at a decided disadvantage when they attempted to compete with Northern and particularly British manufactures, a disadvantage reflected in the substantially higher price of Southern iron products. This price differential meant that Southern mills and foundries always faced an uphill struggle in their battle for sales. Anderson attempted to reduce his production expenses in a number of ways but concentrated primarily on two problems: expensive raw materials and high labor costs. His solution to the former was to go increasingly to the North for much of his pig iron; to meet the latter problem, he broke the opposition of his free workers and introduced large numbers of Negro slaves into skilled rolling mill positions.

I

Anderson had first used slaves extensively while he was still in the Shenandoah supervising the building of the Valley turnpike. At that time, he had expressed a decided preference for slave labor for heavy construction work. "We dont wish to rely on white labor," he wrote his brother in the fall of 1840 when he was attempting to secure hands for the coming year's work.[1] He did not forget his experience with chattel labor when he became the Tredegar's business agent the following March.

The completion of the Armory rolling mill in 1847 provided Anderson with the opportunity to test his theory that slaves could be profitably employed in highly skilled industrial positions. Anderson was only in charge of the Armory Iron Company from 1846 until the spring of 1848, when he relinquished the post to his father-in-law. But during his relatively brief tenure, he exercised his authority as president to install slave labor at key jobs in the Armory mill. This action precipitated one of the antebellum South's most important labor disputes.

In the mid-nineteenth century, the manufacture of finished bar iron from pig metal required a group of skilled laborers possessing both brawn and good judgment. The high carbon content and the presence of impurities in pig iron made the metal too brittle for bending, forging, and rolling. Puddlers performed the first step in removing the impurities. The puddler, assisted by a helper, fed a specially designed furnace with pig iron. When the metal became molten, he worked it with a long hooked rod, stirring the white hot mass and gradually molding it into a pasty ball of about 150 pounds. When the puddler thought the iron had reached the proper consistency, other laborers removed the ball of iron from the furnace, pounded it with a large tilt hammer, ran it through squeezers, and finally passed it back and forth through puddle rolls until it emerged as a rough, elongated "muck bar," free from impurities. After cooling, this muck bar was sheared into shorter pieces which were bound together in a bundle, taken by a heater and reheated until the bars almost fused. Rollers then took the mass of metal and rolled it between grooved cylinders on a finishing mill, producing bar iron.[2]

The puddlers, heaters, and rollers were key laborers in any rolling mill and they jealously guarded their skills, acquired by long years of experience. Anderson's attempt to install slave puddlers at the Armory furnaces stirred the white laborers to immediate action. Anderson had first proposed the introduction of slaves into the Tredegar rolling mill on a large

1. Anderson to F. T. Anderson, Oct. 11, 1840, Anderson Papers, UVA.

2. Earl C. May, *Principio to Wheeling, 1715–1945, A Pageant of Iron and Steel* (New York, 1945), pp. 101–02.

scale in 1842, to cut costs and assist in controlling white labor. The company began purchasing a few slaves and gradually introduced them into the mill in subordinate capacities. The white puddlers, heaters, and rollers had tolerated the presence of slaves in the Tredegar mill at the less skilled positions at the squeezer and puddle rolls. But they steadfastly refused to allow slave puddlers to take up positions in the Armory mill. On Saturday, May 22, 1847, skilled workers at both mills informed Anderson of their determination to strike. The following day they held a meeting and formally resolved that they would not go to work unless the slaves were removed from the puddling furnaces at the new plant. They also voiced their earlier resentment at the introduction of slave laborers into the Tredegar rolling mill by demanding that they be removed from the squeezer and puddle rolls. In addition, the puddlers and heaters called for an increase in the price per ton they were paid for their services. The strikers concluded by tersely informing Anderson and the rolling mill superintendents that they "need not light up the furnaces Monday, nor any other time, until you comply with our resolution." The Tredegar puddlers, heaters, and rollers and the Armory puddlers signed the strike notice.[3]

To make their position perfectly clear and to deny rumors that they were planning violence, the strikers met on May 26 and adopted a supplementary resolution. The difficulties between themselves and their employer were the direct result of Anderson's "wishing to employ and instruct colored people in our stead in the said Tredegar Iron Works," they maintained. They had not attempted to raise a mob and had no idea of injuring their employers. The only object of the strike was "*to prohibit the employment of colored people in the said Works*." [4]

Anderson met the strikers head-on. On May 26, he addressed a letter "*to my late workmen at the Tredegar Iron Works*," informing them that they had fired themselves. He claimed he had not intended to use Negro puddlers at the Tredegar furnaces or to discharge any efficient laborers. But now the strikers had forced him to introduce slave puddlers into the Tredegar rolling mill as well as the Armory mill. He denied that any increase in wages was justified and concluded by requesting all strikers who rented housing from him to vacate as soon as possible.[5]

3. Richmond *Times and Compiler*, May 28, 1847; Bruce, *Virginia Iron Manufacture*, pp. 224–25, 233–34.

4. Richmond *Times and Compiler*, May 28, 1847.

5. Ibid.; Bruce, pp. 225–26.

The Richmond press backed Anderson solidly. "The principle is advocated, for the first time we believe in a slave-holding State, that the employer may be prevented from making use of slave labor," commented and *Times and Compiler* on May 28. "This principle strikes at the root of all the rights and privileges of the master, and if acknowledged, or permitted to gain foothold, will soon wholly destroy the value of slave property." When one of the strikers called at the office of the Richmond *Whig* to request support for the strike, the editors firmly rejected his appeal. "The sympathies of all communities are naturally and properly most generally in favor of the hard working-man, whose toils ought to be fairly requited," wrote the *Whig*; "but in *this* community, no combination, formed for the *purpose* avowed by the authors of the recent strike, can receive the slightest toleration." [6] The Richmond *Enquirer* endorsed Anderson's "just, liberal and proper course" and was convinced that to sanction the strikers' action would render slave property "utterly valueless." [7]

One Northern paper took quite a different view of the Tredegar strike. The New York *Commercial Advertiser* said the labor unrest in Richmond resulted quite naturally from the belief inculcated by slaveholders that all labor was degrading and fit only to be performed by a degraded race. White men therefore would not work with Negroes.[8] The Richmond *Times and Compiler* retorted that prejudice had nothing to do with the strike. It resulted from the false apprehension on the part of the workmen that slaves were to replace them after they taught the Negroes the necessary mechanical skills. "The objection to working *with* negroes did not govern their action: it was the mere fact that negroes were hereafter to take their places." This was not Anderson's intention, the Richmond paper assured its readers. "We are satisfied that there has been no design to get white workmen to instruct negroes who should afterwards displace them, and that every skillful artisan would have been perfectly secure in his station." [9]

Anderson's quick dismissal of the strikers demonstrated that the workers' fears were much more firmly grounded than the Richmond press chose to admit. Anderson followed up his firing of the workers by taking them into court, charging that they had formed an illegal combination in

6. Quoted in Richmond *Enquirer*, May 29, 1847.

7. Ibid.

8. Quoted in Richmond *Times and Compiler*, June 9, 1847.

9. Ibid.

uniting to exclude slaves from his factory. He explained his motivation in a letter to the Richmond *Enquirer:* "It must be evident that such combinations are a direct attack on slave property; and, if they do not originate in abolition, they are pregnant with its evils." [10] Before the mayor's court, the strikers pleaded innocent of any intention to unite in an unlawful combination and expressed regret if what they had done violated the law in any way. Thereupon the mayor dismissed the case. But the lesson was all too plain to other free laborers remaining at the Tredegar works. "It is to be hoped that the case may operate as a warning and that nothing having even the appearance of a combination may again occur to disturb the regular current of business," wrote the *Enquirer.*[11] Anderson won a total victory in his battle with the strikers. The men were not rehired and slaves soon took up important positions in the mills.

II

Following this successful confrontation with his workers, Anderson sent large numbers of slaves into both the Tredegar and the Armory rolling mills. "I am employing in this establishment, as well as at the Armory works adjoining, of which I am President, almost exclusively slave labor except as to Boss men," Anderson informed a Northern correspondent in 1848.[12] During that year, 117 slaves labored at the two plants. (See Table 1.) Two years later, the Tredegar and Armory works employed 100 slaves in a labor force totaling approximately 250 men.

The Tredegar slaves had minimum daily tasks to perform and usually worked a ten-hour day. If they worked overtime or turned out more than their required amount of piecework, they could earn money for themselves. The more skilled Negro laborers had the greatest possibilities for earning personal incomes and the fragmentary payroll records of the company indicate that a number did so. The Tredegar Negroes did not enjoy the degree of freedom granted some industrial slaves in Richmond. Unlike the tobacco factory hands, many of whom were given money to seek their own board and lodging, the slaves employed at the Tredegar slept in tenements near the rolling mill and were fed and clothed by the company. A slave hospital at the works provided medical care.[13]

10. Richmond *Enquirer,* June 12, 1847.

11. Ibid.

12. Anderson to Harrison Row, Jan. 3, 1848, quoted in Bruce, p. 237.

13. Tredegar Payroll, July–Oct. 1852; Bruce, pp. 252–55; Joseph C. Robert, *The Tobacco Kingdom: Plantation, Market and Factory, 1800–1860* (Durham, 1938), p. 203; Richard C. Wade, *Slavery in the Cities: The South 1820–1860* (New York, 1964), pp. 47, 71, 139.

Slave labor was confined largely to two departments, the rolling mill and the blacksmith shop. Of the eighty slaves employed in 1860, Anderson personally owned twenty-eight and Dr. Archer owned four. These hands were primarily skilled puddlers, heaters, and rollers, purchased and trained for rolling mill work over the years since 1847, and they represented the elite among the Tredegar slave population. In 1860, the company hired, usually on an annual basis, some forty-five additional slaves and of this number probably fifteen to twenty-five were blacksmiths, strikers, smith's helpers, and teamsters, and twenty or thirty were porters and common laborers. A group of Negro boys, superintended by a white foreman, built kegs for Tredegar spikes in the cooper shop.[14]

TABLE 1. Slaves Employed at the Tredegar Iron Works, 1838–1860, and at the Armory Iron Works, 1848–1858

Year	*Tredegar Works*	*Armory Works*	*Total*
1838	18	—	18
1839	19	—	19
1840	14	—	14
1841	5	—	5
1842	24	—	24
1843	18	—	18
1844	18	—	18
1845	24	—	24
1846	40	—	40
1847	41	—	41
1848	78	39	117
1849	63	42	105
1850	66	34	100
1851	57	5	62
1852	57	5	62
1853	47	—	47
1854	64	3	67
1855	72	26	98
1856	62	23	85
1857	60	21	81
1858	54	20	74
1859	67	—	67
1860	80	—	80

Sources: City of Richmond, Personal Property Tax Rolls, 1838–1860, VSL; manuscript slave schedules, Henrico County, Va., 1850 and 1860, in "Federal Population Censuses, 1840–1880."

14. Manuscript slave schedules, Henrico County, Va., 1860, in "Federal Population Censuses, 1840–1880"; City of Richmond, Personal Property Tax Rolls, 1860, VSL; Richmond

Prior to the outbreak of the Civil War, Anderson did not attempt to introduce Negroes into other phases of his operations. The 1850s, a period of great expansion of the Tredegar plant, saw the labor force jump from 250 men at the beginning of the decade to 800 in 1860; during this same period, the number of slaves employed dropped from 100 to 80. The departments that received most of Anderson's attention in the '50s, the foundries, machine shops, and the engine and locomotive works, were almost totally devoid of Negro labor. Anderson's decision not to increase his personal investment in slaves during the ten years prior to the war also suggests that there were limits to the cost-cutting potential of this form of labor. By 1850 he had acquired a group of thirty-five rolling mill hands; ten years later he owned only twenty-eight male slaves of working age, plus thirty-two women and children.[15]

Of the more than 700 free white workers at the Tredegar in 1860, Northern- and foreign-born artisans accounted for by far the larger proportion, embracing the whole range of skilled and unskilled positions. Peter Derbyshire, the foreman of the foundry department and the man chiefly responsible for the casting of cannon, was a young Englishman. The superintendent of the rolling mills was a Canadian, Uri Haskins. White laborers working alongside the slaves in the rolling mills grouped in various departments by nationalities: Irish puddlers, Welsh heaters, and English rollers. A large force of Irish and German workers formed the bulk of the Tredegar's ordinary working population.

This pattern of foreign and Northern domination of skilled positions extended throughout the Richmond iron trade. A majority of the molders, boiler makers, finishers, and founders were born outside the Old Dominion. Native-born laborers equaled non-native only among the blacksmiths and the large number of free Negro smiths accounted for this exception.[16] When Anderson needed to replace a foreman or add skilled labor, he almost invariably addressed his inquiries to Northern business acquaintances.[17] In the event of war with the North, Richmond and the South would pay a heavy price for this dependence. The Tredegar partners attempted to build up their native labor force by apprenticing boys

Dispatch, Jan. 11, 1859; Richmond *Enquirer*, Sept. 5, 1860; "List of Negroes Hired," Jan. 1, 1862, Tredegar Contract Books; Bruce, p. 239.

15. Bruce, p. 239; manuscript slave schedules, Henrico County, Va., 1860, in "Federal Population Censuses, 1840–1880."

16. Manuscript population schedule, Henrico County, Va., 1860, ibid.

17. Anderson & Co. to William Sellers & Co., Oct. 13, 1860, March 4, 1861, and to Charles Campbell, March 15, 1861, Tredegar Letterbooks.

for four or five years in the foundries, the blacksmith department, the finishing shop, and the boiler shop, but between January 1859 and the outbreak of the war in April 1861, only eighteen youths entered these departments as apprentices.[18]

Any analysis of the usefulness of slave labor to the Tredegar Iron Works must focus on the rolling mill operation. It was in this department that Anderson concentrated his efforts to reduce costs through Negro labor and it is also the area where the company kept the most precise bookkeeping records on production costs.

In 1848, shortly after he had placed slaves at most of the skilled positions in his mills, Anderson wrote that slave labor "enables me, of course, to compete with other manufacturers." [19] How valid was this claim? Cost figures for the antebellum years indicate that once the slave force was trained and experienced, the Tredegar did achieve some reduction in labor charges:

Labor Cost per Ton of Tredegar Rolled Iron
(tons of 2,000 lbs.)
1844–1852 [20]

1844	$11.96	*1847*	$12.79	*1850*	$10.64
1845	11.98	*1848*	13.38	*1851*	10.04
1846	12.12	*1849*	11.42	*1852*	11.09
3-year average	$12.02		$12.19		$10.59

18. Anderson & Co. to F. J. Hampton, Jan. 26, 1860, ibid.; list of apprentices in Edward R. Archer Account Book, 1861–63, VSL. Hereafter cited as Archer Account Book.

19. Anderson to Harrison Row, Jan. 3, 1848, quoted in Bruce, pp. 237–38.

20. These figures were compiled from production records in the Tredegar Journals, 1844–53. The following is a typical year-end accounting of rolling mill operations:

For the manufacture of 2,463 tons (of 2,000 lbs) of iron in 1844:

pig iron	3,534 tons	$75,650
wages		29,452
coal	143,375 bu	14,731
rent		8,639
repairs		4,417
other (taxes, insurance, water rent, etc.)		9,460
total		$142,349
profit (sales less costs)		$34,411

Slave hires were included under "wages" and, after 1847, a sizable "board account" (usually $2,000 to $3,000) is also given. Slaves owned by Anderson personally were always leased to the company on an annual basis and thus their expense appears under "wages." Depreciation of plant equipment was not taken into account.

During the three years immediately prior to the 1847 strike, labor cost averaged $12.02 per ton. In 1847 and 1848, the period when slaves first took over important jobs in the mills, the Tredegar's labor expenses rose. By 1850, however, Anderson had purchased and trained a select crew of rolling mill hands and the average labor charge per ton fell to $10.59 during the next three years. This average represented a reduction of 12 per cent of the 1844–46 figure.

But despite the lower cost of Tredegar labor in the 1850s, English and Yankee competitors continued to hold a significant price advantage over the Richmond industrialists. In 1860, the commercial columns of the Richmond press quoted Tredegar rolled iron at $85 per ton, while top English refined bar iron cost $75, and common English bar sold for $65 per ton.[21] At the same time, common English bar was quoted on the Baltimore market at $55 to $60 per ton and refined American bar at $60 to $65.[22] Similarly, Tredegar railroad spikes averaged one half to three quarters of a cent higher than the three cents per pound most Northern firms charged.[23] Tredegar rolled iron, like all Southern iron, was priced significantly higher than that produced in any other section of the country. (See Table 2.)

TABLE 2. Bar, Sheet, and Railroad Iron Produced in the United States during the Year Ending June 1, 1860

	Bar iron (tons)	*Railroad iron (tons)*	*Boiler plate (tons)*	*Average price per ton*
New England States	17,340	24,350	6,000	$66.44
Middle Atlantic States	154,297	158,577	22,795	57.70
Western States	41,973	40,000	2,100	69.10
Southern States	14,072	12,180	—	91.52

Source: *Eighth Census of the United States, Manufactures* (Washington, 1865), p. clxxxiii.

In addition to their use of slave labor, the Tredegar owners attempted to overcome the competitive advantage of Northern manufacturers in a number of other ways. They constantly stressed the responsibility of Southern customers to underwrite the region's industrial independence. Tredegar advertisements emphasized the higher quality products resulting

21. Richmond *Dispatch*, March 30, 1860. Quotations remained stable throughout 1860.

22. Baltimore *Daily Exchange*, March 10, 1860.

23. Anderson & Co. to W. L. Clarke, April 23, 1860, Tredegar Letterbooks.

from the use of expensive Virginia charcoal pig iron. And, most important of all, the management accepted the promissory notes and securities of Southern railroads that often lacked adequate financing. Even so, the Richmond industrialists faced rugged outside competition for the iron trade of the South and their resentment against the North grew as the competition mounted.

Part of the price advantage of Northern and English iron manufacturers lay in the very area Anderson attempted to overcome by employing Negro slaves. A rolling mill at Wheeling in the Virginia panhandle reported in 1855 that its free labor cost only $6.00 per ton of finished iron.[24] The Tredegar owners believed English iron producers possessed an even greater labor advantage. "We regret to learn that at the present . . . English Iron can be imported at a very low figure, much lesser [sic] than we can make it, using as we do Virginia Metals & employing labour that costs three times what it does in Europe," wrote Dr. Archer in 1858.[25] Anderson still had to go north for a large number of skilled rolling mill laborers and guarantee them a high wage to induce them to come south. And he often found it difficult to hire white workers because of the presence of slaves in the mills.[26]

The rise in the annual hire of slaves in the decade prior to the war further restricted the cost-cutting potential of this form of labor. A slave normally rented for between 10 and 15 per cent of his total value. The rapid increase in slave values during the late 1850s sent hires upward.[27] By 1860, Anderson had to pay up to $100 a year for ordinary hands, $150 to $170 for blacksmiths, and as high as $300 a year for a skilled slave puddler. Since the company also fed, clothed, and housed all their slaves and paid their medical bills and state taxes, the rise in hires added significantly to the Tredegar's labor expense.[28]

Slaves helped Anderson control strikes, constituted a stable rolling mill work force, and provided some limited opportunity to reduce labor costs.

24. *The Crescent Iron Manufacturing Company with Statistics of Other Manufacturing Companies, Wheeling, Virginia* (Boston, 1855), p. 2.

25. Archer & Co. to McKinney & Boss, Oct. 16, 1858, Tredegar Letterbooks.

26. "Corporate Holdings, 1866," manuscript Tredegar volume, p. 6.

27. Ulrich B. Phillips, *American Negro Slavery* (reprint ed. Gloucester, Mass., 1959), chart facing p. 370; Clement Eaton, *The Growth of Southern Civilization, 1790–1860* (New York, 1961), p. 65; Robert Evans, Jr., "The Economics of American Negro Slavery," in *Aspects of Labor Economics* (Princeton, 1962), pp. 197–203.

28. List of collections for Mrs. E. F. Talley, Jan. 12, 1860, and Anderson & Co. to Scofield & Markam, Dec. 25, 1860, Tredegar Letterbooks; entries for Dec. 1860, Tredegar Journals.

But the savings achieved through the use of this form of labor did not permit Anderson to price his rolled iron below or even at the same level as that of Northern or English manufacturers. He did not find the Negro slave a panacea for all the competitive ills that tormented Southern industry. In particular, slave labor could not compensate for the most glaring weakness of the antebellum South's industrial economy—a pitifully inadequate raw materials base.

III

Up until the middle 1850s, the Tredegar had drawn much of its iron from the charcoal blast furnaces of the Valley of Virginia, the fertile trough between the Blue Ridge and Allegheny mountains stretching the length of the state. The James River and Kanawha Canal brought the numerous furnaces of Botetourt, Alleghany, and southern Rockbridge Counties into direct and inexpensive communication with the Richmond works. Three Virginia railroads tapped the other major iron producing sections of the state: the Virginia and Tennessee penetrated the iron area of mountainous southwest Virginia; the Virginia Central provided transportation from the middle Valley region; and the Manassas Gap cut through the furnace area of the Shenandoah Valley to the north.

This greatly improved transportation and the extensive use of slave labor did not, however, enable the Virginia stacks to compete on even terms with the modern Pennsylvania anthracite furnaces during the 1850s. Virginia founders continued to use charcoal fuel and outmoded techniques and as a result their production costs remained high.[29] Locally produced metal could not hold its own even in the Richmond market against cheaper Northern iron and the Virginia pig iron industry declined markedly in the crucial decade before the war. In 1850, twenty-nine Virginia charcoal furnaces employing 1,129 hands produced 22,163 tons of pig iron; by 1860, only sixteen furnaces employing 529 men remained in blast and production had fallen to 11,396 tons. During the same decade, production of pig in Pennsylvania rose from 285,702 tons to 580,049 tons as anthracite furnaces replaced antiquated charcoal stacks.[30]

29. Samuel S. Bradford, "The Ante-Bellum Charcoal Iron Industry of Virginia" (unpublished Ph.D. dissertation, Columbia University, 1958), pp. 65–67; Temin, *Iron and Steel in Nineteenth-Century America,* pp. 52, 57–62, 83–85.

30. J. D. B. DeBow, *Compendium of the Seventh Census of the United States* (Washington, 1854), p. 181; *Eighth Census of the U.S., Manufactures,* p. clxxx; manuscript returns, Census of Manufactures, 1860, Virginia, VSL; Lesley, *Iron Manufacturer's Guide,* pp. 1–22.

Although Anderson expressed a preference for Virginia iron and advertised that he manufactured from "best charcoal metal," he made heavy purchases of Pennsylvania anthracite pig in 1859 and 1860.[31] Anderson and Company's rolling mill products were, in fact, a mixture of anthracite and charcoal pig, with a strong emphasis on Northern anthracite metal. The company purchased pig iron in thousand ton lots for $19 to $21 per ton in Philadelphia and Baltimore in 1859 and 1860.[32] The price of this iron was considerably below locally manufactured pig. Anderson paid a premium price of $35 to $40 per ton for gun iron from his brother John's Cloverdale and Grace furnaces in Botetourt County and $30 per ton for car wheel iron from the Glenwood furnace in Rockbridge County, owned by his brother Francis. But he did not extend his purchases to other Virginia furnace men at similar rates. Even with the high price Anderson paid for their iron, his brothers required sizable advances to enable them to stay in blast. By June 1860, the Tredegar partners had extended them loans totaling $62,000. Despite the price subsidy and loans, the quality of Glenwood iron had declined so markedly by the late spring of 1860 that the company sought samples of pig suitable for railroad wheels in Pennsylvania.[33]

The Tredegar's dependence on non-Southern labor was equaled by its reliance on Yankee iron. Anderson's works alone consumed more pig metal in 1860 than the sixteen furnaces in blast in Virginia produced. Of the 12,000 tons of iron used at the Richmond plant, probably no more than 4,000 or 5,000 tons came from local stacks. Most of this Virginia-produced pig was for foundry use. The Tredegar rolling mills puddled four tons of Northern iron for every ton of Virginia metal by the fall of 1860 and in the first quarter of 1861, pig iron receipts from the North more than doubled those from within the state.[34] The charcoal iron industry in the Old Dominion was indeed moribund by 1861, as one scholar

---

The figure given for Virginia pig iron production is taken from the manuscript returns. The printed *Eighth Census* gives 11,646 tons.

31. Richmond *Enquirer,* Oct. 4, 1860. During the early 1850s, Anderson's iron enjoyed the reputation of being among the three best charcoal irons rolled in America; see Redlich, *American Business Leaders,* p. 84.

32. Contracts dated June 30, July 13, 1859, Jan. 31, March 22, June 1, 15, Oct. 2, 10, 1860, Tredegar Contract Books; pig iron inventory dated Nov. 23, 1859, Tredegar Letterbooks.

33. Anderson to F. T. Anderson, May 25, June 18, 22, 1860, to John T. Anderson, June 12, 1860, and Anderson & Co. to Felix Wyatt, June 2, 1860, ibid.

34. Tredegar Pig Iron Receipt Book.

has written.[35] Without considerable financial support from Anderson and his partners, the three Virginia furnaces producing specialized, high quality pig would have been unable to continue production.

By the time Anderson and Company paid freight charges on the Northern iron, however, their raw materials costs had risen well above those of their competitors to the north. Mills at Philadelphia, Pittsburgh, Wheeling, and Baltimore could tap the anthracite and the scattering of coke furnaces in Pennsylvania and western Maryland much more cheaply than could the Richmond firm. Anderson's Northern pig iron purchases deprived Virginia furnaces of a major customer but did not bring his production costs down to the level enjoyed by Northern manufacturers.

The Tredegar did succeed in securing a large portion of its coal from sources close to Richmond. Deep pits located in counties immediately adjacent to Richmond had been worked commercially since before the Revolutionary War, despite a high gas and impurities content. In 1860, Virginia ranked fourth among coal producing states, mining 473,360 tons of bituminous coal primarily from the collieries around Richmond. The Midlothian and the Clover Hill mines in Chesterfield County, the two largest pits in the area, produced approximately 86,000 tons in 1860 and supplied Anderson's works with a large percentage of its fuel.[36] Richmond coal tended to be of mixed quality, however, even if mined from the same pit. After receiving a shipment of bad coal from a local mine, one of the partners wrote the mining agent that the last cargo was "no more like the former lot than chalk's like cheese." [37] The company relied on Lehigh Valley coal, shipped by water from Philadelphia, for critical supplies of anthracite for spike furnaces and for foundry use. The Tredegar consumed some 1,500 tons of this Pennsylvania coal yearly.[38] Richmond mines supplied the bulk of the coal used for smith's work, for puddling and heating in the rolling mills, and for melting gun iron.

IV

Although the Tredegar payrolls and pig iron receipts had a strong Northern cast, the sales books had a distinctly Southern look. The bulk of

35. Bradford, p. 185.

36. *Eighth Census of the U.S., Manufactures,* p. clxxii; manuscript returns, Census of Manufactures, 1860, Virginia, VSL; Bruce, pp. 87–109. Pennsylvania produced 10,805,628 tons of coal in 1860, Ohio, 1,265,600 tons, and Illinois, 728,400 tons.

37. Anderson & Co. to Samuel R. Hawks & Son, Oct. 10, 1860, Tredegar Letterbooks.

38. Anderson & Co. to Van Deusen, Norton & Co., Sept. 14, 1859, ibid.; manuscript returns, Census of Manufactures, 1860, Virginia, VSL.

Anderson and Company's orders in 1859 and 1860 came from railroads south of the Potomac.[39] From the foundries and rolling mills came almost every conceivable type of railroad iron, with the single exception of rails. The Armory mill had rolled rails for the Richmond and York River Railroad in the late 1850s, but the new partnership chose not to try to compete with Northern and British rail manufacturers. This was the only area where Anderson and Company did not attempt to meet outside competition for Southern railroad business. The firm manufactured wheels and axles, spikes, freight cars and locomotives, complete iron bridges, and rolled a high quality patented rail chair.[40]

By the summer of 1860, a lack of orders forced the Tredegar partners to curtail their locomotive operations. The company delivered its last locomotive in December 1860 to a Tennessee railroad.[41] The breakup of the locomotive department on the eve of the Civil War would prove a serious blow to Southern railroads when the conflict opened. The workmen in this branch of the business who remained at the Tredegar concentrated on the manufacture of stationary and portable engines for saw, sugar, and grist mills. The company established an agency in New Orleans in January 1860 to cultivate the Gulf Coast sugar and lumber mill trade which Anderson had attempted to build up during the 1840s and '50s.[42]

Bridge building assumed an increasingly large share of the company's attention in the early days of the new partnership. "We are making the bridge iron for nearly all builders in the South and many at the North," Anderson told a Georgia bridge builder in 1860.[43] During 1859 and 1860, the firm entered into contracts to supply the bolts, straps, and iron casting for bridges in Virginia, Tennessee, Georgia, Alabama, and North and South Carolina. The works also executed large orders for major bridge builders north of the Potomac and as far west as Chicago. The Tredegar produced most of the bridge iron for the Baltimore and Ohio Railroad.[44] Anderson used only Virginia charcoal metal in his bridge

39. Tredegar Rolling Mill Sales Books; Tredegar Foundry Sales Books.

40. See advertisements in Richmond *Dispatch,* March 29, 1859, and Richmond *Enquirer,* Oct. 4, 1860.

41. Anderson & Co. to Thomas E. Roberts, Aug. 13, 1860, Tredegar Letterbooks; entry for Dec. 1860, Tredegar Foundry Sales Books

42. Agreement with E. M. Ivens, Jan. 14, 1860, Tredegar Contract Books; Bruce, pp. 209–11.

43. Anderson & Co. to Edward Denmead, March 21, 1860, Tredegar Letterbooks.

44. Contracts dated Sept. 10, 1859, Jan. 13, July 27, Oct. 19, 1860, Tredegar Contract Books; Anderson & Co. to R. E. Roder, Oct. 24, 1859, to L. B. Boomer, Oct. 26, 1859, to M. P. Placide, Nov. 11, 1859, to W. D. Dunn, March 17, 1860, and to Thatcher Perkins, June 2, 1860, Tredegar Letterbooks.

work and this, coupled with fine workmanship, achieved Northern sales which the firm could not match in the highly competitive merchant bar iron market. Except for work done under government contract, bridge building represented the one field in which Tredegar iron competed successfully in the North in the years immediately before the war.

"It seems to be a very hard matter for us to get much on our Virginia Roads—the Yankees do almost all of it," complained one of the Tredegar partners in 1859.[45] As a result of the increasing competition in the Old Dominion, the Richmond industrialists turned more and more toward the cotton states in their quest for customers. But even here the competition was keen. Noting the rush of Northern iron men south in 1859 to secure orders from the lines reaching out from Mobile, Anderson and Company wrote that they were relying on their Southern friends to help Southern industry.[46] Their correspondence constantly emphasized this point—that they were a Southern firm producing for a Southern clientele.[47]

The Richmond press strongly seconded Anderson and Company's appeals for Southerners to buy at home. "Our manufacturers have been neglected by the State, by our railroad companies and by our citizens generally, though they only ask a difference in price equal to the difference in quality," wrote the *Enquirer.* Had Southern roads availed themselves of Richmond's iron facilities earlier, concluded the *Enquirer* editorial, "they would now have good and substantial roads . . . instead of rails fast going to destruction, owing to the miserable and worthless character of the foreign iron, of which they are made." [48] Dr. Archer observed with great pleasure that the Democratic *Enquirer* had "taken very strong *Whig* ground in favor of fostering our domestic manufactures." [49]

Patriotic appeals were not Anderson and Company's most effective technique for securing Southern rail orders, however. The management's willingness to extend liberal credit to Southern roads and accept their securities, often at par, frequently secured large contracts, as indicated by a rich harvest of orders received in January 1860. In that month, the Mobile and Ohio Railroad ordered iron work for one hundred box cars, the Georgia Central contracted for fifty freight cars, and the Charleston and Savannah

45. R. Archer to Sam McKenzie, March 16, 1859, ibid.

46. Anderson & Co. to James Whitfield, Nov. 4, 1859, ibid.

47. See Anderson & Co. to T. F. Jamison, March 8, 1859, to McCowall & Callahan, Oct. 17, 1859, to Robert Hanson, March 23, 1860, and to John D. Gray, Oct. 24, 1860, ibid.

48. Richmond *Enquirer,* Nov. 16, 1858. See also *Enquirer* editorials on Nov. 19, 1858, and April 29, Sept. 30, 1859.

49. R. Archer to William Irvin, Nov. 16, 1858, Tredegar Letterbooks.

ordered twenty-five cars. In addition, Louisville and Nashville Railroad officials signed a contract for all the spikes and chairs for a branch road to Memphis and the Richmond and York River Railroad placed a similar order to complete fifteen remaining miles of its track. In every case, the contracts called for payment in interest-bearing notes maturing in four to eight months from the date of delivery of the iron, and in railroad, city, or state bonds.[50] "The whole of our large capital is now in the hands of our Rail Road friends," Anderson remarked in April 1860.[51]

The Tredegar owners thus managed to effect large sales, particularly in the cotton states, despite prices often 20 per cent higher than Northern manufacturers.[52] In the first quarter of business for the new partnership in 1859, every rolling mill sale in excess of $1,000, with a single exception, went to a railroad or bridge builder south of Virginia, and usually in the deep South.[53] One of the partners expressed satisfaction in 1859 that several Southern roads seemed to have "a disposition to keep their work at home." "It is high time the South should be doing something to encourage their own manufactures," he told a Tennessee customer.[54] But the Tredegar management still faced stiff outside competition for sales in the South.

The efforts which Anderson and his partners made to reduce production costs and market their iron throughout the South were thus only partially successful. Extensive use of Negro slaves in the rolling mills failed to reduce labor costs significantly. The Tredegar owners faced an equally serious problem in the expense of their raw materials. If the works consumed high quality, but costly, Virginia charcoal metal, the price of Tredegar products rose well above Northern and English competition. If Northern anthracite metal went into Anderson and Company's finished iron, quality declined and the price still had to remain high to cover freight charges on the Northern pig. As tension mounted between the North and the South in the 1850s, the Tredegar owners became increasingly willing to seek a political solution to their economic problems. When Anderson and his partners began indulging in that perennial Southern pastime of "calculating the value of the Union," they came up with very few entries on the profit side of their ledgers.

50. Contracts dated Jan. 3, 19, 21, 24, 26, 1860, Tredegar Contract Books.

51. Anderson & Co. to George R. Foster, April 26, 1860, Tredegar Letterbooks.

52. Anderson & Co. to Charles Lewis, May 5, 1860, ibid.

53. Tredegar Rolling Mill Sales Books.

54. R. Archer to George W. Grice, March 9, 1859, and to William Irvin, Nov. 16, 1858, Tredegar Letterbooks.

3

The Politics and Profits of Disunion

I

Even during his first crowded years with the Tredegar, Anderson had always found time for politics. Like most Southern iron men, he was a confirmed Whig in the 1840s and early '50s. His older brothers, Francis and John, were both prominent in Whig political circles in Virginia as early as the 1830s and they undoubtedly had an influence on Joseph's politics. While still at West Point, the Whig doctrine of government support for internal improvements had attracted him and as a young army officer, he had found Whig nationalism appealing. After visiting Charleston in 1836, he expressed his "regret" that such a fine, hospitable people were infected with "the disorganizing and heretical doctrine . . . of nullification." [1] The next year in a rather vague description of his political views, he had declared himself in favor of "moderate & *conservative principles*, by which I understand in this country [to be] medium ground between *locofocoism* on the one hand and aristocracy on the other." [2]

Anderson's early years as an iron manufacturer convinced him of the desirability of another Whig plank, a protective tariff. He was bitterly opposed to the reduction in iron duties carried out by the Democratic Walker tariff of 1846, an act which he referred to "as nothing more nor less than a wicked sporting with the interests of a respectable portion of the country." [3] He enthusiastically supported General Zachary Taylor's candidacy in 1848 and after Taylor's inauguration, Anderson went to Washington to lobby for higher iron duties. "I saw both the President & Secretary of the Treasury and am satisfied they are with us heart and soul on the Tariff as well as [Secretary of the Navy] Preston whom I saw also," Anderson in-

1. Anderson to F. T. Anderson, Dec. 6, 1836, Anderson Papers, UVA.
2. Anderson to F. T. Anderson, Nov. 24, 1837, ibid.
3. Anderson to F. T. Anderson, Oct. 30, 1848, ibid.

formed his brother in the fall of 1849.[4] The increasingly heated sectional debate over slavery in the territories and Taylor's sudden death in 1850 soon shunted tariff revision to the background but Anderson refused to abandon hope. "At present I can only say that I think the prospect of a change in the tariff is much better or was when I was in Washington a week or ten days ago," Anderson noted in June 1850. "The only difficulty is the settlement of the Slavery and territorial question, which I confess looks darker & darker."[5] The Tredegar owner's chief concern during the turbulent months preceding the Compromise of 1850 was still the tariff.

Anderson's lobbying activities were all well and good but they did not satisfy his taste for politics. A Southerner with his drive, ambition, and political interests was not likely to be content to remain merely on the fringes of politics. He sought his first elective office, a seat on the Richmond City Council, in 1847 and won his race. During the next fourteen years, he served five terms on that body. In January 1852, he moved up to the state legislature when the voters of Richmond elected him to fill out the unexpired term of a deceased representative. After campaigning successfully for reelection in 1853, he was appointed to the important Committee on Roads and Internal Navigation and he used this position to promote measures calling for state support for railroads and canals. The Richmond industrialist also participated actively in the strongly Whiggish commercial conventions that shuttled between Southern cities prior to the war.[6]

Although the tariff was Anderson's chief concern among national issues in the late 1840s, he found it impossible to ignore the slavery question. At first he was primarily worried about the potential of the slavery issue to destroy party unity and any chance for enactment of the Whig program, including tariff revision. He found particularly galling charges made by Virginia Democrats that antislavery elements had taken over the Northern wing of the Whig party. Congressional elections in Connecticut in the spring of 1849 proved that these accusations were unfounded, Anderson wrote after a trip to New England. Democratic victories were achieved "by an open union of the Free Soilers or abolitionists with the democrats," he charged. "I hope hereafter we will hear no more in Virginia of the Whig

4. Anderson to F. T. Anderson, Nov. 19, 1849, ibid.

5. Anderson to F. T. Anderson, June 30, 1850, ibid.

6. Freeman, "Cool Head," p. 14; *Journal of the [Virginia] House of Delegates, 1852* (Richmond, 1852), p. 646, *1853–54* (Richmond, 1854), pp. 34, 40, 217, 279, 317, 412–13; Bruce, *Virginia Iron Manufacture*, p. 229.

party in the North being infected with abolitionism, or free soilism, which is the same thing, or but another name for abolitionism." [7] Anderson's hopes for Democratic silence were not to be realized, and by the early 1850s he could no longer attempt to argue away the deep sectional split in his party. Lacking effective leaders and bitterly divided over the slavery issue, the Whigs crumbled as a national political force. For the Richmond manufacturer, the party's inability to protect Southern interests became increasingly crucial. With the Whigs clearly unable to win a Presidential election or control Congress, Anderson dissolved his lifelong political ties and entered the ranks of the opposition.

The events of 1856 changed Anderson from a Whig nationalist to a Democratic sectionalist. He began the year in normal enough fashion, serving as a delegate to the Southern commercial convention meeting in Richmond in January and February. He sat on the resolutions committee and spoke on the floor of the convention in behalf of various economic planks, always avoiding political matters. Anderson directed his remarks solely toward the promotion of various schemes for Southern economic improvement, including the establishment of direct trade with Europe and the construction of a southern Pacific railroad. He probably objected to a resolution demanding repeal or reduction of all duties on railroad iron but the plank calling for the use of Southern manufactures in preference to Northern doubtless had his support. Anderson also sat with J. D. B. DeBow on a committee of nine to summarize the results of the convention and publish an address to the South. The resulting proclamation stated the object of the convention was "to secure to the Southern States the utmost prosperity as an integral part of the Federal Union." [8] This statement probably summarized Anderson's attitude toward disunion at the beginning of that critical election year.

Anderson's Whiggery underwent an abrupt change later in 1856 when the Republican party emerged as a serious challenger on the national political scene. In the three way race between the Republican, John C. Frémont, James Buchanan, and Millard Fillmore, Anderson saw no choice but to abandon the candidate of the American and Whig parties and support the Democrat, Buchanan. Further allegiance to the fading Whig

7. Anderson to F. T. Anderson, April 6, 1849, Anderson Papers, UVA.

8. *DeBow's Review, 20* (1856), 351. For the proceedings of the convention, see Richmond *Whig*, Feb. 1, 4, 1856.

organization would not help in the battle to save the South from Frémont and "Black Republicanism." Anderson and a number of other prominent Richmond citizens announced themselves as Buchanan Whigs, a move which brought immediate scorn from the Richmond *Whig*. "A 'Buchanan Whig' is as complete an anomaly and contradiction as a white-black man or an infidel-christian," quipped the editor.[9]

John T. Anderson, a confirmed Whig, tried unsuccessfully to persuade his brother Joseph to remain within the party. John thought "the fate of our glorious Union" hung on Fillmore's election. "I have been well aware that there is a strong party in the South anxious for a dissolution and that they have for many years been agitating the slave question with the abolitionists with the view of effecting that object," he wrote Joseph. If the secessionists succeeded in their plan, John believed that "it will be the darkest day this country ever saw. It will plunge it in civil and servile war—a war of extermination that our children's children will not see the end of." [10] Joseph did not share this apocalyptic vision, however, and he held to the Democratic party despite his brother's admonitions.

In 1857, Anderson again ran for the General Assembly, but this time as a Democrat. The Richmond *Whig*, angered at his defection, conducted a spirited campaign against him. "Mr. Anderson's Democracy is the result of a deliberate calculation of dollars and cents," the *Whig* editor charged. "He has been receiving several fat contracts from the General Government, and he expects to receive many more, if he holds fast to the Democratic faith." The *Whig* accused Anderson of publicly stating a few years earlier that "when his private interests come in conflict with the public interests, he always made the public interest yield to his private interests." [11] Anderson flatly denied ever having made such a statement and a majority of Richmond's voters evidently believed him. The Democratic challengers swept the entire Richmond delegation out of office, capturing the stronghold of Virginia Whiggery.[12] Anderson took his seat in the House of Delegates and continued to concentrate his efforts on securing state support for internal improvements.[13] He stood for reelection in 1859 but lost

9. Ibid., Sept. 9, 1856.

10. John T. Anderson to J. R. Anderson, Sept. 25, 1856, Robert A. Brock Papers, HL.

11. Richmond *Whig*, May 26, 1857.

12. Ibid., May 29, 1857; Richmond *Examiner*, May 29, 1857.

13. *Journal of the [Virginia] House of Delegates, 1857–58* (Richmond, 1858), pp. 24, 63, 99, 110, 418.

in a close race as a Whig–Know-Nothing ticket won Richmond's three house seats.[14] Anderson nevertheless remained within the Democratic party, for the same reason which had first caused him to abandon the Whigs in 1856. "You and many other patriots will feel compelled to support the Democratic organization," he told his brother, "because of its being the only means of defeating the Black Rep. party." [15]

John Brown's raid on the Harpers Ferry arsenal and armory in October 1859 and the events of the months immediately following confirmed Anderson's worst fears of Republican aims. He reacted with both anger and calculation to Brown's attack. His initial move was to urge Governor Henry A. Wise to push for adoption of a bill requiring that preference be given to Virginia manufacturers for all supplies needed by the railroads, canals, and turnpikes in which the state held stock. Since the state had long given massive support to internal improvement projects, this bill would have virtually excluded Northern and British iron and other manufactured goods from a major state market. A large portion of the Tredegar's railroad trade, lost to outside competitors in the late 1850s, would quickly be restored. Anderson saw the governor personally on this matter and restated his views in a letter on November 18: "Pardon me if I express to you the opinion long entertained that the whole state is most deeply interested in the question not only pecuniarily but as connected intimately with her defence and independence." [16]

An anonymous letter supporting such restrictive legislation appeared simultaneously in the Richmond press. "A Railway Stockholder," Anderson in all likelihood, advised the editor of the *Whig* to look into the subsidy of hundreds of thousands of dollars given "Northern abolitionists" by Virginia railroad officials, "men who systematically expend every dollar *out of the state* that they can so expend, with the least show of reason." In language all too similar to that employed by Anderson in his letter to the governor the following day, the anonymous correspondent concluded by expressing his assurance that if the editor examined this question,

> I am sure you will agree with me in the opinion I have long entertained and often expressed that if Virginia and other Southern States would watchfully attend to the expenditures of the railway corporations and other corporations of their own creation, they would more

14. Richmond *Enquirer*, May 27, 1859.

15. Anderson to F. T. Anderson, June 6, 1857, Anderson Papers, UVA.

16. Anderson to Gov. Henry A. Wise, Nov. 18, 1859, Virginia Executive Papers, VSL.

> effectually establish manufactories and receive all the advantages of a diversified industry, than can be done by any tariff law that Congress ever did or can enact.[17]

The governor chose not to call for such a bill in his December message to the General Assembly. The joint House and Senate committee investigating the Harpers Ferry raid passed a resolution calling for legislation to encourage domestic manufactures and establish Virginia's commercial independence, but the legislature took no steps to implement this resolution.[18]

For weeks after the attack on Harpers Ferry, Anderson anticipated much greater violence to result from the raid. "What will be the effect of the war with the free states which seems to be impending and consequent dissolution of the Union remains to be seen," he wrote in late November.[19] When a general conflict failed to materialize and Anderson was unable to secure restrictive legislation from the state, he and his partners threatened to embark on a personal boycott of Northern suppliers. The Harpers Ferry incident brought into his business dealings the anger Anderson felt toward the personal liberty laws of some Northern states and his fear of Republican national ascendancy, resentment which he had previously channeled solely into his personal political activities. He told a Philadelphia pig iron agent that he and his partners had "some good and true friends of a fair and constitutional lean in the North" but that "in view of recent events, and so long as the Legislatures of those States are inimical to us, and laws remain on their statute books unfriendly to us and denying our just rights, we believe it is becoming a pretty general resolution in our State not to buy anything that we can do without from the Northern cities." [20]

17. Richmond *Whig*, Nov. 17, 1859.

18. "Report of the Joint Committee of the General Assembly of Virginia on the Harpers Ferry Outrages, January 26, 1860," Document 31, *Senate Documents, 1859–60* (Richmond, 1860), p. 24.

19. Anderson to F. T. Anderson, Nov. 25, 1859, Anderson Papers, UVA.

20. Anderson to E. J. Etting, Dec. 12, 1859, Tredegar Letterbooks. Beginning with Pennsylvania in 1824, a number of Northern states enacted personal liberty laws to make it difficult to return fugitive slaves to the South and to prevent the kidnapping of free Negroes. Following the enactment of the Federal Fugitive Slave Act in 1850, several Northern states, Massachusetts and Wisconsin most conspicuously, passed new laws making enforcement of the Federal statute almost impossible; see Alfred H. Kelly and Winfred A. Harbison, *The American Constitution* (New York, 1963), pp. 360–62, 379–80.

As far as Anderson and Company were concerned, however, the effect of such a boycott was severely limited by the large amounts of critical materials unavailable in Virginia. In addition to pig iron and anthracite coal, the partners continued to depend on Northern sources for almost all their new machines and tools, boiler plate, sheet iron, firebrick, copper and tin for bronze ordnance, and even nuts and bolts. The best Tredegar railroad chairs and spikes were produced by machinery built and patented by a Pittsburgh firm, and Anderson and Company continued to use this equipment.[21] Although it did not suit the political preferences of the Richmond industrialists in late 1859, their works leaned much too heavily on the North for essential raw materials to break off the credit and business relationships built up over two decades. After Anderson's initial anger over the Harpers Ferry raid subsided, he wrote no more to the North about Southern boycotts.

II

Following Brown's attack, Anderson became apprehensive about losing his status as a Federal ordnance contractor. Anticipating government purchases, he had built new boring lathes and had made sizable advances to his brother to lay in a large stock of gun iron but so far no orders had come in. The failure of this previously regular source of income would be particularly damaging at this time because receipts had been slow coming in from the railroads during the summer and the company was short of funds.[22]

A November order from the Army Ordnance Bureau for $20,000 worth of 8-inch columbiads temporarily relieved his depression. The company accepted immediately and promised to commence work as soon as the bureau forwarded the necessary specifications. Two weeks later, however, the bureau informed Anderson and Company that the Secretary of War had ordered all cannon cast under the current appropriation to be manufac-

21. Anderson & Co. to Steele & Worth, March 15, Aug. 18, 1860, to Horace A. Beale, April 9, 1860, to Morris & Jones, Dec. 7, 1859, to the American Bolt Co., May 21, June 16, 1860, to E. Pratt & Bros., April 9, 1860, to H. D. Stover, March 17, 1860, to Gray & Wood, April 18, 1860, to David Keener, Dec. 13, 1860, to A. S. & A. G. Whitten, Jan. 7, 1861, to Walter Gwynn, July 4, 1860, and to Dilworth, Porter & Co., Dec. 15, 1865, Tredegar Letterbooks.

22. Anderson to John T. Anderson, Nov. 2, 1859, to A. Anderson, Oct. 21, 1859, and to Capt. D. N. Ingraham, Nov. 19, 1859, ibid.; agreement with John T. Anderson, Feb. 28, 1860, Tredegar Contract Books.

tured after the "Rodman plan." [23] This decision would necessitate a technological revolution in the Tredegar cannon foundry.

The Rodman plan, developed by Captain Thomas Jackson Rodman of the Ordnance Bureau at the Fort Pitt foundry in Pittsburgh, called for the casting of cannon around a hollow core. A stream of cool water was passed through the core while the flask in which the cannon was cast was surrounded by a mass of burning coals. Thus the molten metal cooled from the inside out, relieving the strains produced in cannon under the old method of casting the tube solid, allowing it to cool from the outside in, and then boring it out. The Rodman plan possessed three advantages: it produced stronger cannon; it permitted safe guns of larger size to be cast than heretofore; and it shortened the period required to finish a cannon by cutting sharply the time required for cooling and boring.[24]

The adoption of this method culminated a long search for improved manufacturing techniques initiated after the explosion of a cannon aboard the U.S.S. *Princeton* in 1844 killed Secretary of State Abel P. Upshur and Secretary of the Navy Thomas W. Gilmer. A series of experiments with a 15-inch Rodman gun in 1859 convinced Secretary of War John B. Floyd of the superiority of the new method and he made a firm decision to have it adopted by all founders producing government ordnance. To facilitate the changeover, he authorized the Ordnance Bureau to pay the 20 per cent royalty to the holder of the patent, Charles Knap of the Fort Pitt foundry, and to give all manufacturers the same prices heretofore paid for cannon. Thus any financial difficulties that the founders might encounter in adopting the Rodman plan would be minimized. He also authorized Captain Rodman to visit each foundry and personally supervise the introduction of his methods to insure technical success.[25]

Despite the Secretary's inducements, Anderson did not agree with the decision of his fellow Virginian in the War Department and he set about to secure a reversal of Floyd's order. He opened a correspondence with Knap in Pittsburgh seeking technical and cost data, but at the same time he asked the Ordnance Bureau for time to examine the subject and for permission to cast the cannon for the current $20,000 order by the old

23. Col. H. K. Craig to Anderson & Co., Nov. 3, 18, 1859, Misc. Letters Sent, Ordnance Office, RG 156, NA; Anderson & Co. to Craig, Nov. 4, 1859, Tredegar Letterbooks.

24. Col. J. G. Benton, *A Course of Instruction in Ordnance and Gunnery . . .* (New York, 1867), pp. 135–37, 551–52.

25. Craig to Anderson & Co., Nov. 18, Dec. 12, 1859, Misc. Letters Sent, Ordnance Office, RG 156, NA.

method.[26] Anderson also learned that the other principal Northern founders, R. P. Parrott of the West Point foundry at Cold Spring, New York, and Cyrus Alger at Boston, were skeptical of the new technique. Dr. Junius L. Archer at the Bellona foundry, thirteen miles up the James River from Richmond, concurred in the opinion of his neighbor. With all the founders, north and south, united against Knap at Pittsburgh, Anderson believed that Secretary Floyd would rescind his order.[27]

On December 1, 1859, Anderson dispatched a long letter to his friend Floyd, seeking to secure a reprieve from the order binding him to use the Rodman method. "It is not our opinion here, based on an experience of twenty years nearly in casting guns, that Mr. Knap's plan is an improvement and I think it hard and humiliating in being obliged either to give up the business or give up my own system in favor of what I regard as a Yankee catch penny," he wrote. Knap had failed in 1854 and 1855 to have a single gun accepted by the navy out of an order for fifty-five pieces, Anderson continued, whereas all Tredegar cannon had passed army and navy proofs in recent years, including that portion of the order for fifty-five naval guns given his Richmond foundry after Knap's failure. "I could say much more to you, with which you are not familiar, about the history of making guns—the troubles I have had to encounter by the efforts of this very establishment [Knap] to drive me out of the business in which they have failed and I have triumphed and that when there was no Virginian at the head of the Department," Anderson concluded. "All I have to say now is that I beg for God's sake that you will see that I have a fair chance and I pledge myself to satisfy you that I ought not to be forced into this thing." [28]

The Richmond founder obviously believed his only chance to survive in the competition for army ordnance contracts rested on such special consideration as his fellow Virginian in Washington might grant him. On December 12, however, the chief of the Ordnance Bureau informed Anderson that the Secretary refused to change the order. Anderson and Company would cast by the Rodman method or not at all, as far as the War Department was concerned.[29]

These developments brought the Tredegar senior partner and his associ-

26. Anderson & Co. to Charles Knap, Nov. 29, 1859, and to Craig, Nov. 23, 1859, Tredegar Letterbooks.

27. Anderson & Co. to Cyrus Alger & Co., Nov. 26, 1859, ibid.; J. L. Archer to John B. Floyd, Jan. 30, 1860, Letters from the War Department, Ordnance Office, RG 156, NA.

28. Anderson to Floyd, Dec. 1, 1859, Tredegar Letterbooks.

29. Craig to Anderson & Co., Dec. 12, 1859, Misc. Letters Sent, Ordnance Office, RG 156, NA.

ates to a fuller realization that their political and economic future lay with an independent South. The firm gave positive expression to their belief in a letter sent to the governors of North and South Carolina, Georgia, Florida, Alabama, Mississippi, Louisiana, Arkansas, Texas, Tennessee, and Kentucky on December 8, 1859, at the height of the ordnance crisis with the Federal government: "The time has arrived when the South should be looking to her defences, and we offer our Foundry and our experience to your State, whenever she may require them, and will charge for our guns (iron or brass) shot and shells, the same price we receive from the Government of the United States." [30] This offer brought little immediate response, other than a rush order for grapeshot from Virginia authorities.[31] The Richmond firm could not rebuild its ordnance business in the South in 1859. A year later, Anderson and Company repeated the offer with much more tangible results.

When the company's premature appeal to the Southern governors went unheeded, Anderson resumed his correspondence with the Federal government. Loss of the steady cash income from the Ordnance Bureau remained the major disappointment in the Tredegar's operations during the first six months of 1860. Between January and September 1859, the company had received $42,663 for ordnance and munitions delivered to the army and navy, and Anderson was determined to regain this market in 1860.[32] No doubt he was encouraged when J. L. Archer at the nearby Bellona foundry secured Secretary Floyd's permission in February to cast solid forty-six cannon remaining from an 1857 order.[33] That same month, Anderson again sought relief from the Secretary's order, complaining that he had laid in a thousand tons of gun iron and that experiments still, in his opinion, had not conclusively proved the superiority of the Rodman method. The chief of the Ordnance Bureau replied that, in the opinion of the Secretary of War, the experiments with the Rodman gun were conclusive and that Parrott of the West Point foundry had agreed to adopt the system of hollow casting. The bureau definitely would accept no guns cast solid.[34]

30. Tredegar Letterbooks.

31. Entries for Nov.–Dec. 1859, Tredegar Foundry Sales Books.

32. Entries for U.S. Ordnance Department and Bureau of Ordnance and Hydrography, Tredegar Ledgers.

33. J. L. Archer to Floyd, Jan. 30, 1860, Letters from the War Department, Ordnance Office, and Craig to J. L. Archer, Feb. 3, 1860, Misc. Letters Sent, Ordnance Office, RG 156, NA.

34. Anderson & Co. to Craig, Feb. 23, 1860, Letters from the War Department, Ordnance Office, and Craig to Anderson & Co., Feb. 25, 1860, Misc. Letters Sent, Ordnance Office, ibid.

The Secretary of War's decision had cut off the major source of government revenue. The December 1859 appeal to Southern governors had brought almost no response. And the action of Mark A. Cooper, a Georgia ironmaster seeking to secure brass ordnance for his state in the spring of 1860, must have particularly discouraged the Richmond founder. Anderson and Cooper were friends of long standing and Anderson doubtless expected to receive the order of a sister Southern state. After talking with Anderson in Richmond, however, Cooper continued on north and awarded the contract to a Massachusetts founder who shaved his price one cent a pound below Anderson's. And to add even greater insult, Georgia contracted with Anderson's bitter competitor, Charles Knap at Pittsburgh, for a large number of heavy coast defense cannon.[35] Anderson was ready to give up the manufacture of ordnance after this blow. Only an unexpected naval order for nine 9-inch shell guns, executed between June 18 and November 25, 1860, prevented him from breaking up his ordnance operation.[36]

When John T. Anderson informed his brother in May 1860 that he was considering abandoning the manufacture of gun metal at Cloverdale furnace and selling the property as farm land, Joseph replied that such a course might be advisable, although he thought the land would bring more if sold intact as an iron property. If John did break up the Cloverdale furnace, however, Joseph would make no more guns. "For while we both reluctantly give up the use of an Iron which we have tested so long, 18 years, and we have risked so much to establish, it appears that the good results obtained are not appreciated by the government and our operations of late have been disastrous to both of us." "Do you think we are likely ever to be compensated for such wear and tear of body and spirit?" he asked his brother.[37] Joseph had stockpiled some $35,000 worth of gun iron which he could dispose of only at a great loss and had loaned John a large amount of money. John finally decided not to abandon his furnace; he converted production from gun metal to car wheel and cheaper grades

35. Anderson & Co. to Mark A. Cooper, May 2, 1860, and to J. R. Powell, Nov. 22, 1860, Tredegar Letterbooks; *The War of the Rebellion: A Compilation of the Official Records of the Union and Confederate Armies* (128 vols. Washington, 1880–1901), Series IV, *1*, 169. Hereafter cited as *O.R.*

36. Anderson & Co. to Ingraham, April 14, 1860, Tredegar Letterbooks; entry for Dec. 1860, Tredegar Foundry Sales Books.

37. Anderson to John T. Anderson, May 7, 1860, Tredegar Letterbooks.

of iron to stay in blast.[38] And Joseph did not break up his ordnance operation. But the South came dangerously close to losing its major sources of gun iron and cannon in 1860.

Anderson made still another effort to convince Secretary of War Floyd that the Tredegar should be allowed to cast guns solid. During the first week of June, he went to Washington to explain his case to the Secretary in person. Anderson gave Floyd information he had received that Knap was having difficulty in executing his 1859 order for cannon. Anderson therefore asked the Secretary's permission to cast his share of the 1859 requisition by the old method until either Knap successfully completed his order or, if the Secretary so desired, an experimental gun cast hollow out of Cloverdale metal proved stronger than previous Tredegar cannon. Anderson received some encouragement from Floyd and the Secretary advised him to put his case in writing and he would consider it. Anderson did so immediately upon his return to Richmond.[39] After three tense weeks of waiting, Anderson received the Secretary's terse reply that "it does not appear that the alleged defects or delay in casting at Fort Pitt foundry, are attributable to the mode of hollow casting, and I see no sufficient reason for changing any previous decisions on this subject." [40] The Richmond founder still refused to adopt the Rodman method and the matter appeared closed.

Anderson clearly missed a unique opportunity in 1859 and 1860 to provide the South with the most advanced equipment and technical knowledge for casting heavy ordnance. Following the John Brown incident, Anderson allowed his anger toward the North generally and his antagonism toward a Northern founder and his "Yankee catchpenny" in particular to cloud his judgment. He and his partners installed the most up-to-date equipment in the blacksmith shops, rolling mills, and wheel foundry but refused to modify the process of cannon manufacture, even when the government offered every convenience to expedite the change. The Rodman method was an improved technique, as Northern founders who first resisted its adoption later admitted.[41] The Union Chief of Ordnance testified in 1864

38. Anderson to John T. Anderson, May 18, Sept. 18, Oct 2, 1860, ibid.

39. Anderson to Floyd, June 8, 1860, ibid.; see also Anderson to John T. Anderson, June 12, 1860, and to R. P. Parrott, June 14, 1860, ibid.

40. Craig to Anderson & Co., June 27, 1860, Misc. Letters Sent, Ordnance Office, RG 156, NA.

41. Testimony of R. P. Parrott, Jan. 18, 1865, in "Heavy Ordnance," *Report of the Joint Committee on the Conduct of the War, 1865*, 38th Cong., 2d sess. (3 vols. Washington, 1865), 2, 138.

that the army relied on getting as many firings from one Rodman gun as from three cannon of similar caliber cast solid.[42] Anderson's refusal to change his method of manufacture before the war cost the South dearly in the ensuing conflict.

III

To make up for the loss of their government business, the Tredegar partners stepped up their "buy Southern" campaign in 1860. "We have long been engaged in manufacturing for Southern Roads," Anderson wrote a Georgia railroad man in April, "and for this purpose have invested the earnings of a quarter of a century in an establishment for manufacturing such articles . . . as we consider worthy of the Great South to which we belong." [43] As tension mounted in 1860 with the approach of the fall elections, the Tredegar partners' letters reflected an increased awareness of the economic gain to be derived from their Southern location. "I have always been satisfied that you would prefer patronizing us to Northern men," Anderson told an Alabama railroad superintendent in October. "I know you would and all connected with you and I would not ask (and never will) more than that simple preference. You have repeatedly given me and those connected with me in our varied enterprises, to render the South independent in some respects of the North, that preference, and I thank you for it." [44]

The Richmond press again lent its firm support to Anderson and Company's campaign. "When our whole country is in a state of political excitement, and disunion has almost become a by-word, it would seem to be the dictate of prudence as well as patriotism, to direct the public mind to the encouragement of our own industrial pursuits," wrote the Richmond *Enquirer* in a September 1860 article on the Tredegar works. It called on Southern men to support the Richmond firm with liberal patronage, "and thus keep at home the money which they have heretofore so freely lavished upon Northern establishments hostile to our institutions." [45]

The Richmond City Council showed a willingness to follow the *Enquirer's* advice. In December 1859, the council awarded a $30,000 to

42. Ibid., p. 11.
43. Anderson & Co. to Edwin Dyer, April 26, 1860, Tredegar Letterbooks.
44. Anderson & Co. to Samuel G. Jones, Oct. 29, 1860, ibid.
45. Richmond *Enquirer*, Sept. 5, 1860.

$40,000 contract for water pipe to Anderson and Company, thus relieving some of the financial difficulty threatened by the loss of the Federal ordnance order. The Tredegar bid was the lowest among Richmond offers but every bid from Philadelphia and Baltimore undercut Anderson's, one by as much as 20 per cent.[46]

To secure additional work for the foundry employees, Anderson and Company also subcontracted for Federal orders for shot and shell from manufacturers who were willing to dispose of their requisitions. "We offer you this because we have a good many hands we would rather keep employed though we would make nothing," explained one of the partners.[47] Several manufacturers accepted the company's proposition and this work, along with the Richmond pipe contract, allowed the Tredegar partners to keep their force of pattern makers, molders, and founders intact even though a sharp drop in foundry sales occurred in December 1859 and January 1860.

Despite consistently higher prices for railroad iron than those asked by non-Southern competitors and the loss of the large Federal ordnance contract late in the year, Anderson and Company realized handsome profits in 1859, at least on paper. In the first year of the new partnership, the Tredegar and Armory rolling mills returned a net profit of $56,138 and the foundry operations made a profit of $26,589.[48] These figures are somewhat inflated, however, since much of the company's profit was in the form of promissory notes of Southern railroads, paper which often rested on very rickety financing.

The new year began auspiciously for Anderson and his partners. January brought an influx of railroad orders from the deep South and both foundry and rolling mill production rose sharply beginning in February. In March and April, rolling mill sales topped 1,000,000 pounds both months and remained above 900,000 pounds through May and June. Monthly foundry and rolling mill sales reached a record total of $99,030

46. Report of the Watering Committee, April 8, 1861, in Richmond City Council Minute Books, VSL; entries for May–Dec. 1860, Tredegar Foundry Sales Books; Anderson & Co. to Felix Wyatt, Dec. 9, 1859, Tredegar Letterbooks.

47. Anderson & Co. to Taylor & Humphries, Nov. 22, 1859, ibid.; see also Anderson & Co. to Samuel C. Robinson, Nov. 22, 1859, and to T. J. Hawkins, Nov. 22, 1859, ibid., and contract with Robinson, Dec. 2, 1859, Tredegar Contract Books.

48. See entries for Dec. 1859, Tredegar Journals. For an explanation of "profit" as the term is used here, see note to Table 8.

in June, paced by Southern railroad orders.[49] When the heat of Richmond's summer forced Tredegar workmen to bank the forge and foundry fires in July, the partners had no reason to suspect that sales would not maintain the first half pace during the coming autumn.

Encouraging business prospects prompted the owners to expand certain departments in 1860. They added an extension to the engine finishing shop, purchased new woodworking tools for manufacturing box cars and saw mills, improved the iron and brass foundries, and doubled the capacity of the wheel foundry by building a new cupola and installing up-to-date machinery for boring and drawing wheels onto the axles. In addition, a large steam hammer, capable of executing the heaviest forging, was erected in the blacksmith shop and the horsepower of the rolling mills increased by the construction of a larger water wheel, complemented by a more efficient system of belts for driving the machinery.[50] The Tredegar associates even considered themselves solvent enough to contribute to one of the pet direct trade schemes endorsed by the Southern commercial conventions. In May 1860, they subscribed $5,000 toward a Richmond–Liverpool packet line, an amount equal to the largest Richmond contribution.[51]

IV

In August 1860, Anderson and Company won a contract from the Commonwealth of Virginia which would temporarily compensate for the loss of the army ordnance business. Again, John Brown's raid was the moving force behind a shift in the company's fortunes. As a direct result of the raid, the Virginia General Assembly in January 1860 appropriated $500,000 to equip the State Armory at Richmond with the most improved musket machinery and to purchase arms and munitions. Three commissioners, appointed by the governor, were to supervise the awarding of the contract for the machinery and the acquisition of weapons. Governor John Letcher quickly appointed three outstanding Virginia military figures as commissioners: Colonel Francis N. Smith, superintendent of the Virginia Military Institute; Philip St. George Cocke, a West Point graduate and member of the board of V.M.I.; and George W. Randolph, grandson of

49. Entries for Jan.–July 1860, Tredegar Foundry Sales Books and Tredegar Rolling Mill Sales Books.

50. Anderson & Co. to D. & H. Riker, March 19, 1860, to George W. Grice, March 13, 1860, to Gray & Woods, March 22, 1860, to John Rutherfoord, May 11, 1860, and to W. M. Barron, Sept. 5, 1860, Tredegar Letterbooks.

51. Anderson & Co. to Messrs. Abrahams, May 30, 1860, ibid.

Thomas Jefferson, a navy veteran, and an organizer of a Richmond volunteer artillery regiment after the Harpers Ferry incident.[52]

The Tredegar partners evidently displayed little interest in the project until July 1860, after Secretary of War Floyd turned down Anderson's plea for permission to cast cannon in late June. The only bid received by the commissioners prior to that time came from the prominent Northern firm of James T. Ames and Company of Chicopee, Massachusetts.[53] The Richmond *Enquirer*, learning that the commissioners were on the verge of recommending acceptance of the Ames bid, told the three Virginians that such a decision would "not only involve mortification to our state pride, but very great injustice to the enterprise and skill of our own contractors and workmen." [54] When the New York *Times* repeated the *Enquirer* editorial, commenting that "the South is thus demonstrated to be so poorly prepared for the dangerous experiment of independence, that not only does it lack the ordinary machinery of pacific progress but that even the immediate means of asserting its political individuality must be obtained from the contemptuous commercial enterprise of its rivals," the *Enquirer* called on the commissioners and Virginia entrepreneurs to force the "Northern Abolition Sheet" to swallow its own words.[55] Finally on August 27, the *Enquirer* thanked the *Times* for its "elaborate sneers at the supposed helplessness of the State of Virginia" which assisted in bringing forth a successful bid from J. R. Anderson and Company.

Although the *Enquirer* took credit for initiating the drive to keep the contract in Virginia, Anderson had acquired the services of a skilled armorer to assist the Tredegar in drawing up a bid in July, prior to the *Enquirer's* campaign. James N. Smith, formerly the master mechanic for James T. Ames and Company, agreed to come down to Richmond in July and he and the Richmond firm worked out a proposition for the musket machinery.[56] The *Enquirer* was correct about one thing. The commissioners had recommended that the governor accept the bid of the Massachu-

52. *Acts of the [Virginia] General Assembly 1859–60* (Richmond, 1860), pp. 126–27; entries for Jan. 30, Feb. 11, 1860, Virginia Executive Journal, VSL; *D.A.B.*, *4*, 254–55, *15*, 358–59. Randolph later served briefly (March to Nov. 1862) as Confederate Secretary of War.

53. Philip St. George Cocke, Francis H. Smith, and G. W. Randolph, Commissioners, to Gov. John Letcher, Aug. 17, 1860, Virginia Executive Papers, VSL.

54. Richmond *Enquirer*, Aug. 7, 1860.

55. Ibid., Aug. 11, 1860.

56. Anderson & Co. to J. N. Smith, July 30, Sept. 17, 1860, and to A. Hitchcock, Aug. 7, 1860, Tredegar Letterbooks.

setts firm of Ames and Company. But when Anderson informed Governor Letcher in July that the Tredegar wished to make a bid and requested time to secure an armorer to assist the firm, the governor instructed the commissioners to receive additional proposals.[57]

The commissioners, meeting during the summer at the fashionable Virginia watering resort of White Sulphur Springs, heard Anderson and J. N. Smith personally present a formal bid for the contract in mid-August. Anderson particularly emphasized the importance of keeping the contract within the state. If an emergency should arise, the machinery would be underway in Virginia and could be completed and later duplicated if the state desired increased capacity. A body of skilled Virginia laborers, familiar with the machinery, would be available when the armory began to operate. Anderson sought to dispel any doubts the commissioners might entertain about the ability of his supposedly inexperienced company to produce the machinery by stressing past Tredegar accomplishments: "Whenever we have first proposed to execute any important enterprise for the Genl. Government the same objection has been raised by our Northern competitors, that we were unacquainted with the business, yet we have the official testimonial of triumphant success in every case." Anderson and Company proposed to manufacture the machinery, capable of producing 5,000 rifle muskets per year, for $156,590, a bid slightly higher than that of Ames and Company. In conclusion, Anderson admitted that some of the machinery would have to be purchased outside the state, singling out the machinery for manufacturing stocks as an example. But he and his partners promised "to have as much of it done at home as practicable without injury to the state or serious loss to ourselves." [58]

The commissioners accepted Anderson's bid as well as his logic. They recalled their previous recommendation in favor of Ames and Company and awarded the contract to the Richmond firm in order to encourage Virginia manufactures: "It is due to our own people, and especially to those who have been struggling, and successfully too, in the midst of strong and opposing difficulties to build up industrial establishments within our own limits that we should foster their worthy efforts, by aiding, as far as we may, in educating that class of artisans by whom, in a great degree, the

57. Anderson & Co. to Letcher, July 28, 1860, ibid.; Commissioners to Letcher, Aug. 17, 1860, Virginia Executive Papers, VSL.

58. Anderson & Co. to the Commissioners, Aug. 15, 1860, Tredegar Letterbooks; "Specifications for Musket Machinery," undated [1860], Tredegar Contract Books; entry for Aug. 1860, Tredegar Journals.

wealth and independence of our state may be preserved and advanced." [59] Anderson's "buy at home" campaign had reaped its richest dividend.

The contract called for Anderson and Company to furnish the completed machinery by December 1, 1861. To assist in paying for the machinery as it was finished, the state agreed to meet Anderson's bills by turning over to the company Virginia's stock of over 50,000 old smoothbore flintlock muskets at a valuation of $1.50 each. The state reserved only 10,000 of the obsolete pieces for emergency use until the first 5,000 new rifled muskets were completed. To justify the higher price paid Anderson and Company, the contract also specified that native labor and enterprise should be used to execute as much of the contract as practicable and that the Tredegar should not sublet any part of the machinery outside the state that could be done in Virginia in time to meet the December 1861 deadline. Formal signing of the contract took place on August 23, 1860.[60]

The Virginia contract was quite favorable to Anderson and his partners, primarily because of the clause calling for payment in old muskets valued at $1.50 each. The muskets were to be in good order, and with the increasing tension following the turbulent political conventions of the spring and summer, the market on muskets, flintlock included, was decidedly bullish. One of the partners, John F. Tanner, was already in New York when the contract was signed and Anderson informed him immediately that the muskets were available. He told Tanner to confer about disposing of the weapons with the man who acted as an intermediary in securing the services of Ames and Company's ex-master armorer.[61]

Tanner opened negotiations and Anderson headed north on a two-week trip about September 1 to assist his partner in drawing up a contract for the sale of the muskets. He also wished to secure all the information he could by visiting Northern armories and machine shops. On September 13, Anderson and Company made a contract with the New York arms firm of Cooper and Pond to dispose of the flintlock muskets. Cooper and Pond agreed to sell all the muskets Anderson could ship them, retaining as their commission one quarter of the profits remaining after paying the Richmond firm a minimum of $1.50 per musket plus all freight and insurance charges. In September and October, Anderson and his associates shipped

59. Commissioners to Letcher, Aug. 17, 1860, Virginia Executive Papers, VSL.

60. Contract between the Commissioners and Anderson & Co., Aug. 23, 1860, ibid.; *Calendar of Virginia State Papers, 1652–1869* (11 vols. Richmond, 1875–93), *11*, 186–88.

61. Anderson & Co. to Tanner, Aug. 24, 1860, Tredegar Letterbooks.

3,500 muskets to New York. They sold quickly at $2.40 to $2.50 apiece.[62] If the partners could continue to draw freely on the state muskets, they would net a considerable profit on the armory contract.

Anderson and Company hoped the Virginia contract would lead to orders for arms machinery from other Southern states. The management opened correspondence with Georgia, North Carolina, and Alabama officials but nothing materialized to the south.[63]

V

This contract with the state of Virginia offered an excellent hedge against any financial unrest that might result from the frenzied political activity of the summer and fall of 1860. The Tredegar partners were well aware of the defiant spirit of Southern Democrats prior to the Charleston convention. Anderson participated in both the Richmond city and the state Democratic meetings in February 1860 which voted down resolutions calling on the Virginia Democracy to support unconditionally the nominee of the Charleston convention.[64] The ensuing walkout of Southern delegates at Charleston and their reassembling in Richmond in June provided Anderson and his associates with immediate evidence of the growing political tension in the South.

They would not know, however, how seriously this tension would affect their all-important Southern business until October. As the heat of the Richmond summer subsided, Tredegar workmen rekindled the fires in anticipation of the usual autumn increase in trade. Sales in August and September were good for both foundry and rolling mill products. The first signs of an impending economic crash came when foundry sales dropped from $41,984 in September to $18,836 in October.[65]

Even before Lincoln's election, a financial storm began sweeping across the South that threatened the Tredegar with bankruptcy. "Money matters here are as much deranged as in '57," one of the partners wrote a Tennessee railroad correspondent.[66] The precipitous drop in foundry sales

62. Anderson to F. H. Smith, Aug. 29, 1860, ibid.; contract with Cooper & Pond, Sept. 13, 1860, Tredegar Contract Books; entries for Sept.–Oct. 1860, Tredegar Rolling Mill Sales Books.

63. Anderson & Co. to John W. Anderson, Sept. 18, 1860, to Commissioners for the State of Georgia, Nov. 9, 1860, to Capt. P. H. Colquitt, Dec. 18, 1860, to Gov. John W. Ellis, Dec. 27, 1860, to Senator Marcus Morton, Jan. 16, 1861, and to Horace Ware, Feb. 12, 1861, Tredegar Letterbooks.

64. Richmond *Enquirer*, Feb. 14, 18, 1860.

65. Tredegar Foundry Sales Books.

66. Anderson & Co. to William B. Waldron, Oct. 23, 1860, Tredegar Letterbooks.

was accompanied by the failure of Southern railroads to meet their notes given to the Tredegar for the large amounts of iron delivered earlier in 1860. Richmond banks refused to discount the railroad paper and set prohibitive interest rates of up to 2 per cent per month on short term loans. With local credit sources drying up, Anderson and his associates attempted to realize something on their large holdings of state, municipal, and railroad bonds, but met with no success. Northern creditors who had accepted Anderson and Company's notes for iron, coal, and other raw materials demanded that the notes be met on time. In addition, Anderson's annual note to Charles Y. Morriss for the Tredegar rolling mill fell due on January 1, 1861, and amounted to over $10,000. The Richmond firm suddenly found itself in severe financial straits.[67] Less than a week before the November election they expressed the slender hope that once the political campaign was over, the economic turmoil would abate.[68]

Far from diminishing the Tredegar's financial difficulties, Lincoln's triumph at the polls on November 6 accelerated the company's rush toward economic disaster. The four Virginians running the great iron works met the Republican victory with a mixture of apprehension and expectation. The year of fear and anger initiated by John Brown's attack had climaxed with the long-dreaded election of a Republican president. But at least the waiting was over. The South now had just cause to attempt its own version of a more perfect union, and the Tredegar works stood to benefit materially from the formation of a confederacy of slave states. If the Richmond industrialists went under in the fall of 1860, however, the anticipated growth of their works into the industrial giant of an independent South could be permanently stunted.

The partners' immediate concern was to save their firm from bankruptcy. "We do not perceive that the excitement has added anything to our orders, but it has abated very much our receipts," Anderson wrote shortly after the election.[69] "There is a most terrible financial storm raging here at this time and I hardly know what will become of us," he confided to his New Orleans agent.[70] Tanner embarked on an emergency trip through the

67. Anderson & Co. to J. Bowman Johnston & Co., Nov. 1, 1860, to C. B. Mallet, Oct. 31, 1860, to Charles Jackson, Jr., Nov. 1, 1860, to A. J. McConnell, Nov. 2, 1860, to Waldron, Oct. 23, 1860, to St. John Powers & Co., Oct. 23, 1860, and to J. Wicks, Oct. 25, 1860, ibid.; Richmond City Hustings Court, Deed Book No. 73A, pp. 523–24, microfilm copy, VSL.

68. Anderson & Co. to Johnston & Co., Nov. 1, 1860, Tredegar Letterbooks.

69. Anderson & Co. to Stephen Lee, Nov. 15, 1860, ibid.

70. Anderson & Co. to E. M. Ivens, Nov. 19, 1860, ibid.

cotton states to attempt to collect something from the railroads, but he returned to Richmond empty-handed. By the latter part of November, the firm's receipts were short over $120,000 and during the first week of December, railroads in the deep South defaulted on an additional $40,000 to $60,000 due the Tredegar. Roads canceled orders for iron and sales again fell off. Rolling mill production dipped sharply from 903,183 pounds in October to 673,255 pounds in November, receipts from this branch of the business thus matching the earlier decline in foundry income.[71] As sales dropped, the partners cut back their labor force and notified slave owners that they would not hire extensively for 1861.[72] In trying to collect from defaulting Southern railroads, Anderson stressed the importance of holding his work force together. "What do you suppose would be the effect upon Southern Society for near a thousand hands to be discharged in this crisis?" he asked a large Tredegar debtor.[73]

The most damaging blow of all came during early December. Fast on the heels of the extensive defaults from the lower South and Tanner's fruitless journey, the president of the Louisville and Nashville notified Anderson and Company that the L. and N. could not meet its note for $10,000. Anderson and his partners were counting heavily on the roads in the upper South meeting their obligations and now this final source of income had failed.[74]

The firm turned reluctantly to Richmond's four large commercial banks to save their business. The partners did not wish to pay the exorbitant interest rates being charged or jeopardize their hold on the works but they had little choice. The Farmers' Bank, the Bank of Virginia, the Bank of the Commonwealth, and the Exchange Bank of Virginia loaned Anderson and Company a total of $100,000 on December 7, 1860. The banks agreed to discount sixteen notes of $6,250 each during December 1860 and January 1861. The firm was to repay the notes beginning March 3, 1861, with a note falling due every four days thereafter until the entire loan was repaid. If Anderson and Company desired an extension of the loan and the

71. Anderson & Co. to Maxwell, Saulpan & Co., Dec. 11, 1860, to Jackson, Nov. 24, 1860, to James Guthrie, Dec. 8, 1860, and to W. J. Ross, Dec. 11, 1860, ibid.; Tredegar Rolling Mill Sales Books.

72. Anderson & Co. to T. J. Evans, Nov. 23, 1860, and to M. Fitzgibbon, Dec. 22, 1860, Tredegar Letterbooks.

73. Anderson & Co. to Charles T. Pollard, Dec. 13, 1860, ibid.

74. Anderson & Co. to Guthrie, Dec. 8, 1860, and to Maxwell, Saulpan & Co., Dec. 11, 1860, ibid.

banks consented, the notes could be renewed and the loan continued. As collateral, Anderson, Tanner, and the Archers as J. R. Anderson and Company, and Anderson personally, placed their entire Tredegar property, buildings, and machinery, in a deed of trust to the banks. If the firm failed to pay each note as it fell due in March and April and any of the four banks did not want to extend the loan, the Tredegar works could be sold at public auction.[75] This loan averted the immediate financial threat to the company and gave the partners four months time, maybe more if the banks could continue the advance, to rebuild their business. If the panic persisted, Anderson and Company might not survive.

75. Richmond City Hustings Court, Deed Book No. 76B, pp. 237–41, microfilm copy, VSL.

4

Arming the South

I

The Tredegar partners entertained no doubts about the political course the South would follow after Lincoln's election. John Tanner predicted four days after the election that at least six Southern states would secede immediately, paced by South Carolina and Georgia. "If the great purposes of justice and equality are to be subserved thereby so may it be," was his conclusion.[1] Tanner anticipated a marked increase in Tredegar business from an independent South, as he told a a Georgia railroader: "We feel a deep interest in the events now transpiring in the South and hope it will result in good to our material interests, although for a season it may bring great distress upon all the great interests of the Southern Country, including our Rail Roads." [2] Tanner's oldest son, William, soon to be a member of the firm, was even more emphatic in a letter to a Southern bridge builder:

> We feel that the Union *is now* virtually gone and that the sooner the two sections separate the better, as the recent vote of the North seems to tell us in so many words that we are not to have our rights in the Union as guaranteed to us by the Constitution. If all the Rail Road men in the South will stand by her manufacturers as you seem disposed to do, there will be no necessity for going north of the Tredegar for *anything made of iron or steel.*[3]

A month before South Carolina seceded, young Tanner informed a Charleston customer that the Tredegar would mount the palmetto flag on the dome of a stationary engine about to be shipped from Richmond.[4]

1. Anderson & Co. to John T. Anderson, Nov. 10, 1860, Tredegar Letterbooks.
2. Anderson & Co. to C. N. Pennington, Nov. 13, 1860, ibid.
3. Anderson & Co. to George H. Hazelhurst, Dec. 3, 1860, ibid.
4. Anderson & Co. to H. T. Peake, Nov. 27, 1860, ibid.

Vibrant Southern patriotism was the order of the day at the Tredegar Iron Works.

Lincoln's election convinced Anderson that Virginia and the South should leave the Union. He was equally firm in his belief that the Southern states should reunite quickly in their own confederacy. In early December, he expressed his views clearly to Major Daniel Leadbetter, a former West Point classmate now in charge of the fortifications at Mobile:

> I believe the Union is practically dissolved and that we should address ourselves to the . . . subject of *uniting the South.* In my opinion Virginia will never willingly be separated from her sister states of the South. Soon I believe a large majority of her people will come to the conclusion which I have arrived at (if indeed they are not already of that opinion) that there is an incompatibility in opinion between free and slave states—if you choose, an irrepressibility *in opinion* between them. What else do we learn from the past? Then let all good men and patriots look to the *preservation of the peace* and an equitable division of the assets and liabilities of the old Firm and try it again in two separate confederacies. I hope we shall see a kind feeling expressed toward Virginia in all the Southern states and rely on it—She will stand by the South.[5]

But he entertained no illusions about the unwillingness of the North to go to war if provoked. Anderson constantly stressed his conviction that, although any hope of preserving the Union was gone, all good men, north and south, should see that the separation transpired peaceably.

He was particularly apprehensive about a clash between state and Federal troops over the possession of forts, arsenals, and other public property. "We think the States about to withdraw ought to be careful to abstain from seizing any property in possession of the Genl. Govt. but to resort to negotiation," he wrote his brother John on December 3. The best avenue open to the South, he believed, would be for each seceding state to pass a unanimous resolution advising Congress to return all property within the Southern states. The states had ceded territory to the Federal government in creating the District of Columbia, so Congress could legally return property to the states. If necessary, commissioners should be sent to Washington to negotiate the matter. "This would preserve peace and let each

5. Anderson to Maj. Daniel Leadbetter, Dec. 11, 1860, ibid.

section go in its own way," he concluded.[6] Although his solution was predicated on the false assumption that the South would act rationally in a revolutionary situation and that the North would acquiesce in the dismemberment of the Union, Anderson did touch the heart of the tangible issue that would precipitate a brothers' war no sane man desired. He understood better than most men in that confused winter of 1860 that the decision for war or peace was delicately balanced on the issue of Federal property in the South.

When the South Carolina convention voted to leave the Union in late December, Anderson and his partners threw their unequivocal support behind the secession movement. "You may rely upon Virginia standing side by side with the great sisterhood of Southern States," Tanner told a Louisianian shortly after South Carolina seceded.[7] Anderson expressed similar views to Christopher G. Memminger of South Carolina: "The interests of South Carolina and Virginia are in our opinion so closely allied, that we desire a common destiny, and trust it will not be long before our state shall declare, officially, her resolve to make common cause with you." [8] If the Old Dominion did not secede, Anderson vowed he would secede from Virginia and move south.[9] Robert S. Archer stated that the partners would "move the Tredegar down" if Virginia remained in the Union.[10]

Anderson spoke more soothingly to Northern correspondents, however. Although he participated in the emotional response of the deep South, he realized the ever-increasing chances of war and sought to mollify businessmen in the North. "I note the usual kind tenor of your letter which is fully reciprocated and I trust matters will be settled before long for the mutual benefit of all points of the country," he told a Pennsylvania firm in January. "If we can't lie together in peace would it not be better to separate peaceably? We can still have the same congenial intercourse." [11] Most Americans undoubtedly shared Anderson's desire for peace. But as the Southern delegates gathered in Montgomery in February to form their confederacy and Lincoln and his Republican administration took office in Washington on March 4, the chances of compromise became increasingly remote.

6. Anderson & Co. to John T. Anderson, Dec. 3, 1860, ibid.

7. Anderson & Co. to Judge Henry Boyce, Dec. 29, 1860, ibid.

8. Anderson & Co. to Christopher G. Memminger, Jan. 25, 1861, ibid.

9. Anderson to Judge Joshua Baker, Jan. 29, 1861, ibid.

10. Anderson & Co. to E. F. Raworth, March 29, 1861, ibid.

11. Anderson & Co. to Sefer, McManus & Co., Jan. 22, 1861, ibid.

The Tredegar partners kept a close watch on both capitals. They heartily approved of the election of Jefferson Davis and Alexander H. Stephens and assured Southern friends that "the last one of us is moving energetically too to haul Virginia out of the old Union Wreck." [12] Anderson surveyed the events in Washington and Montgomery with his usual combination of business acumen and Southern spirit. He noted the progress of the Morrill tariff through Congress and inquired what effect it might have on bar iron prices in the New York market.[13] The company sent feelers out to Boston and New York in February to ascertain if they could now sell one hundred or two hundred tons of bar iron in those cities.[14] At the same time, the partners hoped that the Confederate Congress would set a high tariff on Northern manufactures, giving the Tredegar a protected Southern market.[15]

If any question still lingered about the political orientation of the Tredegar owners, an influx of Southern munitions orders soon solidified their commitment to the Confederacy. Before these orders materialized, however, Anderson and Company remained in severe financial straits. The March payments on the $100,000 bank loan were the major threat to Tredegar solvency. The railroads offered little assistance. When the Memphis and Charleston paid its bill late in December 1860, Anderson and Company wrote the superintendent that "we feel like planting a pole in front of your Depot with a lone star flag flying at mast head indicating that yours is the only Road that has promptly met its engagements to us." [16] Tanner summed up the feelings of the company on a bleak December day: "We are in the midst of a heavy snow storm, the weather very cold. Business dull & prospects look gloomy ahead." [17]

The future looked no brighter on New Year's Day, 1861, when Tanner admitted to a Pittsburgh manufacturer that the Tredegar's business had never been so bad.[18] Under such dark economic skies, the partners assembled in the Tredegar offices on January 1 and renewed their partnership agreement for five more years, admitting Anderson's oldest son, Archer,

12. Anderson & Co. to G. Jordan, Feb. 11, 1861, ibid.

13. Anderson & Co. to T. B. Coddington, Feb. 23, 1861, ibid.

14. Anderson & Co. to George Whittemore, Feb. 13, 1861, and to Coddington, Feb. 13, 1861, ibid.

15. Anderson & Co. to E. M. Ivens, Feb. 11, 1861, ibid.

16. Anderson & Co. to W. J. Ross, Dec. 27, 1860, ibid.

17. Anderson & Co. to Ivens, Dec. 21, 1860, ibid.

18. Anderson & Co. to Joseph Dilworth, Jan. 1, 1861, ibid.

and Tanner's eldest boy, William, to the firm.[19] Later that month, John Tanner went South again to try to collect railroad debts and secure orders. The results were as disappointing as on previous trips.[20] "Our friends in the South have thrown on us so many of their engagements to meet that the writer is almost broken down in spirit," Anderson confided to a friend in late January.[21]

II

The financial panic throughout the South and the secession of the cotton states made the execution of the contract for musket machinery of paramount importance both to Virginia and to Anderson and Company. The most difficult problem was obviously going to be getting the machinery from the North which could not be fabricated at the Tredegar works. On August 24, immediately after the contract with Anderson and Company was signed, the ever-vigilant Richmond *Enquirer* expressed pleasure that the money had not gone to the North but was openly skeptical about the extent to which Virginia manufactures would be encouraged. The *Enquirer* predicted that the Richmond firm would have to go to England for most of the machinery. Substantial quantities of machinery would indeed have to come from outside Virginia and time was growing short. On his Northern swing in September, Anderson visited the Springfield armory and talked with the man he had taken the contract from, James T. Ames of nearby Chicopee. They discussed the possibility of Ames furnishing the machinery for manufacturing the stocks and limb work, and Ames made a verbal proposition. When he returned to Richmond in mid-September, Anderson requested written bids on the stock and limb machinery from Ames and a number of Northern firms, including Samuel Colt and Company of Hartford.[22]

Before signing contracts for this machinery, however, Anderson wanted some expert advice. He got it from James H. Burton, formerly master armorer at Harpers Ferry and the Enfield armory in England, who agreed in October to assist the Tredegar in outfitting the Virginia armory.[23]

19. Agreement of partnership, Anderson & Co., Jan. 1, 1861, Anderson Papers, VSL.

20. Anderson & Co. to Tanner, Jan. 25, Feb. 4, 1861, and to T. D. Barley, Feb. 14, 1861, Tredegar Letterbooks.

21. Anderson & Co. to Sidney B. Miller, Jan. 29, 1861, ibid.

22. Anderson to James T. Ames, Sept. 18, Oct. 25, 1860, to Samuel Colt & Co., to P. B. Tyler & Co., and to R. S. Lawrence, Oct. 5, 1860, ibid.

23. Anderson & Co. to James H. Burton, Oct. 27, 29, 30, 1860, ibid.

Anderson immediately sent his armorer on a Northern inspection tour and Burton arrived in Springfield in November. "I will merely suggest to you or remind you of the importance of taking steps to get all the information we want from the U.S. Armories before 4th March," advised the Tredegar senior partner.[24]

As it turned out, Anderson and Company wanted a good deal more than information. Burton, accompanied by Soloman Adams, hired from the Springfield armory to serve as master armorer of the Virginia State Armory, was in Springfield to secure the use of important patterns for casting delicate portions of the machinery and complete drawings of key fixtures and tools to guide the production of the musket machinery. The superintendent at Springfield refused to furnish such assistance without the authorization of the Secretary of War. Adams immediately wrote Secretary of War Floyd asking for an order requiring the officers in charge at Springfield and Harpers Ferry to grant himself and the agents of Anderson and Company access to the patterns and drawings. "I desire to get all the assistance we can from the national armories before our much-honored and esteemed Secretary of War vacates his office for I have no hopes of any assistance after a Black Republican takes possession of the War Department," Adams informed Floyd on November 24.[25]

Bureaucratic wheels turned exceedingly slowly in the War Department in November 1860, and evidently Burton and Adams did not get a quick reply from Floyd. Burton negotiated a tentative contract for the stock and limb machinery with Ames, subject to the approval of the Virginia commissioners and Anderson and Company, and returned to Richmond.[26] George W. Randolph, one of the Virginia commissioners, then repeated the request for free access to the Harpers Ferry and Springfield armories. This time Floyd consented. Burton left immediately for Harpers Ferry and dispatched a large set of drawings back to Richmond.[27] When Virginia troops seized the Harpers Ferry machinery the following April and transported it back to Richmond, these drawings were of inestimable value in reassembling the complicated equipment and replacing damaged parts.

Anderson now addressed himself to securing the commissioners' approval for subletting almost half of his contract to Northern manufacturers.

24. Anderson & Co. to Burton, Nov. 20, 1860, ibid.

25. *O.R.*, Ser. III, *1*, 8–9.

26. Burton to Lawrence, Dec. 10, 1860, and Anderson to Ames Manufacturing Co., Dec. 18, 1860, Tredegar Letterbooks.

27. *O.R.*, Ser. III, *1*, 10; entry for Dec. 1860, Tredegar Journals.

Burton drew up a memorandum outlining the proposed division of production. Anderson and Company would undertake to manufacture all the shafting, gearing, pulleys, and driving machinery, and most of the machinery and tools for the forge, grinding, and polishing departments. The fixtures for the machines and all the gauges, "the most particular and refined portion of the work," were also to be executed in Richmond. In order to meet the December 1, 1861, deadline for having the armory in operation, Burton proposed that machines for producing the stocks and limb work, along with the tools for the machine shop, be ordered from Northern manufacturers. Of the total cost of $156,590, machinery worth $75,498 would come from Massachusetts and Connecticut. If granted sufficient time, Burton believed Anderson and Company could produce all but the stock machinery, but he pointed out that time was now a vital factor. Anderson submitted Burton's memorandum to the commissioners and secured their approval.[28] The commissioners later ordered machinery for rolling musket barrels, adding $14,000 to the total sum of the Tredegar contract. Of this supplemental amount, Anderson thought no more than $3,500 would be expended outside Virginia, and that would go to England.[29]

The governor was having second thoughts, however, about turning over the old state muskets to Anderson and Company for shipment to New York. A flintlock musket could be rifled, altered to percussion, and made a serviceable weapon without great difficulty or expense. Shortly before Lincoln's election, the company informed their New York agent that they could not press the matter of the muskets just at that time. Their fears concerning the withdrawal of the muskets were confirmed after the Republican victory.[30]

Anderson would not abandon this revenue source without a battle, however. His company was in no financial position to wait for the completion of the new machinery before realizing something on the state contract. He

28. Anderson & Co. to Burton, Nov. 29, 1860, Burton to Anderson & Co., Nov. 29, 30, 1860, Anderson & Co. to the Commissioners, Nov. 29, 1860, and to Ames Manufacturing Co., Dec. 18, 1860, Tredegar Letterbooks; "State Arms and Armory," Document 1, *Documents of the [Virginia] House of Delegates (Extra Session), January–April, 1861* (Richmond, 1861), pp. 4–5.

29. S. Adams to Anderson & Co., Dec. 18, 1860, Brock Papers, HL; Anderson & Co. to Adams, Dec. 18, 1860, to Randolph, Dec. 19, 1860, and to Joseph Taylor, Feb. 23, 1861, Tredegar Letterbooks; Randolph to Anderson & Co., Jan. 2, 1861, Tredegar Contract Books.

30. Anderson & Co. to Cooper & Pond, Oct. 30, Nov. 9, 1860, Tredegar Letterbooks.

pressed the commissioners for a change of policy, pointing out that the contract clearly stipulated that his company was entitled to the muskets. The commissioners thought the old weapons were of little use to the state and they passed Anderson's communication on to the governor with the recommendation that he release the muskets. Governor John Letcher disagreed with his commissioners and refused to do so.[31]

Anderson then addressed a long letter to the governor on December 15, frankly stating that his company had to have the muskets to be able to proceed with the fabrication of the machinery. The Tredegar management would need $20,000 on March 1, $40,000 on June 1, and an additional $80,000 by December 1 to pay for machinery being built in Richmond and in the North. The "revolution in the cotton states" had cut off practically all receipts. "We trust you will see the necessity of an immediate response, as in these times, it is absolutely essential to know precisely where means are to be had to meet future obligations maturing in a short time," he concluded.[32]

Faced with the prospect that Anderson and Company would not be able to continue with the construction of the machinery, the governor relented. The partners immediately drew 4,500 muskets and shipped them to New York on December 28 and 31, 1860, and January 10, 1861, realizing over $10,000 on these shipments. With South Carolina's secession an accomplished fact, however, the Virginia authorities again decided that no more muskets should be released, placing this source of income beyond Anderson's reach.[33]

The General Assembly confirmed this decision when the special session opened in January. The House of Delegates immediately demanded an explanation of the sale of muskets to Anderson and Company. After the governor submitted the various documents concerning the contract, the House and Senate passed a joint resolution forbidding any further deliveries to the Tredegar partners until the attorney-general investigated the legality of the transaction.[34] Anderson would send no more Virginia muskets out of the state.

31. Anderson & Co. to Randolph, Nov. 16, 1860, and Randolph to Letcher, Nov. 17, 1860, Virginia Executive Papers, VSL.

32. Anderson & Co. to Letcher, Dec. 15, 1860, ibid.

33. Anderson & Co. to Cooper & Pond, Dec. 29, 1860, Jan. 8, 10, 1861, and to Schuyler, Hartley & Graham, Dec. 31, 1860, Jan. 10, 1861, Tredegar Letterbooks.

34. *Journal of the [Virginia] House of Delegates (Extra Session), January–April 1861* (Richmond, 1861), pp. 107–08, 226; [*Virginia*] *Senate Journal* (*Extra Session*), *1861*

III

A month before South Carolina seceded, the pressing financial needs of the company and Lincoln's victory prompted Anderson to make a final plea to Secretary of War Floyd in the year-long controversy with the United States War Department over the Rodman method of manufacturing cannon. Anderson opened his letter of November 21, 1860, to Floyd on a familiar note: "For a year or more I have had on hand a large quantity of gun-iron which I had reason to expect we would convert into guns for the Government . . . In the present state of things this burden has almost worn me down, and in view of the present aspect of things I do not think it is likely that the Government will ever receive a gun from me after the 4th of March next." Anderson therefore made a last request that before a Republican Secretary of War took office, Floyd would permit the $20,000 worth of cannon ordered in November 1859 to be cast solid. "Won't you do me the favor to answer this request, as it is of the highest importance in the threatening aspect of commercial matters that we should be able to make this large fund to some extent available," Anderson added in a postscript.[35]

Floyd was unmoved by Anderson's plea. Despite "every disposition to accommodate you in your work for this Department," he would not rescind the order.[36] Anderson again turned toward the Southern states to seek orders for ordnance and munitions and this time the governors were ready to listen.

The Virginia armory commissioners gave the first indication that the Southern munitions market was opening up. The legislation authorizing the outfitting of the State Armory also appropriated $180,000 for the purchase of arms, military equipment, and ammunition. Using part of these funds, the commissioners placed a large order for 6- and 12-pounder shot, shell, spherical case, and canister with Anderson and Company in November 1860.[37]

(Richmond, 1861), pp. 314–15; "Governor's Communication Relative to the Sale of Arms to Joseph R. Anderson & Co., February 14, 1861," Document 30, *Documents of the [Virginia] House of Delegates (Extra Session), 1861.*

35. *O.R.*, Ser. III, *1*, 7.

36. Ibid., p. 10.

37. *Acts of the [Virginia] General Assembly, 1861* (Richmond, 1861), p. 127; "State Arms and Armory," Document 1, *Documents of the [Virginia] House of Delegates (Extra Session), 1861*, p. 10; Anderson & Co. to Randolph, Nov. 22, 1860, Tredegar Letterbooks.

In late November and early December, the Tredegar began receiving inquiries from the cotton states about munitions. Anderson informed agents of North Carolina and Alabama that the Tredegar would supply all descriptions of iron and brass ordnance, carriages, and ammunition at the same prices charged the Federal government. The Richmond founder was particularly irate when he learned that several Southern agents had recently gone north to buy their guns and that Northern salesmen were busy in the South. Still smarting from the loss of the Georgia contract earlier in 1860, when a Northern founder undercut him by one cent per pound, Anderson asked to be given the opportunity to meet any rival offer.[38] The first Southern order for cannon came on December 11, when the agent purchasing arms for Georgia signed a contract for three bronze 6-pounder rifled field guns, each complete with carriage, limber, and implements.[39]

Encouraged by this small order, the Tredegar management decided to circularize the Southern governors. "The Southern States are now preparing for defence, and we offer our foundry and experience to your state whenever she may require them," Anderson and Company informed the executives on December 15.[40] A year before, an almost identical letter brought no response. Now, it elicited a flow of orders which enabled Anderson and Company to ride out the economic hurricane unleashed across the South by the Republican electoral triumph. Five days after the letters were dispatched, the South Carolina convention took the Palmetto State out of the Union. The Southern rush to the Tredegar now began in earnest.

The Tredegar gun foundry had remained idle from August to late December 1860. On August 29, workmen cast cannon number 1098, the final 9-inch shell gun remaining from the small order for nine tubes given by the United States Navy the previous April. These nine pieces, bored, finished, and submitted to the usual proof of ten firings, left Richmond on December 14, five destined for the Brooklyn Navy Yard and four going to the Gosport Navy Yard at Norfolk.[41] These nine Dahlgren guns were the last cannon cast at the Tredegar works for the United States government. Two days after Christmas, cannon number 1099, one of the three brass 6-

38. Anderson & Co. to J. R. Powell, Nov. 22, 1860, to A. S. Merriman, Dec. 5, 1860, and to Maj. Daniel Leadbetter, Dec. 11, 1860, ibid.

39. Memorandum of agreement, Anderson & Co. and L. J. Gaskell, Dec. 11, 1860, Tredegar Contract Books.

40. Anderson & Co. to the Governors of N.C., S.C., Ala., Fla., Miss., Ark., Texas, Tenn., and Ky., Dec. 15, 1860, Tredegar Letterbooks.

41. Reports from and Inspections at Foundries, Nov. 1860–Sept. 1861, RG 74, NA.

pounders ordered by the state of Georgia earlier in December, was cast.[42] Production fell off again after the casting of these three pieces but picked up in late January following the receipt of sizable orders.

Georgia increased its order before the turn of the year. General Paul J. Semmes arrived in Richmond in late December to place an order with Anderson and Company for six 18-pounder siege guns and ammunition. When Semmes stressed the importance of quick delivery, Anderson doubtless had some thoughts about Georgia's refusal to give his firm the heavy ordnance the state had ordered from the Fort Pitt foundry earlier in 1860. Georgia wanted the Tredegar siege guns by Lincoln's inauguration. The firm, "apprehending the anxiety of the said State of Georgia to be placed in possession of the materials for her coast defense," promised to do all it could to expedite the order.[43] On the last day of December, Alabama ordered two 10-inch columbiads to strengthen the defenses of Fort Morgan guarding Mobile.[44] By January 1, 1861, the Tredegar had eleven pieces of ordnance on the books or underway for Georgia and Alabama. This was not a large number but was sufficient to indicate a major potential source of revenue in an otherwise barren iron market.

In January and February, the letter sent Southern governors on December 15 brought a flood of inquiries to Anderson and Company. Virginia, North Carolina, Kentucky, Tennessee, Florida, Louisiana, Mississippi, and South Carolina authorities sought information on the Tredegar's capabilities and prices.[45] South Carolina officials placed the largest munitions orders and their purchases alone went a long way toward pulling the Tredegar owners out of financial danger.

IV

South Carolina's urgent requests for ordnance and ammunition came as the result of events in Charleston during early January. On the morning of January 9, artillery fire from state batteries had prevented the unarmed

42. Archer Account Book, VHS.

43. Contract with Gen. Paul J. Semmes, Dec. 27, 1860, Tredegar Contract Books; *O.R.*, Ser. IV, *1*, 169.

44. Anderson & Co. to Gen. R. T. Thom, Dec. 31, 1860, Tredegar Letterbooks; Archer Account Book, VHS.

45. Anderson & Co. to Gov. John W. Ellis, Jan. 16, 17, 1861, to Floyd Tilghman, Jan. 23, 1861, to J. F. Tanner, Jan. 23, 1861, to Col. R. H. Smith, Jan. 31, 1861, to the Governor of Florida, Feb. 4, 1861, to D. W. Adams, Feb. 12, 1861, to Gen. Earl Van Dorn, Feb. 15, 1861, and to C. G. Memminger, Jan. 17, 1861, Tredegar Letterbooks.

Federal relief ship, *Star of the West,* from landing reinforcements and provisions at Fort Sumter. Although he had not used the fort's guns to assist the vessel, Major Robert Anderson, the commander of the Sumter garrison, was greatly angered by this open display of Southern belligerence. That same day he notified Governor Francis Pickens that his cannon would close Charleston harbor and would fire at any South Carolina ship that sailed within range of the fort. After several hours' reflection, Anderson decided he should consult Washington before using force to seal off the harbor and he notified Pickens of his decision. But the threat that the guns of Fort Sumter would be used to strangle the port's commerce had already prompted the governor to take an important step. He had ordered his top ordnance and engineering officers to "report the most favorable plan for operating upon Fort Sumter, so as to reduce that fortress, by batteries or other means in our possession." [46]

The next day they had their report in the hands of David F. Jamison, the planter who had served as president of the session convention and who was now South Carolina's Secretary of War. "Our dependence and sole reliance must be upon Batteries of *heavy ordnance,*" the officers advised, strategically placed, well supplied, and in sufficient number to conduct "an incessant bombardment and cannonade of many hours duration." To fill gaps in the ring of destruction encircling Fort Sumter, they recommended the immediate purchase of seven 10-inch mortars to supplement those cast by the Tredegar in the early '50s and already in place. More shot and shell for guns of all calibers (including a number of other weapons manufactured earlier by the Richmond works) would also be needed. "Report accepted, ordered to be carried out without delay," Jamison scrawled at the bottom of the last page.[47]

On the morning of January 17, the first of a series of urgent telegrams from South Carolina arrived at the Tredegar offices. Christopher Memminger in Charleston wanted to know how soon the works could furnish large quantitites of 8- and 10-inch shot and shell and if cannon powder could be purchased in Richmond. Anderson and Company replied immediately that they had on hand 250 8-inch shot and 450 8-inch shell. They

46. Samuel W. Crawford, *The Genesis of the Civil War; The Story of Sumter, 1860–1861* (New York, 1887), pp. 183–91; W. A. Swanberg, *First Blood—The Story of Fort Sumter* (New York, 1957), pp. 146–52.

47. Report of Col. Walter Gwynn, Col. Edward White, Capt. J. H. Trapier, and Col. Edward Manigault, Jan. 10, 1861, in Confederate States of America, War Department, Ordnance Miscellany, LC.

could make per day 100 10-inch shell, 100 32-pounder shot, and 25 8-inch shot, but this capacity could be doubled in ten days time. One thousand kegs of cannon powder were available in Richmond for immediate shipment. Anderson and his partners knew, as did everyone else in the South who could read a newspaper, of the tense situation in Charleston and they realized that South Carolina might place a tremendous order for munitions. "Will make anything you want—work night and day if necessary, and ship by rail. Prices same as to U.S. Government." Memminger wired back that same evening to send down the shot, shell, and powder at once. He also ordered large quantities of 10-inch mortar and 8-inch columbiad shells for future delivery.[48]

Still another telegram arrived that night from Charleston. Colonel Edward Manigault, South Carolina's ordnance chief, wanted seven 10-inch mortars as soon as the Tredegar could possibly manufacture them. He also inquired whether the company had available for immediate sale any long range ordnance suitable for coast defense. The Richmond ironmakers answered that work would commence at once on the mortars and that they had on hand three 9-inch Dahlgren shell guns, made for the United States Navy in the 1850s but never accepted. Manigualt wired back not to send the Dahlgrens.[49]

Tredegar workers labored all the next day in a pouring rain, loading powder, shot, and shell onto a special train at the Richmond and Petersburg depot. At five o'clock in the afternoon, the engine chugged across the James, carrying the first of many Tredegar cargoes south to Charleston harbor.[50]

On January 24, six days after the special trainload of munitions left Richmond, Anderson and Company commenced almost daily shipments of shot and shell to South Carolina. With almost one thousand tons of gun iron on hand, stockpiled since 1859, little delay occurred in beginning work on the seven mortars. Tredegar molders cast the first one less than a week after the receipt of Manigault's telegram and by February 9 it was on a flatcar headed for Charleston. Two more were shipped five days later.[51]

48. Anderson & Co. to Memminger, Jan. 17, 1861, Tredegar Letterbooks.

49. Ibid.; Anderson & Co. to Manigault, Jan. 17, 1861, ibid.

50. Anderson & Co. to Memminger, Jan. 19, 21, 24, 1861, ibid.

51. Anderson & Co. to Manigault, Jan. 19, 1861, and to Gov. Francis Pickens, Feb. 16, 1861, ibid.; entries for Jan.–April 1861, Tredegar Foundry Sales Books; Archer Account Book, VHS.

Despite the exertions of Anderson and Company, Governor Pickens was dissatisfied with the flow of munitions into Charleston and he dispatched a special messenger to Richmond to investigate the delay. The agent arrived on February 19 and wired the governor immediately that the Tredegar was not to blame for any tardiness.[52] Anderson assured the governor that "we have not been remiss in executing the urgent orders of South Carolina, but . . . have redeemed the pledge given in the outset to spare no effort by day or by night to place the State in a posture of defence, as far as it depended on this Foundry." Anderson correctly placed responsibility for the delay on the railroads south of Petersburg.[53] The Tredegar shipments had to travel over the tracks of five different railroad companies to reach Charleston, with changes of cars at Petersburg and Wilmington.[54] The South Carolina agent directed his attention toward hurrying the shipments along from junctions south of Petersburg.

Anderson left Richmond on February 25 with a trainload of munitions for Charleston, carrying with him invoices amounting to $18,863 for articles delivered to South Carolina up to that time. Upon his arrival in Charleston, he conferred with Governor Pickens on the additional ammunition needs of Southern batteries and arranged for the payment of the state's sizable account with his firm.[55] When the Tredegar senior partner toured the gun emplacements ringing the harbor, he saw a number of familiar ordnance pieces. In addition to the new 10-inch mortars, five of which had already arrived, a number of Tredegar weapons cast for the state in 1851 and 1852—8-inch columbiads, 8-inch siege howitzers, 24-pounder siege guns, and 10-inch mortars—were also mounted and ready for action.[56]

Before he left Charleston, Anderson rowed out to Fort Sumter to call on his old West Point artillery instructor, Major Robert Anderson. The Richmond ironmaker did not attempt to conceal the object of his trip to the city.

52. J. J. Evans to Pickens, Feb. 19, 1861, Tredegar Letterbooks.

53. Anderson & Co. to Pickens, Feb. 19, 1861, ibid.

54. Robert C. Black, *The Railroads of the Confederacy* (Chapel Hill, 1952), end map.

55. Entries for Jan.–Feb. 1861, Tredegar Foundry Sales Books, and for Jan.–April 1861, Tredegar Journals; Anderson to Pickens, April 8, 1861, Tredegar Letterbooks.

56. Because the South Carolina forces had captured a number of 8-inch columbiads, 8-inch howitzers, and 24-pounder guns when they occupied Fort Moultrie, Castle Pinckney, and the Charleston arsenal, it is impossible to tell exactly how many Tredegar tubes of these calibers were in the batteries. As few as 19 and as many as 27 of the 47 pieces used in the bombardment could have been cast at Anderson's foundry. See Halsey, "South Carolina Began Preparing for War in 1851," *Civil War Times Illustrated, 1* (April 1962), 12.

Despite this admission, Major Anderson greeted him cordially and invited him to stay for dinner, all of which disgusted Captain Abner Doubleday, one of the more belligerent members of the Sumter garrison. As Joseph departed, the Federal officers gave a hearty farewell and "God bless you!" to the man who was furnishing the major portion of the shot and shell that would soon batter their fort into submission.[57]

Anderson and Company continued to forward ordnance and large quantities of munitions to the South Carolina port during March and April. At Pickens' urgent request, the final two mortars and a large shipment of ammunition left Richmond by special train on March 2. The governor also had second thoughts about the three Dahlgren shell guns lying idle in Richmond and told the partners to send them down also.[58] A Union officer scanning the Southern batteries from the fort in early April noted that a "lone but potent nine-inch Dahlgren" was now bearing on Sumter.[59] The Tredegar owners celebrated Lincoln's inauguration day by exchanging telegrams that resulted in further deliveries of munitions. Two weeks later, just as the company was completing the January order for ammunition, Colonel Manigault placed still another large order for 10-inch mortar and 8-inch columbiad shells.[60]

"We sincerely hope that our strenuous efforts to carry out your wishes about these shipments promptly, have proven satisfactory," Anderson and Company wrote Manigault in late March, "& that we may be able to contribute still further, towards the defence of yours, & other sister states, against the abolition horde which threaten [sic] to invade us."[61] The Tredegar's performance had been more than satisfactory. Between January 17 and April 9, the Richmond firm dispatched the seven urgently needed mortars, three Dahlgren guns, and 11,516 rounds of cannon and mortar ammunition to Charleston.[62]

57. Abner Doubleday, *Reminiscences of Forts Sumter and Moultrie in 1860–61* (New York, 1876), p. 120. The Tredegar senior partner was not related to Maj. Robert Anderson.

58. Entry for March 1861, Tredegar Journals; Anderson & Co. to Pickens, Feb. 21, March 2, 1861, to D. F. Jamison, March 4, 1861, and to Manigault, March 4, 1861, Tredegar Letterbooks.

59. Swanberg, p. 294; *O.R.*, Ser. I, *1*, 280–81. The other two Dahlgrens were mounted in the "Star of the West" battery on Morris Island guarding the main ship channel; see ibid., p. 27.

60. Allan Nevins, *The War for the Union: The Improvised War, 1861–1862* (New York, 1959), p. 41; W. E. Tanner to John F. Tanner, March 22, 1861, Supplementary Tredegar Records, VSL.

61. Anderson & Co. to Manigault, March 21, 1861, SCA.

62. Entries for Jan.–April 1861, Tredegar Foundry Sales Books.

V

At the same time the foundries began filling Southern ordnance contracts, Anderson and Company unexpectedly received a request from the Federal government for gun metal. Two days after the partners informed Southern governors that the facilities of the Tredegar were at their disposal, the head of the Bureau of Ordnance and Hydrography wrote Anderson and Company seeking fifty tons of Cloverdale gun iron for experimental purposes. The company replied immediately that they would sell the navy the iron for $50 per ton. This valuable metal, enough to cast ten 8-inch columbiads, was shipped to the Washington Navy Yard on December 28, and brought the company over $2,500.[63]

The owners also agreed to furnish shot and shell to the Federal government. On December 31, they accepted an order from Dr. Junius L. Archer of Bellona foundry to supply the ammunition for cannon Archer was completing for the United States Army. In January, projectiles cast for the Federal government and Southern states lay side by side on the floor of the Tredegar foundries.[64]

These transactions, particularly the sale of ammunition to the Federal government in 1861, demonstrate that Anderson and his partners did not let their secessionist sympathies stand in the way of a profitable business deal. They needed every dollar they could possibly scrape together in late 1860 and early 1861 and these two sales would bring immediate cash payment. Like most Northern businessmen during these same months, the Richmond ironmakers were simply putting first things first.[65] The solvency of their firm ranked ahead of loyalty to an as yet unformed Southern Confederacy.

Ordnance sales clearly offered the Tredegar owners their best opportunity to ride out the financial panic and Anderson pressed hard for addi-

63. Capt. G. A. Magruder to Anderson & Co., Dec. 17, 1860, Letters and Telegrams Sent to Inspectors, RG 74, NA; Anderson & Co. to Magruder, Dec. 18, 1860, Tredegar Letterbooks.

64. Anderson & Co. to J. L. Archer, Dec. 31, 1860, and to Capt. A. B. Dyer, Jan. 5, 1861, ibid.

65. The shipment of Northern arms to the South following secession, for example, reached such proportions that the New York superintendent of police warned that "if something is not done by somebody to arrest this traffic, we shall be nearly destitute of small arms at the North in a short time." John A. Kennedy to Thurlow Weed, Jan. 24, 1861, quoted in Philip S. Foner, *Business & Slavery: The New York Merchants & the Irrepressible Conflict* (Chapel Hill, 1941), n. 15, p. 299. See also below, pp. 78–79.

tional Southern contracts. He sent an ordnance price list to his New Orleans agent, Edward M. Ivens, and urged him to open discussion at once with state authorities in Louisiana. "Drive the ordnance negotiation as hard as possible," Anderson advised; "it is our mainstay now." Ivens secured an order from Louisiana for columbiad carriages but was not able to sell any cannon.[66] The company also advised John Tanner, who had gone south originally to persuade railroads to pay their bills and place new orders, to concentrate on selling ordnance to state officials. Tanner visited Louisville, Nashville, Jackson, New Orleans, Mobile, and Tallahassee, and repeated the offer made by letter in mid-December to supply guns and munitions. He obtained an order for caissons from Florida's ordnance agent and negotiated a large contract with General Earl Van Dorn of Mississippi for eighteen brass field pieces, ammunition, and five battery forges.[67]

Additional orders from North and South Carolina and Georgia came in quick succession in late January and early February. A South Carolina naval officer contracted for bronze boat howitzers after visiting the works and Colonel Manigault placed an order for bronze field artillery. These two orders totaled twenty-four pieces.[68] An ordnance officer came up from North Carolina in January to inspect the Tredegar plant and confer with the management about artillery. Following these discussions, a member of the firm, Robert S. Archer, went to Raleigh and there signed a contract with Governor John Ellis for twelve bronze field pieces and four columbiads, all complete with carriages, implements, and ammunition.[69]

One of the largest state orders came from Georgia in February and included the heavy guns the state had refused to buy from Anderson earlier in 1860. When public protest in Pittsburgh prevented Charles Knap at the Fort Pitt foundry from delivering the columbiads he was casting for the state, Georgia officials sent an urgent inquiry to Richmond asking if the Tredegar could manufacture the cannon. These guns were desperately needed for the Savannah defenses. The company replied that it made

66. Anderson & Co. to Ivens, Dec. 30, 1860, Jan. 25, Feb. 12, 1861, Tredegar Letterbooks.

67. Anderson & Co. to Tanner, Jan. 22, Feb. 4, 1861, to R. B. Hilton, March 7, 1861, and to Van Dorn, Feb. 15, 1861, ibid.; contract with the State of Mississippi, Feb. 4, 1861, Tredegar Contract Books.

68. Anderson & Co. to Capt. James H. North, Jan. 30, 1861, to Manigault, Feb. 8, 1861, and to D. N. Ingraham, June 22, 1861, Tredegar Letterbooks.

69. Anderson & Co. to Lt. Charles C. Lee, Jan, 21, 1861, ibid.; contract with J. R. Anderson & Co., Feb. 2, 1861, in Ordnance Book, 1861, John W. Ellis Papers, NCA. See also Ellis to Lee, Jan. 19, 1861, and endorsement of Lee on Anderson & Co. to Lee, Jan. 21, 1861, ibid.

"every description of U.S. service gun—iron & brass, and some others." With pointed reference to Georgia's unsuccessful and time-consuming attempt to secure the guns in Pittsburgh, the Tredegar owners estimated that they could finish the large order in about eight weeks, "unless you postpone it till our hands are full of orders for our own and other states." [70] Governor Joseph E. Brown and his military advisers were in no mood for delay; Georgia's chief ordnance officer arrived in Richmond within the week. On February 7, he signed a contract for five 10-inch columbiads, ten 8-inch columbiads, four 24-pounder flank defense howitzers, and twelve light 12-pounder bronze guns—a total of thirty-one cannon, all complete with appropriate carriages, implements, and ammunition.[71]

The night the Georgia contract was concluded, Anderson wrote his partner John Tanner in high spirits:

> This has been quite an exciting day. We had a visit from Capt. W. R. Boggs, Ordn. Officer of Georgia who contracted with us for ordnance to the extent of about $35,000 and agrees to pay as they are shipped in New York funds. We have now including the 18 p^s you telegraphed us you had taken at Vicksburg 66 Bronze Pieces on our books. But we will finish them very fast. The smaller ones at least we will cast two per day of and I think we can start tools enough to turn & bore from 9 to 12 per week—at least I hope so. We are driving everything we have in the Foundry. All we want now is money till our cash acceptances are in. Our bill on the State of Georgia for the Brass Battery (3) for Capt. Wallace, was over $3,000 which I hope we will soon get. I never saw a more beautiful battery, whether reference be had to the guns or carriages. South Carolina remits promptly, much more so than the old U.S. By the by we have not gotten pay for our Pig Iron yet.[72]

Anderson's elation reflected the prospect that Southern ordnance deliveries would rescue his firm from threatened financial ruin. The first three cannon cast for a Southern state, Georgia's brass battery, brought in over $3,000. South Carolina remitted its January bill very quickly while the Federal government had not yet paid for the gun iron delivered to the

70. Anderson & Co. to Adj. Gen. Henry C. Wayne, Jan. 31, 1861, Tredegar Letterbooks; *O.R.*, Ser. IV, *1*, 169.

71. Contract with Capt. W. R. Boggs, Feb. 7, 1861, Tredegar Contract Books.

72. Anderson to Tanner, Feb. 7, 1861, Tredegar Letterbooks.

Washington Navy Yard at approximately the same time. The contracts with the Southern states for cannon and munitions provided solid financial confirmation of the political and social predilections of the Tredegar partners.

Under the impetus of these large Southern orders, the Tredegar began tooling up for full-scale war production well before the outbreak of hostilities. In January 1861, the partners undertook to double the ordnance and munitions capacity of their works. Laborers prepared additional patterns and flasks for cannon, shot, and shell and converted the facilities of the new car wheel foundry to ammunition production. Within a month after the receipt of South Carolina's first order, the works could turn out daily twice the previous amount of shot and shell. By mid-March, the ordinary capacity of the foundries and boring mill for casting and finishing 8- and 10-inch columbiads had been doubled. Workers went on a night shift at a 50 per cent increase in wages to rush the orders to completion.[73]

Southern ordnance orders also put the Tredegar in the market for gun metal again. Like the Richmond works, Virginia's gun iron blast furnaces began to gear for war several months before hostilities began. John T. Anderson commenced manufacturing gun metal again at his Cloverdale furnace in Botetourt County in January and by the middle of the next month, canal boats were delivering the first of this new blast to the Tredegar.[74] Anderson and Company also contracted for gun metal with an important founder in southwest Virginia, David Graham of Wythe County. Graham had furnished the Bellona foundry with gun iron during the late 1850s and reputedly produced a high quality metal.[75]

For a staggering amount of other essential raw materials, however, the Tredegar partners had to look to the North. Baltimore and New York dealers supplied the copper and tin for bronze ordnance. Most of the parts for gun carriages came from the North, including flange and angle iron from Pennsylvania and New Jersey, sheet copper and cut timber from New York, and hubs and spokes from Philadelphia. Cooper and Pond, Anderson and Company's New York sales agent for Virginia muskets, supplied field artillery implements and friction tubes and fuses for the thousands of

73. Anderson & Co. to John W. Eastman, Jan. 22, 1861, to W. T. Little, Jan. 24, 1861, and to Manigault, Jan. 30, April 3, 1861, ibid.; W. E. Tanner to John F. Tanner, March 16, 1861, Supplementary Tredegar Records, VSL.

74. Tredegar Pig Iron Receipt Book.

75. Anderson & Co. to David Graham, Jan. 21, Feb. 23, March 9, 1861, Tredegar Letterbooks; Graham to Anderson & Co., March 5, 1861, Tredegar Contract Books.

shells sent to Southern states in the early months of 1861.[76] The Richmond firm also acted as intermediary for South Carolina in the purchase of 250 Colt navy pistols from the Hartford factory during the first part of February.[77] The North–South arms traffic was extremely brisk in the first quarter of 1861.

Continuing munitions orders and prompt payment by state authorities enabled the partners to meet their deadline with Richmond's bankers. By April, bills on South Carolina alone totaled almost $50,000.[78] Georgia added to its already sizable ordnance orders in late February and March with requests for five more columbiads, sixteen 42-pounder guns, and a stationary engine for the ordnance department at Milledgeville.[79] By the middle of March, Anderson and Company were delivering to Southern states three to five heavy guns per week, with requisite ammunition, carriages, and implements.[80] Comparative foundry and rolling mill sales figures reflected the heavy dependence on ordnance production. During the first four months of 1861, foundry sales totaled $166,544, while rolling mill sales amounted to only $71,385. During the same months the previous year, the situation had been almost exactly reversed. In January–April 1860, foundry sales were $62,859 while rolling mill sales reached $154,695.[81] Unlike the defaulting Southern railroads, the states met their bills promptly. During the critical month of March when the first payments on the $100,000 loan fell due, income from the Southern states, especially South Carolina, enabled the Tredegar owners to settle their notes to the banks and pay their labor force.[82]

76. Anderson & Co. to David Keener, Dec. 13, 28, 1860, Feb. 19, 1861, to A. S. & A. G. Whiten, Dec. 29, 1860, Jan. 7, Feb. 4, 1861, to Morris Wheeler & Co., Feb. 6, 1861, to Horace Beale, Feb. 16, 1861, to H. H. Puryear, Feb. 27, 1861, to James J. Reeves, March 19, 1861, to Cooper & Hewitt, March 18, 1861, to Cooper & Pond, Dec. 20, 25, 1860, Jan. 7, 14, 15, 1861, and to Manigault, Feb. 7, 1861, Tredegar Letterbooks.

77. Anderson & Co. to Col. Samuel Colt, Feb. 1, 1861, to Manigault, Feb. 2, 12, 14, 18, 1861, and to Colt Patent Firearms Co., Feb. 4, 5, 15, 1861, ibid.

78. Entries for Jan.–April 1861, Tredegar Foundry Sales Books.

79. Anderson & Co. to Boggs, Feb. 27, 1861, and to Wayne, March 26, 1861, Tredegar Letterbooks.

80. Tredegar Foundry Sales Books; W. E. Tanner to John F. Tanner, March 16, 1861, Supplementary Tredegar Records, VSL.

81. Tredegar Foundry Sales Books; Tredegar Rolling Mill Sales Books.

82. Entries for March 1861, Tredegar Journals; Anderson & Co. to Manigault, March 11, 14, 20, 22, 1861, Tredegar Letterbooks; W. E. Tanner to John F. Tanner, March 22, 1861, Supplementary Tredegar Records.

VI

The Richmond industrialists wasted no time in seeking to include the new Confederate government among their ordnance customers. John Tanner was in Montgomery on February 20 when the Provisional Congress authorized the War Department to contract for guns and munitions. That same day he offered the services of the Tredegar to Secretary of War L. P. Walker. The Richmond establishment had twenty years' experience in the manufacture of ordnance and projectiles, Tanner informed the Secretary. "An order for these articles including the Gun carriages, can be executed with dispatch . . . We are now engaged in manufacturing for the Southern States & hold ourselves in readiness to execute an order for the Southern Confederacy should you be pleased to confide one to us." [83] Tanner telegraphed Richmond inquiring how soon the foundries could produce columbiads for the Confederacy. The company was still occupied with the large Georgia order for heavy cannon and one of the partners replied that they could not finish a gun for the Confederate government within five weeks.[84] As a result, Tanner failed to secure an immediate order from the Secretary of War.

Secretary Walker soon got a laudatory report on the Tredegar works from Raphael Semmes, sent north by President Davis to contract for cannon, munitions, and arms machinery. Semmes wrote from Richmond on February 28 that the Tredegar was a large, well-appointed establishment, employing seven hundred men and possessing "great facilities for founding cannon and casting shot and shell." Semmes recommended the works highly.[85] Before Walker could order his purchasing agent to contract with the Tredegar, the senior partner of J. R. Anderson and Company had arrived in the Confederate capital to promote the business of his firm.

Anderson had already departed for Charleston when Semmes reached Richmond. The Tredegar head continued on to Montgomery in early March to confer personally with the Secretary of War. On March 7, he and Walker signed a contract for thirty 10-inch columbiads, with the first two guns to be ready by April 1 and two each week thereafter. Payment was to be two thirds cash and one third 8 per cent Confederate bonds. The next

83. Tanner to Secretary of War, Confederate States, Feb. 20, 1861, Letters Rec'd., Secretary of War, RG 109, NA.

84. Anderson & Co. to Tanner, Feb. 19, 1861, Tredegar Letterbooks.

85. *O.R.*, Ser. IV, *1*, 119.

day the contract was modified to include carriages for each gun and Anderson agreed to take one half of the payment for the carriages in bonds. This first contract with the Confederate government represented almost $60,000 worth of ordnance.[86]

After a trip to Mobile and New Orleans to attempt to collect some back bills, Anderson revisited Montgomery and Charleston and again talked with government officials in both cities. When he saw Secretary of the Navy Stephen R. Mallory on April 1, he informed him of the Tredegar's facilities for manufacturing steamship engines and left an ordnance price list. Three days later, the Secretary ordered ten cannon with boat carriages and ammunition.[87]

Continuing on to Charleston, Anderson had interviews with Governor Pickens and General Pierre G. T. Beauregard. Pickens was concerned about the quality of Tredegar ammunition because some of the 10-inch shells had burst prematurely during practice firings. Anderson learned from Beauregard that the trouble resulted from inexperienced South Carolina gunners firing lighter mortar shells from columbiads. He carried an order for 10-inch columbiad shells back to Richmond and the casting of these projectiles commenced when Anderson arrived back at the Tredegar on April 6.[88] On April 8, Beauregard wired Anderson and Company to use all haste to forward the shells to Charleston. The next day, the partners shipped a lot of 210 of the needed shells and informed Beauregard that casting would continue.[89]

While on his six weeks trip through the cotton states, Anderson noted the martial spirit everywhere in evidence. He no longer had any illusions about the two sections separating peaceably but he and his associates had little idea when the first blow would be struck.[90] Three days before the first shell burst over Fort Sumter, Anderson and Company told their Baltimore agent not to ship any more copper to Richmond until the following week. They had enough on hand to keep the brass gun foundry busy for

86. Contracts with Secretary of War L. P. Walker, March 7, 8, 1861, Tredegar Contract Books.

87. Anderson & Co. to Walker, March 22, 1861, Letters Rec'd., Secretary of War, RG 109, NA; Anderson & Co. to J. R. Anderson, March 29, 1861, Tredegar Letterbooks; copy of prices left with S. R. Mallory, April 1, 1861, Tredegar Contract Books; Archer Account Book, VHS.

88. Anderson & Co. to Pickens, April 8, 1861, Tredegar Letterbooks.

89. Anderson & Co. to Manigault, April 9, 1861, and to Beauregard, April 10, 1861, ibid.; Tredegar Foundry Sales Books.

90. Anderson & Co. to R. C. Brinkley, April 11, 1861, Tredegar Letterbooks.

two weeks and did not wish to stockpile an excess quantity.[91] On April 10, however, the telegraphic dispatches from Charleston in the Richmond papers carried the news that the Federal government was determined to reinforce the Sumter garrison. "A conflict is inevitable," reported the correspondent of the Richmond *Dispatch.* "Our warmest sympathies are with you," William E. Tanner answered a Charleston friend.[92] Anderson busied himself the day before the attack on Sumter arranging quietly for the purchase of two thousand kegs of Dupont cannon powder at the request of the Confederate Secretary of War.[93] At 4:30 the next morning, a South Carolina officer jerked the lanyard of a 10-inch Tredegar mortar on James Island, sending a shell arching through the darkness that exploded over Fort Sumter.[94] The most momentous bombardment in American history had begun, an assault made possible by almost three months of Tredegar production.

91. Anderson & Co. to Keener, April 9, 1861, ibid.

92. Anderson & Co. to W. T. Little, April 10, 1861, ibid.

93. Anderson to Walker, April 11, 1861, ibid.

94. Martin Abbot, "The First Shot at Fort Sumter," *Civil War History, 3* (1957), 41–45; Clarence C. Buel and Robert U. Johnson, eds., *Battles and Leaders of the Civil War* (4 vols. New York, 1887), *1,* 76. Hereafter cited as *Battles and Leaders.*

5

Abundant Enthusiasm, Limited Resources

I

"We have just heard that Fort Sumter was attacked yesterday and are glad suspense is to cease," Anderson wrote on the 13th. But Virginia delayed. "I still feel low spirited about our Convention but hope that the current events will awaken them. Much excitement among our people." [1]

Anderson did all he could to encourage this excitement. As soon as he learned of the fall of Fort Sumter, he hurried to the capitol to ascertain what course Virginia would follow. When Governor Letcher informed him of his determination to support the Union, Anderson decided to organize a mass demonstration to marshal public support behind secession. He hired the State Armory band to lead a procession up Main Street to the Tredegar works. There, to the strains of the *Marseillaise*, some three thousand Richmonders cheered as Tredegar workmen hoisted the Stars and Bars over the spike factory. Cannon recently finished for Southern states delivered a seven gun salute and a large cannon was fired in honor of Virginia, "in hopes that her representatives would soon do their duty," explained the Richmond *Dispatch*.[2] Anderson spoke a few words and then introduced several secessionist members of the state convention who urged Virginia's immediate withdrawal from the Union. J. Randolph Tucker, Virginia's attorney-general, elicited prolonged cheers from the crowd when he told them that cannon cast at the Tredegar had breached the walls of Fort Sumter.[3]

At the conclusion of the festivities at the works, the "Tredegar boys" and the band led the crowd to Capitol Square, acquiring on the way the

1. Anderson to John J. Walker, April 13, 1861, Tredegar Letterbooks.

2. Richmond *Dispatch*, April 15, 1861; entries for April 1861, Tredegar Journals.

3. Anderson to James Lyons, Dec. 23, 1863, Tredegar Letterbooks; Richmond *Enquirer*, April 16, 1861; Richmond *Dispatch*, April 15, 1861.

cannon of a local artillery regiment for another noisy celebration. A hundred-gun salute echoed over Richmond's hills and the mob called lustily for the governor, "Honest John" Letcher. He appeared briefly in response to this raucous serenade but would promise no more than to do his duty toward Virginia, no matter what the personal cost. Letcher retired but numerous secessionist orators quickly took his place. The demonstrators heard several harangues and raised the Confederate flag over Jefferson's capitol as dusk fell. Before dispersing, the assembled Richmonders shouted approval of a resolution, "that we rejoice . . . at the triumph of the Southern Confederacy over the accursed government at Washington in the capture of Fort Sumter." [4] That night, torchlight parades flourishing the new flag of the Southern Confederacy crowded Richmond's streets.[5]

"We hoisted the Confederate Flag from the top of our spike factory on Saturday evening . . . and hope before next Saturday she may float above the Va. Convention," wrote William Tanner on April 15.[6] Lincoln's call for 75,000 volunteers that same day changed Governor Letcher's mind about supporting the Union, and the Virginia convention went into secret session. A "Southern Rights" convention, with Anderson serving as a Richmond delegate, met in Richmond on April 17 and prepared to pass an extralegal secession ordinance if the convention did not take quick action. But the official body voted to secede on the 17th.[7] "The flag of the Southern Confederacy waves over the State Capitol and we will defend it to the last extremity," telegraphed young Tanner exultantly.[8]

The Tredegar partners immediately offered their works to the Confederate government. Archer Anderson, J. R. Anderson's son and a member of the firm since January 1, left for Montgomery on April 19, with full powers to convey the entire plant to the government, either by lease or purchase. If Confederate officials bought or rented the Richmond establishment, Anderson and his associates expected to continue to operate the Tredegar under their personal supervision.[9] The extent to which the government should finance and control private industry had not been deter-

4. Richmond *Examiner*, April 15, 1861.

5. Richmond *Enquirer*, April 16, 1861.

6. Anderson & Co. to E. F. Raworth, April 15, 1861, Tredegar Letterbooks.

7. Alfred H. Bill, *The Beleaguered City: Richmond, 1861–1865* (New York, 1946), pp. 39–41; Richmond *Examiner*, April 16–18, 1861.

8. Anderson & Co. to H. T. Peake, April 20, 1861, Tredegar Letterbooks.

9. Anderson to L. P. Walker, April 18, 1861, and Anderson & Co. to James A. Seddon, Dec. 23, 1862, Letters Rec'd., Secretary of War, RG 109, NA.

mined at this early stage of the conflict, however. The Charleston *Courier* voiced "strong objections against any undertaking by the government of duties which can be fulfilled by private enterprise," and Congress tabled a request from the owner of an iron works near New Orleans that the government buy his plant.[10] The brief successful war that most Southerners anticipated would not require the government to go meddling in private business. Confederate officials declined Anderson and Company's offer and the owners retained complete control of the works.

The atmosphere around the Tredegar offices was decidedly bellicose in the weeks immediately after the surrender of Fort Sumter. "We are a unit here in defense of our liberties and will die before subjugation," Anderson wrote in late April, and one of his partners promised that the Tredegar was "busily preparing to give Old Abe a warm reception when ever he may feel disposed to call on us." [11] In a letter to a Tennessee railroad man in May, John Tanner expressed the determination of the Tredegar management to resist the North at all costs: "It pains us to know that any slave state has been subjugated, like Missouri & Maryland. We consider it far more honorable to die with honor than live in disgrace & we feel pledged to this policy, as we find your noble state is also. We are daily expecting an attack, but the God of Battles will defend the right." [12]

At the same time, Anderson pleaded with Northern business acquaintances to use their influence to prevent a "bloody contest." [13] "We still trust to the returning good sense of the public to settle our troubles without bloodshed," Anderson wrote the Massachusetts firm that had subcontracted for part of the Virginia musket machinery.[14] "Cant the good men interpose and have the troops withdrawn and save the country?" he asked.[15] Anderson's reluctance to believe that civil war could really come to America was shared by the leaders of both sections of the divided country. But war had arrived. "All of our worst fears as expressed in our several conversations are fully realized and we are in the midst of Civil War. This sad

10. Lester J. Cappon, "Government and Private Industry in the Southern Confederacy," in *Humanistic Studies in Honor of John Calvin Metcalf*, University of Virginia Studies, *1* (1941), 175.

11. Anderson to Nelson Beale, April 27, 1861, and Anderson & Co. to Samuel Tate, May 6, 1861, Tredegar Letterbooks.

12. Anderson & Co. to William B. Waldron, May 18, 1861, ibid.

13. Anderson & Co. to James Jeffries & Sons, April 30, 1861, ibid.

14. Anderson & Co. to James T. Ames, April 30, 1861, ibid.

15. Anderson & Co. to Merrick & Sons, April 30, 1861, ibid.

event compels us to change our plan of operations and to use our whole establishment & every instrumentality at our command for the protection of our country against the invasion of a merciless foe now threatening our subjugation or destruction," wrote John Tanner.[16]

II

The unique facilities of the Tredegar works were of incalculable importance to the new nation. In the early months of the war, the entire burden of heavy cannon production fell on the Richmond plant. The government attempted to stimulate the manufacture of ordnance at other points in the Confederacy by granting contracts to iron founders who proposed to begin the production of guns. The Secretary of War contracted with Mark A. Cooper of the Etowah Iron Works in Georgia for 8- and 10-inch columbiads, field artillery, and ammunition on April 21, 1861, but Cooper was unable to fulfill his contract. The Navy Department ordered columbiads and 32-pounder naval guns from two New Orleans firms, Leeds and Company and Bennett and Surges, but these firms met only limited success with their ordnance operations before the city fell. Bellona foundry near Richmond went back into production in 1862 and a new government foundry at Selma, Alabama, began casting heavy cannon in July 1863, but the Tredegar works remained the backbone of Confederate ordnance production throughout the war. Field artillery presented fewer manufacturing difficulties than heavy siege and seacoast weapons. The Ordnance Bureau was able to secure field pieces from a number of plants in Georgia—its own arsenals at Macon and Augusta and private iron works at Columbus and Rome—from small foundries in Mobile, Vicksburg, Memphis, New Orleans, and Columbia, South Carolina, and from Bellona foundry in Virginia. But the Tredegar produced many times the total number of weapons manufactured at these establishments.[17]

Fortunately for the South, the Confederate government did not have to depend exclusively on Tredegar production for all its heavy coast defense weapons. Evacuating Federal troops left a rich legacy in Southern forts

16. Anderson & Co. to W. D. Dunn, April 27, 1861, ibid.

17. List of contracts made by Secretaries of War, Dec. 13, 1862, Letters Rec'd., Secretary of War, RG 109, NA; Josiah Gorgas, "Notes on the Ordnance Department of the Confederate Government," *Southern Historical Society Papers, 12* (1884), 82, 93–94; Frank E. Vandiver, *Ploughshares into Swords: Josiah Gorgas and Confederate Ordnance* (Austin, Texas, 1952), pp. 62–63, 169–70, 240; Jennings C. Wise, *The Long Arm of Lee; The History of the Field Artillery of the Army of Northern Virginia* (New York, 1959), pp. 78–79; William A.

and arsenals in the form of 429 pieces of seacoast ordnance. In addition, approximately fifty 8-inch columbiads cast at Bellona foundry for the Federal government and detained by Virginia authorities in April 1861 were available for service. The South came into its greatest store of heavy ordnance on April 21, 1861, when Virginia troops occupied the Gosport Navy Yard at Norfolk. The Virginia militiamen who marched into the navy yard found 1202 cannon on hand, along with great stores of ammunition, gun carriages, implements, and 282,149 pounds of cannon powder. These ordnance pieces quickly filled batteries along the Virginia coast and 136 guns were shipped to the Richmond defenses. Virginia officials also dispatched a large number of cannon to vital points in other Southern states. When Virginia turned the navy yard over to the Confederate government on June 30, 1861, only 489 of the original 1202 pieces remained.[18]

The Confederacy's limited capacity for producing heavy ordnance was equaled by the dearth of facilities for manufacturing railroad iron. The only rolling mills of any magnitude in the Southern nation were the two at the Tredegar, the Gate City rolling mill in Atlanta, a smaller mill at the Etowah Iron Works near Cartersville in north Georgia, the Shelby rolling mill in Alabama, and the Cumberland rolling mill, close to Fort Donelson, Tennessee. Only one of the Tredegar mills and the Atlanta mill had ever rolled rails.[19] The facilities at the Richmond plant had been converted to the production of bar iron and rail chairs during the 1850s and would require considerable adaptation before rails could be rolled again. Small forges dotted the mountains of Virginia, North Carolina, and Tennessee, producing bar iron for local consumption and manufacturing agricultural implements and household items, but their product was negligible and of no use to the railroads. The Alabama iron industry had hardly been born. (See Table 3.)

Albaugh, III, and Edward N. Simmons, *Confederate Arms* (Harrisburg, Pa., 1957), pp. 195–277; *Official Records of the Union and Confederate Navies in the War of the Rebellion* (31 vols. Washington, 1894–1927), Series II, *2*, 53. Hereafter cited as *O.R.N.*

18. *O.R.*, Ser. IV, *1*, 228; "Report of Ordnance and Ordnance Stores on hand at the Gosport Navy Yard on the 21st of April, 1861 . . ." and "Report of Expenditures of Ordnance and Ordnance Stores from the 21st of April to 30th of June, 1861, inclusive," Document No. 25, *Documents of the [Virginia] House of Delegates, 1861–62* (Richmond, 1862).

19. Lesley, *Iron Manufacturer's Guide*, pp. 244–46, 259; Black, *Railroads of the Confederacy*, pp. 22–25; Frank E. Vandiver, "The Shelby Iron Works in the Civil War: A Study of a Confederate Industry," *Alabama Review, 1* (1948), 15.

TABLE 3. Bar, Sheet, and Railroad Iron Produced in the Southern States, Border States, and Pennsylvania during the Year Ending June 1, 1860

State	Number of establish-ments	Capital invested	Hands employed	TONS OF IRON PRODUCED Bar	Railroad	Boiler plate	Sheet iron	Total
Southern States								
Virginia								
Tredegar Iron Works	1	$ 435,000	800	6,000	—	—	—	6,000
Other	16	163,725	154	1,709				1,709
Total Virginia	17	$ 598,725	954	7,709				7,709
North Carolina	25	165,250	129	1,096	—	—	—	1,096
Georgia	2	102,200	104	30	2,000			2,030
Alabama	2	33,000	15	93	—	—	—	93
Tennessee	35	284,835	344	5,144				5,144
Total Southern States	81	$ 1,184,010	1,546	14,072	2,000	—	—	16,072
Border States								
Maryland	7	$ 4,260,000	455	8,335	—	—	2,350	10,685
Missouri	2	525,000	275	6,678	—	—	—	6,678
Kentucky	5	1,350,000	640	12,000	—	900	1,200	14,100
[West Virginia]	2	435,000	420	—	10,180	—	—	10,180
Total Border States	16	$ 6,570,000	1,790	27,013	10,180	900	3,550	41,643
Pennsylvania	87	$10,974,013	10,177	112,276	133,577	13,000	7,000	266,253

Sources: *Eighth Census of the United States, Manufactures*, pp. clxxxiii, 625; manuscript returns, Census of Manufactures, 1860, Virginia, VSL.

Unfortunately for the South, the industrial resources of the border states were never added to the Confederate war machine. (See Table 3.) In 1860, the Gate City mill at Atlanta produced 2,000 tons of rails. During the same year, two rolling mills at Wheeling, Virginia, produced 10,180 tons of rails. Wheeling had a total of five rolling mills with a capacity of well over 20,000 tons of rails per year and three nail works. Maryland had four rolling mills manufacturing sheet iron, an article not made in the South, and the Baltimore area had two modern rolling mills, a spike mill,

TABLE 4. Pig Iron Produced in the United States during the Year Ending June 1, 1860

States	*Number of establish-ments*	*Number of workers employed*	*Tons of pig iron produced*
Pennsylvania	125	7,593	580,049
Maryland	11	615	30,500
Kentucky	18	465	33,471
Missouri	2	175	18,000
Virginia	16	524	11,646
Georgia	2	60	1,100
Alabama	4	95	1,742
Tennessee	17	991	22,302
Total Southern States	39	1,670	36,790
Total New England States	14	786	26,600
Total Middle Atlantic States	157	9,381	736,869
Total Western States	76	4,017	187,300

Source: *Eighth Census of the United States, Manufactures*, p. clxxx.

and a large nail works. Both Maryland and Kentucky possessed thriving pig iron industries, each producing in 1860 almost as much metal as the entire product of the states which later joined the Confederacy. (See Table 4.) Kentucky was blessed with seven modern rolling mills, four of which were centered just below Cincinnati. A rolling mill at Louisville produced boiler plate, another strategic item not manufactured in the seceding states, and a mill at Paducah and one in Lyon County on the Cumberland River rolled bar, sheet, and plate iron. The iron industry had made rapid strides in Missouri in the 1850s, with the erection of modern blast furnaces south of St. Louis and the emergence of St. Louis as a rolling mill center.[20] The accession of Maryland, Kentucky, and Missouri to the Confederacy and the retention of West Virginia would have given the new nation vital industrial support, in addition to untold political and strategic benefits. The economic balance would still have been weighted in favor of the North but not nearly so heavily.

III

Less than a month before the outbreak of the war, Anderson and Company had informed a job seeker that there were so many unemployed mechanics in the city that they did not want to induce any more to come to Richmond.[21] This labor surplus did not last for long. Five or six Irish puddlers left for the North on the eve of the conflict and the company advertised for first class smiths and smith's helpers, pattern makers, and woodworkers in March and April.[22] By the first week of May, the Tredegar labor force had gone on a seven-day week, working until ten o'clock in the evening. The management had considered the ordnance department fairly well staffed at the outset of hostilities, primarily because state orders for cannon and munitions in the first quarter of 1861 had forced the hiring of additional artisans. Of the approximately 900 men working at the Tredegar when the war began, 540 were engaged in ordnance production. But in May, Anderson reported difficulty completing cannon after they were cast because of a shortage of finishers. Machinists, blacksmiths, and molders were also in short supply.[23] The company wrote during the summer that they could use twenty-five or thirty good men—machinists, vise and lathe hands, chippers, and filers. In October, they were still advertising for men with these skills, as well as for brass molders and the much-needed finishers.[24]

A number of factors accounted for this growing shortage of skilled arti-

20. Manuscript returns, Census of Manufactures, 1860, Virginia, VSL; Lesley, pp. 137–38, 241–44, 254–55, 257–60; James D. Norris, *Frontier Iron: The Maramec Iron Works, 1826–1876* (Madison, Wis., 1964), pp. 116–17.

21. Anderson & Co. to J. N. Powell, March 19, 1861, Tredegar Letterbooks.

22. Anderson & Co. to Albert Johnson, April 7, 1861, to R. J. Capron, April 16, 1861, and to the Publisher, Petersburg *Express*, April 10, 1861, ibid.; Richmond *Dispatch*, March 5, 1861.

23. Anderson & Co. to C. T. Cunningham, May 3, 1861, to C. G. Memminger, May 9, 1861, to E. F. Raworth, May 4, 1861, to Mitchell & Smith, May 13, 1861, to Hugh Harper, May 6, 1861, and to Thomas B. Rowland, May 17, 1861, Tredegar Letterbooks.

24. Anderson & Co. to W. Johnson, July 13, 1861, ibid.; Richmond *Dispatch*, Oct. 22, 24, 1861.

sans. The city's iron works had depended on aliens for much of their labor and some Northern and foreign-born workers headed north after Fort Sumter. The crush of military orders that descended on the Tredegar and Richmond's numerous smaller foundries and machine shops quickly increased the demand for experienced operatives and the demand grew even more when the government's shops began production. The Virginia State Armory, soon to be transferred to the Confederate government, the Confederate Arsenal, established in a group of tobacco warehouses near the Tredegar, and the ordnance works of the army and navy competed among themselves and with private companies for an insufficient number of qualified artisans. In September 1861, the Irish foundry workers at the Tredegar struck in mass and told the managers they had jobs waiting for them at the nearby armory. To hold them, Anderson had to grant the men higher wages.[25] Distrust of some Northern mechanics presented an added difficulty. The Tredegar management discharged three men in July "on account of supposed disloyalty to the South" and notified other Richmond iron manufacturers of their action to prevent the men from securing jobs in the Confederate capital.[26]

The owners took several steps to fill gaps in the Tredegar labor force. As a start, they accepted an increased number of boys as apprentices. In the first year of the war, some fifty youths were apprenticed to various departments, almost three times the number taken between 1859 and April 1861.[27] The management also hired some twenty-two additional Negroes, including two blacksmiths, in November 1861. These additions boosted the slave population at the works to almost one hundred.[28] Since the total number of workers had risen to approximately one thousand men by the end of the year, slaves still represented about 10 per cent of the working force. The owners doubtless would have hired more slaves had they not found it difficult to acquire hands before the customary months of December and January.

They increased the number of slave workers by one third at the first of the year:

25. Anderson & Co. to James H. Burton, Sept. 18, 1861, Tredegar Letterbooks; labor charges for Aug.–Sept. 1861, Tredegar Foundry Sales Books.

26. Anderson & Co. to Talbot & Bro., July 17, 1861, Tredegar Letterbooks.

27. Archer Account Book, VHS.

28. Contract with Thomas J. Bagley, Nov. 8, 1861, Tredegar Contract Books; entry for Dec. 1861, Tredegar Journals.

List of Negroes Hired at Tredegar Iron Works
January 1, 1862[29]

SLAVES:	
Rolling mill hands	48
Blacksmiths	6
Blacksmiths' helpers	7
Strikers	12
Smith shop laborers	19
Foundry laborers	6
Teamsters	7
Boatmen	1
Common laborers	21
Total	131

FREE NEGROES:	
Rolling mill hands	1
Blacksmiths	1
Blacksmiths' helpers	1
Carpenters	1
Total	4

Slaves were still concentrated primarily in the rolling mill and blacksmith shops, as had been the case under peacetime conditions, but their numbers had increased. Bonds given slave owners by Anderson and Company promised to feed and clothe the hands during the year and contained a clause stipulating that if the enemy disturbed Tredegar operations, the company reserved the right to return the slave and pay for his services up to the time of evacuation.[30] As the war progressed and white artisans became increasingly difficult to secure, the Tredegar's reliance on slave labor grew.

The rush of Tredegar operatives to volunteer for military service was a major source of trouble during the early months of the war. The most skilled cannon rifler left the works as a militia volunteer in late April, and ten days later the entire force of ten blacksmiths working on iron gun carriages enlisted as a unit.[31] State authorities acted quickly in an attempt to

29. Tredegar Contract Books. This total of 131 slaves corresponds closely to the 128 listed in City of Richmond, Personal Property Tax Rolls, 1862, VSL.

30. Blank slave bond, Supplementary Tredegar Records.

31. Anderson & Co. to Letcher, April 22, 27, May 6, 15, 1861, and to Capt. L. Bossieux, May 8, 1861, Tredegar Letterbooks.

arrest this overmobilization. Governor Letcher issued a proclamation on April 25 exempting from state service all persons engaged in making military equipment. On May 1, the Virginia state convention passed an ordinance expanding the governor's proclamation. Under this law, all persons employed in any factory manufacturing arms, munitions of war, and other vital commodities necessary for the defense of the state were declared exempt from military duty, unless the governor ordered them into militia service. In a supplemental act passed on June 26, 1861, the convention included persons engaged in mining coal, iron, lead, saltpeter, and salt in this broad exemption.[32]

The press also joined in the effort to dampen the military ardor of vital laborers. The Richmond *Examiner* cautioned in a sober and prophetic editorial on April 26 that "men who are actually occupied with pursuits necessary for the well-being of the whole state should not be encouraged to let their work go to the dogs and hurry off to camps in a moment of blind and unreflecting enthusiasm." "Wars seldom begin and never end in an hour, a day or a week," warned the *Examiner*, and "the first draft that goes to make up an army will not be the last. War devours men."

Once a man had enlisted, the Tredegar management found the process of regaining his services difficult and tedious. The cannon rifler, John McDonald, who had worked at the Tredegar for many years, was the object of an extended correspondence following his April enlistment. After Anderson and Company dispatched letters to Governor Letcher, Major General Robert E. Lee, the Adjutant General of the Confederate Army, and Major Josiah Gorgas, chief of the Ordnance Bureau, McDonald was discharged on July 15 and returned to the works.[33] Securing the return of the ten gun-carriage blacksmiths was more difficult. The captain of their company refused to discharge them, and finally the company had to take its case to the Secretary of War. On August 22, the owners informed Walker that "we are now unable to fulfill the orders of the Government for want of mechanics and submit the whole question to you." Five of the men were dis-

32. Richmond *Examiner*, April 25, 1861; "Ordinances adopted by the Convention of Virginia, in Secret Session, April and May 1861," appendix to *Acts of the [Virginia] General Assembly, 1861*, p. 27; "Ordinances adopted by the Convention of Virginia, at the Adjourned Session in June and July 1861," appendix, ibid., p. 58.

33. Anderson & Co. to Letcher, May 15, 1861, to Gen. R. E. Lee, May 15, 1861, to Col. George Deas, July 8, 1861, and to Maj. Josiah Gorgas, July 8, 1861, Tredegar Letterbooks; "Compiled Service Records of Confederate Soldiers who Served in Organizations from the State of Virginia," *National Archives Microfilm Publications*, M-324 (Washington, 1961).

charged the following day and returned to Richmond.[34] The War Department was generally willing to discharge needed laborers in 1861 if the Tredegar pressed the matter. But later, when the demand for fresh troops increased with the approach of the spring campaigns in 1862, the Tredegar's labor problem became acute.

The management found their most effective tool for retaining skilled native-born workers at the outset of the war was the Tredegar Battalion. Anderson and his associates organized this group as a volunteer militia unit during the heady days following Fort Sumter. Anderson, as major, commanded the battalion and Robert S. Archer, William E. Tanner, Peter Derbyshire, the foundry superintendent, and William Prescott, foreman of the machine shops, captained the four companies. The battalion totaled almost 350 men, all Tredegar operatives. The firm spent $3,000 to outfit the unit and the Richmond City Council voted an additional $2,000 for uniforms and equipment. The state issued the men muskets and bayonets and, at Anderson's request, gave them six old iron 6-pounder cannon lying at the State Armory for an artillery battery. These cannon, mounted and equipped with harness, were soon turned over to the Confederate government, however. Robert S. Archer later appealed to the Secretary of War for a battery of heavy siege artillery to assist in the defense of Richmond but was turned down. He repeated his request to the Richmond City Council, seeking funds to finance the purchase of the cannon, but again met no success. The Tredegar Battalion remained strictly an infantry group.[35]

The men served their first duty patrolling the works, but not until after a serious arson attempt. Anderson and Company requested a detail of four watchmen from the city on May 11 to assist in protecting the plant but no military guard was posted. On Saturday night, May 18, a volunteer regiment drilling on Gamble's Hill overlooking the works saw flames in the pattern shop. They spread the alarm and assisted in putting out the blaze before it spread. A few hours later, watchmen discovered two more fires in the heart of the plant and found the adjacent fireplug disabled. Early discovery prevented serious damage but the attempt alerted the owners and state officials to the pressing need for a guard. The Richmond *Dispatch*

34. Ibid.; Anderson & Co. to Walker, Aug. 22, 1861, Tredegar Letterbooks.

35. Anderson & Co. to Lee, May 8, 1861, to William Salmon, May 28, 1861, and to Letcher, July 16, 1861, ibid.; entries for Tredegar Battalion June–Sept., Dec., 1861, Nov. 1862, Tredegar Journals; "Issues from Richmond Armory, April 1–June 13, 1861," and "Anderson's Application for Iron Cannon, May 8, 1861," Virginia Executive Papers, VSL; minutes of Feb. 20, 1862, Richmond City Council Minute Books, VSL.

Joseph R. Anderson in the uniform of a brigadier general, Confederate States Army, photographed by Mathew B. Brady in the summer of 1865.

The Tredegar works in the summer of 1865 as seen from the Richmond and Petersburg Railroad tracks. The whitewashed wooden buildings at the left on Brown's Island (sometimes called Neilson's Island) are part of the Confederate ammunition laboratories.

suggested that lynch law be applied to the arsonists. Anderson asked Governor Letcher to muster the Tredegar Battalion into state service and detail the four companies back to the works for guard duty. Letcher's military advisory council submitted the matter to Lee, then in command of Virginia's forces, and he recommended that only one of the four companies be used for such duty. This was done and Company D of the Tredegar Battalion instituted a close watch. Passes were hereafter required for access to the works. These measures put an end to arson attempts for the duration of the war.[36]

IV

An important change in the management of the Tredegar works took place in September 1861 when Joseph R. Anderson went on active military service. The guard patrols, drills, and Fourth of July picnics which comprised the military activities of the Tredegar Battalion did not come close to satisfying Anderson's martial appetite. He decided to request a field command and wrote the Secretary of War on August 21, 1861. "At the Head of the 'Tredegar Iron Works' I have used every exertion in my power to promote the interest of the country," he informed Walker. "But as I have been educated a soldier and see that the Government finds it necessary to confer military command on citizens who have not had the advantage of military education, I think it is time now for me to claim some exemption from purely business occupations and to ask for a command in the field." Anderson observed that three of his West Point classmates, Montgomery C. Meigs, John W. Phelps, and Thomas W. Sherman, had recently been appointed brigadier generals in the Union Army, "neither of whom would, I believe, consider it boastful in me to compare my qualifications, as a soldier, with theirs." [37]

Lee, among others, questioned whether Anderson could render more effective service to the South by entering the army than he could by remaining at the head of the Tredegar works. He urged Anderson to continue on in Richmond unless he could make satisfactory arrangements for

36. Anderson & Co. to the Mayor of Richmond, May 11, 1861, to the Governor and Council of the State, June 3, 1861, and muster rolls for Company D, Tredegar Battalion, June–Aug. 1861, Tredegar Letterbooks; Anderson & Co. to Letcher, May 20, 1861, Virginia Executive Papers, and entries for May 21, 1861, Virginia Executive Journal and Journal of the Advisory Council of Virginia, VSL; Richmond *Dispatch*, May 20, 1861; blank Tredegar pass, Confederate States Miscellany, LC.

37. Anderson to Walker, Aug. 21, 1861, Field and Staff Officers File, RG 109, NA.

managing the critically important Tredegar operations.[38] Anderson replied that as long as John Tanner and Dr. Archer were at their jobs, the Tredegar would be in capable and energetic hands. These assurances apparently satisfied the President for Davis appointed Anderson a brigadier general in the Provisional Army on September 3, 1861. John B. Jones, the War Department diarist, noted Anderson's appointment with the terse comment that the West Pointer "does not look like a military genius." [39] He was ordered to North Carolina on coast defense duty and given command of the District of Cape Fear.[40] The Richmond *Dispatch* echoed Lee's reservations about Anderson leaving his works, noting that the Tredegar's senior partner was "now to be transferred to a higher, though not more useful, sphere of action." [41]

Anderson departed for North Carolina but retained an active interest in the Tredegar. In December 1861, he wrote the Secretary of War from Wilmington expressing his fear that another arson attempt might be made on the works and asking for an increased guard. "It would take a long time to replace the machinery in these works and much of it has no duplicate in this country." Anderson admitted that his financial interest in the Tredegar was considerable, "but at present the country has a greater stake in it." [42] The government was very much aware of the importance of the Tredegar works. After less than one year of active duty, Anderson would be back in Richmond in command of his industrial army.

With Anderson's removal from Richmond, John Tanner assumed overall direction of Tredegar operations. Tanner, then fifty-two years old, was Anderson's closest business associate. He had risen from bookkeeper to superintendent of the rolling mill and finally had become a partner in the works. Tanner's black horses and carriage soon became a familiar sight in Richmond, dashing between government offices and depots and the Tredegar.[43]

Dr. Robert Archer directed his attention primarily to ordnance production. After he had brought his mill into the partnership of Anderson and

38. Lee to Anderson, July 15, 1862, quoted in Bruce, *Virginia Iron Manufacture*, p. 376.

39. John B. Jones, *A Rebel War Clerk's Diary*, ed. Howard Swiggett (2 vols. New York, 1935), *1*, 77.

40. Samuel Cooper to Anderson, Sept. 3, 1861, Letters Sent, Adjutant and Inspector General, RG 109, NA.

41. Richmond *Dispatch*, Sept. 6, 1861.

42. Anderson to Judah P. Benjamin, Dec. 17, 1861, Letters Rec'd., Secretary of War, RG 109, NA.

43. Bill, *Beleaguered City*, p. 58.

Company in 1859, he and his son, Robert S. Archer, had taken increasingly active roles in the manufacture of cannon. Dr. Archer was an inventor of some distinction, having designed rifle shot for Tredegar cannon and a safety device to prevent premature explosions of cannon shell.[44] When General Anderson left for the North Carolina coast in early September, he believed that with Dr. Archer's assistance, Tanner could cope with any problems that might arise. Unfortunately for Tredegar production, the senior partner overestimated his associates' ability to make independent decisions.

V

Lincoln's April 16 ban on trade with the South and his subsequent blockade proclamations did not affect the Tredegar's operations until several weeks after the war began. Anderson received 5,000 pounds of high quality tin from Baltimore when Federal authorities permitted the Bay Line steamers to sail into Norfolk until April 30, but he failed to secure 100,000 pounds of Baltimore copper before this last avenue was closed.[45] The next month, the Richmond industrialists turned down a large lot of tin in New Orleans because they considered the price too high. "Your people are making calculations for a long blockade," one of the partners wrote their New Orleans agent.[46]

In May, the Tredegar owners began to realize the full extent of their dependence on the North for strategic materials. Late that month, the brass foundry exhausted its slim store of copper and the casting of bronze field pieces ceased. Until a supply of copper could be secured, the Tredegar had to furnish the batteries going into the field with iron ordnance. The company developed 3- and 6-pounder iron rifled guns, banded with wrought iron jackets at the breech for added strength, and an iron 12-pounder howitzer and manufactured these weapons in large quantities in the summer and fall of 1861. In October, the Tredegar was able to obtain copper in limited quantities from the South's only source, the Ducktown mines in Polk County, Tennessee, close to Chattanooga. With tin supplied by the Ordnance Bureau, the casting of bronze cannon resumed on December 7,

44. Archer, "History of the Archer and Silvester Families," VHS; Richmond *Enquirer*, Sept. 28, 1861.

45. Anderson & Co. to Thompson & Oudesluys, April 17, 25, 1861, and to David Keener, April 27, 1861, Tredegar Letterbooks; J. W. H. Porter, *A Record of Events in Norfolk County, Virginia, 1861–1862* (Portsmouth, Va., 1892), p. 25.

46. Anderson & Co. to E. M. Ivens, May 21, 1861, Tredegar Letterbooks.

1861, over six months after the exhaustion of the Baltimore copper in May.[47]

The Tredegar soon discovered that other metals were in equally short supply. Steel needed for retooling boring lathes and rifling machines, lead for rifle projectile sabots, sheet zinc for ammunition boxes, and gas pipe for fitting cannon shell detonators all became difficult, and sometimes impossible, to secure in the South. After buying whatever they could find, the Richmond associates had to depend on the Ordnance Bureau for these materials. But government arsenals and armories had first call on the slender stocks of these precious metals and the lead mined near Wytheville, Virginia, was insufficient even to maintain adequate production of musket ammunition.[48]

Some items previously obtained in the North presented less of a problem. Lumber mills near Richmond could furnish gun carriage timber, usually inadequately seasoned, and the Tredegar machine shops turned out the necessary metal parts. The rolling mills began manufacturing boiler plate, the first ever made at the Tredegar, in the fall of 1861. Grindstones were secured in southwest Virginia and workers recut old files to give them added life. Nuts for fitting bridge bolts, supplied before the war by a Massachusetts manufacturer, now had to be tediously cut by hand at the Richmond works.[49]

The shortage of firebrick was a source of constant concern to the Tredegar management throughout the war. In late April 1861, Anderson and Company asked their Baltimore supplier to ship them 30,000 firebrick and to get the vessel off immediately. The shipment never arrived. With the foundries and rolling mills in constant use, the need for new brick to reline the furnaces soon became a pressing matter. The partners first attempted to manufacture their own but abandoned the project when it proved unfeasible. By September, some furnaces stood idle for want of brick. Later that fall, the company ordered a supply from a Georgia manufacturer but high

47. Anderson & Co. to Letcher, May 24, 1861, to Col. S. G. French, July 8, 1861, to Gorgas, Sept. 7, 1861, to Michael Cohen, Sept. 21, 1861, to Capt. E. J. Raht, Sept. 17, 1861, and to H. Nutt, Oct. 3, 1861, ibid.; Tredegar Gun Foundry Book.

48. Vandiver, *Gorgas*, p. 123; Anderson & Co. to Gorgas, Sept. 16, 1861, to Ellis & Moore, Nov. 8, 1861, and to Ivens, Sept. 9, 20, Nov. 14, 1861, Tredegar Letterbooks.

49. Anderson & Co. to Gorgas, Sept. 27, 1861, to L. W. Glazebrook, Nov. 19, 1861, and to W. J. Ross, Aug. 24, 1861, ibid.; contract with D. B. Corrie and Henry Ball, Sept. 23, 1861, Tredegar Contract Books; Archer Account Book, VHS.

freight charges and the uncertainty surrounding any long railroad shipments in the Confederacy rendered dependence on such a distant source impracticable. Anderson and Company turned finally to wartime Virginia porcelain corporations and furnished iron and subscribed stock in several to assist them in organizing and beginning production.[50] The works secured a supply of firebrick from several of these corporations but found the bricks of very poor quality. "Our furnaces frequently give out in a few days when they ought to last us many months," complained one of the Tredegar partners in 1864.[51] The problem of obtaining an adequate supply of good firebrick was never solved and this deficiency hindered production for the duration of the war.

Coal pits near Richmond could supply much of the fuel required by the Tredegar but the blockade cut off Northern anthracite used in the spike furnaces and for general foundry purposes. Anderson and Company first bought up such meager stores of anthracite as they could find in Richmond and then attempted unsuccessfully to persuade Baltimore agents to run a cargo through the blockade.[52] When these efforts failed to produce sufficient supplies, the firm decided to rebuild the anthracite-consuming spike and foundry furnaces to take coke, which could be manufactured out of bituminous coal available nearby. Adequate quantities of coke soon became unobtainable on the open market and Anderson and Company built coking furnaces and produced their own. During the summer and early fall, Richmond agents agreed to supply the works with large amounts of coal for the coming winter.[53] The partners felt much more secure about coal deliveries than they did about their supplies of other vital materials, including pig iron.

50. Anderson & Co. to F. B. Deane, Jr. & Son, Sept. 16, 1861, to George Yonge, Nov. 8, 1861, to Barnes & Co., Dec. 3, 1862, Jan. 6, Feb. 27, 28, 1863, and to William Withrow, Jr., Dec. 20, 1864, Tredegar Letterbooks; contracts with Isaac Williams, July 26, 1861, and Barnes & Co., April 23, 1862, Tredegar Contract Books; R. S. Archer, holdings of Confederate States Porcelain Co. stock, Watson-Archer Papers, VHS.

51. Anderson & Co. to Withrow, Oct. 3, 1864, Tredegar Letterbooks.

52. Anderson & Co. to M. Sloat, May 1, 1861, to M. Brown, May 21, 1861, to J. C. Turner, May 2, 1861, and to Thompson & Oudesluys, May 14, 1861, ibid.

53. Anderson & Co. to Deane, May 18, 1861, to J. J. Werth, May 25, Sept. 10, 1861, to Daniel Cram, June 8, 1861, to M. C. Selden & Co., Sept. 10, 1861, and to D. S. Woolridge, Sept. 10, 1861, and agreements with J. W. Cottrell, July 17, 1861, Clover Hill Coal Co., Sept. 17, 1861, and Woolridge, Oct. 9, 1861, ibid.; contract with Cottrell, Nov. 8, 1861, Tredegar Contract Books; Richmond *Enquirer*, Sept. 28, 1861.

VI

The high level of production demanded by government orders placed Anderson and Company immediately in need of tremendous quantities of pig iron. The Tredegar partners had depended increasingly on Northern sources of supply in the years immediately prior to the war and this dependence placed their operations in severe jeopardy when the blockade choked off the flow of pig metal from Philadelphia and Baltimore. Tredegar cannon foundries faced a potential shortage of gun metal before the war was a month old. John T. Anderson, whose Cloverdale furnace produced the Tredegar's best gun iron, was more interested in pursuing a political career than he was in manufacturing pig. He ceased production at both the Cloverdale and Grace furnaces after short blasts early in 1861 and took his seat in the House of Delegates in 1861 as a representative of Botetourt County.[54] Anderson and Company had a substantial supply of Cloverdale and Grace gun iron, stockpiled since the 1859 dispute with the United States War Department over the Rodman method, but the rapid production of cannon in the months surrounding the opening of the war quickly exhausted this metal. The short blast at Cloverdale furnace in January and February produced only some forty tons of gun iron—about enough to cast five 10-inch columbiads. A canal boat deposited the last load of this metal at the Richmond works on March 22, 1861.[55]

To insure a continuing supply of gun iron, Anderson and Company contracted in early March for one hundred tons of gun metal from David Graham's furnaces in southwest Virginia that had previously produced gun metal for Bellona foundry. Contracts signed later in 1861 included all the gun iron Graham might make during that year. These orders were supplemented by agreements signed in May and August with John Wissler, owner of the Columbia furnace in Shenandoah County, for 900 tons of gun iron and a September contract with the proprietor of the Fort furnace, located near Strasburg in the Valley. Graham's iron began arriving at the works in late May and the Columbia metal followed close behind in June.[56]

The use of these brands was a decided risk. Tredegar founders had not

54. *Journal of the [Virginia] House of Delegates (Extra Session), 1861,* p. 292; ibid., *1861–62* (Richmond, 1862), p. 355.

55. Tredegar Pig Iron Receipt Book.

56. Ibid.; contracts with Graham & Son, July 17, Oct. 28, 1861, John Wissler & Co., May 1, Aug. 27, 1861, and J. S. Davidson, Sept. 30, 1861, and Graham to Anderson & Co., March 5, 1861, Tredegar Contract Books.

Plan of the Tredegar Iron Works, circa 1864–65

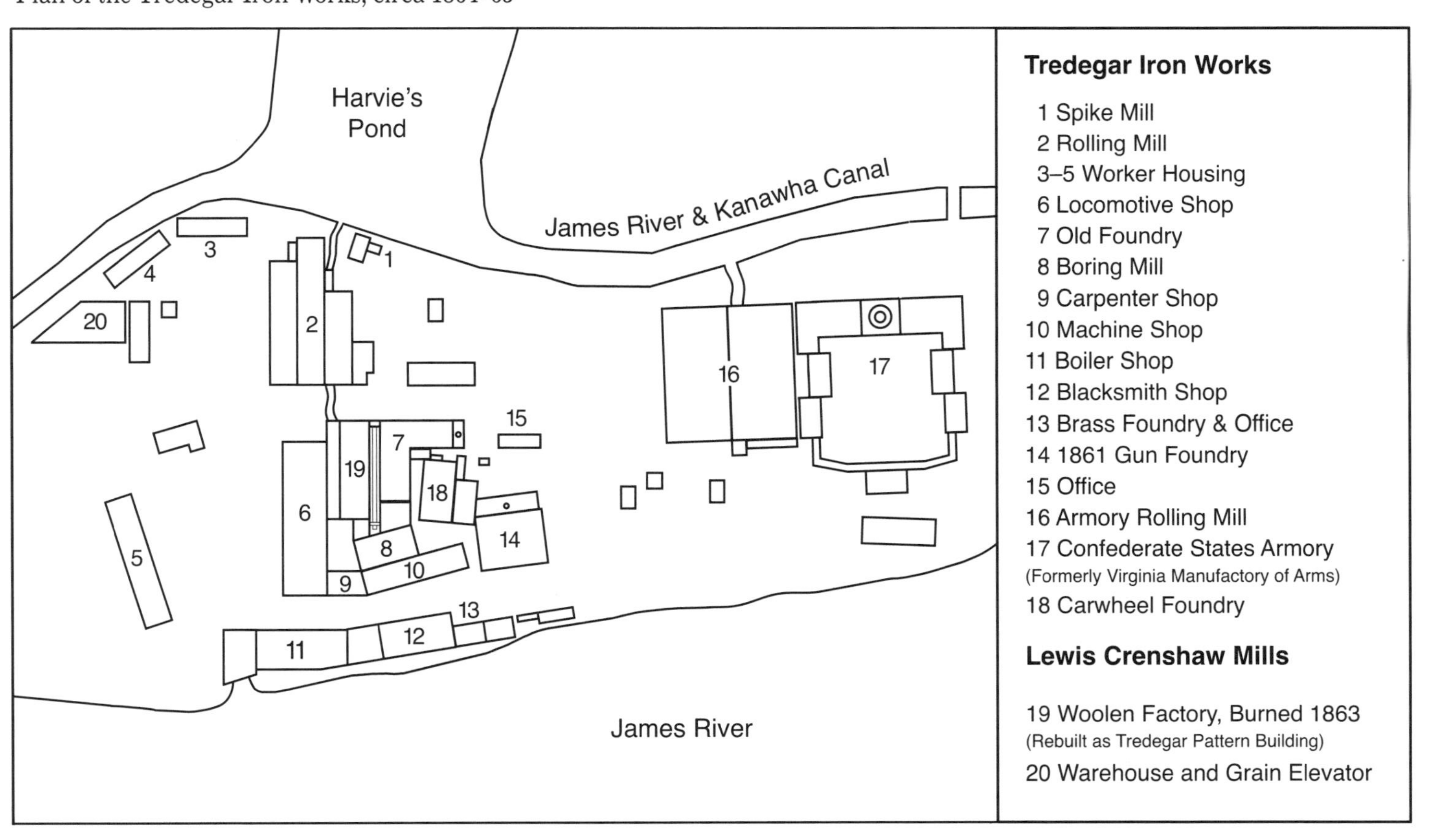

Outline map of Virginia showing the location of the Tredegar forges, blast furnaces, and coal mines during the Civil War.

A. Columbia Furnace
B. Fort Furnace
C. Caroline Furnace
D. Clay Forge
E. Mount Torry Furnace
F. Australia Furnace
G. Jane Furnace
H. Rebecca Furnace
I. Roaring Run Furnace
J. Grace Furnace
K. Catawba Furnace
L. Cloverdale Furnace
M. Glenwood Furnace
N. Dover Mines
O. Tuckahoe Mines

cast the Graham, Columbia, and Fort metal into cannon prior to the war. The Tredegar's only experience with Graham's metal occurred in 1859, when the company manufactured a test slab of the iron for experiments by the Ordnance Bureau. Workmen reported this metal very hard, tough, and difficult to work at that time. This iron had, however, established an excellent reputation in a Bellona trial cannon cast for the Federal government that withstood one thousand rounds so Anderson felt reasonably safe about using Graham's iron in artillery.[57] The Columbia and Fort iron was completely untested for ordnance purposes. The only known way to prove the qualities of a new brand of gun iron was to cast a cannon and subject it to extensive test firings. Even then, slight variations in the method of manufacture or in the fuel, fluxes, and ore used could produce unsafe metal.[58] But the Confederacy needed ordnance and Tredegar gun founders had to use such iron as the management could find. By late June, they had exhausted stocks of Cloverdale and Grace and were forced to cast cannon with Graham, Columbia, Glenwood, and occasionally Fort pig.[59]

Anderson and his partners undoubtedly had misgivings about using this metal. Leeds and Company, proprietors of the large New Orleans foundry and machine shops, asked Anderson and Company for details on cannon manufacture shortly after the war began. The Richmond firm replied that during twenty years of gun casting, "the main difficulty we have experienced has been in obtaining an iron suitable for the purpose & its proper treatment when obtained." After many years of experiments, Anderson and Company had found only one metal entirely reliable for ordnance—the Cloverdale. "There may be other metals that it would be safe to use, but they are unknown to us." [60] When one of Leeds' first cannon burst, Anderson and Company remarked that "our friends will ascertain after a while that all metals wont answer for fabricating ordnance." [61] If the Richmond firm had been able to follow its own advice, subsequent explosions of Tredegar ordnance probably would not have occurred.

Although John T. Anderson did not wish to operate his valuable furnace, Joseph Anderson attempted to get the Cloverdale back in blast by arranging for an experienced founder to lease and operate the furnace.

57. Anderson & Co. to Capt. A. B. Dyer, Sept. 28, 1860, Tredegar Letterbooks; Graham to Anderson & Co., March 5, 1861, Tredegar Contract Books.

58. Benton, *Ordnance and Gunnery*, p. 145.

59. Tredegar Gun Foundry Book.

60. Anderson & Co. to Leeds & Co., May 1, 1861, Tredegar Letterbooks.

61. Anderson & Co. to Ivens, July 4, 1861, ibid.

After making inquiries in April and May, he located two brothers, Isaac and Thomas Steers in Alleghany County, who expressed an interest in renting the furnace. On June 21, 1861, just as the stock of Cloverdale metal at the Tredegar gave out, Anderson made a verbal agreement with the brothers Steers to operate the furnace for two years. Anderson and Company agreed to take a total of 2,000 tons of gun metal during 1861 and 1862, and 140 tons in both 1863 and 1864, at $50 per ton. Anderson failed to secure a written contract, however, and Tredegar gun operations would suffer from this error before the year was out. He believed the large obligation incurred to get Cloverdale back in production, guaranteeing payments of $100,000 before inflation took hold, was a heavy enough burden for the company to bear and he did not extend the terms of the Cloverdale agreement to cover Grace furnace.[62] The enterprising Steers supplemented the agreement with Anderson and Company later in 1861 by signing contracts with the Bureau of Ordnance and Hydrography to supply the navy with 3,600 tons of Cloverdale gun iron over three years beginning January 1, 1863, and 3,600 tons of number one Grace iron starting in April 1862.[63]

VII

The prospect of receiving a substantial stock of proven gun metal alleviated one of the company's major concerns but great quantities of cheaper grades of iron were still needed for other foundry operations and for rolling mill work. In the uncertain days immediately after the bombardment of Fort Sumter, Anderson and Company had turned away offers of pig and scrap iron.[64] Lincoln's proclamations forbidding Northern trade with seceded states and announcing a blockade of Southern ports quickly changed the minds of the Tredegar management. In late April and early May, the owners began buying up every ton of pig and scrap they could lay their hands on in Virginia and signed numerous contracts for future delivery.[65]

62. Anderson & Co. to Thomas & Isaac Steers, April 26, May 23, June 21, 1861, and to John T. Anderson, May 27, Oct. 28, 1861, ibid. Francis T. Anderson had tried to sell Glenwood furnace to Isaac Steers in December 1860 and had enlisted Joseph's aid in attempting to close the deal. The Tredegar senior partner had known Steers for some years and at that time had "a high opinion of him as a business [and] iron man." See John T. Anderson to William A. Glasgow, Dec. 29, 1860, Glasgow Family Papers, WLU.

63. *O.R.N.*, Ser. II, *2*, 74.

64. Anderson & Co. to Fowle & Co., April 15, 1861, Tredegar Letterbooks.

65. Contracts with Crenshaw & Co., April 24, 1861, Wissler & Co., May 1, 1861, F. T. Anderson, May 3, 1861, Graham & Son, June 17, 1861, and D. & H. Forrer, n.d.,

The Richmond manufacturers hoped to supplement Virginia's pig iron production with large tonnages from Tennessee and Georgia. The Tredegar works alone could consume the entire output of every furnace in blast in Virginia in 1860. Tennessee's pig iron production of 22,302 tons in 1860 was twice that of the Old Dominion. (See Table 4, p. 89.) In the summer, Anderson and Company purchased substantial lots of pig from founders in northern Georgia and middle Tennessee and after ascertaining that there was a supply of Scotch pig in New Orleans, ordered their agent to ship 200 tons to Richmond.[66]

In every case, shipment of this metal by rail took a seemingly interminable length of time and transportation costs were much higher than the value of the metal warranted. Scotch pig, desperately needed for rifled artillery projectiles, was shipped from New Orleans in mid-September. After a near incredible series of misdirections and delays, this metal began arriving in Richmond on November 4; the last lot did not reach the works until January 20, 1862. Freight on the bulk of this iron, purchased at $25 per ton, was $30 to $35 per ton. Of the 500 tons of metal contracted for in Tennessee in early September and shipped that month, the railroads lost almost 120 tons in transit. The final load of the 380 tons that eventually got through arrived at the Tredegar works on April 24, 1862, after Anderson and Company had shipped iron to repair burned bridges in East Tennessee. The Georgia pig was equally slow in arriving, although all but 20 of the 250 tons ordered was delivered.[67]

This experience convinced Anderson and Company that it could not rely on Georgia and Tennessee furnaces for large quantities of pig iron in 1862. They had made extensive inquiries about future blasts in both states in October 1861 and Robert S. Archer had left for Tennessee late that month to sign contracts for the coming year.[68] High freight charges, the complete uncertainty of regular railroad deliveries, and, most important, the increased prospect of a revival of the Virginia pig iron industry

---

Tredegar Contract Books; Anderson & Co. to E. F. Raworth, May 7, 1861, to S. C. Pritchard, May 20, 1861, to J. S. Davidson, June 1, 1861, to Watkins James, July 4, 1861, and to F. B. Deane, Jr., & Son, June 1, 1861, Tredegar Letterbooks.

66. Anderson & Co. to Mark A. Cooper, July 8, 1861, to Dr. John W. Lewis, Aug. 21, Sept. 9, 1861, to Hillman Bros., Aug. 3, 1861, and to Ivens, Sept. 11, 13, 25, 1861, ibid.; contract with Pointer Bros., Sept. 9, 1861, Tredegar Contract Books.

67. Anderson & Co. to Samuel Tate, Nov. 9, 1861, Tredegar Letterbooks; entry for Dec. 1861, Tredegar Journals; Tredegar Pig Iron Receipt Book.

68. Anderson & Co. to Pointer Bros., Oct. 14, 1861, to C. Powell, Oct. 22, 1861, and to J. W. Lewis, Oct. 26, 1861, Tredegar Letterbooks; entry for Nov. 1861, Tredegar Journals.

caused Anderson and Company to abandon these more distant sources of supply. In early November, the partners in Richmond telegraphed Archer not to sign any contracts in Tennessee and to return to Virginia.[69]

As the prospects of obtaining Georgia and Tennessee metal grew increasingly remote, Anderson and Company directed more of their attention to the blast furnaces of Virginia. The Tredegar management estimated in October 1861 that the works would need 12,500 to 15,000 tons of pig iron during the coming year.[70] They began soliciting contracts for complete blasts of Virginia furnaces in mid-October. John Tanner prodded founders throughout the Valley and southwest Virginia to resume operations.[71] Since common charcoal pig iron had risen on the Richmond market from a prewar April price of $28 to $34 per ton, depending on quality, to $40 to $45 per ton in September, the Tredegar superintendent could make a fairly convincing case.[72] "We think you will never have another such an opportunity to get your property in blast," he told a Shenandoah furnace owner.[73] "We are please[d] that our furnace men can at last get a full return for their labour and capital & hope the time may never return when the productions of the Northern States or Europe shall flow into our Country to the exclusion of our own," he wrote another ironmaster.[74]

The Richmond press echoed Tanner's optimistic forecast of the state's economic future. "Secession will at once make Virginia the leading manufacturing State in the Union," predicted the *Examiner*. Secession will "give to Richmond, especially, a leading character as a manufacturing city, at the same time that it will relieve it from the formidable commercial

69. Anderson & Co. to R. S. Archer, Nov. 1, 2, 1861, Tredegar Letterbooks.

70. Anderson & Co. to Mallory, Oct. 15, 1861, and to Thomas Steers, Oct. 15, 1861, ibid.

71. Anderson & Co. to David Anderson, Oct. 15, 1861, to D. & H. Forrer, Oct. 15, 26, Nov. 1, 1861, to J. S. Davidson, Oct. 15, 1861, to B. P. Newman, Oct. 15, 1861, to R. W. Sanders, Oct. 23, 1861, to Wissler & Co., Oct. 15, 1861, to Shaw & Co., Oct. 26, 1861, to Shaw & Kunkell, Oct. 28, Nov. 9, 16, 1861, to Crenshaw & Co., Nov. 2, 1861, to Thomas & Hurst, Nov. 14, 1861, and to T. Belew & J. J. Stoneburner, Nov. 18, 1861, ibid.

72. Quotations given in Richmond *Dispatch* and Richmond *Enquirer*, April–Dec. 1861.

73. Anderson & Co. to Forrer, Oct. 15, 1861, Tredegar Letterbooks.

74. Anderson & Co. to Wissler, Oct. 25, 1861, ibid. Federal blockaders, not the Confederate tariff, gave Southern industry this protected market. The permanent Constitution of the Confederate States specifically prohibited the erection of tariff barriers to foster domestic industries. Bills passed by Congress on March 15 and May 21, 1861, followed the hallowed Southern creed of a tariff for revenue only. These acts placed only a 15 per cent ad valorem duty on pig metal, iron products, and coal. See *O.R.*, Ser. IV, *1*, 139, and James M. Matthews, ed., *Statutes at Large of the Provisional Government of the Confederate States of America . . .* (Richmond, 1864), pp. 69, 130.

competition of Northern rivals." [75] The realization of this rosy prediction depended, however, on the ability of a woefully underdeveloped raw materials base to replace Northern sources of supply and furnish major manufacturing plants such as the Tredegar with the necessary iron and coal. John Tanner's calls to Virginia furnace men were intended to elicit just such a supply of iron to feed the ever-demanding furnaces of the Tredegar.

VIII

Before Anderson and Company committed themselves heavily for supplies of pig metal, they wanted assurances from the government that the War and Navy Departments would place large orders during the coming year at remunerative prices. On October 15, the Tredegar owners outlined to Secretary of the Navy Mallory their efforts to increase the supply of pig iron and the obstacles thus far encountered. They proposed to offer attractive contracts to Virginia founders to induce them to start furnaces forced out of blast during the previous decade by the flood of cheap Northern anthracite pig. But Anderson and Company were unwilling to guarantee high prices for future deliveries of metal "unless the Government would contract with us for the manufacture of articles equal to . . . these purchases at corresponding rates." Previous Tredegar contracts with the War and Navy Departments had followed the pattern set by the contract signed March 7, 1861, calling for delivery of a specified amount of cannon and munitions at a stated price within a set period of time. These contracts were no longer profitable, the partners claimed, because of advances in labor and raw materials costs. They therefore asked that their contracts be reviewed, that their prices be modified, and that the government agree to place sufficient orders at new, satisfactory prices to enable the company to enter into the necessary agreements with furnace men. "It is not our disposition in times like the present at least to come under obligations to conduct our operations on a more extended scale or come under unnecessary pecuniary engagements but we regard it as our imperative duty to place our works at the disposal of the country," they concluded. The partners appended a new set of tentative prices to the letter but two days later, they requested that prices be fixed at a future date and that the new contract, embracing their proposals, set the government's annual purchases at $2,000,000.[76]

75. Richmond *Examiner*, April 19, 1861.

76. Anderson & Co. to the Secretary of the Navy, Oct. 15, 17, 1861, Tredegar Letterbooks.

The Secretaries responded immediately to Anderson and Company's request for a new arrangement. On October 26, 1861, the War and Navy Departments signed a joint contract with the company for "cannon, shot, shells, bar, bolt and boiler iron, and iron plates for covering vessels," to run for two years from January 1, 1862. The terms of the agreement followed the company's requests almost to the letter. The government promised to buy annually $2,000,000 worth of Tredegar products for two years, purchases which would be more than adequate security for Anderson and Company's pig iron contracts. In addition, the Secretaries consented to turn over to the Tredegar as much of the pig iron contracted for by the government as the company might require to fill military orders. The War and Navy Departments also agreed to adjust future prices paid for Tredegar products on the basis of advances in labor and raw materials costs. This would give the company protection against inflation and compensation for the loss of profitable open market sales. The Tredegar management repeated an earlier pledge to build a new gun foundry and boring mill, which would double the ordnance capacity of their plant and give them facilities for casting the heaviest descriptions of cannon. They also promised to rebuild their rolling mills to permit the manufacture of larger and thicker armor and boiler plate.[77] This contract represented an important departure from the Anderson and Company's previous agreements with the government and opened the way for later contracts which would revolutionize Tredegar operations.

This agreement placed the Richmond industrialists in a position to contract with Virginia founders for large amounts of pig iron and they wasted no time. During the last week of October and the first week of November 1861, Anderson and Company signed contracts which promised the Tredegar works the complete 1862 blasts of six furnaces at prices averaging $45 per ton, the top price then paid on the Richmond market.[78] A final agreement, made in December, guaranteed the works a supply of charcoal

77. *O.R.N.*, Ser. II, 2, 73; list of contracts made by Secretaries of War, Dec. 13, 1862, and Anderson & Co. to Benjamin and Mallory, Dec. 21, 1861, Jan. 25, 1862, Letters Rec'd., Secretary of War, RG 109, NA; Anderson & Co. to Gorgas, March 16, 1863, and to Mallory, March 25, 1863, Tredegar Letterbooks.

78. Contracts signed Oct. 23, 26, 28, 30, Nov. 2, 18, 1861, Tredegar Contract Books. The six furnaces were the Beauregard, Columbia, Glenwood, Graham, Caroline, and Marion. The company loaned two furnace owners $2,000 each to assist them in getting their long-cold furnaces back into blast. The iron masters were to repay the loans by deducting a set amount from the price of the first deliveries of iron.

blooms for manufacturing boiler plate and bands for heavy cannon.[79]

The Tredegar owners estimated that these six furnaces would furnish in the neighborhood of 10,000 tons of metal during the coming year.[80] They were satisfied that this amount, coupled with supplies of Cloverdale, Graham, Columbia, and Fort gun metal contracted for earlier in 1861, would allow the Tredegar to operate at full capacity in 1862. Production at the Confederacy's largest iron works would depend in large measure on the degree to which the founders honored these contracts.

79. Contract with Wissler & Co., Dec. 18, 1861, ibid.

80. Anderson & Co. to Crawford, Nov. 4, 1861, Tredegar Letterbooks.

6

Production: A Year of Trial

I

After the war, Jefferson Davis wrote that "the first difficulty" confronting the Confederate government was "how to supply arms and munitions of war." [1] The procurement of war matériel was certainly among the most crucial problems facing the new nation. If Confederate troops were to be armed and the coastline defended, the War Department had to have great quantities of ordnance and ammunition and had to have them at once.

Although the Tredegar works offered the South unique facilities for large-scale production of cannon and munitions, the government's ordnance needs exceeded the company's capacity from the very outset of the war. In late April, when Major Josiah Gorgas gave Anderson the largest single order the Tredegar gun foundries had ever received—two hundred 8-inch, one hundred and fifty 10-inch, and twenty 15-inch columbiads—the owners had to undertake an immediate expansion of their ordnance establishment.[2] The facilities for casting, boring, and finishing heavy cannon could then turn out six to eight small cannon and about six heavy cannon per week. To give them increased manufacturing capacity, Anderson and his partners rented Bellona foundry, thirteen miles up the James River from Richmond, in April 1861, but soon abandoned Bellona in favor of expanding the Tredegar plant. In May, machine shop workers commenced constructing new boring and finishing lathes and rifling machinery, as well as machinery for fabricating wrought iron cannon carriages. Anderson also leased a small foundry and machine shop near the Tredegar for ordnance work and placed his nephew, Francis T. Glasgow, in charge.[3]

1. Jefferson Davis, *A Short History of the Confederate States of America* (New York, Belford Co., 1890), p. 76.

2. Anderson to Gorgas, April 26, May 1, 11, 1861, Tredegar Letterbooks.

3. Richmond *Enquirer*, Sept. 28, 1861; Anderson & Co. to J. L. Archer, April 26, 1861, to R. H. Staton, June 5, 1861, to R. E. Lewis, May 14, 1861, to Mallory, July 3, 1861, to

The Tredegar management was decidedly unenthusiastic about the Ordnance Bureau's request for 15-inch cannon. "The War Department is urging us to make immediate arrangements for fabricating some large Guns similar to those made for the United States and now in use against our batteries, at Old Point & other places," one of the partners wrote in October. "We are greatly indisposed to enter into such an engagement with the Government and would decline doing so if we felt at liberty, but we do not as the Guns cannot be obtained elsewhere." [4] The largest ordnance heretofore cast at the Tredegar were 10-inch columbiads, smoothbore coast defense cannon weighing when finished approximately 15,000 pounds. The 15-inch columbiad, developed by Charles Knap at the Fort Pitt foundry in Pittsburgh, was produced by the Rodman method of hollow casting that Anderson had refused to accept in 1859 and 1860. It weighed some 50,000 pounds and fired a 320-pound shell over three and one-half miles.[5]

Anderson's almost total ignorance of the Rodman method was the chief obstacle preventing production of the heaviest descriptions of ordnance. His founders were completely unequipped for, and unacquainted with, this technique. They now had to attempt to develop the necessary tools, facilities, and technology under the pressure of wartime demands for other cannon and shortages of skilled personnel and critical materials. Work on a new gun foundry and boring mill began in October after the War Department approved Anderson and Company's price of $10,000 for the first 15-inch columbiad and $5,000 for each one thereafter.[6] This price would help offset the cost of development and production. Manufacture of these powerful weapons would have to await the completion of these improvements. In the meantime, the Tredegar faced many more immediate tasks.

Overlapping state and Confederate orders confused Tredegar ordnance operations during the early months of the war. Large state orders given before the firing on Fort Sumter remained unfilled. Georgia and South Carolina turned over the cannon remaining from their previous contracts to the national government but North Carolina, Tennessee, Florida, Mississippi, Louisiana, and Virginia demanded delivery of their ordnance and

---

Gorgas, Aug. 14, 1861, and to C. B. Turner, Sept. 26, 1861, Tredegar Letterbooks; *O.R.N.*, Ser. II, *1*, 579; Archer Account Book, VHS.

4. Anderson & Co. to Lewis E. Harvie, Oct. 2, 1861, Tredegar Letterbooks.

5. Mark M. Boatner, III, *The Civil War Dictionary* (New York, 1959), p. 168; Harold C. Peterson, *Notes on the Ordnance of the American Civil War* (Washington, 1959).

6. Anderson & Co. to Gorgas, Sept. 5, 1861, Tredegar Letterbooks.

munitions, and North Carolina increased its order in May.[7] "Every State is clamoring for arms," one of the Tredegar partners wrote a Mississippi officer on April 17.[8] Virginia authorities placed an immediate embargo on all ordnance shipments out of the state when the convention adopted the ordinance of secession. Guns already on cars for Georgia and the Confederate government were detained and state officers seized gun carriages awaiting shipment to Mississippi and Louisiana. The Virginia Ordnance Department sent a rush order for brass field artillery to outfit the volunteer companies flooding into Richmond and had the Tredegar rebore and rifle a number of old iron and brass guns stored at the State Armory.[9] The War Department finally clamped down on these state orders in the late summer and early fall of 1861 and hereafter the Tredegar gun foundries cast solely for the Confederate government.[10]

During the opening months of the war, the Tredegar concentrated its production for the Confederate government on heavy coast defense artillery. (See Table 5.) Under peacetime conditions, the Tredegar took two months to cast and finish a 10-inch columbiad. The exacting process began by forming a mold of sand. A wooden pattern was imbedded in moistened sand and the entire mold was encased in a flask, composed of interlocking sheets of metal which could be removed one at a time to permit the withdrawal of various pieces of the wooden pattern. When the mold was completed, it was placed vertically in a pit with the breech at the bottom. On the day of casting the furnace was charged with gun iron and the iron melted. A 10-inch columbiad took a charge of some 19,000 pounds of metal which required approximately six hours to melt. The furnace was tapped and the iron run first into a reservoir and from there taken down by a trough to the mold, which was filled from the bottom. A workman agitated the iron with a long rod as it rose in the mold to bring impurities in the metal to the top. Filling the mold took only five or ten minutes. The entire flask was then surrounded by sand and charcoal to prevent too rapid cool-

7. Entries for April–Dec. 1861, Tredegar Foundry Sales Books; Anderson & Co. to Warren Winslow, May 20, 1861, and to Gorgas, June 27, 1861, Tredegar Letterbooks.

8. Anderson & Co. to Col. S. G. French, April 17, 1861, ibid.

9. Anderson & Co. to Charles G. Talcott, April 23, 1861, and to Col. Charles Dimmock, April 22, 30, 1861, ibid; entries for April–Nov. 1861, Tredegar Foundry Sales Books; Burton to Dimmock, April 22, 1861, Virginia Executive Papers, VSL.

10. Anderson & Co. to Capt. A. D. Moore, July 26, 1861, and to French, Aug. 17, Sept. 18, 1861, Tredegar Letterbooks.

ing and left in the pit for five or six days. When sufficiently cool, the flask was hoisted out of the pit and the cannon removed. After the head containing any impurities was cut off, workmen began the tedious work of boring the interior, turning the exterior, planing the trunnions, chipping the piece, and drilling the vent.[11]

TABLE 5. Ordnance Cast for the Confederate States at the Tredegar Iron Works, 1861–1865 *

	1861		*1862*		*1863*		*1864*		*1865*	
Month	*Field*	*Siege & Seacoast*	*Field*	*Siege & Seacoast*	*Field*	*Siege & Seacoast*	*Field*	*Siege & Seacoast*	*Field*	*Siege & Seacoast*
January	3	13	13	17	19	11	16	—	16	2
February	4	14	10	11	10	10	20	12	10	3
March	7	15	31	7	33	7	—	6	4	—
April	{5 **	39 **	70	2	6	4	24	13	—	—
May			40	2	8	2	—	4	—	—
June	—	13	35	7	18	6	21	12	—	—
July	—	13	9	10	6	9	3	10	—	—
August	—	10	7	15	3	5	8	—	—	—
September	—	9	1	5	16	16	16	2	—	—
October	—	12	2	8	19	18	6	3	—	—
November	10	18	14	10	28	18	15	6	—	—
December	16	13	11	14	4	10	9	7	—	—
	45	169	243	108	170	116	138	75	30	5
Total	214		351		286		213		35	

* The various types of artillery produced by Anderson and Company are given in the Appendix, pp. 323–24.

** Foundry records for April–May 1861 are incomplete and these figures are approximations based on existing fragmentary sources.

Sources: Archer Account Book, VHS; Tredegar Gun Foundry Book. See Bruce, *Virginia Iron Manufacture*, p. 461, for a somewhat different set of figures.

For a 10-inch columbiad these various steps required four hundred to five hundred hours of difficult and often delicate labor. The absolute minimum amount of time required to produce a cannon of this size by Anderson's methods was one month of continuous labor. By the fall of 1861, the Tredegar foundry force, working day and night, was turning out 10-inch columbiads in the shortest possible time. Cannon number 1306, a 10-inch columbiad, was cast on November 16, 1861; on December 16, this same gun, complete with iron carriage, chassis, and implements, was

11. Benton, *Ordnance and Gunnery*, pp. 195–200; "Gun Tests for the United States, 1857–58," manuscript Tredegar volume.

loaded onto a flatcar at the Richmond and Petersburg Railroad station, destined for General Albert Sydney Johnston at Nashville.[12]

Confederate authorities placed sufficient orders with Anderson and Company in 1861 to keep the gun foundries more than occupied. By early May, the company had accepted Ordnance Bureau requisitions for four hundred columbiads and Major Gorgas supplemented these orders in the summer and fall with requests for field and siege artillery. In August, the Tredegar books contained orders for ninety-two pieces of field artillery, including 3-inch iron rifled guns and 12-pounder iron and brass howitzers, fifty 8-inch siege howitzers, twenty 8-inch rifled columbiads, and twenty 10-inch rifled columbiads. The Navy Department ordered fifty 9-inch Dahlgren shell guns and fifty 32-pounder cannon in December 1861.[13]

The rifled columbiad was the outgrowth of an attempt by Anderson and Company to produce heavy guns of long range and great accuracy prior to the development of the new facilities for Rodman casting. In July 1861, Anderson informed Gorgas that the Tredegar had developed machinery capable of rifling 8- and 10-inch pattern columbiads and he suggested that the Ordnance Bureau order a number of these weapons. The 8-inch pattern columbiad was to be bored to 5.82 inches, the caliber of a 32-pounder gun, and the 10-inch to 6.40 inches, or 42-pounder caliber. (See Appendix.) Anderson did not believe full bore 8- and 10-inch columbiads would stand the added strain of firing rifled projectiles. He predicted that a battery of rifled columbiads placed on Willoughby Point, a narrow spit of land opposite Old Point Comfort and Fort Monroe, could drive Yankee shipping from Hampton Roads and open Norfolk harbor for unrestricted Confederate use.

President Davis, Secretary of War Walker, Lee, and Gorgas all expressed interest in the project and Anderson proceeded to manufacture the guns. Lee ordered General Benjamin Huger at Norfolk to prepare concealed emplacements across from Fort Monroe and promised that the cannon would be sent down as quickly as possible. By the second week in August, the Tredegar had finished three rifled columbiads. But Huger evidently believed a battery on Willoughby Point would be too exposed to

12. Tredegar Gun Foundry Book; Tredegar Order Book; shipping bill in "J. R. Anderson & Co.," Confederate Citizens File, RG 109, NA.

13. Gorgas to Anderson & Co., Aug. 3, 15, 1861, Tredegar Contract Books; Anderson & Co. to Gorgas, June 27, 1861, Tredegar Letterbooks; Tredegar Order Book; Archer Account Book, VHS.

naval and infantry attack and the Tredegar cannon never got into range of the fort.[14]

Confederate commanders along both the Atlantic and Gulf coasts pressed for Tredegar cannon. "The winter of 1861–2 was the darkest period of my department," wrote Gorgas of the Ordnance Bureau. "Heavy guns . . . were called for in all directions—the largest guns for the smallest places." [15] Colonel A. J. Gonzales spent two months at Anderson's works in the summer of 1861, securing ordnance for the defense of Charleston harbor and the South Carolina coast. Heavy Tredegar cannon, mounted on special carriages and moved by hordes of men and horses, protected the vital Charleston and Savannah Railroad throughout the war.[16] Secretary of War Walker, an Alabamian, was particularly concerned about the defenses of Mobile and in August he ordered sixteen Tredegar columbiads to Fort Morgan and Fort Gaines.[17] In addition to the shipments to Charleston and Mobile, the Tredegar dispatched heavy cannon to Norfolk, Savannah, Galveston, and Pensacola, St. Augustine, Fernandina, and St. Marks, Florida. General Joseph R. Anderson drew on his works for 8- and 10-inch cannon for various defensive positions along the North Carolina coast. Lee, sent to take command of the South Atlantic coast late in 1861, asked for and received a number of Tredegar guns.[18]

Anderson and Company also dispatched heavy ordnance to the western theater of operations. The Tredegar made frantic efforts to supply gaps in the defenses of Forts Henry and Donelson, guarding the Tennessee and Cumberland Rivers. "We still want 12, 18, and 24 pounders as siege pieces and for the arming and flanking our forts. Where shall we get them?" Major General Leonidas Polk asked Gorgas in October.[19] The only reply the Ordnance Bureau chief could make was the Tredegar works. The Richmond firm forwarded several columbiads and siege howitzers to the Tennessee forts but not nearly enough to satisfy the field com-

14. Anderson & Co. to Gorgas, July 5, 1861, and to Lee, July 26, 1861, Tredegar Letterbooks; Tredegar Foundry Sales Books; *O.R.*, Ser. I, *2*, 997, 1001; Lee to Anderson & Co., July 26, 1861, Misc. Letters Sent, Headquarters, Virginia Forces, April–Nov. 1861, RG 109, NA.

15. Gorgas, "Notes on the Ordnance Department," *Southern Hist. Soc. Papers, 12*, 75.

16. Ella Lonn, *Foreigners in the Confederacy* (Chapel Hill, 1940), p. 241; Tredegar Foundry Sales Books; Archer Account Book, VHS.

17. Walker to Gorgas, Aug. 15, 1861, Letters Sent, Secretary of War, RG 109, NA; Leadbetter to Gorgas, Sept. 14, 1861, Letters Sent, Engineer Department, ibid.

18. Tredegar Foundry Sales Books; Benjamin to Gorgas, Sept. 30, 1861, Letters Sent, Secretary of War, RG 109, NA; *O.R.*, Ser. I, *6*, 367–68, 375–76.

19. Ibid., *4*, 446.

manders. When the combined land and naval forces of General Ulysses S. Grant and Flag Officer Andrew H. Foote attacked the two forts in February 1862, the defenders had only a handful of effective artillery pieces.[20] The War Department, responding to pressures from all over the South, had spread the Tredegar's ordnance thinly over the entire Confederate border.

Gorgas also sought large numbers of field artillery from Anderson and Company. The old cannon from the Virginia State Armory, rebored and rifled by the Tredegar, formed the artillery backbone of the Confederate Army of the Potomac until the Richmond founders could supply new ordnance. The Tredegar foundries outfitted the Washington Artillery of New Orleans and the battery of Wade Hampton's Legion with new field pieces just prior to the Manassas engagement. In August, several more artillery companies came to the works seeking cannon.[21]

A substantial number of the Tredegar field pieces were intended for General Joseph E. Johnston's forces in Northern Virginia. Shortly after the opening battle near Manassas, Johnston had urged that the artillery of his Army of the Potomac be doubled. The Ordnance Bureau concurred and looked to Anderson's works for most of these weapons.[22] Brigadier General William N. Pendleton, Johnston's artillery chief, arrived in Richmond in late August to hasten the outfitting of the new batteries. "Have had a great deal to do here in pushing up artillery preparation," he reported. "Will have several batteries at Manassas next week, & several others the week after &c. Several difficulties obstruct the way," he continued. "Want of tin to make brass. Only one good foundry here, deficiency of hands &c &c . . . Still by hook or by crook we get along." [23] By September, Anderson and Company had begun monthly deliveries of ten to fifteen pieces of field artillery to the ordnance depot in Richmond for reassignment.[24]

20. Tredegar Order Book; Tredegar Foundry Sales Books; *O.R.*, Ser. I, 7, 849; Shelby Foote, *The Civil War, A Narrative: Fort Sumter to Perryville* (New York, 1958), pp. 189–90, 194, 203–04; *Battles and Leaders, 1*, 370–71.

21. Tredegar Foundry Sales Books.

22. Gen. J. E. Johnston to Col. W. N. Pendleton, July 31, 1861, and Pendleton to Albert T. Bledsoe, Aug. 11, 1861, William N. Pendleton Papers, DUL; Pendleton to Mrs. W. N. Pendleton, Aug. 12, 1861, William N. Pendleton Papers, UNC.

23. Pendleton to Sandie Pendleton, Aug. 22, 1861, ibid.

24. Tredegar Foundry Sales Books.

II

Secretary of the Navy Mallory's determination to build an ironclad fleet brought the Tredegar's capabilities for producing armor plate and marine engines into prominence in 1861. In May of that year, the Secretary asked Congress to authorize the construction of an "iron-armored ship." [25] The energetic Mallory was not about to wait for Congress to act, however. On June 10, 1861, he instructed Lieutenant John Mercer Brooke, an able and inventive naval officer, to aid the Navy Department in designing an ironclad vessel. John L. Porter, superintendent of naval construction, and William P. Williamson, chief engineer, were ordered from Norfolk to Richmond for consultation in late June. Porter, it turned out, had come up independently with a model for an armor-plated ship. When he, Brooke, and Williamson met in the Confederate capital on June 23, Brooke and Porter found their ideas in harmony. Both proposed a steam ram with sloping iron-plated sides, mounting powerful cannon.

Discussion then proceeded to the practical question of building such a vessel. Williamson suggested that the machinery of the U.S.S. *Merrimack*, raised on May 30 from the shallows of Norfolk harbor, be repaired and utilized to save time. Porter asked why the entire vessel could not be used, and the three officers agreed on the idea. On June 25, they submitted this proposal to Mallory and the Secretary gave his immediate approval. He ordered Brooke to superintend the manufacture of the armor plate and the preparation of ordnance, Porter to supervise the actual construction of the vessel at Norfolk, and Williamson to direct the repair of the *Merrimack's* engines.[26]

The Tredegar works quickly became a key element in the *Merrimack* operation. On July 23, 1861, shortly after work began at the Gosport Navy Yard on the ship, Anderson and Company contracted with Mallory to supply the iron necessary for sheathing the vessel. The navy agreed to pay 6½ cents per pound for the armor plate and to cover the expenses of a superintendent to oversee the fitting up of the iron at the Tredegar.[27]

The company immediately began searching for the large quantity of iron needed to manufacture the plate and found the railroads of northern

25. *Battles and Leaders, 1,* 631.

26. Virgil Carrington Jones, *The Civil War at Sea* (3 vols. New York, 1960–62), *1,* 155–58; Porter, *Norfolk County,* pp. 329–32; *O.R.N.,* Ser. II, *2,* 174–75.

27. Anderson & Co. to Mallory, July 24, 1861, Tredegar Letterbooks.

Virginia a ready-made, if sometimes involuntary, source. General Thomas J. Jackson provided a good portion of the metal with the spirited stripping of the Baltimore and Ohio Railroad which his troops accomplished in the summer and fall. The War Department ordered the quartermaster in charge of the B. and O. pillage to turn all refuse rails over to Anderson and Company.[28] Robert S. Archer went to Winchester in October and purchased all the iron the owners of the threatened Winchester and Potomac Railroad might tear up. The company also acquired the old rails of the Virginia Central and some three hundred tons of scrap iron from burned portions of the Gosport Navy Yard.[29]

To enable the rolling of plates of the desired sizes, eight inches wide, and varying lengths, the doors of the Tredegar heating furnaces had to be rebuilt to permit the entry of the large pile of iron. The pile for the plates was formed by surrounding rails, cut to the desired length, with pig and scrap iron already puddled and rolled into bars. The entire pile was heated once, passed through roughing rolls, reheated, and then worked into finished plate.[30]

Lieutenant Brooke's original plan called for covering the vessel with three inches of iron, formed by three one-inch plates. These plates could be rolled rapidly and the spike holes punched with a machine used previously for punching railroad chairs. He had second thoughts, however, about the ability of three inches of iron to withstand heavy punishment and in September he ordered a large quantity of two-inch plates, to build four inches of armor. Brooke conducted a series of experiments at Jamestown Island in early October which confirmed his suspicions. Solid shot fired from an 8-inch columbiad in one of the batteries on the island penetrated three inches of iron but failed to pierce four inches.[31]

The shift to two-inch plates necessitated an added delay and expense, however. These pieces could not be punched and required drilling. The

28. Anderson & Co. to Maj. Thomas R. Sharp, Sept. 17, 1861, and to the Secretary of War, Sept. 19, 1861, ibid.; contract with A. C. Myers, Sept. 21, 1861, Tredegar Contract Books; Johnston, *Virginia Railroads*, pp. 23–24.

29. Anderson & Co. to Capt. S. S. Lee, Oct. 21, 1861, Tredegar Letterbooks; contract with W. L. Clarke, Sept. 28, 1861, Tredegar Contract Books; entry for Oct. 1861, Tredegar Journals.

30. Statement of James H. Wade, Oct. 27, 1925, in "Letters, Clippings, etc. Involving the Tredegar Company."

31. *O.R.N.*, Ser. I, *1*, 785–86; T. Catesby Jones, "The Iron-Clad Virginia," *Virginia Magazine of History and Biography*, *49* (1941), 298–301; Brooke to Mrs. J. M. Brooke, Oct. 1, 1861, John M. Brooke Papers, UNC.

shipbuilders were constantly reworking and perfecting their design and every change called for a shift in the position of the spike holes. In September, Anderson and Company reported that they had had to change the position of the holes in some plates three or four times and were awaiting a decision on further modifications. The change to thicker armor, the constant shifting of holes, and a rise of some 20 per cent in the cost of materials since the July estimate was given, prompted the company to advance their price to 7½ cents per pound in September.[32]

Manufacture of the armor proceeded rapidly in the fall of 1861. The first plates were rolled in September and production occupied the Tredegar rolling mills to the exclusion of practically all other work until February 1862.[33] "We are now pressed almost beyond endurance for the heavy iron work to complete one of the war vessels *now ready for operations*. When that is completed we expect to commence on another vessel which will keep us till the end of the year," wrote one of the partners to a disappointed railroad customer in October. "It is a most fortunate thing that we could render this assistance to our little Navy—It could not have been done elsewhere in the Confederacy." [34] This assertion was not completely true. The newly built Gate City rolling mill at Atlanta was turning out armor for two powerful ironclads under construction at New Orleans and a Tennessee mill on the Cumberland River was rolling plates for gunboats being built at Memphis.

The Tredegar partner would have been more accurate if he had qualified his statement by explaining that Southern railroads could not have delivered the iron to Norfolk from any point much farther away than Richmond. Getting the armor from the Tredegar works to the Gosport Yard was difficult enough. Transportation problems arose with the very first shipment. The most direct route from Richmond to Norfolk was over the Richmond and Petersburg and the Norfolk and Petersburg roads. Anderson and Company applied to the superintendent of the R. and P. for transportation early in October. "The Navy Department is pressing us to send forward the heavy iron for the steamer Merrimac. We have some 70 to 100 tons of the iron now ready to ship. We will have it all ready in the next 5 or 6 weeks," wrote a member of the firm. "You will please state if you

32. Anderson & Co. to D. N. Ingraham, Sept. 11, 13, 1861, Tredegar Letterbooks.

33. Anderson & Co. to J. P. King, Nov. 7, 1861, ibid.; Tredegar Rolling Mill Sales Books; Richmond *Enquirer*, Sept. 28, 1861.

34. Anderson & Co. to Col. M. B. Pritchard, Oct. 11, 1861, Tredegar Letterbooks.

have a sufficient No. of flats to forward the iron promptly." [35] Superintendent Thomas H. Wynne replied that his road did not have enough flatcars and this initial shipment and subsequent cargoes were much delayed.[36]

Naval authorities became worried over the delays and pressed the Tredegar for faster delivery.[37] The company in return asked for government transportation orders, got them, and then began routing some of the plates over the Richmond and Danville to Burkeville and from there via the Southside Railroad to Petersburg.[38] This helped but did not solve the problem. "We have iron for the Navy Yard that has been lying on the bank for 4 weeks—several sizes are ready to go down," wrote one of the exasperated partners in mid-November; "the Rail Road has been unable to transport it." [39]

A shortage of flatcars caused these extended delays. Southern railroads were short of rolling stock before the war and military shipments from Richmond often deprived the roads of cars for long periods of time. Flatcars used to transport heavy Tredegar cannon to many distant points in the lower and western sections of the Confederacy were slow returning. Finally the Navy Department arranged for the Petersburg Railroad to carry iron to Weldon, North Carolina, where the Seaboard and Roanoke could pick it up and take it on to Norfolk. This added the flatcars of two new roads to the project and the iron now moved more rapidly to Norfolk.[40]

The bulk of the *Merrimack's* armor was rolled in the last two months of 1861 and the first month of 1862. Anderson and Company delivered the final lot of plates on February 12, 1862. In all, the Tredegar mills rolled 723 tons of iron for the vessel and received $123,015 for the job, paid for primarily in Confederate bonds.[41]

Lieutenant Brooke, who attended the rolling of the plates for the *Merrimack,* also developed the powerful rifled guns for the ship at the Tredegar works in the fall of 1861. Brooke planned to employ the standard naval

35. Anderson & Co. to T. H. Wynne, Oct. 12, 1861, ibid.

36. Anderson & Co. to Comdr. F. Forrest, Nov. 5, 7, 9, 19, 22, 23, 1861, ibid.

37. Anderson & Co. to John L. Porter, Nov. 5, 21, 1861, ibid.

38. Anderson & Co. to Capt. George Minor, Oct. 28, 1861, ibid.

39. Anderson & Co. to S. March, Nov. 16, 1861, ibid.

40. Anderson & Co. to Minor, Nov. 30, 1861, ibid.

41. Anderson & Co. to Mallory, Oct. 28, 1861, ibid.; Tredegar Rolling Mill Sales Books; entries for Nov.–Dec. 1861, and Feb. 1862, Tredegar Journals.

weapon, the 9-inch Dahlgren gun, for most of the *Merrimack's* armament. This smoothbore cannon fired shell and heated shot, the standard ammunition used against wooden ships. He also envisaged a battery of rifled guns, possessing greater accuracy and longer range than smoothbores, which could fire both shells and solid projectiles or "bolts." Brooke designed a heavy rifled cannon for the *Merrimack* with a wrought iron ring shrunk onto the piece at the breech, in the manner perfected by the Northern founder R. P. Parrott for his rifled field artillery. These rings increased the safety of the cannon by strengthening the area of the power chamber for the heavier charge and greater stress involved in firing rifled projectiles. Secretary Mallory ordered the first two "Brooke guns," as they were soon called, on September 21, 1861, and increased the order in October and November.[42]

Anderson and Company proceeded at once to build the patterns and alter the flasks and boring lathes needed to cast and finish these cannon. Between September 1861 and March 1862, the Tredegar gun foundry cast fourteen Brooke guns. These pieces were of 6.40-inch and 7-inch caliber and were delivered to Gosport, along with the necessary bars for banding the breeches. The 6.40-inch Brooke was the standard 32-pounder naval cannon, rifled and banded; the first 7-inch Brookes were of the 9-inch Dahlgren pattern, bored to only 7 inches, rifled, and strengthened with a wrought iron jacket. Four of these Tredegar cannon, two 7-inch and two 6.40-inch Brookes, went aboard the *Merrimack,* in addition to six 9-inch Dahlgren smoothbores.[43] The Tredegar also cast a number of shells for the *Merrimack's* rifled cannon but no solid shot was produced prior to the ironclad's first engagement with the enemy. Officers of the Confederate Bureau of Ordnance and Hydrography did not anticipate the sudden appearance of the *Monitor* and therefore called on the works only for shells, the type of projectile which would be most effective against the wooden fleet assembled at Hampton Roads.[44]

When the *Merrimack* met the Federal ironclad on March 9, after inflicting great damage on the wooden *Cumberland, Congress,* and *Minnesota* the previous day, the Confederate gun crews had no wrought iron bolts

42. Benton, *Ordnance and Gunnery,* p. 550; *O.R.N.,* Ser. II, *2,* 175; Anderson & Co. to Mallory, Sept. 22, Oct. 29, Nov. 9, 1861, and to Minor, Oct. 11, 1861, Tredegar Letterbooks.

43. Tredegar Gun Foundry Book; Tredegar Foundry Sales Books; Tredegar Rolling Mill Sales Books; Archer Account Book, VHS; Catesby ap R. Jones, "Services of the 'Virginia' (Merrimac)," *Southern Historical Society Papers, 11,* (1883), 66.

44. *O.R.N.,* Ser. II, *1,* 786.

with which to load their rifled guns. These projectiles could have penetrated the turret of the enemy's ship. Their only available ammunition, shells, bounced off the *Monitor's* armor plate, just as the shells fired from the 11-inch Dahlgren smoothbores of Ericsson's craft failed to pierce the sloping sides of the Confederate vessel.[45]

After the battle ended in a draw, the navy sent a rush order to Richmond for solid shot. The Tredegar quickly fabricated a number of bolts and furnished another Richmond machine shop with bars for manufacturing the same article. These projectiles along with fifty-three tons of new plates to repair cracked armor and wrought iron shutters for the *Merrimack's* gun ports were quickly dispatched to Norfolk.[46] Lieutenant Brooke sought some slim consolation for the oversight of not supplying the bolts earlier. "It is perhaps better that the 'Monitor' was not captured, by the guns at least of the Merrimac-'Virginia.' Now they believe the Monitor to be strong enough and will probably regard her as a standard. She is not strong enough and they have yet to learn that the Virginia employed only shell," he wrote a friend who served aboard the *Merrimack*.[47]

When the Confederate ironclad steamed out to challenge the *Monitor* in April and early May, her guns were equipped to deal with the Federal craft. The *Monitor* failed to answer the challenge, however. Lincoln had ordered the ship to be extremely cautious about renewing the duel with the *Merrimack* and the Union vessel remained in shallow water. The *Monitor* alone stood between the rebel monster and General George B. McClellan's wooden transports and the President refused to jeopardize the entire Peninsular campaign by risking a rash renewal of the action. Nor, indeed, were Confederate military authorities willing to commit their only ironclad to a life or death struggle against the *Monitor*. As a result, the two vessels never renewed their duel. When McClellan's movements finally forced the evacuation of Norfolk, the cumbersome *Merrimack*, drawing twenty-three feet of water, lost her base and could not retreat up the James. On May 11, 1862, her crew blew up the vessel to prevent her from falling into Federal hands.[48]

45. Jones, *Civil War at Sea, 1*, 419–28, 431–36; William C. White and Ruth White, *Tin Can on a Shingle* (New York, 1957), pp. 66–76, 90–101.

46. Entries for March–April 1862, Tredegar Foundry Sales Books, and for March 1862, Tredegar Rolling Mill Sales Books.

47. Brooke to Lt. R. D. Minor, March 17, 1862, Minor Family Papers, VHS.

48. Jones, "Services of the 'Virginia,'" pp. 73–74; Allan Nevins, *The War for the Union: War Becomes Revolution, 1862–1863* (New York, 1960), p. 56; Roy P. Basler, ed., *The*

III

Secretary Mallory considered one Tredegar job of equal importance to the production of the *Merrimack's* armor. The powerful ironclad C.S.S. *Mississippi,* on the ways near New Orleans, was easily the most ambitious marine project under construction in the new nation. The *Mississippi* and a sister ship, the *Louisiana,* were rams designed to carry batteries of twenty guns each. Mallory believed, with some justification, that these two vessels could prevent the capture of New Orleans by sea and disperse the Union blockading fleet. Flag Officer David Farragut reported after taking New Orleans that "the Mississippi . . . was to be the terror of the Seas, and no doubt would have been to a great extent."[49] In October 1861, work began on the mighty vessel at Jefferson City, just above the New Orleans city limits. The designers contracted for the engines and small side shafts in New Orleans, but Richmond's Tredegar works was the only establishment in the Confederacy capable of manufacturing the *Mississippi's* great fifty-foot center shaft.[50]

To save time, Mallory allocated to the project the shafts of the steamer *Glen Cove,* which had burned in the James River in 1861, but it still took two to three months just to prepare the Tredegar to execute the job. After work finally began in January 1862, Mallory pressed the firm to keep men employed on the shaft night and day, sparing no expense. The job was a difficult one. The twelve-inch shafts of the *Glen Cove* had to be laboriously turned down by hand to nine inches and then spliced and welded into the dimensions required for the *Mississippi.* Fifty men labored on the shaft for two months, receiving time-and-a-half for night work and double time for Sunday labor. Mallory visited the works practically every morning to check on its progress and he grew increasingly anxious as the difficult work dragged on.[51] "The Tredegar Works have disappointed us terribly," he informed the builders on March 15. "The shaft is not ready, and, although promised from day to day, may not be ready for a week."[52] A week later it was finished. "The shaft leaves on Monday morning, the 24th, complete;

Complete Works of Abraham Lincoln (9 vols. New Brunswick, N.J., 1953–55), *5,* 154; Jones, *Civil War at Sea, 2,* 3–8, 11–12, 16–20; White, pp. 117–20.

49. Charles L. Dufour, *The Night the War Was Lost* (Garden City, N.Y., 1960), p. 336; *O.R.N.,* Ser. I, *18,* 158, Ser. II, *2,* 150.

50. Dufour, pp. 99–103; *O.R.N.,* Ser. II, *1,* 534–35.

51. Ibid., pp. 637–39, 763, 773–75.

52. Ibid., p. 605.

a beautiful piece of work. Strain every nerve to finish the ship," Mallory wired New Orleans on March 22.[53]

The shaft went through on its special railroad car with little delay, but to no avail. Farragut's fleet passed Forts Jackson and St. Philip on April 24, and the way to New Orleans was open. Naval officials ordered the unfinished *Mississippi* burned to prevent capture by the enemy. The powerful vessel never fired a shot.[54]

The *Merrimack* and the *Mississippi* were not the only vessels which the Tredegar outfitted during the first year of the war. Tredegar workers rolled some of the armor plate for the C.S.S. *Arkansas*, under construction at Memphis, sheathed the sides of the steamer *Patrick Henry* with iron, and performed boiler and machinery repairs on four other naval vessels in the summer of 1861.[55] Production of armor for the C.S.S. *Richmond*, being built at Norfolk, began when the work for the *Merrimack* was completed. On November 21, 1861, Anderson and Company agreed to build the machinery for the *Richmond* and added engines and boilers for three more gunboats to their order books on January 27, 1862.[56]

IV

The rifled and banded Brooke guns were by far Anderson and Company's most successful ordnance innovation during the early part of the war but several other projects were undertaken at the request of the government and private individuals. The navy, with responsibility for defending over 3,500 miles of coastline, led the way with numerous inventions. Commander Matthew Fontaine Maury had the Tredegar build the first tanks for his torpedo experiments in the summer of 1861, and when he organized the navy's Torpedo Bureau in 1862, the Richmond works built submarine mechanisms that mined many Southern rivers and harbors. The torpedo proved to be one of the Confederacy's most effective coastal defense weapons, sinking or damaging a total of thirty-four Union vessels.[57]

53. Ibid., p. 606.

54. Dufour, pp. 296–97.

55. Anderson & Co. to Capt. John T. Shirley, Oct. 31, 1861, Tredegar Letterbooks; Tredegar Rolling Mill Sales Books; Tredegar Foundry Sales Books. The four steamers, all employed as part of the James River fleet, were the *Logan*, *Teaser*, *David Currie*, and the *Jamestown* (rechristened the *Thomas Jefferson*).

56. Anderson & Co. to William P. Williamson, Nov. 20, 1861, and to Mallory, Nov. 21, 1861, June 8, 1863, Tredegar Letterbooks; contract with C.S. Navy, Jan. 27, 1862, Tredegar Contract Books.

57. Frances Leigh Williams, *Matthew Fontaine Maury, Scientist of the Sea* (New Brunswick, N.J., 1963), p. 377; Eugene B. Canfield, *Notes on Naval Ordnance of the*

In the fall of 1861, work began on a submarine at the Tredegar. W. G. Cheeney, a master in the navy, designed the ship and supervised its construction. Cheeney's submarine was to be used in conjunction with Maury's torpedoes to destroy enemy ships in Virginia waters. Although the vessel evidently was launched, there is no record that it ever saw active service. The designer, Cheeney, was in charge of torpedoes strung in the James River below Richmond in June 1862.[58]

The army also drew on the Tredegar works for some novel military hardware. The gun foundries produced light brass mountain howitzers and brass mountain rifles for use in rugged western Virginia and East Tennessee in the fall of 1861, and an experimental wrought iron mountain howitzer, strengthened with a wire binding at the breech. These cannon were light weapons designed to be carried by pack animals over terrain inaccessible to regular mounted field artillery.[59] D. R. Williams supervised the construction of the first of his light, rapid fire, breechloading guns at the works in September 1861. Anderson and Company built a total of twenty Williams guns in 1862 and 1863. Four of these were sent to General Sterling Price's army in the Trans-Mississippi Department and the remainder were turned over to the inventor. This remarkable weapon, firing eighteen to twenty shots per minute, was the first machine gun ever successfully employed in battle. The rapid rate of fire tended to expand the breech, however, and prevented the mechanism from relocking. As a result, the guns saw only limited service.[60]

American Civil War (Washington, 1960), pp. 12–15; Richard L. Maury, *A Brief Sketch of the Work of Matthew Fontaine Maury During the War* (Richmond, 1915), pp. 6–7; Anderson & Co. to Col. Thomas S. Rhett, Dec. 29, 1862, and to Beauregard, Jan. 12, 1863, Tredegar Letterbooks. During the Civil War, "torpedo" referred to what is now called a mine. For a full discussion of the Confederate use of torpedoes, see Milton F. Perry, *Infernal Machines: The Story of Confederate Submarine and Mine Warfare* (Baton Rouge, 1965).

58. Ibid., pp. 92–93; Ernest T. Walthall, *Hidden Things Brought to Light* (Richmond, 1933); *O.R.N.*, Ser. I, 7, 546; entries for Oct. 1861, Tredegar Journals, and for Nov. 1861, June 1862, Tredegar Foundry Sales Books; bills of Anderson & Co., Feb. 27, May 13, 1862, Subject File, Box 128, Naval Records Collection, RG 45, NA. The Archer Account Book, VHS, contains a drawing of the submarine's propeller.

59. Tredegar Gun Foundry Book; bill of Anderson & Co., April 1862, in "J. R. Anderson & Co.," Confederate Citizens File, RG 109, NA; Jac Weller, "The Field Artillery of the Civil War," *Military Collector and Historian, 5* (1953), 66; Archer Account Book, VHS.

60. Agreement with D. R. Williams, Aug. 21, 1862, Tredegar Contract Books; entries for Dec. 1862, Jan.–March 1863, Tredegar Foundry Sales Books; Anderson & Co. to Capt. James Ker, Dec. 26, 1862, Tredegar Letterbooks; Col. S. Shriver to Gov. William Smith, Virginia Executive Papers, VSL; Wise, *Long Arm of Lee*, pp. 32–33; Boatner, *Civil War Dictionary*, p. 928.

The vital work done at the Tredegar to outfit other war industries in the Confederacy was of far greater importance to the Southern military effort than these ordnance innovations. Federal evacuation of Harpers Ferry on April 18, 1861, placed the musket and rifle machinery of the arsenal and armory in the possession of Virginia. The musket machinery, capable of producing 15,000 weapons per year, was transferred to the Virginia State Armory at Richmond and the rifle machinery was sent on to Fayetteville, North Carolina. Anderson and Company's lucrative contract to outfit the State Armory immediately became a dead letter. James H. Burton, now in charge of the armory, recommended that the state abrogate its contract with the Tredegar owners. But the Federals had damaged much of the machinery, some tools were injured in transit, and several vital parts of the complete machinery, primarily tilt and drop hammers and shafting, were left at Harpers Ferry when Confederate troops evacuated. Fortunately some of the machines under way at the Tredegar works were of the class needed and two drop hammers had arrived from Ames and Company of Massachusetts a week before the firing on Fort Sumter. Anderson and Company could build and install the necessary shafting. Burton therefore recommended that certain tools and additional fixtures be accepted or ordered from the Tredegar.[61]

The governor and his military advisory council followed Burton's advice and requested Anderson and Company to surrender their contract but to supply certain needed machinery. This the company agreed to do, if the state would pay for all work already done and guarantee that the Tredegar would not be held responsible for any obligations previously incurred for the state. Governor Letcher accepted these terms and in June when the armory was turned over to the Confederate Ordnance Bureau for the duration of war, the national government took over the state's responsibilities to the Tredegar partners.[62]

The company proceeded with the tools, fixtures, and other machinery needed to perfect the Harpers Ferry equipment. Lathes, hammers, vises,

61. Burton to Dimmock, June 14, 1861, and to John R. Chamblis, June 19, 1861, Documents Nos. 43, 31, *Documents of the [Virginia] Convention, 1861* (Richmond, 1861); entry for May 1861, Tredegar Journals.

62. Anderson & Co. to the Executive Council, May 29, 1861, and resolutions adopted by the Convention, June 29, 1861, Virginia Executive Papers, VSL; Anderson & Co. to Letcher, June 17, 1861, Tredegar Letterbooks; *O.R.*, Ser. IV, *1*, 504–05; deed of transfer from Virginia to the Confederate States, Sept. 2, 1861, Letters Rec'd., Secretary of War, RG 109, NA.

pulleys, shafting and hangers, a new water wheel, and other important parts were fabricated at the works in the summer and fall of 1861, work which enabled the government to use the machinery as fully as the availability of skilled manpower would permit. In all the company realized some $40,000 on the original $156,000 contract.[63]

Equally important was the work executed for the Ordnance Department's new powder mill at Augusta, Georgia. The South's few small mills were totally inadequate to the task of supplying the huge quantities of powder needed to sustain the great armies being mustered into service. Gorgas handed the vexing problem of powder production to Major George Washington Rains, a native of North Carolina, a West Pointer, and former iron works president. Rains hoped at first to secure the heavy rolls, bed circles, and shafts from iron establishments in Tennessee or Georgia, but after visiting various plants in those states, he informed Gorgas that the machinery could be procured only at the Tredegar. Anderson and Company commenced work on Rains' order for twelve rolls weighing 10,000 pounds each, six bed circles, and ten shafts in September 1861. The Richmond firm finished the job the following February. With the Tredegar's assistance, Rains had one of the world's finest powder mills in operation by April 1862.[64]

The uncertainty that any one area would be free from attack and the inability of the railroads to transport large quantities of raw materials or finished munitions to distant plants and armies forced the Confederate ordnance bureaus to establish shops over a wide geographic area. The exigencies of the war had dispelled any initial qualms the government had about jumping into manufacturing. The small arms industry in the South was practically nonexistent. The Tredegar works supplied various descriptions of iron to many of the government establishments, including the armories at Fayetteville and Asheville, North Carolina, the Macon, Georgia, arsenal, and the naval ordnance shops at Charlotte, which housed the valuable machinery removed from the Gosport Navy Yard when Norfolk was evacuated. The extensive government facilities at Richmond, including the

63. "Machinery, Tools, &c. supplied the Virginia State Armory by J. R. Anderson & Co.," Sept. 30, 1861, Document No. 40, *Documents of the [Virginia] Convention, 1861.*

64. *O.R.*, Ser. IV, *1*, 557; Gorgas to Maj. G. W. Rains, Sept. 30, 1861, George Washington Rains Papers, UNC; Anderson & Co. to C. Shaler Smith, Nov. 13, 1861, Tredegar Letterbooks; Tredegar Foundry Sales Books; Vandiver, *Gorgas*, pp. 76–77; J. W. Mallet, "Work of the Ordnance Bureau of the War Department of the Confederate States, 1861–5," *Southern Historical Society Papers, 37* (1909), 4.

armory, arsenal, and the army and the navy ordnance workshops, also received important items from Anderson and Company that helped them initiate production.[65]

V

Southern railroads placed overwhelming demands on the Tredegar's facilities from the outset of the war. When the conflict commenced, inquiries poured into Anderson and Company from railroad men in all parts of the South, asking for wheels, axles, chairs, spikes, rails, cars, and locomotives. The Tredegar partners replied that the urgent necessities of the government must first be met. "As soon as we get off some of our orders for the defence of the country, which now engross our every thought, we will turn our attention to other subjects and think we can supply many articles heretofore obtained at the North," John Tanner told an Alabama superintendent.[66] The Tredegar management could already foresee the enormous trade that would come to their works as soon as they were able to handle it. "In war or peace we are preparing to make ourselves independent of Lincoln's friends and as soon as this rush at arming the country is done we will propose to supply you many articles heretofore obtained at the North," the Tredegar superintendent repeated to another railroader.[67]

Tanner pointedly told rail managers that their antebellum neglect of the Tredegar was a major cause of present scarcities. "It had been well for our Southern Roads, if long ago they had been more liberal in patronizing Southern establishments. With but few exceptions, preference has generally been given to those who are now our bitterest enemies," he wrote in May 1861.[68] The Richmond *Dispatch* echoed Tanner's admonition in an editorial on January 25, 1862. "It was in vain the John Brown raid threw athwart the whole sky the first lurid glare of the rising comet of war," wrote the editor. The South "never bought a dollar's worth less of Northern men on that account." "It was in vain that Southern journalists invoked the Southern people to break loose from their dependence on Northern artisans, and manufacture for themselves, if they would secure to themselves that might

65. Entries for Feb., Aug., Sept., 1862, Tredegar Rolling Mill Sales Books, and for Nov. 1862, Tredegar Order Book; Vandiver, *Gorgas*, pp. 240–41; Cappon, "Government and Private Industry," Univ. of Va. Studies, *1*, 163–64; Mallet, pp. 5–6; *O.R.N.*, Ser. II, *2*, 547–52.

66. Anderson & Co. to Thomas H. Millington, May 20, 1861, Tredegar Letterbooks.

67. Anderson & Co. to Daniel Cram, June 8, 1861, ibid.

68. Anderson & Co. to Millington, May 20, 1861, ibid.

which, among nations, is the only defense of right." Now the South was desperately short of railroad iron and existing facilities were inadequate to meet the heavy demand.

The Tredegar was unequipped to meet some of the railroads' requests. The works had not manufactured a locomotive since 1860 and the machinists and boiler makers were now preoccupied with more pressing orders. "We are so much engaged in defending the country that we cant stop to build Locomotives," one of the partners wrote in May.[69] The foundries were engaged almost totally with ordnance work, and the new car wheel foundry, converted to ammunition production during the rush to outfit South Carolina for the Sumter bombardment, was working night and day to supply Confederate armies. Tredegar carpenters, formerly freight car builders, now devoted their skills to the manufacture of gun carriages.

But after work began on the deluge of state and Confederate orders that swamped these departments during the first weeks of the war, the Tredegar management was able to give some attention to railroad requests. The military had not yet placed large orders for rolling mill products. In late May, the partners agreed to supply a Georgia road with chairs and spikes for twenty miles of track and accepted several other large railroad contracts.[70] By early September, the Tredegar mills were rolling railroad axles and limited production of car wheels had resumed. "Shall be pleased to furnish you with spikes, bar iron, bridge bolts, wheels & axles or anything in our line," Anderson and Company optimistically informed a Georgia railroad official in late August.[71] The company's sales indicated that this was no idle boast. From April through September, the rolling mills delivered 1,022 long tons of iron to private customers, primarily railroads, and only 152 tons to the government. The Virginia Central and the Virginia and Tennessee, two roads carrying heavy military traffic, were the largest private Tredegar customers.[72]

Secretary of the Navy Mallory's decision to stake the naval fortunes of the Confederacy on ironclads soon reversed the Tredegar's sales pattern, however. The partners quickly discovered that they could not supply both

69. Anderson & Co. to C. F. Vance, May 18, 1861, ibid.

70. Anderson & Co. to M. G. Dobbins, May 31, 1861, to W. D. Dunn, June 25, 1861, and to W. L. Clarke, Sept. 17, 1861, ibid.

71. Anderson & Co. to G. J. Fulton, Aug. 30, 1861, ibid.

72. Figures compiled from Tredegar Rolling Mill Sales Books, and railroad accounts in Tredegar Ledgers. During this same period, various Tredegar departments consumed 312 long tons of the company's rolling mill production.

the government and the railroads with adequate supplies of rolled iron. By the end of September, one of the partners wrote a Georgia railroad superintendent, the works were "overwhelmed with business, all for the Government, except a small corner for Rail Roads, which indeed are a portion of the Government." [73] The railroads' corner grew increasingly smaller. Urgent navy requests for rapid production of plates for the *Merrimack* and her sister ship, the *Richmond,* forced Anderson and Company to refuse large railroad contracts. Once the manufacture of the *Merrimack's* armor commenced, private rolling mill sales declined sharply, reversing the pattern of the previous six months. During the last quarter of 1861, the government purchased 784 long tons of Tredegar rolled iron, while private production was only 535 long tons.[74]

The Richmond industrialists succeeded in filling a vital government request for railroad iron in January 1862 when their facilities provided the spikes and chairs to anchor the world's first military railroad. Following the battle at Manassas, Confederate troops wintered at Centerville, approximately six and one-half miles from the Orange and Alexandria tracks at Manassas Junction. To facilitate the supply of thousands of soldiers quartered around Centerville, General Joseph E. Johnston advised the construction of a railroad from Manassas Junction. The Quartermaster Department began work on the line in December, with rails supplied by Jackson from the Baltimore and Ohio and 150 kegs of spikes and 3,410 chairs furnished by Anderson and Company. Traffic began moving over the line the following month and the road had a busy but brief life. When the Confederates withdrew from Centerville in early March, the Federals tore up the line and returned the rails to the B. and O.[75]

VI

Tredegar prices did not rise spectacularly in 1861, but did climb substantially above prewar rates. The partners made their first advance in late April, upping prices for standard railroad spikes from 3¾ cents to 4 cents per pound. "Materials are advancing very rapidly and if this abominable Yankee Blockade is continued we hardly know where it will stop," Tanner explained to Tredegar customers.[76] By December, spikes

73. Anderson & Co. to Alfred L. Tyler, Sept. 30, 1861, Tredegar Letterbooks.

74. Anderson & Co. to Dunn, Oct. 8, 1861, ibid.; Tredegar Rolling Mill Sales Books. Tredegar consumption amounted to 165 long tons.

75. Tredegar Rolling Mill Sales Books; Johnston, *Virginia Railroads,* pp. 35–36.

76. Anderson & Co. to Dobbins, May 21, 1861, Tredegar Letterbooks.

had risen to 6½ cents per pound and bar to 6 cents per pound for both the government and private customers. Articles purchased only by the military advanced more slowly, however. Brass cannon rose from the April price of 46 cents to 60 cents per pound in September, but the price of iron cannon, fixed by prewar contract, remained at 6½ cents per pound. (See Figure 1, p. 221.) "We are doing all in our power to keep down rates, for while we are paying double & over for everything we purchase, we have made no such advance in our rates & do not propose doing so unless we are overruled by others," wrote one of the members of the firm in mid-November.[77]

Their price increases for articles sold on the open market were, however, well in line with the rise in the general price index in the eastern Confederacy in 1861.[78] Charcoal pig iron jumped from an average price of $30 per ton in March to $40 to $45 per ton at the end of the year, an increase of 30 to 50 per cent. Wages advanced for selected groups of skilled workers but did not climb as rapidly as raw materials costs. The September strike by the foundry workers forced the Tredegar management to grant its first across-the-board wartime pay increase. Wages for skilled personnel, such as molders, machinists, finishers, pattern makers, and boiler makers, rose from $2.50 per day to $3.00 during that month. The next general wage increase did not come until July 1862.[79]

Tredegar prices on non-military items rose more than enough to cover increases in labor and raw materials costs in 1861, and the company earned substantial profits on munitions delivered to the government. The profit on a ton of Tredegar rolled iron which cost $79.80 to produce in 1861 was $53.57.[80] Private customers consumed three pounds of rolled iron for every two pounds sold to the government in 1861. (See Table 6.) The steady price of 6½ cents per pound for iron cannon cut the profit margin on ordnance, but the company compensated for this with other items. "The irons for carriages we make tremendous profits upon," William Tanner wrote his father in March 1861.[81] The margin remained high after the war broke out. An 8-inch siege carriage which cost the Tredegar $269.99 to make in January 1862 sold to the Confederate Ordnance Bu-

77. Anderson & Co. to George Yonge, Nov. 13, 1861, ibid.

78. Eugene M. Lerner, "Money, Prices, and Wages in the Confederacy, 1861–1865," *Journal of Political Economy, 63* (1955), 24.

79. Wage charges in Tredegar Foundry Sales Books.

80. Tredegar Inventory Book.

81. W. E. Tanner to J. F. Tanner, March 22, 1861, Supplementary Tredegar Records.

reau for $400 and a 32-pounder barbette carriage and chassis costing $425.44 sold for $700. Anderson and Company also earned a handsome return on artillery projectiles. A 6.40-inch bolt cost $11.73 to make in the summer of 1862 and sold to the government for $18. Cast shell for the 7-inch Brooke guns which the *Merrimack* carried into battle cost the navy $20 each; labor and raw materials cost the Tredegar $15.30. The 7-inch steeltipped wrought iron bolt, weighing 115 pounds, developed for piercing armor plate following the duel between the *Monitor* and the *Merrimack,* was the most expensive projectile manufactured by the Tredegar. It cost the firm $53.40 to make but the navy paid $95 for each such projectile.[82]

TABLE 6. Tredegar Rolling Mill Production, 1859–1866
(in tons of 2,240 lbs.)

Year	*Sales to Confederate government*	*Sales to railroads and private individuals*	*Consumed by Tredegar operations*	*Total*
1859	—	—	—	4,210
1860	—	—	—	4,658
1861	—	—	—	3,592
April–December 1861	936	1,556	477	
1862	1,497	1,323	900	3,720
1863	1,350	1,178	617	3,145
1864	783	1,203	679	2,665
January–March 1865	108	179	—	287
August–December 1865	—	—	—	1,067
1866	—	—	—	3,663

Sources: Tredegar Journals; Tredegar Rolling Mill Sales Books; Tredegar Inventory Book.

With both production and prices at high levels, the firm earned the greatest profits in the Tredegar's twenty-five year history during 1861. Foundry sales were spectacular—$848,694, which netted Anderson and Company $322,777. Profits on rolling mill sales of $435,422 were $175,455. Total profit at the end of 1861, including earnings for hauling and loading cannon and munitions and interest on outstanding accounts, was $518,019.[83]

82. Archer Account Book, VHS; Tredegar Foundry Sales Books.

83. Tredegar Inventory Book. For an explanation of profit, see note to Table 8. This 1861 figure was only slightly inflated; a dollar in gold could be bought for $1.25 in currency at Richmond banks in December 1861. See "Confederate Inflation Chart," *Official Publication No. 13,* Richmond Civil War Centennial Committee (Richmond [1963]).

VII

With the earnings acquired during 1861, Joseph Anderson settled the major outstanding debts against himself and his firm, with the exception of almost $50,000 due Northern creditors. On January 1, 1862, Anderson secured a release from the lien held by the Richmond banks against the Tredegar works for the $100,000 loan granted in December 1860, when bankruptcy threatened the company. This debt was fully paid during 1861.[84] Anderson and Company attempted to pay Northern creditors in April and May 1861 but the enactment of sequestration legislation by the Confederate Congress in late May and August cut short these remittances. Debts totaling $49,531, incurred in the North for pig iron, coal, and military supplies delivered before the outbreak of hostilities, remained on the Tredegar's books until December 1861, when the company placed the total sum at the disposal of the government.[85]

Anderson's Northern creditors wasted no time in trying to recoup their losses. The Tredegar senior partner held considerable timber acreage on the B. and O. Railroad in Alleghany County, Maryland, and the Northern parties attached the land in retaliation. Anderson promised a Philadelphia creditor that "when the war is over we expect to settle every dollar due by us in whatever quarter and to whomever due." [86] But despite these assurances, his Maryland lands were sold at auction and William E. Dodge, the New York copper and iron magnate, bought extensive tracts of the property. The matter was not fully settled until after the war. If it was any consolation to the injured parties in the North, the Richmond firm lost $30,000 worth of machinery when the Federals occupied New Orleans in April 1862. The Tredegar's agent, on the advice of the Richmond office, had been holding the machinery off the market in anticipation of increasingly higher prices.[87]

Manufacture of ordnance and munitions at the foundries and machine shops was easily the most successful Tredegar operation during 1861. The gun foundries cast 214 cannon for Southern states and the Confederate government and thousands of rounds of ammunition. Heavy guns were

84. Indenture dated Jan. 1, 1862, Anderson Papers, VSL.

85. Anderson & Co. to Ames Manufacturing Co., May 23, 1861, and to P. Gibson, Aug. 17, 1861, Tredegar Letterbooks; entry for Dec. 1861, Tredegar Journals. For a discussion of Confederate sequestration procedures, see Richard C. Todd, *Confederate Finance* (Athens, Ga., 1954), pp. 159–65.

86. Anderson & Co. to Felix Wyatt, April 23, 1863, Tredegar Letterbooks.

87. Anderson & Co. to Ivens, April 26, 1861, ibid.; entry for Dec. 1862, Tredegar Journals.

dispatched to forts from Galveston to Aquia Landing. Field artillery, mounted on Tredegar-built carriages and equipped with shot, shell, and implements, went from the Richmond plant to every section of the new nation. The works served as a center for ordnance experiments and made significant contributions to the South's military capacity by outfitting key government establishments with needed tools and equipment. The rolling mills recorded large sales to railroads and delivered the armor plate for the *Merrimack.*

But, despite these successes, Anderson and Company failed to maintain a consistently high level of production. Neither the foundries nor rolling mills were worked to their capacity. Rolling mill sales reached only 3,592 long tons in 1861; the previous year, the mills had sold 4,658 long tons, despite extremely poor business during November and December when panic struck the Southern economy. (See Table 6.) Much more serious were the sharp monthly fluctuations in the manufacture of cannon. (See Table 5, p. 111.) The problem at both the rolling mills and foundries was the same—an inadequate supply of raw materials.

7

Government Aid

Of all the elements needed to maintain a high level of Tredegar production, pig iron was unquestionably the most important. Without this vital metal, the Confederacy's key heavy industrial plant could contribute practically nothing to the war effort. Anderson and Company's frustrating and costly attempts to secure iron from Tennessee and Georgia had convinced the Richmond manufacturers that they would have to rely on a revived Virginia blast furnace industry for pig metal. When this rebirth failed to materialize, the resulting threat to the Tredegar's output quickly produced a dramatic shift in the government's policy toward private enterprise and brought about a revolutionary expansion of the company's activities.

I

An incident in the fall of 1861 gave a strong indication that Tredegar production would soon face grave raw materials problems. The trouble lay at Cloverdale furnace, the chief source of Anderson and Company's gun iron. Isaac and Thomas Steers, the Cloverdale lessees, made a verbal agreement with the Tredegar owner in June 1861 to supply the works with 2,000 tons of gun metal, to be delivered during the next eighteen months. As week after week passed and no Cloverdale pig came down the James River and Kanawha Canal, the Tredegar management grew increasingly anxious. Anderson and Company's gun founders were forced to feed their furnaces with inferior brands of iron, primarily Graham, Columbia, and Fort pig, but supplies of these metals soon ran dangerously low. In August, the Tredegar's prospects for obtaining iron received a severe blow when Graham's Wythe County furnace broke down, and by the middle of the month stockpiles of gun iron were completely exhausted. From August 16 to September 12, not one cannon was cast at the Tredegar works.[1] "We regret that as yet we have heard of no shipment of iron from the Clover-

1. Tredegar Gun Foundry Book.

dale," one of the partners wrote the Steers in September. "We can cast no more guns until we get it and must beg that you ship at once all you possibly have ready. We are much concerned for this delay." [2] On September 26, a shipment of the long-awaited metal finally arrived at the works. Small loads continued to come down the canal during October but it was scarcely enough to whet the appetite of the voracious Tredegar furnaces.[3]

The management in Richmond suspected that something was wrong at the furnace and proceeded to investigate the Cloverdale operation. They soon discovered that the brothers Steers had yielded to the temptation to speculate with their iron on the open market. Even worse, the profiteering pair had stopped making gun metal and had converted production to cheaper grades of iron for sale in Richmond. The Cloverdale lessees had also made contracts with other parties for future deliveries of ordinary pig at a price above that guaranteed by Anderson and Company for gun metal.[4]

The Steers' profiteering severely jeopardized Tredegar ordnance operations and the company's status as a government contractor. The partners asked John T. Anderson, the Cloverdale owner, to try to persuade the lessees to return to the manufacture of gun iron. Tanner outlined the plight of the company in a long confidential letter to John Anderson on October 28:

> Our relations with the War Department are of a delicate character—we have assured them that we had contracts for all the Gun Metal that we could melt, relying upon this agreement with Steers & one with Graham which he cant fill because his wheel house has been burned & he can deliver no more till March but will then resume. We cant afford to have an open rupture with Steers, because we are bound to the War Department to deliver them Guns. You, we know, appreciate our position and we beg that you will see Steers & if there be any difficulty in the way of his making the metal, do him any assistance or advice at your command & if you can close all matters of contract with him please do so on such terms as you may consider for our interest.[5]

Colonel Gorgas at the Ordnance Bureau became alarmed at the delay in Tredegar cannon production and visited the company's offices on the eve-

2. Anderson & Co. to T. and I. Steers, Sept. 16, 1861, Tredegar Letterbooks.
3. Tredegar Pig Iron Receipt Book.
4. Anderson & Co. to Thomas Steers, Nov. 8, 1861, Tredegar Letterbooks.
5. Anderson & Co. to John T. Anderson, Oct. 28, 1861, ibid.

ning of November 7. The partners gave Gorgas a full account of their difficulties and the next day he wrote a letter to Anderson and Company, intended for the Steers' eyes:

> On the basis of the information you have given me relative to the misunderstanding of the contract between yourselves and the parties with whom you have contracted to supply you with No. 1 Cloverdale Iron, I beg leave to say that the threatened deficiency in the supply of this iron would be an event of the most disastrous character to the defence of the Seacoast. No other iron will give the necessary confidence in the strength of heavy guns.
>
> I trust the gentlemen with whom you have contracted for the supply needed by the government for its heavy guns will reconsider the matter and comply with the wants of the country, even if their understanding of the contract is at variance with what appears on its face to be the proper construction.
>
> The matter is of real importance, & I beg you will communicate to me the final determination of this question for the information of the War Department.[6]

The entreaties of Anderson and Company and Colonel Gorgas accomplished very little. Only small lots of Cloverdale gun metal arrived at the works before the end of the year.[7]

The Tredegar's inability to secure large quantities of Cloverdale iron took on added importance when cannon made with Graham metal proved to be completely unreliable. "We regret to inform you that several of the guns manufactured from your metal have recently burst, the one at Columbus Kentucky with results that are distressing," Anderson and Company informed Graham on November 14. The failure of these cannon "seriously affects a reputation for making Guns which has been obtained by years of patient efforts & a large expenditure of money," the partner continued. "This result is a most serious one both for ourselves and the country. Worse than all we have used a considerable portion of the metal & the guns are now all in the field." A week later, the Tredegar management informed Graham that "another large gun made from your metal burst at Port Royall in the hottest of the battle with the fleet." [8] The army ordnance in-

6. Gorgas to Anderson & Co., Nov. 8, 1861, ibid.
7. Tredegar Pig Iron Receipt Book.
8. Anderson & Co. to Graham & Son, Nov. 14, 22, 1861, Tredegar Letterbooks.

spector at the works promptly rejected two heavy cannon cast with Graham iron.[9] Either Anderson and Company or the government, or both, would have to do something to clear up the Cloverdale situation very soon or most of the large caliber cannon fabricated in the Confederacy would be untrustworthy.

II

Despite the grave implications of the Cloverdale situation, the Tredegar owners refused to acknowledge, at least officially, just how close they were to a severe pig iron shortage. In December 1861, John Tanner claimed that his chief worry was that the government would not give Anderson and Company sufficient orders to keep the works fully occupied. The contract of October 26, 1861, required the firm to furnish the Confederate States a total of $2,000,000 worth of iron products per year. "To accomplish this it will be necessary that our establishment together with those we are constructing be employed in every department," Tanner informed the Secretaries of the War and Navy Departments on December 21. He asked that the firm be granted orders for five hundred iron guns, ranging in size from a 24-pounder to the still uncast 15-inch gun, with three hundred projectiles for each piece and a carriage for each army gun. Such bronze or iron field artillery as the Ordnance Bureau might require would be in addition to the five hundred heavier cannon. Tanner requested that the navy allot annually the machinery for twenty gunboats, one hundred tons of chain cable and boiler plate, one thousand tons of assorted bar iron for navy yards, and not less than 4,500 tons of gunboat plates. He entertained no doubts in December about the Tredegar's ability to meet these extremely ambitious quotas.[10]

The Ordnance Bureau took Tanner at his word. On February 4, 1862, Colonel Gorgas ordered a total of four hundred heavy cannon and mortars, complete with implements, 58,500 rounds of ammunition for these weapons, and 295 carriages and mortar beds. This requisition was to be filled by January 1, 1863.[11] Field artillery needed in addition to those remaining from 1861 orders would be requested as the occasion demanded. The Navy Department was evidently more skeptical of Tanner's claims.

9. Anderson & Co. to Gorgas, Nov. 29, 1861, ibid.

10. Anderson & Co. to Benjamin and Mallory, Dec. 21, 1861, Letters Rec'd., Secretary of War, RG 109, NA.

11. Gorgas to Anderson & Co., Feb. 4, 1862, Tredegar Contract Books.

Secretary Mallory contracted on January 27, 1862, for engines and boilers for only three gunboats.[12] The rolling mills were still at work on the *Merrimack's* plates and had to roll the armor for the *Richmond* once the first job was complete.

By late January, however, Anderson and Company had serious reservations about their ability to produce in 1862 the $2,000,000 worth of iron called for in their government contract. In a long letter to the War and Navy Departments dated January 25, the partners asked that their contract be extended an additional year beyond the two years stipulated in the October 26, 1861, agreement and cited six factors influencing their request:

First, the government was contracting for the blasts of Virginia furnaces for three years and the company was having difficulty purchasing for shorter periods.

Second, even though contracts signed in the fall of 1861 would supply additional pig iron to the Tredegar, "we shall still be compelled to put in operation on our own account furnaces enough to supply a large deficiency of metal which will doubtless exist in this section of the country."

Third, the company would incur considerable expense in constructing the new gun foundry, boring mill, and rolling mill for armor and boiler plate and this expenditure would not be justified unless the works were kept fully employed for at least three years.

Fourth, the Tredegar management, in placing the plant at the disposal of the government, surrendered a large and remunerative business, built up over twenty-five years, which would probably be permanently lost.

Fifth, "in consequence of the great scarcity of labour and materials at present, it will be impossible to supply during the present year our full quota under the contract but this deficiency can be supplied during the two years next ensuing."

Finally, the owners stated that prices charged the government were much below present market rates and would continue to be as long as military purchases were so extensive. In conclusion, the Tredegar partners pointed out that they had given freely of their technical knowledge to public and private establishments that would soon be their rivals.[13]

This letter gave the Confederate government clear warning that the

12. Contract with C.S. Navy, Jan. 27, 1862, ibid.

13. Anderson & Co. to the Secretaries of War and Navy, Jan. 25, 1862, Letters Rec'd., Secretary of War, RG 109, NA.

South's most important industrial plant was on the verge of severe production difficulties. The basic problems were insufficient raw materials, iron in particular, and an inadequate labor force. Labor shortages had occurred in some departments, including the rolling mills when the production of the *Merrimack's* plates commenced, but the Tredegar partners' primary concern was their iron supply.[14] Tanner's optimistic forecast of December was abandoned, as far as it applied to 1862.

III

Reviving the dormant Virginia pig iron industry was proving a far more difficult task than either the Tredegar owners or the founders anticipated when Anderson and Company signed contracts in the fall of 1861 for the full blasts of numerous furnaces. The problems facing a furnace owner attempting to get his furnace into blast were numerous and difficult. He first had to assemble a free and slave labor force. This usually required an application to the War Department for details of men formerly employed at the furnace, a process that was almost always ensnarled in red tape and produced, at best, only a portion of the men requested. To acquire slaves, the furnaces had to compete with the Corps of Engineers, which was hiring large numbers of men to work on fortifications, as well as large private hirers—the railroads, the canal company, and the Richmond factories, in particular. The owner then had to secure teams and wagons, a task made difficult by widespread government impressment of vehicles and animals for military purposes, and provide food and forage. If the agents of the Commissary Department had been active in the vicinity of the furnace, provisioning could be difficult and expensive. Acquiring enough salt to prepare large quantities of meat for storage required the approval of state or Confederate authorities. If the bellows, water wheel, and other essential parts of the furnace machinery could be repaired and the blast finally begun, there was often the possibility that a Federal cavalry foray could reach the vicinity, especially in the northern Shenandoah Valley.

The solutions to these problems were often beyond the capacity of individual furnace owners. Furnace men bombarded the Tredegar management with requests for assistance—to secure details of men, wagons, and teams from the army, to keep commissary agents out of their county, for salt requisitions, furnace parts, and money to help them inaugurate their operations. The Richmond industrialists responded to these requests as

14. Anderson & Co. to Mallory, Aug. 26, 1861, Tredegar Letterbooks.

best they could, but more often than not they could supply only limited assistance.[15]

By late January 1862, the firm saw that in all probability the contracts signed the previous year would not keep their works adequately supplied with metal. In 1861, Anderson and Company had contracted for the 1862 blasts of ten furnaces, hoping to realize 12,500 to 15,000 tons of iron from these agreements. During the first quarter of 1862, the Tredegar received iron from only four of the ten and pig iron receipts from all sources totaled less than one thousand tons. Deliveries of the all-important Cloverdale gun metal were trifling. The Cloverdale lessees delivered only thirty-eight tons in January and after a shipment of sixteen tons arrived on February 15, all deliveries ceased.[16] By the end of the month, Tredegar gun founders again charged their furnaces with a new, unproven brand of iron.[17] In a number of instances the furnace owners had not been able to overcome the obstacles impeding the revival of their facilities. When furnaces did get into blast, the temptation to speculate with the iron on the open market proved to be stronger in some cases than the contracts with Anderson and Company, which had already fixed a price. The result was a crisis in Tredegar production which climaxed in March and April 1862.

On March 4, 1862, Colonel Gorgas of the Ordnance Department placed an advertisement in the Richmond press inviting bids on 200,000 tons of pig iron, 50,000 tons of blooms, and 50,000 tons of bar iron.[18] He received a partial answer to his notice before the end of the month when Anderson and Company informed the government that they could not meet their contractual obligations. "The Department has just received formal notice from the Tredegar Works that in consequence of the nonfulfillment of contracts made by them with furnaces for iron they are unable to comply with their contract," the Secretary of the Navy informed President Davis on March 21. "They now have to take possession of furnaces and mine and work the ore," and the government would have to aid them in

15. Anderson & Co. to the Secretary of War, Aug. 27, Sept. 25, Nov. 29, 1861, and to Stoneburner & Belew, Nov. 18, 28, 1861, ibid.; Anderson & Co. to the Secretary of War, Jan. 3, April 3, 1862, Letters Rec'd., Secretary of War, RG 109, NA; Wissler & Co. to Letcher, June 5, 1861, and Watkins James to Letcher, July 17, 1861, Virginia Executive Papers, VSI.

16. Tredegar Pig Iron Receipt Book.

17. Tredegar Gun Foundry Book.

18. Richmond *Examiner*, March 4, 1862.

this undertaking.[19] This startling intelligence brought an immediate response from both the Administration and Congress. The survival of the Confederate nation depended too heavily on Tredegar production to permit the government to ignore the company's plight for long. Within a month, Congress enacted far-reaching legislation to assist the Southern iron and coal industries.

IV

In February and August 1861, Congress had authorized the President or the Secretary of War to make advances of up to one third the value of contracts in order to stimulate the manufacture of ordnance, small arms, and munitions but had made no provision for agreements with producers of raw materials.[20] After taking office in September 1861, Secretary of War Judah P. Benjamin had nevertheless interpreted the terms of this legislation broadly. Early in 1862, he began signing contracts for pig iron which advanced furnace owners substantial loans. One such contract with a North Carolina ironmaster called for a government loan of $100,000 in 8 per cent bonds to enable the founder to put his furnace and forge in operation. He agreed to furnish the army set amounts of iron, including gun metal, over the next three years at a stated price and promised that no iron would be delivered to any party other than the Confederate government until the stipulations of the contract had been met. The Secretary of War agreed to exempt from military service all men employed at these furnaces and works.[21]

The requirements of an ironclad navy prompted the Bureau of Ordnance and Hydrography to even greater activity in this field. Captain George Minor, the capable chief of the bureau, made contracts with iron men in Virginia, North Carolina, Tennessee, Alabama, and Georgia, in an attempt to secure a plentiful supply of iron for the navy's own shops and for large contractors such as Anderson and Company.[22] In December 1861, Minor agreed to turn over to the Tredegar 7,000 tons of pig iron to

19. *O.R.N.*, Ser. II, *2*, 171–72.

20. Matthews, ed., *Statutes at Large*, pp. 28–29.

21. Abstract of agreement between Benjamin and B. J. Jordan, Jan. 24, 1862, and list of contracts made by Secretaries of War, Dec. 13, 1862, Letters Rec'd., Secretary of War, RG 109, NA; *O.R.N.*, Ser. II, *2*, 249; Gorgas, "Notes on the Ordnance Department," *Southern Hist. Soc. Papers*, *12*, 75.

22. *O.R.N.*, Ser. II, *2*, 73–74, 248–49.

be manufactured for the navy at Buena Vista furnace in Rockbridge County, Virginia, during 1862, 1863, and 1864.[23] Less than a month later, Minor included among his pig iron contractors Joseph Reid Anderson, who consented to deliver to the navy 3,000 tons of pig iron from his Catawba furnace in Botetourt County within two years from April 1, 1862.[24]

Both Secretary of War Benjamin and Secretary of the Navy Mallory realized early in 1862 that additional government action was needed to insure a supply of pig iron adequate to the needs of the Confederate war industries. The contracts already signed would not begin to equate supply with demand, even if founders met the ambitious quotas set in the agreements. "The supply of iron . . . will soon be far short of our wants both for cannon and for the construction of gun-boats," the Secretary of War warned President Davis on March 12, 1862. Benjamin's totally inadequate solution to the problem was the suggestion that Congress pass legislation to encourage planters to shift their slaves from areas threatened by invasion to iron-producing regions, where the labor could be used to dig ore and chop wood.[25]

Secretary of the Navy Mallory was much broader in his recommendations for Congressional action than his counterpart at the War Department. "The materials of construction, the artisans, the workshops, the instructed officers, and the seamen—all essential to the creation of a naval establishment—demand time and the fostering hand of the Government, whatever may be its resources, to develop and bring into useful operation," he reported to the President on February 27, 1862. "An estimate may be made of the iron thus required for Naval purposes and the consequent development of the iron and coal deposits of our country by the fact that about 1,000 tons have been used in plating the Virginia." [26] The Ordnance Bureau gave further indication of the Confederacy's need for iron early in March 1862 when Gorgas placed the advertisement requesting bids on

23. Tredegar Contract Books.

24. *O.R.N.*, Ser. II, *2*, 248. Anderson had purchased the Catawba property in 1847 but, like so many other Virginia charcoal furnaces, this stack had gone out of blast during the next decade. After unsuccessfully attempting to sell or rent the property in 1861, Anderson agreed with the Navy Department to put the furnace back into operation. See Bruce, *Virginia Iron Manufacture*, p. 228; Richmond *Examiner*, Oct. 5, 1861; Richmond *Dispatch*, April 3, 1862; Anderson & Co. to C. R. Mason, May 15, 1861, and to Capt. George Minor, Nov. 28, 1861, Tredegar Letterbooks.

25. *O.R.*, Ser. IV, *1*, 988–89.

26. *O.R.N.*, Ser. II, *2*, 151.

200,000 tons of charcoal pig iron, 50,000 tons of iron blooms, and 50,000 tons of bar iron. In 1860, the states which later formed the Confederacy had produced only 36,790 tons of pig and 16,072 tons of bar and railroad iron. (See Tables 3, p. 88, and 4, p. 89.)

Pressure mounted on many sides for the Confederate government and private industry to take steps to increase supplies of pig and finished iron. Railway executives took a prominent role in this movement. The inability of the Tredegar works and the mills in Georgia and Tennessee to manufacture both gunboat plates and railroad iron was the primary factor behind a series of railroad conventions held in late 1861 and early 1862. A meeting of railroad men in Richmond in December 1861 adopted resolutions urging the passage of congressional legislation that would advance capital for the construction of iron mills. When a similar convention assembled in the capital the following February, the Richmond *Dispatch* commented that if the meeting could come up with a plan to remedy the South's iron shortage, "it will have done as much towards solving the great problem of national freedom, as any class of individuals have done since the breaking up of the old Union." [27] President Davis submitted the resolutions of the December convention to Congress and recommended that the House and Senate take action to aid the construction of rolling mills and locomotive works. The President offered no advice on the form or extent of such financial assistance, however. "The exigency is believed to be such as to require the aid of the Government," he concluded.[28]

Despite the President's recommendation that something be done to increase the supply of railroad iron and Benjamin's and Mallory's warnings of impending shortages, Congress acted only after the Secretary of the Navy reported on March 21, 1862, that the Tredegar would not be able to meet its production quotas.[29] A thoroughly alarmed Congress now moved rapidly to provide assistance to the Southern iron industry. "No more important subject could engage the public attention than that of developing the iron product and manufacture," Senator Benjamin H. Hill of Georgia told his colleagues.[30] On April 19, 1862, less than a month after Mallory reported that Anderson and Company was desperately short of pig metal,

27. Richmond *Dispatch*, Jan. 27, 1862.

28. James D. Richardson, ed., *Messages and Papers of the Confederacy* (2 vols. Nashville, 1905), *1*, 152–53.

29. *O.R.N.*, Ser. II, *2*, 171–72.

30. "Proceedings of the First Confederate Congress," 1st Sess., *Southern Historical Society Papers*, *45* (1925), 37–38, 47–48.

Congress passed a bill which, hopefully, would provide for sufficient iron to feed the Southern war machine.

This act established the government's position toward the South's basic raw materials and manufacturing industries for the duration of the war. The bill authorized the government to loan up to 50 per cent of the capital needed to erect or expand "all establishments or mines for the production of coal and for the production and manufacture of iron." Terms were extremely liberal. Manufacturers were to repay the interest-free loans in the products of their establishments, at prices set at the time of the loan. In addition, the President could sign contracts for coal and iron to run for as long as six years and make advances of up to one third the value of such contracts.[31] Ten days after the passage of this legislation, Anderson and Company signed a far-reaching agreement with the War and Navy Departments which led to new responsibilities and new problems for the Richmond industrialists.

V

Critically important industrial concerns such as Anderson and Company had a distinct advantage over the government when contract bargaining commenced. Clearly the War and Navy Departments needed the Tredegar's production much more than the company needed the government's business. The partners made excellent profits on supplies furnished to the government but could realize much greater sums if they devoted more of their company's production to private customers. To insure that the South's military needs would be met, Confederate officials were willing to grant almost any legal demand the Tredegar management might make.

The threat of government confiscation of the works as a military necessity always existed but was never taken seriously by the Tredegar owners. More than once during the war Anderson and his partners offered to divest themselves of their plant, either by sale or lease to the government, but always received official encouragement, usually in the form of a price increase, to carry on.[32] The War and Navy Departments pressed the Tredegar constantly for more ordnance and munitions but never evidenced any inclination to take over the complex and many-faceted Tredegar oper-

31. James M. Matthews, ed., *Public Laws of the Confederate States of America,* 1st Cong., 1st Sess. (Richmond, 1862), p. 38.

32. See Anderson & Co. to Seddon, Dec. 23, 1862, Letters Rec'd., Secretary of War, RG 109, NA.

ation. Any increase in production of ordnance stores that might result from governmental control of the works would hardly have justified the political risk involved in attempting such a move. Charges of military despotism and subversion of individual property rights would have sounded loud and long in the halls of the Virginia legislature and the Confederate Congress, where Anderson had many friends. He also had access to President Davis, and prominent military officers frequently dined at Anderson's handsome residence on Franklin Street.[33] In addition to his political influence, Anderson possessed the power of wealth. In 1860, he reported the value of his real and personal estate as $755,000, the second highest total in Richmond.[34]

The government was by no means impotent when bargaining with private enterprise, however, even when faced with a powerful concern like the Tredegar. The secessionist views of the Tredegar owners which had matured into a strong Southern nationalism insured the government a sympathetic response when it requested military goods. Reinforcing the political and social predilections of the Andersons, Tanners, and Archers was their expectation of a great increase in the Tredegar's business once the war was won and their works dominated the Southern iron trade. The settling of Tredegar bills against the Army and Navy Ordnance Bureaus in Confederate treasury notes and bonds was also a basic consideration. If the war was lost, the company's sizable bank account would be worthless, unless of course the management put their assets into a more permanent form such as property, gold, or cotton. The capture of Richmond and a Union victory might well see the Tredegar confiscated, if not destroyed. In short, the success of the Confederate armies was very much in the economic, political, social, and emotional interests of the Tredegar management.

In addition to the Tredegar's very real stake in a Confederate triumph, the government had two important tools with which to exert pressure on private industry: control of the industrial labor force in the South; and increasing control over raw materials, the pig iron industry in particular.

The power to draft and detail gave the War Department considerable influence over Southern industrial concerns. The first conscription act in American history, passed on April 16, 1862, following the battle of Shi-

33. Anderson & Co. to [?], June 7, 1861, Tredegar Letterbooks; John C. Breckinridge to Anderson, Jan. 20, 1864, and John B. Hood to Anderson, Jan. 19, 1864, Anderson Papers, UVA.

34. Manuscript population schedules, Henrico County, Va., Eighth Census, 1860, in "Federal Population Censuses, 1840–1880."

loh, empowered the President to draft and place in military service for three years all white men, residents of the Confederate States, between the ages of eighteen and thirty-five. A supplementary act passed five days later exempted a wide variety of civilians from the draft, including all persons engaged in working iron mines, furnaces, and foundries, under rules to be prescribed by the Secretary of War. [35] The draft age limit was raised to forty-five in a supplementary act of September 27, 1862, and exemptions were tightened in a bill passed on October 11. The approval of the chief of the Ordnance Bureau was now required before artisans employed in private munitions plants were exempt from conscription. Workmen at iron furnaces were liable for the draft unless they were employed at works conducted under the authority of state officials or were manufacturing iron for the Confederate government.[36] As the war deepened in 1863 and 1864 and military commanders demanded more and more men to fill their shattered armies, exemptions became increasingly difficult to secure.

The Secretary of War's authority to detail skilled mechanics from the ranks was an extremely important consideration when the Tredegar owners and the heads of the War and Navy Departments sat down for contract negotiations. Exemption for workers presently employed at the vital Tredegar plant was taken for granted in 1862. But correcting the overmobilization which occurred during the opening months of the conflict and securing new artisans to keep the expanded Tredegar facilities fully employed was quite another matter. The Secretary of War's recognition of the labor needs of the company and his willingness to exert pressure on field commanders to release men from the ranks were necessary if the Tredegar owners were to maintain a high level of production and profit.

Military authorities began systematically organizing their control over the production of pig iron in April 1862 when Congress authorized the formation of a Niter Bureau as a division of the Ordnance Department.[37] Although the enabling legislation only granted the new bureau power to stimulate the production of niter for manufacturing gunpowder, the duties of the officers forming the corps soon expanded to include the development of all the mineral resources of the Confederacy. Under the command of Major Isaac M. St. John, another one of the superbly efficient officers Gorgas attracted to the ordnance service, a mining desk was established at the

35. Matthews, ed., *Public Laws,* 1st Cong., 1st Sess., pp. 29–32, 51–52.
36. Ibid., 1st Cong., 2d Sess., pp. 61–62, 77–79.
37. Ibid., 1st Cong., 1st Sess., pp. 27–28.

Niter Bureau before the end of the summer of 1862.[38] Congress formally recognized the enlarged scope of the bureau's activities in April 1863, when it passed legislation establishing the Niter and Mining Bureau as an independent bureau of the War Department and specifically charged the bureau "with all duties and expenditures connected with the mining of iron, copper, lead, coal, etc., so far as it shall be deemed necessary to supply the military necessities of the country." [39] The Bureau of Ordnance and Hydrography, which made the navy's extensive contracts with iron founders, also took an active role in promoting the development of the South's iron and coal resources. In the fall of 1862, the navy had a three-man geological team in the Virginia mountains searching for new ore deposits from which gun iron could be made.[40]

Once the War and Navy Departments began signing contracts with furnace owners throughout the iron-producing regions of the Confederacy in late 1861 and 1862, the Tredegar management either had to produce its own pig metal or reach a firm agreement with the government for a supply. When the furnaces under contract to Anderson and Company failed to deliver the metal to the Richmond plant in the first quarter of 1862, the management could not turn to other founders for metal because the government already had contracts for their iron. "Every thing must stop unless we go into the mountains & purchase and operate Blast furnaces to make Pig Iron," Anderson wrote in the summer.[41] The Tredegar's new contract with the War and Navy Departments was intended to facilitate this dramatic expansion of the Tredegar's operations.

VI

During the month between the Tredegar's formal notice to the government and the signing of the new contract, negotiations between the company and the War and Navy Departments centered around the basic problem of increasing pig iron supplies. The Tredegar owners maintained that under ordinary circumstances they would not be willing to undertake the manufacture of pig metal, an enterprise they considered outside the scope of their legitimate operations. If, however, the War and Navy Departments considered it necessary to enable the Tredegar to supply ordnance and munitions, the company would reluctantly consent to produce pig iron if

38. *O.R.*, Ser. IV, *2*, 21, 26–27.

39. Matthews, ed., *Public Laws*, 1st Cong., 3d Sess., p. 114.

40. *O.R.*, Ser. IV, *2*, 143.

41. Anderson to Gen. Lawrence O'B. Branch, July 23, 1862, Lawrence O'B. Branch Papers, NCA.

the government would purchase and equip the furnaces. Anderson and Company would operate the facilities at their own expense.

The Secretaries did not take the partners' professed reluctance to go into the manufacture of pig iron too seriously. The company had been willing to sign a contract with the navy to operate the Catawba furnace in February and the partners thought at that time they stood an excellent chance of gaining a good profit on the furnace's production.[42] Mallory and the new Secretary of War, George Wythe Randolph, turned down the company's suggestion that the government buy and outfit the furnaces. They offered instead to advance Anderson and Company the capital to meet all the expenses necessary to commence pig iron production, under terms outlined in the act of April 19, 1862. The Tredegar management finally accepted this proposition and the contract was drawn accordingly.[43]

The contract between Anderson and Company and the government signed April 29, 1862, was a precedent-setting document, establishing the basic pattern which the Confederate government later used to induce the expansion of other Southern iron establishments.[44] The Tredegar owners agreed to deliver all the guns, shot and shell, bar, bolt, rod, boiler iron, and iron plates for covering vessels, which the army and navy might require, within the increased capacity of the Tredegar works, to the extent of $2,000,000 annually. The contract was to be in force until December 31, 1864. The government, obviously worried about the bursting of Tredegar cannon, secured a promise from Anderson and Company that in the future all guns would be manufactured from iron such as heretofore used in guns made for the United States. The company repeated its pledge, remaining unfulfilled from the October contract, to increase the capacity of the works to enable the casting and finishing of 15-inch guns and the rolling of armor plate up to 2½ inches thick, 12 inches wide, and 10 feet long. To compensate the partners for this expansion and to cover increases in raw material and labor costs, the Secretaries agreed to a slight increase in the prices paid for Tredegar iron products. The provision of the October 1861 contract providing for future price adjustments to meet increased production costs was continued.

The section dealing with the Tredegar's move into pig iron production formed the heart of the new contract. Because the company could not rely

42. Anderson & Co. to John T. Anderson, Oct. 28, 1861, Tredegar Letterbooks.

43. Anderson & Co. to Seddon, Dec. 23, 1862, Letters Rec'd., Secretary of War, RG 109, NA.

44. *O.R.N.*, Ser. II, *2*, 210–11; Vandiver, "Shelby Iron Works," *Ala. Review*, *1*, 18, 24; Cappon, "Government and Private Industry," Univ. of Va. Studies, *1*, 166–67.

on obtaining pig metal from other sources, the partners agreed to undertake to produce "a large proportion" of the iron required to meet their production quotas. To facilitate these furnace operations, the War and Navy Departments advanced Anderson and Company $300,000, one half in treasury notes and one half in Confederate bonds, to be invested in the purchase and maintenance of blast furnaces. The Richmond industrialists were not required to repay this interest-free loan until the expiration of the contract on December 31, 1864.

In the closing paragraphs of the agreement, the Tredegar owners agreed that "the orders of and work for the Confederate States shall at all times have priority . . . over all other work or orders." This was an important concession to the government. Anderson and Company promised to keep their establishment fully employed during the period of the contract, to enable them "to manufacture the quantity of articles proposed to be supplied under this agreement," amounting to $2,000,000 worth of guns, ammunition, and iron per year. Bills would be settled two thirds in treasury notes, one third in Confederate bonds. The requisition of Colonel Gorgas for four hundred cannon given on February 4, 1862, was to serve as the basis for production for the Ordnance Department until further notice.

In conclusion, the Secretary of War and the Secretary of the Navy promised to exercise their extensive control over two vital segments of the Southern economy to aid Tredegar production. First, they agreed to transfer to Anderson and Company so much of the pig metal the government had purchased from other parties as the Richmond industrialists might require to execute the contract. In addition, the Secretaries consented to exempt or detail from military service such men as the Tredegar owners considered indispensable to enable them to carry out the terms of the agreement. These two provisions more than compensated the company for the guarantee of priority for government business. Although the contract represented hard bargaining on both sides, Anderson and Company received considerably more than they were forced to give.[45]

VII

The Tredegar owners moved immediately to acquire blast furnaces. Two days after the contract signing, Tanner informed the Secretaries that the company had purchased four furnaces and the teams necessary for transportation. Obviously, the Tredegar management had made some de-

45. Contract with the War and Navy Departments, April 29, 1862, in "J. R. Anderson & Co.," Confederate Citizens File, RG 109, NA.

tailed advance arrangements in anticipation of the government loan. Tanner asked that the cost of the furnaces and teams, $175,000, be turned over to the company and the Treasury did so at once.[46] Anderson redeemed one of his prewar investments when the company purchased his Catawba furnace property for $25,000. The Tredegar went after the Cloverdale and Grace furnaces also, acquiring these two properties from John T. Anderson for $94,500. Thomas Steers, the founder at Cloverdale and Grace who had performed so unsatisfactorily, received $30,000 for a tract of land near the furnaces in Botetourt County and for the mules, wagons, provisions, and other items in the inventory at the two furnaces. The purchase of a fourth property, Australia furnace in Alleghany County, completed the Tredegar's first acquisitions.[47]

A logical continuation of the expansion of Tredegar operations came six months after the signing of the April document. With winter approaching, both Anderson and Company and the government were gravely concerned about the capacity of the Richmond coal mines to supply the needs of the Tredegar works, the government shops, and the civilian population. Under terms of a supplementary agreement made on September 22, 1862, the War and Navy Departments loaned the company an additional $200,000 to purchase a coal field and to add three or more blast furnaces to the four already owned, plus a forge for making blooms. Anderson and Company agreed to sell the government any coal raised over and above the needs of the works. Because of the large expenses to be incurred by the company to increase their furnace commitments and to begin coal mining, the Secretaries agreed to extend the provisions of the contracts of October 26, 1861, and April 29, 1862, to January 1, 1868, the maximum six years permitted by law. In addition, the War and Navy Departments granted an across-the-board price increase of 30 per cent on all Tredegar iron products furnished the government. These new prices were to continue "until the fluctuations in the value of material and labor may justify a further change." [48]

Using the $200,000 provided by the September contract plus $125,000 still remaining unspent from the April loan, Anderson and Company purchased one coal property, rented another, and bought or leased six more blast furnaces. The Dover coal field in Goochland County, which had been

46. Anderson & Co. to the Secretaries of War and Navy, May 1, 1862, and endorsements, ibid.

47. Entries for May 1862, Tredegar Journals; deed of Thomas Steers to Anderson & Co., May 12, 1862, Anderson Papers, VSL.

48. Contract with the War and Navy Departments, Sept. 22, 1862, in "J. R. Anderson & Co.," Confederate Citizens File, RG 109, NA.

worked since the eighteenth century, was purchased for $90,000 in October 1862. This property consisted of approximately 1,100 acres and had fifteen shafts, the deepest of which was four hundred feet. The James River and Kanawha Canal provided direct communications with the Tredegar works. The Dover land also contained an excellent farm and the company anticipated raising food there to help feed the miners and the operatives at the Richmond plant. The Tuckahoe or Trench mines, a tract of some 250 acres in Henrico County, twelve miles from Richmond and three miles from the canal, was leased for five years in January 1863. There were several shafts on this property, including one over two hundred feet deep.[49] The Tredegar management leased Francis T. Anderson's Glenwood furnace in Rockbridge County, and the Columbia furnace and forge and the Caroline and Fort furnaces in Shenandoah County. All the stock and equipment at these properties were purchased. The final two acquisitions, the Rebecca and the Jane furnaces owned by Francis T. Anderson, completed Anderson and Company's purchases.[50] By the end of January 1863, the Tredegar had spent the entire $500,000 loan and had gained control of ten blast furnaces and two coal properties.

VIII

General Joseph R. Anderson returned to Richmond in the midst of these expanding activities. His brigade had been called up from North Carolina in late April 1862 and assigned to A. P. Hill's Light Division, to assist in the defense of Richmond. Anderson's troops fought well when they went into combat during the Seven Days' Battles for the Confederate capital. His brigade saw its first action at Beaver Dam Creek on June 26. In this engagement and in the fierce fighting in the swamps at Gaines' Mill the next day, Anderson led his men like a seasoned professional. Three days later when he took his men into battle again, this time at Frayser's Farm, Anderson suffered a slight head wound and was temporarily disabled.[51] His retirement from active service came two weeks later.

49. "Corporate Holdings, 1866," manuscript Tredegar volume; entry for Dec. 1862, Tredegar Journals; Bruce, p. 88.

50. Anderson & Co. to the Secretaries of War and Navy, Dec. 26, 1862, Jan. 7, 1863, Feb. 14, 1863, and to Seddon, Jan. 12, 1863, Tredegar Letterbooks; entries for Nov. 1862, Jan. 1863, Tredegar Journals; agreements with Stoneburner & Belew, Sept. 25, 1862, and with Francis T. Anderson, Jan. 15, 1863, Tredegar Contract Books.

51. *O.R.*, Ser. I, *9*, 463, *11*, pt. ii, 877–81; Bruce, pp. 461–62; Clifford Dowdey, *The Seven Days: The Emergence of Lee* (Boston, 1964), pp. 180, 183, 224–28, 302.

The critical situation at the Tredegar, not his injury, prompted Anderson to resign his commission. While he was convalescing at his headquarters near Richmond, John Tanner rode out to brief him on the company's situation. Tanner's recitation of the Tredegar's production difficulties was unsettling, to say the least. After listening to his superintendent's report, Anderson felt he had no choice but to return to the works, as he informed the War Department on July 14. When he first offered his services to the President, he thought satisfactory arrangements had been made for the direction of the company's affairs, he explained in his letter of resignation. But since that time, the acquisition of blast furnaces, "each constituting a heavy and responsible business of itself," had "revolutionized" Tredegar operations and it appeared that the company would also have to mine its own coal. "Since these changes have occurred I cannot doubt as to where I can render most service to the country nor could I do otherwise than give my personal attention to the works, after having been notified, as I have been, by the Gentleman left in general charge, that he cannot continue to discharge the duties without my personal attention," Anderson concluded.[52] "I am grieved to say," he repeated to a fellow officer, "that circumstances (my duty to the country) seem to make it imperative for me to leave the field before the war is terminated and return to my duties at the Tredegar Works." [53] In a warm letter to Anderson, Lee thanked him for his military service but agreed that he could best serve the Confederacy by devoting his time and energy to a solution of the Tredegar's problems.[54] Secretary of War Randolph followed the advice of the commander of the Army of Northern Virginia and accepted Anderson's resignation.

The Tredegar senior partner returned to his works at a critical moment. His company's move into the production of raw materials proved far more difficult than the Richmond industrialists ever imagined. The myriad problems involved in rehabilitating the newly acquired blast furnaces and coal mines taxed the abilities of Anderson and his partners to the limit. Their performance would largely determine the extent of the Tredegar's contribution to the Confederate cause.

52. Anderson to Gen. S. Cooper, July 14, 1862, Field and Staff Officers File, RG 109, NA.

53. Anderson to Branch, July 23, 1862, Branch Papers, NCA.

54. Lee to Anderson, July 15, 1862, quoted in Bruce, p. 376.

8

Provisions and Pig Iron

"It is but for the people of the South to make continued exertions to produce in a short time all the iron they need," predicted the Richmond *Examiner* on November 28, 1862. "Too much capital and labour cannot be invested in this enterprise." The *Examiner's* solution to the Confederacy's increasingly acute iron shortage was essentially correct, but the unbounded optimism of the editor was very much out of place. Capital and labor were indeed needed to develop the mineral resources of the South and the government was willing to supply the capital. Labor was quite another matter, however, and was only one of many problems involved in getting a furnace or coal mine into operation, as Anderson and his partners quickly discovered. The Tredegar owners had to rebuild stacks and replace machinery at furnaces long out of blast, find competent managers, acquire teams and wagons for hauling ore, timber, and pig iron, and, most difficult of all, provide food and clothing for their hundreds of furnace laborers and obtain transportation for these items.

Anderson and Company's attempts to overcome these obstacles achieved only partial success. The result was a perpetual shortage of pig iron at the South's most important manufacturing plant which neither the company nor the government could remedy. For the duration of the war, the Tredegar Iron Works never received enough metal to operate at much more than one third of capacity.[1]

I

Extensive preparations had to be made at each furnace before the blast could commence. Basic furnace machinery first had to be put in order. At eight of the ten Tredegar furnaces, water powered the bellows and sent air

1. Anderson & Co. to Seddon, Dec. 23, 1862, Letters Rec'd., Secretary of War, RG 109, NA; Anderson & Co. to Maj. Snowden Andrews, Jan. 24, 1863, Tredegar Letterbooks. Pig iron receipts are given in Table 7.

blasting through the furnace, blasts which created and maintained the high temperatures necessary to melt iron ore. Only the Australia and Fort furnaces were steam powered and used improved "hot blast" techniques for preheating the furnace charge. Anderson and Company considered Fort furnace, located in the northern Shenandoah Valley, too exposed to the enemy and never attempted to operate the property. But the Australia furnace, located in Alleghany County near the West Virginia border, needed a new engine and the Tredegar management decided to convert both Grace and Glenwood furnaces to steam power so that they could operate when their streams froze in the winter or went dry in the summer. The coal mines also needed engines to pump water from the pits and lift coal to the surface. The Tredegar machine shops reconditioned some old engines, built others, and fabricated cylinders and pipes for several furnaces. Four stacks, the Cloverdale, Grace, Glenwood, and Columbia, were in blast when acquired by Anderson and Company but the other six were in varying states of disrepair. The Catawba, Jane, and Rebecca furnaces in Botetourt County had not made metal for ten years, were dilapidated, and required very extensive rebuilding. And both Australia and Caroline needed substantial work before they would be ready for production.[2] The physical task of rebuilding and equipping the furnaces and mines with machinery was only the first of many difficulties encountered by the Tredegar owners.

II

William Weaver, an experienced Virginia ironmaster, wrote before the war that he had followed various occupations during his lifetime but could say "without hesitation that it requires more capacity and judgment to conduct an extensive ironwork establishment to advantage than any other business in this section of the country." [3] The manager had full responsibility for the entire operation and the ability and drive of this man determined the output of a furnace. Anderson and Company's initial task was to assemble a competent group of furnace superintendents. An excellent first step was the appointment of Francis T. Glasgow as a general agent to as-

2. F. T. Glasgow to Anderson & Co., Jan. 23, 1863, Tredegar Letters re Furnaces; Anderson & Co. to Glasgow, Feb. 13, 1863, Tredegar Letterbooks; entries for Oct.–Nov. 1862, June 1863, Tredegar Foundry Sales Books; Archer Account Book, VHS; Lesley, *Iron Manufacturer's Guide*, pp. 72–73; Bradford, "Ante-Bellum Charcoal Iron Industry," p. 48. For an explanation of hot blast, see Temin, *Iron and Steel in Nineteenth-Century America*, pp. 58–59.

3. Quoted in Bradford, p. 78.

sume overall direction of the five Tredegar stacks in Botetourt and the two furnaces in nearby Rockbridge and Alleghany counties. Glasgow, a native of Rockbridge County and Anderson's nephew, had previously been associated with the Tredegar owner in machine shop operations and had supervised the work of an auxiliary shop near the works since the outbreak of the war. He knew the iron business thoroughly and would prove his competence during the three difficult years that followed. Another agent, Charles Crum, was hired to supervise furnace operations in the northern Shenandoah Valley.

Anderson believed that a competent furnace manager could increase the production of a poorly run stack as much as 50 per cent.[4] The Tredegar head discovered, however, that good furnace men were hard to come by in 1862. Many of the Northern-born ironmasters had left the Valley when the war broke out and the Confederate Army claimed most of the remaining native-born managers. Several of the company's furnaces suffered from inadequate management throughout the war, despite the unceasing efforts of the Tredegar owners to correct this deficiency.

III

The Tredegar partners did not expect the government to assume responsibility for maintaining their furnaces but they did anticipate at least the benevolent neutrality of the War Department once their operations began. "When there are impediments in the way of our making Iron for the Government which it seems to be in the power of the Government to remove we will take the liberty of bringing them to your attention promptly," they informed the Secretary of War soon after the first blast furnaces were purchased.[5] But when the Richmond industrialists instituted their search for food, clothing, and draft animals, they soon discovered that the government offered more hindrance than help.

The company faced a staggering provisioning problem. The total labor force dependent on the Tredegar would soon number over two thousand free and slave workers, plus their families. The management set a ration of six to seven pounds of beef or three pounds of bacon and one and one-half pecks of corn meal per man per week. To meet these quotas and keep the laborers adequately fed in 1863 would require the accumulation of over

4. Anderson & Co. to Capt. William Steptoe, Nov. 12, 1864, Tredegar Letterbooks.

5. Anderson & Co. to Randolph, Aug. 1, 1862, Letters Rec'd., Secretary of War, RG 109, NA.

300,000 pounds of bacon, 600,000 to 700,000 pounds of beef, and some 40,000 bushels of corn, plus additional corn and hay for horses and mules.[6]

The management solved one problem fairly quickly. A supply of salt was acquired from the North Carolina coast by manufacturing salt pans for a number of parties in Wilmington and taking payment in kind.[7] Pork, beef, corn, and other foodstuffs were not so easily acquired, and neither were the horses and mules needed at every Tredegar facility.

The owners had to search beyond Virginia's borders for both provisions and draft animals, and in September 1862, the company secured permission from the War Department to send a purchasing agent into Kentucky. By late September, the agent, Jacob S. Atlee, had crossed the mountains and reached Pound Gap. He had the misfortune, however, to enter Kentucky at the same moment General Braxton Bragg led the Army of Tennessee into the state. The indecisive battle at Perryville on October 8 and Bragg's retreat the following day doomed any chance Atlee might have of tapping the rich stores he saw everywhere in abundance. The Confederate dollar depreciated with every mile Bragg made back toward Tennessee and the Tredegar agent had no choice but to follow the army.

Fortunately, he found hogs and livestock in large numbers in East Tennessee and extreme southwest Virginia and made heavy purchases. Although he had the specific permission of the Secretary of War to buy stock, General Edmund Kirby Smith, the commander of the Department of East Tennessee, ordered his arrest when he attempted to drive his sixty mules and horses and two thousand hogs into Virginia. Confederate military authorities charged Atlee with attempting to remove the livestock illegally from East Tennessee.[8]

6. Anderson & Co. to Maj. B. F. Noland, Sept. 1, 3, 1864, Tredegar Letterbooks; Glasgow to John Bass, Feb. 16, 1864, Tredegar Furnace Letterbook. These individual quotas closely approximated the weekly ration given antebellum slaves; see Eaton, *Growth of Southern Civilization*, p. 59.

7. Agreement with Worth & Daniel, Aug. 22, 26, 1862, Tredegar Order Book; entries for Oct.–Nov. 1862, Tredegar Foundry Sales Books; Anderson & Co. to H. P. Tasker, Nov. 28, 1862, Tredegar Letterbooks.

8. Randolph to Anderson & Co., Sept. 15, 1862, and to Gen. E. Kirby Smith, Nov. 12, 1862, Letters Sent, Secretary of War, RG 109, NA; J. S. Atlee to Kirby Smith, Nov. 29, 1862, and Anderson & Co. to Randolph, Nov. 11, 1862, and endorsement, Letters Rec'd., Secretary of War, ibid.; Atlee to Anderson & Co., Nov. 29, 1862, Anderson Papers, VSL; Anderson & Co. to Atlee, Nov. 27, 1862, to Seddon, Dec. 4, 1862, and to Glasgow, Dec. 6, 1862, Tredegar Letterbooks; entries for Dec. 1862, Tredegar Journals.

Anderson was thoroughly aroused when he learned of Atlee's detention and he wasted no time informing Secretary of War Seddon of the serious consequences of this action. Without the hogs and draft animals, it would be impossible to continue operations, warned the Tredegar senior partner. This protest had the desired effect. Seddon telegraphed General Kirby Smith promptly that the animals "were for use in Works of highest importance to the Government" and were to be released immediately. Kirby Smith freed Atlee and his stock but complained that the agent's extensive acquisitions had advanced the price of pork in his department. As a result the War Department prohibited further Tredegar provisioning in Tennessee.[9]

The company had secured more than enough pork to feed all hands during the coming year, however, so exclusion from Tennessee did not worry the partners. Over two thousand hogs were butchered at the Tredegar plant and furnaces in December 1862 and the meat was sold to free workers at cost. Slaves were fed at company expense but could buy extra meat with their overtime wages if they desired.[10] When the President made an appeal for food for the army in April 1863, Anderson and Company turned over 25,000 pounds of bacon to the War Department and offered an additional two thousand pounds to the city of Richmond for feeding soldiers' families.[11] No shortage of meat occurred in 1863.

The next item on the Tredegar agenda was corn. The Richmond office instructed furnace managers to collect what supplies they could locally and told agents originally sent out to hire slaves to purchase corn whenever possible.[12] Managers of the three furnaces in the rich Shenandoah Valley had little difficulty securing meat, grain, and hay. The six furnaces in Botetourt, Rockbridge, and Alleghany counties were not so easily supplied, however, chiefly because local military officers opposed large Tredegar purchases. When the manager of Cloverdale furnace attended a public sale in Roanoke, the local quartermaster refused to allow him to buy corn and

9. Anderson & Co. to Seddon, Dec. 4, 1862, and to Atlee, Dec. 5, 15, 1862, Tredegar Letterbooks; endorsement of Seddon on R. Heth to Seddon, Dec. 5, 1862, Letters Rec'd., Secretary of War, RG 109, NA.

10. Entry for March 1863, Tredegar Daybooks; Anderson & Co. to P. S. Derbyshire, Dec. 20, 1862, and to William T. Patton, Dec. 22, 1862, Tredegar Letterbooks.

11. *O.R.*, Ser. IV, 2, 477; Anderson & Co. to Seddon, April 14, 1863, and to David J. Saunders, April 9, 1863, Tredegar Letterbooks.

12. Anderson & Co. to William Jordan, Nov. 27, 1862, to Charles Crum, Nov. 27, 1862, to D. J. Hartsook, Nov. 28, 1862, to J. M. Poindexter, Dec. 9, 1862, to Tasker, Dec. 19, 1862, to Glasgow, Dec. 24, 1862, and to W. W. Forbes, Jan. 3, 1863, ibid.

told him that wagons would soon be sent into Botetourt County to impress corn which some farmers were holding off the market. Anderson forwarded this letter to the Secretary of War and included his own angry protest. The Botetourt furnaces would go out of blast at once if supplies could not be secured, he wrote. "It is our duty to remind the Department that if these Furnaces are stopped not another cannon can be made for the Government and in fact nothing else of importance." He requested an immediate order prohibiting impressment of supplies accumulated at the furnaces or purchases by government agents within thirty miles of each furnace and west of the Blue Ridge Mountains.[13]

The Secretary of War refused to meet all of Anderson's demands. He instructed the general commanding the Department of Western Virginia to halt impressments of Tredegar provisions, because "the iron furnaces in western Virginia owned by this firm, are essential to supply iron for government work." But Seddon was unwilling to issue a broad order prohibiting all government purchases or impressments in Botetourt and Alleghany counties, despite protests by Anderson and Company in December that confiscation of their supplies was continuing.[14]

The grain shortage at the Tredegar furnaces became increasingly critical. "I have more concern about a supply of grain than on any other Subject & I am depending on you to devise some means of securing it," was Francis Glasgow's New Year's greeting from the western mountains. Almost 10,000 bushels of corn were purchased in Virginia by the end of January but another 25,000 to 30,000 bushels were still needed. No more corn could be secured in the vicinity of the furnaces. "It appears to me that the success of your business here depends on obtaining grain from North Carolina," Glasgow informed Richmond in late January 1863.[15]

Anderson and Company again had to rely on distant sources of supply and once more face the bureaucratic and military opposition that invariably accompanied their attempts to maintain the far-flung Tredegar operations. Soon after Jacob Atlee returned from Tennessee, Anderson dispatched his capable agent to western North Carolina with orders to pur-

13. Anderson & Co. to Seddon, Dec. 6, 1862, ibid.; Patton to Anderson & Co., Dec. 3, 1862, Letters Rec'd., Secretary of War, RG 109, NA.

14. Seddon to Gen. Samuel Jones, Dec. 10, 1862, Letters Sent, Secretary of War, ibid.; Anderson & Co. to Seddon, Dec. 24, 1862, and endorsements, Letters Rec'd., Secretary of War, ibid.; Anderson & Co. to Seddon, Dec. 12, 31, 1862, Tredegar Letterbooks; Glasgow to Anderson & Co., Jan. 17, 1863, Tredegar Letters re Furnaces.

15. Glasgow to Anderson & Co., Jan. 1, 11, 22, 24, 31, 1863, ibid.

chase 20,000 bushels of corn. Atlee reported back that large quantities of corn were selling in North Carolina for $1.00 to $1.50 per bushel, compared with $2.50 to $3.00 per bushel paid Virginia farmers in the vicinity of the furnaces.[16] The local quartermaster at Tarboro put an abrupt halt to the agent's activities, however, after Atlee had purchased 2,000 bushels. The local officer protested that such large purchases raised the price of corn in his district and the Quartermaster General's office supported him. A thoroughly exasperated Anderson bluntly told the Secretary of War that 4,500 bushels of corn per month were absolutely necessary to maintain the Richmond works, the two coal pits, nine canal boats, and six of the nine Tredegar furnaces dependent on the company for food. After a prolonged correspondence, the Secretary agreed to turn over to the Tredegar agent 8,000 bushels, which together with the 2,000 bushels already purchased would give the company exactly half the quantity originally sought in North Carolina.[17]

The first carload of North Carolina corn arrived in Richmond on April 13, four months after the agent left the capital. Deliveries of the much-needed corn continued for several months but were painfully slow. By the end of May, less than 5,000 bushels had arrived from Tarboro. "Nothing is so important to us now as to get that corn," the company informed Atlee on May 30. The Richmond office instructed Glasgow to advise all furnace managers to be very economical in using supplies until an adequate quantity of corn could be secured.[18]

Anderson and Company turned finally to the lower South in their search for corn, a move which eventually had important effects on Tredegar production. Tanner learned from a Georgia Congressional delegate in April that abundant quantities of corn were available in southwestern Georgia. He immediately dispatched letters informing the presidents of the Macon and Western and the Central of Georgia railroads that the Tredegar had to find some means of feeding over 2,500 company employees. Tanner requested them to purchase a total of 25,000 bushels of corn, to be forwarded up the Western and Atlantic road to Tennessee and then on to

16. Glasgow to Anderson & Co., Jan. 31, 1863, ibid.; Anderson & Co. to Glasgow, Jan. 3, 1863, to Robert Tannahill, Jan. 9, 1863, to E. R. West, Jan. 16, 1863, and to George Chambers, Jan. 16, 1863, Tredegar Letterbooks.

17. Anderson & Co. to Atlee, Feb. 17, March 12, 21, 27, 28, April 9, 10, 1863, and to Maj. Charles S. Carrington, Jan. 21, Feb. 19, March 28, 1863, ibid.

18. Anderson & Co. to Atlee, April 13, 17, May 30, 1863, and to Glasgow, March 31, 1863, ibid.

Lynchburg, where Tredegar canal boats could distribute the grain to Richmond and the furnaces. "For these purchases we would be willing to supply to the Rail Roads transporting it, the value of the corn and freight thereon, in such necessary articles of our manufacture as are as indispensable for their maintenance as the corn is for ours," Tanner told the presidents.[19]

The Georgia railroad men jumped at the chance to acquire scarce iron supplies. Final arrangements were made at a convention of Southern rail executives which assembled in Richmond in late April. President Richard Cuyler of the Central of Georgia Railroad agreed to finance the purchase of 15,000 bushels of corn by a Tredegar agent and receive payment for the grain in spikes, wheels, and bar iron. Other Georgia roads were included in the arrangement and the Tredegar agreed to pay all freight charges in iron. Colonel William M. Wadley, the government's supervisor of railroads, approved the scheme and provided the names of some additional railroad officials who might be of some help in furthering the project.[20]

The first Tredegar agent reached Georgia in early May. All the corn the company needed could be purchased in southwestern Georgia at $2.00 per bushel, he reported soon after his arrival. Promises of Tredegar iron products quickly accomplished all transportation arrangements in Tennessee and Virginia. By the middle of June, eleven carloads of corn were on the way to Richmond, with more due to follow shortly. The Tredegar owners believed their long quest for corn had finally ended.[21]

Federal advances in East Tennessee quickly dispelled any illusions the management entertained about easy transportation from the deep South. The first shipment of Georgia corn reached Knoxville in late June, just after Federal cavalry burned three bridges east of that important rail center on the East Tennessee and Virginia Railroad. Local military officials immediately impressed the shipment of corn for the use of their troops. The bridges were repaired, however, and the company's agent soon had another trainload on the way. The Secretary of War issued an order enjoining all government officers not to interfere with the Tredegar corn.

19. Anderson & Co. to Isaac Scott, March 28, 1863, and to R. R. Cuyler, April 10, 1863, ibid.

20. Anderson & Co. to Virgil Powers, April 13, 1863, to Cuyler, April 23, 1863, to Campbell Wallace, April 22, 1863, to John J. Woodruff, April 22, 24, 1863, to R. Peters, May 8, 1863, and to Maj. J. S. Rowland, May 12, 1863, ibid.; Black, *Railroads of the Confederacy*, pp. 119–20.

21. Anderson & Co. to Glasgow, May 19, 21, 1863, to Woodruff, May 19, 28, June 4, 20 1863, and to W. P. Woodruff, June 16, 1863, Tredegar Letterbooks.

Shipments finally began arriving at Lynchburg in August but shortly thereafter, General Ambrose Burnside's forces took Knoxville, closing the Tennessee route. The Tredegar partners doubtless wondered if their vexing supply problems would ever end. The corn was now directed to Richmond by the eastern rail network and a new group of railroads joined the "iron for corn" plan.[22]

Despite the seemingly endless series of setbacks, the Tredegar secured some 14,000 of the needed 20,000 bushels of corn from Georgia during 1863.[23] This vital supply permitted the Tredegar blast furnaces, coal mines, canal boats, and the Richmond plant to continue in operation. Anderson and Company confidently expected to increase their purchases in Georgia in 1864.

As early as the spring of 1863, the firm began bartering for produce. "Notice to planters and others," the company advertised in the Richmond press. "We will exchange coal, iron or nails, for corn, corn meal, hay, flour, beef or bacon, for the supply of our iron works in Western Virginia and in this city, on fair terms." [24] The first nail machine, manufactured at the Tredegar machine shops, went into production in April 1863 and nails quickly became the standard item of Tredegar agricultural exchange.[25]

In planning for their 1864 operations, Anderson and his partners were willing to commit the resources of their works as fully as need be to secure provisions. "If we await the movements of the quartermaster here, we will all starve," one of the partners told a company agent.[26] The Richmond office informed purchasing agents they had unlimited stocks of iron at their disposal for bartering. In late 1863 and early 1864, a Tredegar commissary agent insured a supply of meat by purchasing large numbers of beef cattle and hogs in southwest Virginia and North Carolina and a sizable delivery of Tredegar iron secured salt from the works at Saltville, Virginia.[27]

22. Anderson & Co. to Glasgow, June 23, 1863, to Col. A. C. Myers, June 23, 1863, to G. Jordan, July 9, 1863, to Powers, July 20, 1863, and to J. H. Jamison, July 28, 1863, ibid.; Seddon to Anderson & Co., July 28, 1863, Letters Sent, Secretary of War, RG 109, NA; Gen. Braxton Bragg to Anderson & Co., Aug. 14, 1863, and J. R. Bell to Anderson & Co., Aug. 19, 1863, Brock Papers, HL.

23. Anderson & Co. to Powers, Dec. 19, 1863, Tredegar Letterbooks.

24. Richmond *Dispatch*, Jan. 28, 1864.

25. Anderson & Co. to Thomas Dodamead, April 25, 1863, Tredegar Letterbooks; Archer Account Books, VHS.

26. Anderson & Co. to Bell, Nov. 14, 1863, Tredegar Letterbooks.

27. Anderson & Co. to Glasgow, March 7, 1864, and to J. Armstrong, Oct. 1, 1864, ibid.;

An April 1865 view of the Tredegar works from the banks of the James River, taken by Alexander Gardner. The building at the left on the water housed the blacksmith shop and the brass foundry. The new gun foundry with its prominent furnace stack stands in the center. The machine shops are located just behind the new gun foundry, parallel to the blacksmith shop and the brass foundry. The large stack at the far right belongs to the old foundry. The rafters of the new pattern shop are in the right background, behind the old foundry, probably under construction on the foundations of the Crenshaw Woolen Factory, which burned in 1863.

A Mathew B. Brady photograph of the Tredegar works, taken in the summer of 1865. In addition to the buildings shown in the previous photograph, this view includes the Tredegar office building (the two-story brick building in the center), part of the Confederate States Armory (formerly the Virginia State Armory, originally called the Virginia Manufactory of Arms) at the extreme right and the Armory rolling mill (the twin-roofed, open-ended structure at the right). The spike mill is seen just above the Armory mill's roof line, and Lewis Crenshaw's grain elevator and warehouse is the tall, brick building in the center background. In the foreground are the ruins of the Confederate ordnance depot.

A May 1865 view of the western end of the Tredegar works, looking across the James River and Kanawha Canal and Harvie's Pond, taken by the photographic firm of Levy and Cohen, Philadelphia. Pig iron, coal, and other raw materials were transported to Tredegar along the canal, and water from the canal powered the mill's waterwheels. Two freight boats are docked on Harvie's Pond, the turning basin above the works, and the large building to the far left is the spike mill. A multi unit row of worker housing stands on the left bank of the canal; the fenced enclosure and small, chapel-like building behind the tenement suggests a domestic compound, probably for enslaved workers. The tall brick building to the left and behind the worker housing is Lewis Crenshaw's grain elevator and warehouse.

A view of the Tredegar works looking south, with Belle Isle in the background. The spike factory stands along the canal in the right side of picture, and the old foundry, with its prominent furnace stack, appears on the left. The pattern building, built on the foundations of the Crenshaw Woolen Factory, is to the right of the old foundry. The low roof of the Tredegar rolling mill extends between the spike mill and pattern building. The finished brick wall along the canal and the reconstructed pattern building suggest a postbellum date.

Obtaining Georgia and South Carolina corn was again the most critical problem. "The time that the Furnaces can get into blast will depend very much upon the speed with which you can forward corn to them," Glasgow reported in early February 1864.[28] When Tredegar agents entered the deep South in December 1863, they carried substantial quantities of nails and bar iron with them and thus encountered little difficulty engaging large amounts of corn. Key railroads promised every aid in getting the provisions to Richmond but performance often fell short of prediction. The first shipments of Georgia corn did not reach Richmond until mid-March 1864 and Glasgow was forced to delay new blasts at the Tredegar furnaces until the grain arrived.[29]

Although periodic grain shortages occurred in the spring and fall, Anderson and Company succeeded in feeding over two thousand laborers and their dependents throughout 1864. Even in the bitter winter months when Lee's troops were desperately short of food and operatives at the government's Richmond shops threatened hunger strikes, free and slave Tredegar workers were generally well supplied with corn meal, pork, and beef.[30] This provisioning, accomplished only after extended delays and the cutting of much bureaucratic red tape, strained the managerial talents of Anderson and his partners to the limit. Their success was certainly among the most notable of the Tredegar's wartime achievements.

IV

Threats to Tredegar furnace operations came from some unexpected quarters. Confederate cavalry horses, fattening up in infirmary camps near the company's stacks in late 1863 and early 1864, seemed to Glasgow to be a greater danger than Federal troopers. "Suddenly there came an influx of cavalry—they spread like locusts over the land," he reported in Febru-

---

Glasgow to Anderson & Co., Aug. 2[?], 1863, Tredegar Furnace Letterbook; entries for Dec. 1863, June 1864, Tredegar Journals.

28. Glasgow to Anderson & Co., Feb. 2, 1864, Tredegar Furnace Letterbook.

29. Glasgow to Anderson & Co., April 26, May 5, 10, 1864, and to W. M. Bryan, June 3, 1864, ibid.; Anderson & Co. to Tasker, March 16, 1864, to C. O. Sanford, March 17, 1864, to A. H. Anderson, Sept. 14, 1864, to Glasgow, Oct. 7, 1864, to Noland, Nov. 17, 1864, to Charles G. Talcott, Jan. 2, 1865, and to R. R. Bridges, Nov. 1, 1865, Tredegar Letterbooks.

30. Anderson & Co. to Noland, Sept. 1, 1864, to Glasgow, Oct. 7, 1864, to Sanford, Dec. 15, 1864, and to Talcott, Jan. 2, 1865, ibid.; W. LeRoy Broun, "The Red Artillery; Confederate Ordnance During the War," *Southern Historical Society Papers, 26* (1898), 373; Clifford H. Dowdey and Louis H. Manarin, eds., *The Wartime Papers of R. E. Lee* (Boston, 1961), pp. 877, 883, 890.

ary 1864. These horses succeeded in "consuming everything like food in that section." [31] And although the Adjutant and Inspector General's office had issued orders specifically exempting from impressment all supplies of government iron and munitions contractors and despite individual exemptions granted by the Niter and Mining Bureau to each Tredegar furnace, Confederate cavalry officers impressed large amounts of the company's grain and forage.[32]

A verbal hassle ensued after Anderson and Company lodged an immediate and angry protest.[33] General J. E. B. Stuart countercharged that Tredegar agents had accumulated a surfeit of supplies at the furnaces in Augusta, Rockbridge, Botetourt, "and doubtless many more counties." Starving cavalry horses had some claim on these excessive stores, Stuart maintained.[34]

Stuart, it turned out, had a good case. Anderson and Company's quartermasters had long been outbidding army agents for limited local stores, despite extensive government schedules published in 1863 and 1864 establishing maximum prices for food, clothing, and other articles needed by the military. Tredegar purchasing agents simply ignored these rates until the summer of 1864 when the government made a concerted attempt to restrict prices allowed by private contractors to the published schedules. "This order will effectually bar all further purchases by us if it is applied to your agents as we cannot buy a bushel of grain or a pound of meat at Govt. rates," Glasgow informed the partners in Richmond.[35] The Tredegar management circumvented this order immediately by instructing their agents to offer farmers iron and nails at prices considerably below open market rates in return for their produce.[36] This method proved so successful that the army's Subsistence Department later asked Anderson and Company for twenty tons of bar iron to assist officers bartering for supplies.[37]

31. Glasgow to Anderson & Co., Feb. 11, 1864, Tredegar Furnace Letterbook; Anderson & Co. to the Secretaries of War and Navy, Dec. 9, 1864, Tredegar Letterbooks.

32. Anderson & Co. to Forbes, April 8, 1863, to Glasgow, April 29, June 25, 1863, and to Seddon, June 3, 1863, ibid.; Glasgow to Anderson & Co., May 13, 1863, Tredegar Letters re Furnaces; *O.R.*, Ser. IV, *2*, 511.

33. Anderson & Co. to Carrington, Feb. 20, 1864, Tredegar Letterbooks.

34. *O.R.*, Ser. I, *51*, pt. ii, 860.

35. Glasgow to Anderson & Co., Aug. 24, 1864, Tredegar Furnace Letterbook.

36. Glasgow to Bryan, Aug. 24, 1864, ibid.; Anderson & Co. to Glasgow, Aug. 20, 1864, Tredegar Letterbooks.

37. Anderson & Co. to Capt. James Sowers, Jan. 20, 1865, ibid.

V

The Tredegar management overcame some supply deficiencies in 1863 and 1864 with less difficulty than that encountered in repairing food shortages. With shoes virtually unavailable on the open market, the company had to make some provision for footwear for both the slave and free labor force. Large amounts of leather were also required for harnesses and machine belting. When they were unable to purchase sufficient quantities of leather, the Tredegar owners established a tannery at their Richmond works and purchased two others, one at Buchanan and another at Covington, Virginia. Slaves, working under the direction of a white tanner, provided most of the labor for these three facilities. Richmond's canine population was threatened by this new Tredegar venture. "Wanted—Hides of all kinds, for which the highest market prices will be paid. Horse, mule, and dog skins will be readily bought," read a Tredegar advertisement.[38] Hides of animals slaughtered to feed Tredegar hands were delivered to the tanneries and hooves were converted into glue for use on gun carriages. A shoe and harness shop, manned by Negro slaves, was established at Cloverdale furnace.[39]

Securing ample clothing for the slave labor force also presented a constant problem. The management acquired some cotton cloth in Petersburg by sending shafting and other needed iron products to factories there and the company instructed Tredegar purchasing agents to buy cloth as well as food whenever possible.[40] But cloth shortages persisted and Anderson and his partners used this deficiency in an attempt to gain shipping privileges on government blockade-runners in 1863 and 1864.[41]

When the Army of Northern Virginia crossed the Potomac in June 1863, Tredegar purchasing agents trailed closely behind. Charles Crum, chief furnace agent in the lower Shenandoah Valley, and two employees from the Richmond plant visited Hagerstown, Chambersburg, and other cities on Lee's invasion route. When Crum asked for a want list, the Trede-

38. Richmond *Dispatch*, March 21, 1864.

39. Glasgow to Anderson & Co., Jan. 9, 22, 24, 31, April 3, 1863, Tredegar Letters re Furnaces; Anderson & Co. to Armstrong, Dec. 5, 1863, Tredegar Letterbooks.

40. Glasgow to Anderson & Co., Jan. 1, May 25, 1863, Tredegar Letters re Furnaces; Anderson & Co. to Atlee, March 17, 1863, and to Lynch & Callender, March 18, 1863, Tredegar Letterbooks.

41. See below, pp. 198–209.

gar management replied "we need everything." The agents returned in July with paint, tools, and other badly needed materials.[42]

VI

Union cavalry menaced the areas where Tredegar furnaces were located as early as the spring of 1862. In May of that year, the slaves and teams at Grace furnace were evacuated when raiding Federal troopers reached Covington, only sixteen miles from the furnace. Operations at Australia furnace in Alleghany County were also suspended during the raid, but both stacks escaped destruction.[43]

The company's most vulnerable furnaces were those in the northern Shenandoah Valley region and these properties received the first of many Federal torches that fired Tredegar holdings. Fort furnace near Strasburg was never put into blast because of its exposed position, but the Columbia furnace and forge and Caroline furnace, all in Shenandoah County, were vital elements in the Tredegar operation. Columbia produced some gun iron and most of the blooms used in banding heavy rifled cannon and manufacturing boiler plate; Caroline iron was employed in railroad car wheels. Cavalry forays caused the evacuation of these furnaces in December 1862 and March 1863 but no damage resulted.[44] Then, late in November 1863, a large party of Federals captured some eighty head of cattle near Columbia but did not reach the furnace. Two weeks later, the Tredegar's luck ran out. Union raiders found and burned the Columbia property. The management in Richmond ordered pickets posted at their other furnaces so that the alarm could be sounded in time to evacuate, but no further destruction took place in 1863. Rebuilding of the Columbia machinery began at once and the furnace and forge were operating again early in 1864.[45]

Disaster struck the Tredegar furnace operations in the summer of 1864. The catastrophe took the form of a large Union raiding party sent by Major General David Hunter from West Virginia to capture Lynchburg

42. Anderson & Co. to Crum, June 23, 1863, and to Capt. R. Turk, June 23, 1863, Tredegar Letterbooks; Glasgow to Anderson & Co., July 3, 1863, Tredegar Furnace Letterbook; entries for Nov.–Dec. 1863, Tredegar Journals.

43. Anderson & Co. to Gorgas, May 26, 1863, Letters Rec'd., Secretary of War, RG 109, NA.

44. Anderson & Co. to Crum, Dec. 6, 10, 13, 29, 1862, March 16, 26, April 1, 1863, Tredegar Letterbooks.

45. Anderson & Co. to Glasgow, Nov. 24, Dec. 11, 19, 1863, to Armstrong, Dec. 17, 1863, and to Crum, Dec. 28, 1863, ibid.; Tredegar Pig Iron Receipt Book.

and disrupt railroad communications in western Virginia. A mixed force of cavalry and infantry left West Virginia in early June and cut through the gaps in the western slopes of the Blue Ridge Mountains. The Federals defeated a Confederate force under "Grumble" Jones near Staunton on June 5 and occupied the town the next day. "There is a good deal of uneasiness felt here in consequence of a reverse we met with near Staunton on Sunday," Glasgow wrote from Botetourt County on June 7. But the Tredegar furnace agent understood that sufficient reinforcements were moving up to check the enemy advance and he made no attempt to evacuate the furnaces.[46] This error proved costly. The Union troopers' invasion route took them through the heart of Virginia's iron country and they surprised three Tredegar furnaces. Cloverdale furnace, the South's chief supplier of gun metal, Grace furnace, another producer of cannon iron, and Mount Torry furnace, purchased in December 1863, were left in smoldering ruins. Many of the slaves escaped and the raiders captured large numbers of draft animals and destroyed extensive stores of provisions.[47]

The management ordered an immediate assessment of damages and learned that the Yankees had done a thorough job. They decided nevertheless to attempt to rebuild these three key furnaces and secured a loan of $150,000 from the Niter and Mining Bureau to assist them in the task. The work proceeded very slowly.[48] Before the new machinery could be completed at the Richmond works, the Federals struck again, this time in the northern Shenandoah Valley. Sheridan's troops destroyed Columbia furnace in October, the second time this property had suffered destruction at the hands of the enemy. Again, the cavalry failed to reach Caroline furnace but the Tredegar management considered it too exposed and after working up the stock of ore and charcoal at the site, abandoned the property.[49] Not one of the furnaces destroyed in 1864 got back into blast before the end of the war.

The Tredegar works and, in turn, the Confederate cause suffered an ir-

46. Glasgow to Anderson & Co., June 7, 1864, Tredegar Furnace Letterbook.

47. *O.R.*, Ser. I, *37*, pt. i, 96–97, 139–41, 144–47, 155; Anderson & Co. to W. O. Harvey, Sept. 10, 1864, to Gen. J. L. Kemper, Dec. 2, 1864, and to Mrs. T. L. Skinner, Dec. 4, 1864, Tredegar Letterbooks; Glasgow to Anderson & Co., Jan. 19, 1865, Tredegar Furnace Letterbook.

48. Glasgow to Anderson & Co., July 21, 23, Sept. 1, 1864, ibid.; Anderson & Co. to Glasgow, Jan. 7, Feb. 4, 1865, Tredegar Letterbooks; entries for Jan., March, 1865, Tredegar Foundry Sales Books.

49. Anderson & Co. to Glasgow, Oct. 10, 31, 1864, and to Col. Richard Morton, Nov. 4, 14, 1864, Tredegar Letterbooks.

reparable loss in the destruction of these blast furnaces. By November 1864, only five of the eleven furnaces acquired by Anderson and Company during the war were in blast and two of the five had never performed satisfactorily and could not be counted on for much iron.[50] In an effort to bolster their supply of metal, the Tredegar partners acquired two properties in late 1864. They leased Clay forge, located in Augusta County, as a bloomery in September and rented an Alleghany County furnace, Roaring Run, noted for its car wheel iron, in December.[51] Production of metal at these two sites was negligible, however, and total Tredegar pig iron production was again far below the management's expectations. The works received only 3,127 long tons of iron from its own furnaces in 1864 and receipts of pig and scrap from all sources amounted to only 7,238 tons. (See Table 7.)

TABLE 7. Iron Receipts at the Tredegar Iron Works, 1859–1866 (in tons of 2,240 lbs.)

Year	*Received from Confederate government*	*Received from Tredegar furnaces*	*Total*
1859	—	—	7,557
1860	—	—	9,674
1861	—	—	6,134 *
1862	855	981	6,522
1863	1,737	3,636	7,677
1864	1,121	3,127	7,238
January–April 1865	164	54 **	411
August 1865–December 1866	—	—	10,214

* Of this total, 971 tons were received during January–March 1861.
** 1,136 tons of metal were still at Tredegar furnaces at the close of the war.
Sources: Tredegar Pig Iron Receipt Book, Inventory Book, Ledgers, Journals, and "Shipments and Receipts, Pig Iron, 1863–64," in Tredegar Letters re Furnaces.

VII

By late 1864, Anderson and his partners had become thoroughly disillusioned about the prospects for manufacturing pig iron during the coming

50. Anderson & Co. to Morton, Nov. 14, 1864, ibid.

51. Anderson & Co. to John D. Brooks, Sept. 3, 1864, to Col. I. M. St. John, Oct. 20, 1864, to W. S. Watkins, Dec. 20, 1864, and to Glasgow, Dec. 23, 28, 1864, ibid.; entries for Dec. 1864, Jan., Aug., 1865, Tredegar Journals.

year. The seemingly overwhelming task of provisioning for 1865 was the chief cause of their disenchantment. Anderson and Company estimated in September 1864 that the Tredegar's more than two thousand laborers and six hundred horses and mules would require 80,000 bushels of corn and 15,000 bushels of wheat. To provide an adequate meat ration for the men, more than 300,000 pounds of bacon and 600,000 pounds of beef were needed.[52] The owners had overcome a similar challenge in 1864, but they were anything but confident about repeating their performance in the year ahead.

The management nevertheless launched a two-pronged attack on this provisioning problem in the fall. First, they informed the Commissary Department of the quantities of foodstuffs needed and asked for assistance. This, they advised, the government could provide in two ways—either by allocating stores in the lower South to the firm and providing transportation north, or, preferably, by turning over to Anderson and Company meat and grain collected in the vicinity of the furnaces under the 10 per cent tax in kind on agricultural produce.[53] Second, John Tanner headed south in October to look after some Tredegar cotton speculations and to do what he could about securing food.[54]

Initially, the owners were optimistic about both efforts. Tanner returned to Richmond in late November and reported that he had "succeeded in effecting arrangements for all the provisions we require." [55] Prior to his return, the Quartermaster Department, to minimize competition from Tredegar purchasing agents, proposed to turn over to Anderson and Company at cost 4,000 bushels of corn monthly in South Carolina. The department offered to meet additional Tredegar needs by a large supplementary transfer of corn to the firm in Georgia, also at cost. Lee's army had preempted North Carolina supplies and that state was declared off limits to Tredegar agents. The company accepted this offer with alacrity.[56] Anderson and his partners also had hopes of securing part of the local tax in kind because agents of the Niter and Mining Bureau had received au-

52. Anderson & Co. to Noland, Sept. 1, 3, 1864, Tredegar Letterbooks.

53. Ibid.; Glasgow to Anderson & Co., Sept. 20, 1864, Tredegar Furnace Letterbook.

54. Anderson & Co. to Glasgow, Oct. 10, 1864, and to John J. Walker, Nov. 26, 1864, Tredegar Letterbooks; entry for Nov. 1864, Tredegar Journals. The company's cotton speculations are discussed below, pp. 199–209.

55. Anderson & Co. to John J. Walker, Nov. 26, 1864, Tredegar Letterbooks.

56. Anderson & Co. to Maj. I. H. Carrington, Oct. 19, 1864, and to A. Sydney Robertson, Dec. 12, 1864, ibid.

thority to collect "tithes" and purchase supplies from detailed farmers in order to support government-controlled furnaces.[57]

Within the space of one week, the company's various plans for securing food collapsed and fresh obstacles arose. The worst news came from Georgia. An agent sent south to forward both the supplies promised by the Quartermaster Department and foodstuffs purchased earlier by Tanner reported in late November on the swath of destruction Sherman's troops had cut through Georgia. Demolition of mile after mile of two key lines, the Georgia Railroad connecting Atlanta with Augusta and the Georgia Central Railroad running from Macon to Savannah, had completely severed rail communication with the southwestern part of the state, where the company had contracted for large stores. In addition, the enemy had consumed or destroyed Tredegar provisions awaiting shipment along the Georgia Railroad.[58] The attention which Sherman purposely lavished on the ruin of Georgia's rail network was not misplaced. By disrupting the Tredegar's line of supply for the duration of the war, he dealt the already tottering Confederate munitions industry a near-fatal blow.

The news from Georgia was compounded by equally bleak tidings from western Virginia. On December 2, Glasgow reported the arrival of General Jubal Early's foraging cavalry in the vicinity of the Tredegar furnaces. "This brings up the question of feed again & I think it my duty to urge you to consider this question gravely before making engagements for another years work here," he wrote. The capable furnace agent proceeded to outline in detail the chief difficulty facing his operations and he recommended drastic action:

> Unless you can provide a sufficient supply of grain you cannot succeed in making iron & all your labor here will only end in trouble and loss—last year there was a large crop of corn & we secured considerable local supplies; there is no surplus grain here now—and in long forage the Government agents have been so diligent that I think there is very little surplus not sold to us which has not been seized & if a part of Early's Cavalry is to forage here this winter you may rest assured there will not be long forage left to subsist our teams. Do you see your way clear for a regular supply of corn for the furnaces from Georgia—if not I would say by all means try to turn over your

57. Glasgow to Anderson & Co., Sept. 20, Nov. 2[?], 1864, Tredegar Furnace Letterbook.

58. Anderson & Co. to J. R. Bell, Dec. 2, 1864, Jan. 19, 1865, Tredegar Letterbooks; Black, *Railroads of the Confederacy*, pp. 259–60.

> furnaces to the N & M Bureau & make some arrangement with them for a part of the product. I know the importance to you to secure a supply of pig iron, but is the assurance of a reasonable supply of iron from these furnaces sufficient to justify the large expenditures necessary to support them the coming year—I don't think the five furnaces [Cloverdale, Grace, Catawba, Rebecca, and Glenwood] have yielded over 2000 tons Iron the present year. I wish only to impress upon you that an irregular and uncertain supply of corn will not accomplish what you have in view in undertaking the heavy responsibility of continuing your Blast Furnaces & that their product with such a supply will not justify the undertaking.[59]

Glasgow's advice to relinquish the furnaces to the government unless a supply of Georgia corn was assured came just as the Tredegar management learned of Sherman's depredations.

Word from the Quartermaster Department destroyed Anderson and Company's last hope for supplies. In early December, the Quartermaster General ruled that food and forage could not be impressed for Tredegar furnaces nor could any part of the 10 per cent tax in kind be relinquished for private use.[60] This decision effectively closed off the last possibility that the company could provision in Virginia.

The Richmond office decided to follow Glasgow's counsel. "By agreement with the War & Navy Depts we have been operating certain furnaces in this state since 1862, for the purpose of supplying these works with pig metal," began Anderson and Company's letter of December 9 to the Secretaries of the War and Navy Departments. "But we find it impractical to continue these operations longer . . . and respectfully ask that the Govt. release us of them." The Tredegar owners cited two primary reasons why they wished to stop manufacturing pig iron. The first was "the difficulty of obtaining provisions." Government agents gleaned practically all the food raised in the neighborhood of the furnaces and foraging cavalry horses finished off what little remained. The company therefore had to acquire stores at long distances and undergo enormous trouble and expense to transport them to Virginia. Once supplies arrived, impressing officers seized them "under the plea of military necessity." Serious delays and frequent disruptions of furnace operations resulted. The firm's second reason for abandoning production of pig metal concerned labor: "We also fear

59. Glasgow to Anderson & Co., Dec. 2, 1864, Tredegar Furnace Letterbook.

60. Anderson & Co. to Carrington, Dec. 3, 1864, Tredegar Letterbooks.

that in consequence of the Raid by the enemy the present year in the vicinity of our Furnaces, by which we have lost many negroes, we shall be unable to hire hands [for] the coming year unless owners are guaranteed against loss."

The management therefore proposed that the government lease the Tredegar furnaces for a rent amounting to 20 per cent of the iron produced. The remaining 80 per cent would also be turned over to Anderson and Company at a price fixed by the government. The firm promised to use three fourths of the latter amount on military work and apply the remainder to railroad supplies and to the maintenance of Richmond works. Because of the present state of affairs in the Confederate States, the partners believed that their furnace operations "may be conducted more successfully on Govt account than on our own—the latter mode having become in our judgment totally impracticable." [61]

"We are applying to the Govt. to take our furnaces with, we fear, but little prospect of success," the company informed Glasgow on the same day they wrote the Secretaries.[62] They were correct in this assessment. The Secretary of War declined to lease the furnaces but he did promise aid to the Tredegar managers in their quest for food and forage. Seddon reversed the earlier decision not to permit Anderson and Company's furnaces to receive supplies collected under the tax in kind or by Niter and Mining Bureau agents. Hereafter, the Tredegar stacks were to have the same status as those contracting directly with the government mining service. He further ordered the Quartermaster General to authorize the distribution of almost 20,000 bushels of corn and over 500,000 pounds of hay to the Tredegar's furnaces and canal boats.[63]

Although Anderson and his partners welcomed the Secretary of War's promise of aid, the government's action was largely a repetition of the familiar Confederate pattern of too little and too late. Had the War Department taken measures to assure the furnaces food and forage in 1862, the history of Anderson and Company's pig iron operations might have been something other than a series of delayed and inadequate blasts brought on largely by insufficient supplies. Time, resources, and energy which the Tredegar management devoted to provisioning could have been directed

61. Anderson & Co. to the Secretaries of War and Navy, Dec. 9, 1864, ibid.

62. Anderson & Co. to Glasgow, Dec. 9, 1864, ibid.

63. Anderson & Co. to Maj. J. Wilcox Brown, Dec. 21, 1864, to Morton, Dec. 17, 1864, and to Glasgow, Dec. 19, 23, 1864, ibid.

instead to tasks more intimately connected with military production. The War Department's laissez-faire policy toward the needs of private contractors precluded such an optimum allocation, however. When the government finally reversed this stand, the collapse of the Confederate nation was less than four months away.

As soon as the government guaranteed at least a portion of the needed furnace supplies, the Tredegar management moved to prepare for the coming year's blasts. They hoped to keep all their furnaces in operation except the two most exposed stacks in the Shenandoah Valley.[64] "We are anxious to get as much iron made as possible before the Yankees cripple us again," they told their furnace superintendent in late December.[65] By mid-January, workmen at the Richmond plant had completed new machinery for two of the furnaces destroyed by the Federals the previous year and were finishing up equipment for a third.[66]

Several furnaces went into blast in January, but severe operational difficulties arose before the month was out. The Quartermaster General's office did not issue final orders permitting Anderson and Company to draw on the tax in kind until January 12, 1865.[67] By that time, the furnaces were desperately short of grain and forage. "I fear you do not appreciate our condition," Glasgow wrote the Richmond office on January 19. "Let me impress upon you again that we cannot make iron & can make but little preparation for it, nor can we send you the iron now made until you can supply corn." The teams had been worked on short rations for months and were in "very low order," he reported. Without grain to rebuild their strength, they could not work much longer.[68]

Authority to draw on government depots for food failed to remedy this grave situation. By the time the Quartermaster General's orders arrived in western Virginia, local quartermasters in the vicinity of the furnaces had already collected and appropriated the tithes to military agencies. The only large stores still in quartermasters' warehouses were in remote counties along the West Virginia border, Glasgow reported, and the officer in charge of this region refused to surrender forage to the company. He did not construe the order from Richmond as binding but on only as giving

64. Anderson & Co. to Crum, Dec. 27, 1864, ibid.

65. Anderson & Co. to Glasgow, Dec. 27, 1864, ibid.

66. Anderson & Co. to St. John, Jan. 10, 1865, ibid. The completed machinery was for Cloverdale and Mt. Torry furnaces but was not erected at the stacks until after the war.

67. Anderson & Co. to Glasgow, Jan. 11, 1865, ibid.

68. Glasgow to Anderson & Co., Jan. 19, 1865, Tredegar Furnace Letterbook.

him authority to deliver food to Tredegar furnaces and he refused to do so without positive and specific orders.[69] An irate letter to the Quartermaster General produced no results.[70] "We are living from hand to mouth now & dont know where our provisions are to come from a week ahead," Glasgow wrote in February.[71]

One source of food remained. Anderson and Company had purchased several thousand bushels of grain in South Carolina in 1864, and the government had also promised to furnish some supplies to the company there. The Tredegar management ordered its agents to use every possible means to forward the foodstuffs to Richmond, but the North Carolina and the Piedmont railroads, the only route open, were so clogged with military freight that the company's stores could not get through. Corn, rice, bacon, and sugar accumulated at Charlotte until early January when a fire roared through the warehouse district there. The blaze consumed 6,000 bushels of Tredegar corn and all the rest of the firm's supplies.[72] This loss broke the back of the company's provisioning operation, as they informed Glasgow in a plaintive letter late in January. "We fully appreciate the difficulties of your situation without feed—but what can we do? The Roads have done nothing for several months—now we have lost much by the fire at Charlotte & have almost to begin de novo." [73] A last hope, for some 3,000 bushels of grain believed safe in Greensboro, disappeared by February.[74]

The end of the Tredegar's usefulness to the Confederacy was near at hand. Good blasts began at several of the company's stacks in 1865 but because of short grain and forage rations, draft animals could move only small tonnages of metal to the James River and Kanawha Canal. The severe winter of 1864–65 kept this vital artery frozen into February.[75] The consequences for Confederate military production were disastrous. Only fifty-four tons of Tredegar-produced iron reached the Richmond works during 1865. (See Table 7.)

69. Glasgow to Anderson & Co., Jan. 20, 1865, ibid.

70. Anderson & Co. to Gen. A. R. Lawton, Jan. 26, 1865, Tredegar Letterbooks.

71. Glasgow to Crum, Feb. 9, 1865, Tredegar Furnace Letterbook.

72. Anderson & Co. to Shay & Williamson, Jan. 7, 1865, to J. R. London, Jan. 10, 1865, to Glasgow, Jan. 11, 12, 1865, and to Capt. James Sowers, Jan. 18, 1865, Tredegar Letterbooks; Jones, *Diary*, 2, 382.

73. Anderson & Co. to Glasgow, Jan. 24, 1865, Tredegar Letterbooks.

74. Ibid.; Glasgow to Anderson & Co., Feb. 17, 1865, Tredegar Furnace Letterbook.

75. Glasgow to Crum, Feb. 9, 1865, ibid.

VIII

The War and Navy Departments promised in the April 1862 contract to provide the Tredegar works with substantial quantities of pig iron. Although Anderson and Company assumed primary responsibility for supplying their own metal, the government agreed to supplement the blasts of Tredegar furnaces with enough iron to enable the foundries and rolling mills to meet their military production quotas.[76] The Tredegar owners took the Secretaries at their word and sent frequent applications for pig metal to the military store in Richmond and to the local iron depot of the Niter Bureau.[77] When these appeals failed to elicit a steady flow of government pig to the works, Anderson informed the Ordnance Bureau in October 1862 that failure to receive this metal would seriously threaten Tredegar production.[78] His Richmond facilities could use two thousand long tons of metal per month. Half that amount the company expected to receive from their own stacks; the other half would have to come from government-controlled furnaces.[79] He requested that as a partial solution to the Tredegar's iron problem, the government transfer all its contracts with Virginia furnace owners to his firm. Gorgas thought such a transfer would "doubtless be advantageous to the public interest," but the Secretary of War refused to guarantee the Tredegar the total product of Virginia's none too numerous blast furnaces.[80]

When the iron shortage forced a complete halt in Tredegar rolling mill production in January 1863, alarmed Confederate authorities promised to work out a system of priorities on the allocation of government pig metal.[81] Major Isaac M. St. John, chief of the Niter Bureau, assured Anderson that all pig iron received by the bureau and not required by the more urgent demands of the government's shops would be turned over to

76. Contract with the War and Navy Departments, April 29, 1862, in "J. R. Anderson & Co.," Confederate Citizens File, RG 109, NA.

77. Anderson & Co. to Maj. W. S. Downer, June 24, July 4, 1862, and receipts given to Col. Richard Morton for pig iron furnished by Confederate States, Jan. 27, 1863, Tredegar Letterbooks; Tredegar Pig Iron Receipt Book.

78. Anderson & Co. to Gorgas, Oct. 15, 1862, Letters Rec'd., Secretary of War, RG 109, NA. See also Anderson & Co. to Seddon, Dec. 23, 1862, Jan. 9, 14, 1863, ibid.

79. Anderson & Co. to Maj. Snowden Andrews, Jan. 24, 1863, Tredegar Letterbooks.

80. Anderson & Co. to Gorgas, Oct. 15, 1863, and endorsements, Letters Rec'd., Secretary of War, RG 109, NA.

81. Anderson & Co. to Gorgas and Capt. George Minor, Jan. 28, 1863, Tredegar Letterbooks.

the Tredegar. "This is entirely satisfactory to us," replied Anderson. He expected any claim superior to the Tredegar's, "if there be any higher," to be met first, and he would accept the judgment of Colonel Gorgas in this matter.[82]

St. John failed to back up his promises with much iron. During the first few months after the Niter Bureau set up its priority schedule, the various Confederate agencies controlling iron turned over several hundred tons to the company, although most of this metal would never have reached Richmond if the Tredegar's small boat fleet had not floated it from the mountain furnaces to the canal.[83] But the Tredegar's capacity was measured in thousands, not hundreds, of tons. In January 1863, Anderson and Company made specific application to the War Department for the blasts of four Virginia furnaces; John Tanner informed the Secretary of War in October that the company was still looking for the first ton of this iron and that the government had not even replied to the January letters. "The execution of our Contract with the Army and Navy is interfered with, by the delay on the part of the Government to deliver this metal," he concluded.[84]

When Secretary of War Seddon asked the Ordnance Bureau for comment on the Tredegar communication, Colonel Gorgas replied that Anderson and Company had received and was still receiving a large portion of the iron produced at government furnaces. But the remainder of Gorgas' reply revealed a certain defensiveness about the small tonnages of iron delivered to the works. He countercharged that the Tredegar owners had not yet delivered the first 15-inch gun, promised within four months of the April 1862 agreement, and "they are not in a condition to demand a strict fulfillment of the letter of the contract." [85] After reading Gorgas' comments, the Secretary of War concluded this correspondence with Anderson and Company by repeating the terse endorsement of Colonel St. John on the same letter: "Iron will be turned over to you as the necessities of the Government will allow." [86]

82. Anderson & Co. to St. John, Jan. 31, 1863, Letters Rec'd., Secretary of War, RG 109, NA.

83. Anderson & Co. to Mallory, Feb. 7, 1863, to Comdr. F. Forrest, Feb. 14, 1863, to Lt. John Ellicott, April 6, 7, June 1, 1863, and to Glasgow, April 11, 1863, Tredegar Letterbooks; Glasgow to Anderson & Co., March 11, May 27, 1863, Tredegar Letters re Furnaces.

84. Anderson & Co. to Seddon, Jan. 9, 14, Oct. 17, 1863, Letters Rec'd., Secretary of War, RG 109, NA.

85. Endorsement of Gorgas on Anderson & Co. to Seddon, Oct. 17, 1863, ibid.

86. Endorsement of St. John, ibid.; Seddon to Anderson & Co., Oct. 26, 1863, Letters Sent, Secretary of War, ibid.

Despite the Ordnance Bureau's contention that the Tredegar received an inordinate share of government iron, deliveries remained small throughout the war. In 1862, the works received 855 tons of government metal. Receipts of iron from furnaces controlled by the Niter and Mining Bureau and the Bureau of Ordnance and Hydrography were almost as disappointing in 1863 and 1864. (See Table 7, p. 166.)

The truth of the matter was that the government simply did not have the iron to give. Furnace owners under contract to the Confederate States faced a cost-price squeeze that made them reluctant to stay in blast and the difficulties that harassed Tredegar furnace operations affected all Virginia stacks. Production problems overwhelmed a number of ironmasters in the Old Dominion late in 1863.[87] The next year, inadequate labor, draft animals, and subsistence, the exhaustion of ore banks and convenient timber for making charcoal, and the movements of the enemy combined to prevent all but three of the eighteen Virginia furnaces in production from making full blasts and caused thirteen stacks to remain completely idle. As a result, pig iron production in Virginia from January 1863 through September 1864 amounted to only 6,897 long tons.[88] Even if the Tredegar had received every ton of this metal, it would have allowed the works to operate at full capacity for only three to four months.

IX

"The most serious embarrassment to be apprehended in reference to the ordnance supplies is the deficiency of iron," Secretary of War Seddon reported to the President in January 1863.[89] Neither the government nor the Tredegar management ever succeeded in correcting this deficiency. Following the signing of the April 1862 contract with the War and Navy Departments, the company made herculean efforts to acquire, equip, man, and supply blast furnaces. Yet the Tredegar plant, able to consume annually between 20,000 and 24,000 long tons of pig iron, never had even 8,000 tons of metal to work with in any year of the war.[90] (See Table 7, p. 166.)

Richmond, paced by the sprawling Tredegar establishment, had grown

87. Anderson & Co. to St. John, Dec. 11, 1863, Tredegar Letterbooks; St. John to David Graham, Dec. 8, 1863, Graham Records and Papers, UVA.

88. *O.R.*, Ser. IV, *3*, 700, 832.

89. Ibid., *2*, 291.

90. Anderson & Co. to Seddon, Dec. 23, 1862, Letters Rec'd., Secretary of War, RG 109, NA; Anderson & Co. to Andrews, Jan. 24, 1863, Tredegar Letterbooks.

into a major iron manufacturing center during the ten years before the war. But during the same decade, furnace after furnace in Virginia had gone out of blast. The gap between the diminishing raw materials base of the Southern economy and the growing productive capacity of the South's heavy industrial plants had widened as important consumers like the Tredegar went north for cheap anthracite pig iron. Virginia furnace men, faced with an inadequate demand for their expensive charcoal pig, had largely ignored the technological advances which spurred on the Pennsylvania pig iron industry in the 1850s. The only modern furnace using coke and hot blast in the Old Dominion in 1860, the Potomac furnace in Loudoun County, was lost during the first weeks of the war.[91] Rich seams of coking coal in the mountains of southwest Virginia lay untapped and inaccessible. The pool of skilled labor from which managers, founders, and other vital personnel had to come was quite small at the opening of the conflict and was further decimated by the emigration of Northern-born ironmasters and the military mobilization of Southern manpower. Poor blasts at several Tredegar furnaces resulted directly from incompetent management.[92] When war engulfed the South, the company possessing the widest business experience in the Confederacy, backed by the resources of the government, could do very little to close the raw materials gap. The work of decades could not be accomplished in a few strife-torn years.

The failure of the Confederacy's railroads to provide adequate communication with the lower South further compounded the Tredegar's pig iron shortage. The overburdened and underequipped railways could not provide a constant flow of supplies to Virginia to repair all the deficiencies created in the western counties by zealous quartermasters. As a result, blasts were delayed, furnace workers lost time because of inadequate food and clothing, and underfed mules and horses were ravaged by disease or put to pasture when they were needed for furnace work.[93] Disappointing blasts meant in turn that metal was not available to keep the military adequately supplied, much less permit the large-scale manufacture of spikes, rails, cars, wheels, and other products desperately needed by Southern roads. Tracks and rolling stock continued to deteriorate, furnace supplies became more difficult to secure, and the cycle repeated itself.

91. Manuscript returns, Census of Manufactures, 1860, Virginia, VSL; Lesley, *Iron Manufacturer's Guide*, p. 63.

92. Glasgow to F. T. Anderson, Oct. 10, 1863, Anderson Papers, UVA.

93. Glasgow to Anderson & Co., Jan. 1, April 19, May 25, 1863, Tredegar Letters re Furnaces.

Nor were the railroads capable of tapping distant sources of pig iron. Production of metal in the potentially rich but still underdeveloped Alabama iron regions was four times Virginia's output of pig, but the Tredegar did not use a single ton of Alabama iron during the war. Only insignificant amounts of Georgia, Tennessee, and North and South Carolina iron reached Richmond.[94]

The underdeveloped state of the Southern pig iron industry constituted the single most important obstacle to Tredegar production throughout the war. In December 1863, the Tredegar management halted the conversion of the Armory rolling mill into a heavy gunboat plate mill, "because there was no prospect of obtaining metal to keep it employed." [95] Almost a year later, Secretary of the Navy Mallory reported that the rolling mills at Richmond could turn out almost any quantity of gunboat plates, "but the material is not on hand." [96] Cannon production also suffered. From a wartime high of 351 tubes cast in 1862, ordnance manufacture declined to 286 pieces in 1863 and to 213 in 1864. (See Table 5, p. 111.)

Historians have frequently pointed to the relative weakness of the South's manufacturing economy as a major cause of her defeat, and unquestionably the industrial balance was weighted heavily in favor of the North. But this emphasis on the Confederacy's overall industrial impotence has largely ignored the disparity between the potential of the manufacturing plant and the ability of the raw materials sector to feed it.[97] The Confederate States possessed some significant industrial assets. The Tredegar and Bellona foundries, two of the five plants casting heavy cannon for the United States government in 1859, lay within the borders of the Old Dominion. Virginia, Tennessee, Georgia, Alabama, and Louisiana all had important rolling mills, foundries, and machine shops. The Tredegar works and other private and government establishments had the capacity to turn out large quantities of high quality ordnance, munitions, gunboat

94. *O.R.*, Ser. IV, *3*, 700; Tredegar Pig Iron Receipt Book.

95. Anderson & Co. to Gorgas, Dec. 8, 1863, Tredegar Letterbooks.

96. *Report of the Secretary of the Navy, November 5, 1864,* quoted in Lester J. Cappon, "History of the Southern Iron Industry to the Close of the Civil War" (unpublished Ph.D. dissertation, Harvard University, 1928), p. 220.

97. Charles W. Ramsdell, *Behind the Lines in the Southern Confederacy* (Baton Rouge, 1944), pp. 99–100, 103; Cappon, "Government and Private Industry," Univ. of Va. Studies, *1*, 156; Nevins, *Improvised War*, p. 415; Richard N. Current, "God and the Strongest Battalions," in David Donald, ed., *Why the North Won the Civil War* (Baton Rouge, 1960), pp. 3–4, 20–22; E. Merton Coulter, *The Confederate States of America, 1861–1865* (Baton Rouge, 1950), pp. 199, 202–04.

plates, railroad supplies, and other strategic and badly needed items. But without sufficient pig iron to feed even the most vital manufacturing plants, production of the tools of war was doomed to remain inadequate. The raw materials base of the Southern economy could not support the industrial superstructure, and this basic weakness contributed mightily to the ultimate collapse of the Confederate nation. As a result, when the rattle of musketry and the flash and roar of cannon announced a violent collision of blue and gray armies, the Union forces almost invariably possessed overwhelming advantages in matériel. The superb élan of the Southern fighting man could compensate for only so much hard iron.

9

Cannon for Lee

The Ordnance Bureau assigned Anderson and Company two major tasks in 1862 and 1863. Since the Tredegar foundries remained the South's chief sources of large caliber guns, the government placed substantial orders for heavy siege and seacoast artillery. In addition, the armies in the northern Confederacy, the Army of Northern Virginia in particular, relied primarily on the Richmond works for field artillery. As the war progressed, Tredegar gun founders gave more and more attention to the ever-changing strategic demands of Lee's army.

I

The opening of the Peninsular campaign in the spring of 1862 focused Tredegar production on the immediate task of providing for the defense of Richmond. In the fall and winter of 1861, a number of heavy Tredegar cannon had gone into defensive positions on the lower part of the neck of land created by the York and the James rivers. The landing of General George B. McClellan's massive Union army at Fort Monroe in late March 1862 and his subsequent push up the Peninsula brought a hurried strengthening of the Confederate defensive line at Yorktown. New Tredegar cannon, primarily 8- and 10-inch columbiads and 4.62-inch rifled siege guns, were rushed to John Bankhead Magruder and D. H. Hill in an effort to defend the Yorktown line against McClellan's hundred-gun siege.[1]

Hill complained almost immediately about his new weapons. "We are no match for the Yankees at an artillery play with our wretched ordnance, poor in quality and feeble in quantity," he wrote the Secretary of War on April 15.[2] Nine days later he informed the Secretary that two cannon had

1. Entries for Oct., Dec., 1861, April 1862, Tredegar Foundry Sales Books, and for April 1862, Tredegar Order Book; *O.R.*, Ser. I, *4*, 674.

2. Ibid., *11*, pt. iii, 442.

exploded, killing two gunners and wounding four. "There must be something very rotten in the Ordnance Department," Hill charged. "It is a Yankee concern throughout, and I have long been afraid that there was foul play there. Our shells burst at the mouth of the gun or do not burst at all. The metal of which the new guns are made is of the most flimsy and brittle character and the casting is very bad." [3] When more Tredegar cannon were shipped to Yorktown, Hill left the pieces lying on a wharf because he was afraid to fire them. In all, four or five Tredegar rifled cannon burst during the month-long siege.[4]

"As to the worthlessness of many of the Tredegar guns I full[y] agree with Genl Hill," Gorgas wrote the Secretary of War on May 1. "That establishment has not sustained its old reputation." But the Ordnance Bureau chief categorically denied that even the slightest trace of disloyalty existed either at the Tredegar works or the government laboratories. He cited the shortage of good iron and the failure to find an experienced officer to supervise the casting of ordnance as the primary reasons for unsafe Tredegar cannon.[5] Secretary of War Randolph backed up Gorgas' conclusions but he also ordered the foundries to stop casting the 4.62 rifled siege guns, the chief troublemakers.[6]

The Tredegar's inability to secure high quality gun iron was the primary cause for the bad cannon, as Gorgas pointed out. The guns sent to Yorktown were not cast out of Cloverdale metal; the lessees of that all-important furnace were at that time speculating with their iron on the open market.[7] At the end of April 1862, Anderson and Company signed the contract with the government which put the responsibility for supplying iron to the works squarely on the shoulders of the Tredegar management. The company purchased Cloverdale furnace immediately and on May 21, 1862, the first shipment of the new blast of Cloverdale gun iron arrived at the works.[8] The explosions of Tredegar cannon at Yorktown unquestionably hastened both the government's and the company's determination to reach

3. Ibid., p. 461. Gorgas, the head of the Ordnance Bureau, was a native of Pennsylvania. For a discussion of Hill's charges and Gorgas' reply, see Vandiver, *Gorgas*, pp. 111–12.

4. *O.R.*, Ser. I, *11*, pt. iii, 465; *O.R.N.*, Ser. II, *1*, 718–19.

5. Vandiver, *Gorgas*, p. 112.

6. *O.R.*, Ser. I, *11*, pt. iii, 464.

7. Foundry numbers of guns sent to Yorktown given in Tredegar Foundry Sales Books and Gun Foundry Book show that most of the castings were primarily of Liberty iron, plus small amounts of Glenwood, Cloverdale, or Columbia pig.

8. Tredegar Pig Iron Receipt Book.

an agreement that would provide for adequate supplies of proven gun metal.

Bad iron was the main cause for the weak Tredegar guns produced in the first months of 1862 but improper manufacturing methods and shoddy workmanship were also involved. In March, the bursting of a Tredegar field piece during a routine proof firing prompted the Ordnance Bureau to investigate Anderson and Company's production techniques. Gorgas was shocked to discover that iron for a number of field guns—3-inch rifles, 6-pounder guns, and 12-pounder howitzers—had been melted in a cupola furnace instead of in the Tredegar's specially constructed gun iron furnace. He immediately instructed ordnance officers in the field to prove their new Tredegar artillery and informed the War Department of his action.[9]

Secretary of War Judah P. Benjamin could hardly contain his rage when he received Gorgas' communication. He promptly fired off a scathing letter to the Richmond firm in which he charged them with knowingly using dangerous casting procedures. "It is bad enough that our brave defenders should expose their lives to the fire of the enemy under such odds as exist against us, but to furnish them arms more dangerous to themselves than to the enemy is utterly inexcusable," wrote the aroused War Department chief. "I say nothing at this time of your responsibility for lives that may be lost by the bursting of your field batteries, but I give you notice that I shall have every gun in the service received from your shops severely tested and hold you liable to replace every one that shall fail to stand, besides charging you with all the cost of making the test." [10] As a result of the inspections ordered by Benjamin and Gorgas, the Tredegar foundries had to recast a number of cannon made in February 1862.[11]

Even after the Secretary's stern warning, ordnance officers continued to complain about the poor quality of Tredegar guns and ammunition. Workmen began casting with Cloverdale iron as soon as the May shipment arrived but Colonel Thomas S. Rhett of the Ordnance Department saw little improvement in the castings. "I will be frank and say that I am in doubt about the guns. Those lately cast have been so bad that I am in doubt about the propriety of trying again. My own reputation as well as yours is at

9. Gorgas to Capt. E. P. Alexander, March 12, 1862, Edward Porter Alexander Papers, UNC.

10. Benjamin to Anderson & Co., March 12, 1862, Letters Sent, Secretary of War, RG 109, NA.

11. Tredegar Gun Foundry Book.

stake & the welfare of the country deeply involved," Rhett told the Tredegar management. "With good iron & the skill of your workmen we ought to have the best & safest guns in the world." [12] According to the disenchanted D. H. Hill, Tredegar artillery was anything but the best and safest in the world. During the first twelve months of the war, he wrote, "frequent burstings caused a 'Richmond gun' to be viewed with mingled scorn and apprehension." [13] The poor performance of the works during Anderson's tour of active duty undoubtedly influenced the War Department's decision to allow him to resign his commission in July 1862. His managerial talents were badly needed at the Richmond plant.

In early May, the Confederate commander, Joseph E. Johnston, ordered the evacuation of the Yorktown line and the Southern forces retreated to new defensive positions around Richmond. The Tredegar gun foundries had a dual role to perform in the tension-filled days before the battle for the Confederate capital. Ordnance workers had to provide both siege guns for the heavy batteries in the earthworks ringing the city and supply the outnumbered Confederate troops with additional field artillery. Ammunition, carriages, and artillery implements were also badly needed. Activity at the sprawling Tredegar plant quickened daily as McClellan's troops approached the capital. "I have very urgent orders for the following projectiles" and "Genl. Lee is very anxious on this subject" became common phrases in the Ordnance Department's Tredegar correspondence.[14]

The Tredegar helped insure that Richmond would not be taken from the James when the rolling mills filled a rush order in March and April for iron bolts and shoes for obstructions sunk at Drewry's Bluff. The earthen fortifications at the bluff also received Tredegar cannon just in time for the successful duel with the *Monitor*, the *Galena*, and three other Federal gunboats on May 15.[15]

Anderson and Company provided vital assistance to the hard-pressed Confederate forces before and during the Seven Days' Battles. Additional Tredegar heavy ordnance was dispatched to key batteries guarding the land approaches to the capital. The company's skilled slave crew of gun movers became the most prized hands in the city. They were constantly on

12. Rhett to Anderson & Co., June 10, 1862, Tredegar Order Book.

13. Daniel Harvey Hill, *Bethel to Sharpsburg* (2 vols. Raleigh, 1926), *1*, 125.

14. Capt. W. N. Smith to Anderson & Co., June 18, 1862, and Maj. Briscoe Baldwin to Anderson & Co., June 23, 1862, Tredegar Order Book.

15. Col. Alfred G. Rives to Anderson & Co., March 7, 21, 1862, Letters Sent, Engineer Department, RG 109, NA; entries for March–May 1862, Tredegar Foundry Sales Books.

the move, hauling ordnance from the works to the emplacements and shifting cannon from one battery to another. Tredegar mechanics laid down siege platforms, sighted cannon, and made repairs at the batteries.[16] Gun founders concentrated on field artillery during April, May, and June. Seventy-two cannon were cast in April alone, the highest monthly total achieved by the Tredegar foundries during the war. Many of the pieces produced during these crucial months were bronze 6-pounder guns and 12-pounder howitzers, made from the bells of Southern churches.[17]

Tredegar workers hammered out a novel piece of military hardware for General R. E. Lee just before the Seven Days' campaign opened. Lee wanted a weapon to aid in checking any Federal movement up the Richmond and York River Railroad and he proposed the construction of an ironclad railway car mounting a heavy gun. The Navy Department, which controlled the armor plate needed to sheath the battery, accepted responsibility for constructing the car. The chief of the Bureau of Ordnance and Hydrography immediately put his most able officer, John M. Brooke, on the job. Lieutenant Brooke drew up the necessary plans and Tredegar carpenters and machinists went to work on the project on June 12, a week after Lee first suggested the battery. Two-inch armor plate rolled for the gunboat *Richmond* was appropriated to cover the sloping roof and the sides of heavy timber. In ten days the finished car was on the York River tracks, with the menacing snout of a Tredegar 32-pounder Brooke gun protruding through its porthole.

The world's first railroad battery went into action on June 29, 1862. The car moved forward with Confederate infantry at Savage Station as "Prince John" Magruder belatedly launched an attack against the rearguard of McClellan's retreating army. The battery proved its worth in this bloody fight, helping to clear a bridge of enemy troops, and the army officer in charge of the gun expressed enthusiasm over the experiment.[18]

II

Confederate artillery was badly outgunned during the Seven Days. Anderson and Company had outfitted the Southern field batteries with a

16. Entries for June 1862, ibid.

17. Tredegar Gun Foundry Book.

18. Entries for June 1862, Tredegar Rolling Mill Sales Books, Tredegar Foundry Sales Books, and Tredegar Order Book; Comdr. George Minor to R. E. Lee, June 24, 1862, Alexander Papers, UNC; Baldwin to Pendleton, June 25, 1862, Pendleton Papers, UNC; *O.R.*, Ser. I, *11*, pt. ii, 664, 717–18, pt. iii, 574, 610, 615; Johnston, *Virginia Railroads*, p. 59.

large number of new tubes on the eve of the battles around Richmond but some of these pieces were faulty and almost all of them were obsolete before they went into service. During the first eighteen months of the war, the Tredegar gun foundries had concentrated on three models: an iron 3-inch rifled gun, a 12-pounder howitzer, and a 6-pounder smoothbore gun. These weapons were no match for the 12-pounder bronze Napoleon guns and the iron 20-pounder Parrott rifles which Federal artillerists possessed in increasingly large numbers.[19] The technical superiority of the Union weapons was all too evident on the first day of July 1862, when Federal artillery massed on Malvern Hill gave their Confederate counterparts a severe mauling.[20]

The 12-pounder bronze Napoleon gun, perfected by the French army in the 1850s, had several important advantages over existing Confederate smoothbore ordnance. Its range and accuracy were considerably greater than the 6-pounder gun and 12-pounder howitzer. Although the old 12-pounder gun, model 1841, had comparable range, the Napoleon weighed some five hundred pounds less and was much easier to transport and maneuver. The weight of the cannon became increasingly important as irreplaceable Southern artillery horses broke down under the rigors of constant campaigning. A load of canister delivered by a Napoleon at close range had a devastating effect on advancing infantry. "At the distance at which the serious work of artillery was done, it was an overmatch for rifled artillery," wrote Gorgas.[21] The rifled and banded Parrott guns, possessing greater range and accuracy than the smoothbore Napoleon, were effective pieces for long distance bombardments.

The Ordnance Department took immediate steps after Malvern Hill to effect basic changes in the field artillery of the Army of Northern Virginia. Ten days after the bloody climax to the Seven Days, the bureau instructed Anderson and Company to cease casting 12-pounder howitzers and 6-pounder guns altogether and to prepare the necessary patterns and begin manufacturing 12-pounder Napoleons. "I trust you will make every exertion to supply them within a short time," the ordnance inspector told the

19. Tredegar Gun Foundry Book; E. P. Alexander, *Military Memoirs of a Confederate* (New York, 1907), pp. 245, 279; L. VanLoan Naisawald, *Grape and Canister: The Story of the Field Artillery of the Army of the Potomac, 1861–1865* (New York, 1960), pp. 29, 245–46; Dowdey, *Seven Days,* pp. 311, 322.

20. Ibid., pp. 332–34; Douglas Southall Freeman, *Lee's Lieutenants* (3 vols. New York, 1942–44), *1,* 596–97; Alexander, pp. 158–60, 245.

21. Gorgas, "Notes on the Ordnance Department," *Southern Hist. Soc. Papers, 12,* 93.

Photograph of the interior of the 1861 gun foundry, taken by Huestis P. Cook. Two large cranes, each of 30-ton capacity, operated in the gun foundry, lifting heavy gun castings from pits in the foundry's floor. Molten iron flowed into the building from air furnaces on the exterior of the back wall; the iron ran down troughs into molds (called flasks) in the pits. Tredegar foundries produced more than one thousand guns of various types during the Civil War. A 1907 journal article noted that the building was currently used for "general castings."

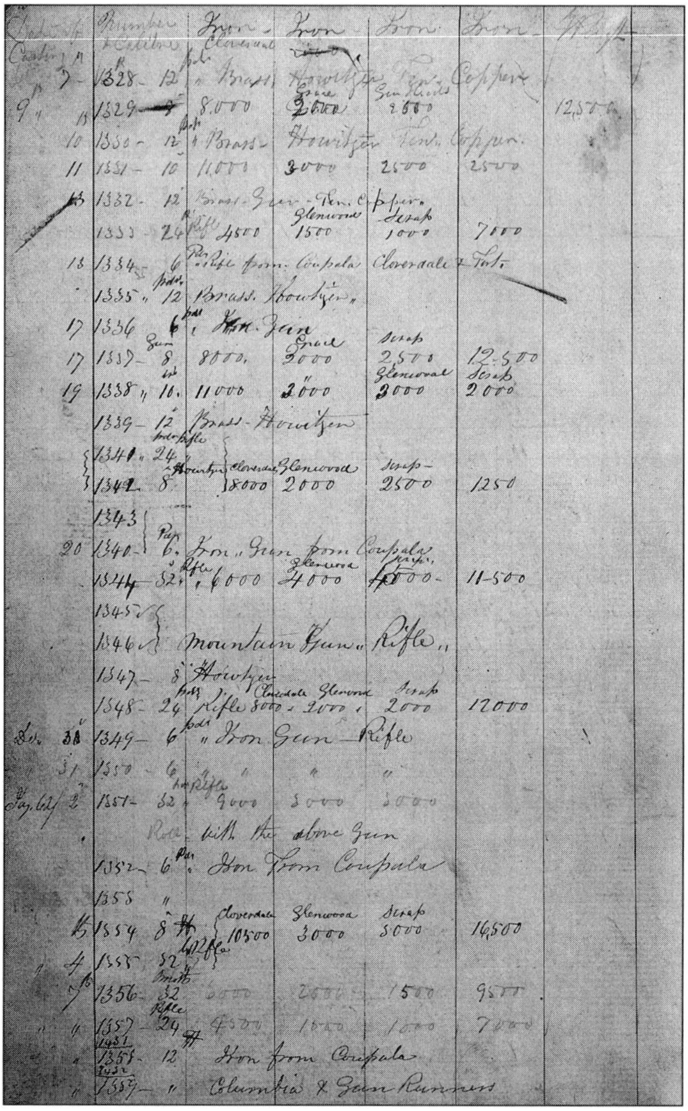

Entries in record book of guns cast, 1861–65. The Library of Virginia (formerly the Virginia State Library), holds more than one thousand volumes and a half-million additional items in the Tredegar Iron Company collection, including rare records from the Civil War period. Tredegar workers recorded the gun's identifying number, along with the size and type of each gun cast, and frequently included the name of the furnace that produced the pig iron used in the casting.

Tredegar partners.[22] The next day, the Ordnance Department ordered seven 30-pounder Parrott rifles, patterned after a Federal gun captured at Manassas which the Confederates had dubbed "Long Tom." The 30-pounder Parrott was essentially a siege gun, but on July 30, 1862, the bureau included 20-pounder Parrotts in the new requisition.[23] The Tredegar had a major task to execute for Lee's army and the future effectiveness of the field artillery of his forces would depend primarily on Anderson and Company's performance.

The initial changeover in Tredegar ordnance manufacture was accomplished very rapidly. Workmen at the Richmond plant quickly built patterns and prepared flasks for the new weapons. On July 26, just two weeks after the initial government order, the first 30-pounder Parrott was cast. Tredegar foundrymen cast the first bronze Napoleon on August 9 and the first 20-pounder Parrott by the end of that month.[24]

The Ordnance Bureau urged Anderson and Company to manufacture these weapons as quickly as possible.[25] General William N. Pendleton, Chief of Artillery of Lee's army, was particularly anxious to secure some 20-pounder Parrott rifles before the Army of Northern Virginia invaded Maryland, but the Tredegar could not finish the guns in time. The Richmond plant delivered the first two 30-pounders in September but did not finish any 20-pounders until the following month, when four were turned over to the government.[26] Southern troops at Sharpsburg came under a withering Union artillery fire which the Confederate gunners could not silence. "Pray that you may never see another Sharpsburg," Stephen Lee, a Confederate gunner, told a fellow officer. "Sharpsburg was Artillery Hell." [27] The Tredegar guns were not there.

Despite the swift retooling of the Tredegar plant, the modernization of the field artillery of the Army of Northern Virginia was proceeding at a snail's pace. The chief obstacle was a familiar one—insufficient raw materials. Although copper, tin, and gun iron were all in short supply, copper was a particularly critical item. Government laboratories had first call on the South's meager copper resources for the manufacture of percussion

22. Rhett to Anderson & Co., July 10, 1862, Tredegar Order Book.

23. Rhett to Anderson & Co., July 11, 30, 1862, ibid.

24. Tredegar Gun Foundry Book.

25. Rhett to Anderson & Co., July 29, 30, 1862, Tredegar Order Book.

26. Rhett to Anderson & Co., Aug. 27, 1862, ibid.; entries for Sept.–Oct. 1862, Tredegar Foundry Sales Books.

27. Quoted in Alexander, p. 247. See also Naisawald, pp. 200, 203, 208.

caps. Each Tredegar Napoleon, although somewhat lighter than its Federal counterpart, required over one thousand pounds of copper. Gun founders had produced the first Napoleon in August 1862; by the end of the year, they had cast a total of only ten. During the entire month of September, just six cannon of all descriptions were cast at the Tredegar works, and October production was a mere ten pieces.[28] The next month, when Pendleton pressed the Ordnance Bureau for the Napoleons, Colonel Rhett replied that there were none on hand in Richmond. "We have ordered some from the 'Tredegar' but it is impossible for me to say *when* they will be ready." [29]

Anderson and Company's inability to speed up ordnance production alarmed Lee and he proposed a means of circumventing the raw materials shortage in December 1862. "During the past campaign I have felt, in every battle, the advantages that the enemy possessed over us in their artillery. This arose in part from their possessing more experienced artillerists and better prepared ammunition, but consisted chiefly in better guns," Lee told the Secretary of War. He recommended that if copper and tin could not otherwise be procured, the Tredegar should melt down the army's light bronze weapons and recast them into 12-pounder Napoleons. "I urgently recommend to the Department the consideration of this subject, and that measures be immediately taken to improve our field artillery. The contest between our 6-pounder smoothbores and the 12-pounder Napoleons of the enemy is very unequal, and, in addition, is discouraging to our artillerists." Lee also wanted four Napoleons without delay "for a particular purpose," and some 20- and 30-pounder Parrotts.[30]

The letter crossed Secretary of War Seddon's desk and went to Colonel Gorgas. The efficient Ordnance Department chief replied that he had already anticipated Lee's desires and almost a month before had instructed Anderson and Company to work night and day on Napoleons and Parrotts. He would request that the light bronze guns be forwarded to Richmond from the lines at Fredericksburg and from the Valley, and be recast. The four Napoleons Lee wanted were not immediately available but would be made as soon as possible.[31]

The "particular purpose" behind Lee's request for the four cannon was

28. Tredegar Gun Foundry Book.
29. Rhett to Pendleton, Nov. 16, 1862, Pendleton Papers, UNC.
30. *O.R.*, Ser. I, *21*, 1046–47.
31. Ibid., p. 1047.

his attempt to placate Stonewall Jackson. Jackson had objected strenuously to a proposed shift of captured Napoleons from his old Army of the Valley, even though the transfer was intended merely to equate the artillery strength of the divisions in his Second Corps. Lee tactfully avoided further mention of the subject to his officers and requested the Napoleons from Richmond.[32] In response to a query from the Ordnance Bureau, Anderson promised to give immediate attention to Lee's request, but pointed out that no raw materials were available at the Tredegar. "You had better hurry on the old Guns that are to be melted over to make the 'Napoleons,'" Anderson told Gorgas.[33] The four guns were cast during the ensuing month and delivered to the government in January.[34]

The Army of Northern Virginia received a few Parrott rifles in time to answer the mighty Union cannonade that descended on Fredericksburg in mid-December. For two months prior to the battle, ordnance officers had been urging Anderson and Company to speed up delivery of these powerful rifles. Four 20-pounder Parrotts were turned over to the Ordnance Department in October and two 30-pounders were completed late in November.[35] Lee ordered the 30-pounders to the front immediately. On the evening of November 28, thirty Tredegar slaves labored for almost five hours at the Richmond, Fredericksburg, and Potomac station, loading the two cannon on a special train and filling two box cars with ammunition. The guns arrived at Fredericksburg the next day, were tested, and put into previously prepared emplacements on Marye's Heights. When Union troops attempted to storm the naturally strong Confederate position on December 13, the two Parrotts went into action. Confederate artillerists used the heavy guns with devastating effect on the assaulting Federals for several hours, but both guns burst during the battle, one on the thirty-ninth round, the other on the fifty-fourth. Lee, Longstreet, and other high officers were standing near one of the cannon when it exploded, but miraculously all escaped injury.[36]

32. Ibid., p. 1044; Freeman, *2*, 323–24.

33. Anderson & Co. to Gorgas, Dec. 8, 1862, Tredegar Letterbooks.

34. Tredegar Gun Foundry Book; Tredegar Foundry Sales Books.

35. Gorgas to Anderson & Co., Oct. 2, 1862, Rhett to Anderson & Co., Oct. 8, 30, Nov. 1, 4, 5, 1862, and R. K. Hudgins to Anderson & Co., Oct. 23, 24, 1862, Tredegar Order Book; Tredegar Foundry Sales Books.

36. Entry for Nov. 1862, ibid.; Alexander, p. 302; *O.R.*, Ser. I, *21*, 564–66. The rapid rate of fire maintained during the battle probably overheated these cannon and caused the explosions.

By January, Colonel Gorgas had assembled enough of Lee's light bronze ordnance to allow Anderson's founders to make at least a start on the much-needed Napoleons.[37] Lee kept a watchful eye on the progress of the operation. In January, while Union troops were struggling through their "mud march" in an attempt to ford the Rappahannock above Fredericksburg, Lee wrote Gorgas that the Napoleons would greatly aid in opposing the Federal crossing.[38] The head of the Ordnance Bureau in turn prodded the Tredegar management and Tanner replied that "we are pushing ahead the Napoleons for Gen Lee & have remelted nearly the whole of the old Guns. We will require at once either copper or more old guns." Gorgas ordered his military storekeeper to issue the Tredegar all copper not absolutely necessary for other critical manufactures.[39] Lee wanted forty Napoleons in sixty days time, Gorgas told the Tredegar management on January 19. Could that number be delivered inside of two months? Anderson thought so. "Be kind enough to inform General Lee that the subject engaged my immediate attention and the efforts of my partners and all connected with the establishment will be unceasing to accomplish his wishes." [40]

Anderson saw in the urgent demands of the commanding general a chance to raise another problem. "I think the guns will all be ready within the time he names if we should not have trouble about workmen," the Tredegar chief informed Gorgas. "I take this occasion Colonel to beg you to invoke the aid of General Lee in detailing men to assist us here. By a small reduction of the field force the efficiency of this Establishment could be greatly enlarged, but nearly all our applications for men have of late been denied—even in the case of men reported unfit for field duty." [41] The subsequent performance of Anderson's foundries indicated that this department was not severely undermanned. The senior partner attempted to use this occasion to persuade Lee to change his policy toward details but his effort failed. Lee had fewer than 60,000 men to oppose over 130,000 Federals and he steadfastly refused to lessen the number of his troops or weaken their morale by detailing men back to Richmond during the harsh winter of 1862–63.

37. Alexander to Pendleton, Jan. 7, 1862 [sic], Pendleton Papers, DUL.

38. *O.R.*, Ser. I, *21*, 1109.

39. Anderson & Co. to Gorgas, Jan. 24, 1863, and endorsement, in "J. R. Anderson & Co.," Confederate Citizens File, RG 109, NA.

40. Anderson to Gorgas, Jan. 26, 1863, Tredegar Letterbooks.

41. Ibid.

A continuing shortage of raw materials was the chief reason why production of Lee's new Napoleons dragged during the first two months of 1863. Only nine were cast in January and in February the number dropped to seven. Anderson and Company maintained that the delay resulted from tardy deliveries of the promised materials. "We ought to have 10 tons copper & a corresponding quantity of tin to work from at all times," one of the partners told the Ordnance Bureau in February.[42] Lee asked President Davis to look into this matter. "To increase the efficiency of the army as much as possible, a supply of suitable guns will be required for the opening of the spring campaign," Lee wrote anxiously on March 2. "To replace the 6 pdr smoothbore with Napoleons, which I am trying to do, will require 70 Napoleons in addition to those we now have. I will be greatly obliged to your Excl. if you could accelerate their manufacture." [43]

The close attention of the President and the commanding general of the Army of Northern Virginia finally remedied the slow delivery of copper and tin to the Tredegar. Large numbers of guns were now pulled out of the lines at Fredericksburg and taken from the Shenandoah Valley and shipped to Richmond. All the light bronze pieces of Jackson's Corps were sent to the capital by the middle of February and many of those of Longstreet's Corps and the General Reserve followed during the next two months.[44] The Tredegar management continued to press the Ordnance Department for more materials, including steel needed for retooling the boring lathes.[45] At the request of the Confederate government, old bronze cannon used as corner posts in Richmond were wrenched from the ground and carted down to the works.[46] During the first half of 1863, the Tredegar foundries received over 80,000 pounds of copper and tin, chiefly in the form of obsolete cannon.[47]

Tredegar gun founders now showed what they could accomplish when

42. Anderson & Co. to Rhett, Feb. 12, 1863, ibid.

43. Lee to Davis, March 2, 1863, Robert E. Lee–Jefferson Davis Correspondence, 1862–65, VSL.

44. *O.R.*, Ser. I, *25*, pt. ii, 617–18; Baldwin to Pendleton, March 6, 1863, Pendleton Papers, UNC; Tredegar Receiving Book; entries for March 31, May 28, 1863, Tredegar Day Books.

45. Anderson & Co. to Snowden Andrews, Jan. 14, 1863, to W. S. Downer, Jan. 20, 1863, to Rhett, Feb. 12, 1863, and to Gorgas, Feb. 21, 1863, Tredegar Letterbooks; Anderson & Co. to Downer, Jan. 5, Feb. 23, 1863, in "J. R. Anderson & Co.," Confederate Citizens File, RG 109, NA.

46. Resolution passed April 13, 1863, Richmond City Council Minute Books, VSL.

47. Entries for March, May, July, 1863, Tredegar Journals.

provided with adequate materials. They had been able to produce only sixteen Napoleons in the first two months of 1863 but cast thirty-four in March and April. Of the forty guns requested by Lee in January, thirty-five were finished and delivered within the sixty days he specified.[48] When this original quota was met, Gorgas thought Lee wished deliveries of Napoleons to cease. Lee promptly corrected this false impression. "Lt Col Baldwin informs me that after next week the Ordnance Department will cease to furnish 12 pdr. Napoleon guns to this army as by that time it will have furnished all that were promised," Lee wrote Gorgas on March 26. "I do not know anything of this promise but my wish & understanding has been that all the bronze 6 pdrs in the army were to be exchanged for Napoleons. If the exchange ceases next week there will remain eleven 6 pdr howitzers which are of no use to us. I hope you will be able to give me Napoleon guns for those also." [49] Thirteen Napoleons were promptly cast at the Tredegar works in April and May to replace the remaining 6-pounders. By the end of April, the exchange was almost completed.[50] Forty-nine of the fifty Napoleons cast during the first four months of 1863 were bored, mounted, and turned over to Lee's artillerists in time to participate in the spring and summer campaigns.[51]

III

Joe Hooker opened his drive on Richmond during the last week in April, just as the Tredegar works was attempting to finish the recasting of Lee's ordnance. The Union general tried to get behind the strong Confederate position at Fredericksburg by sending approximately one third of his 130,000 men across the Rappahannock above the city, at fords near Chancellorsville. Lee and 50,000 of his troops moved to check Hooker's attempted envelopment. The first day of the battle of Chancellorsville climaxed when Jackson, after leading some 26,000 men on a concealed march around the Federal army, launched a surprise attack which rolled up the exposed right flank of the Union forces. The fall of night and the mortal wounding of Jackson by a mistaken volley from his own troops halted the fighting on May 2.[52]

48. Tredegar Gun Foundry Book; Tredegar Foundry Sales Books.

49. Lee to Gorgas, March 26, 1863, Letters and Telegrams Sent, Army of Northern Virginia, RG 109, NA.

50. *O.R.*, Ser. I, *25*, pt. ii, 749.

51. Tredegar Foundry Sales Books.

52. Freeman, *Lee's Lieutenants*, *2*, 524–83. Hooker left a third of his army to attack the Confederate forces entrenched at Fredericksburg and held the remaining third in reserve, to

The next day promised to be a bloody contest. At dawn Confederate troops would have to attack a now strongly entrenched foe, backed by massive artillery, through the tangled underbrush of the Wilderness. But Hooker inadvertently surrendered the strongest position on the field on the morning of May 3. The Union general wanted to establish a tighter defensive perimeter and he ordered his artillery off Hazel Grove, a cleared eminence overlooking a right angle in the Federal lines. Porter Alexander, who had conducted an extensive reconaissance during the night looking for possible positions for Confederate artillery, recognized the importance of the location. Alexander alerted Jeb Stuart, the new commander of Jackson's Corps, to the possibility of massing artillery at Hazel Grove and enfilading the Union lines. Stuart promptly ordered all available guns to the strategic hill. Soon the gentle rise was crowned with new Tredegar Napoleons and iron rifled guns. A withering fire crashed into the enemy's lines, scarcely 1,500 yards away, softening the position for the Confederate infantry assaults. Federal artillery, for the first time in the war, was definitely being outfought.[53]

At Hazel Grove, "the finest artillerists of the Army of Northern Virginia were having their greatest day." [54] A young Confederate cannoneer wrote home after serving his two Napoleons at Hazel Grove that "the most noteworthy feature of the Battle was the efficiency of our Artillery; owing to the issue of good guns replacing bad & to the organization into Battalions we massed it & produced effects unknown & unhoped before." [55] Another Southern officer who had manned a Tredegar Napoleon during the battle was equally enthusiastic about the new field pieces. The Yankees "have always acknowledged our superiority in Infantry, but said they surpassed us in Artillery, but this time we fought them with equal guns & ammunition," he wrote. "Some of their art^{y} officers who were captured said we took them completely by surprise with our artillery & that nothing on earth could stand against the shower of missiles we gave them." [56] The success of the Confederate guns at Chancellorsville was in large measure attributable to the Tredegar's prompt recasting of Lee's cannon. If the Richmond works could continue to supply the Army of Northern Virginia with additional

---

be used at either position. Lee pulled all but 10,000 of his men out of the naturally strong Fredericksburg defenses.

53. *O.R.*, Ser. I, *25*, pt. i, 823; Wise, *Long Arm of Lee*, pp. 507–11.

54. Freeman, *2*, 592.

55. C. G. Chamberlayne, ed., *Ham Chamberlayne—Virginian* (Richmond, 1932), p. 176.

56. Lt. John H. Munford to Sallie R. Munford, May 14, 1863, Munford-Ellis Papers, DUL.

improved ordnance, the chances of a successful Southern invasion of the enemy's homeland would be materially improved.

IV

Production of iron cannon during March and April stood in marked contrast to the rapid manufacture of bronze Napoleons. Only fifteen iron weapons were cast during those months and this total included just two Parrott rifles.[57] Lee reported in late April 1863 that his forces had received only three 10-pounder Parrotts.[58]

This severe production slowdown occurred just as Tredegar workmen were winding up construction of new ordnance facilities. Although all preparations for casting and finishing the long-awaited 15-inch Rodman gun were not yet completed, the large gun foundry begun in October 1861 was almost finished by January 1863. A new Tredegar-built air furnace, capable of melting 100,000 pounds of iron at a single lighting, was in operation and additional casting pits and heavy duty cranes were ready for use. The new gun mill building was still in the process of construction, but was well on its way to completion at the first of the year.[59]

The difficulty, as usual, was a shortage of raw materials. Production of gun metal at Cloverdale furnace had fallen far short of the demands of the Tredegar foundries. This furnace labored under several severe handicaps. The property had been worked continuously for over two decades and timber and ore in the immediate area of the stack were exhausted. Raw materials for the furnace had to be hauled considerable distances over dirt roads that turned into quagmires during rainy winter and spring months. Because the company could not secure the detail of an experienced founder for nearby Catawba furnace, the founder at Cloverdale had to handle both blasts and production at the two furnaces suffered accordingly.[60] Bad weather in January 1863 ended the blast at Cloverdale furnace completely. When roads in the vicinity of the furnace became impassable during the last week in January, stocks of charcoal gave out and could not be replenished until the weather improved. Francis Glasgow esti-

57. Tredegar Gun Foundry Book.

58. *O.R.*, Ser. I, *25*, pt. ii, 749.

59. Entries for Dec. 1862, Dec. 1863, Tredegar Journals; Anderson & Co. to Albert L. West, March 17, 1863, Tredegar Letterbooks; "Corporate Holdings, 1866," manuscript Tredegar volume, p. 5.

60. Glasgow to Anderson & Co., Feb. 7, March 11, April 19, 1863, Tredegar Letters re Furnaces.

mated in early February that it would be at least six weeks before the furnace could make iron again.[61]

The Tredegar owners realized that a crisis in their ordnance production was rapidly approaching which they were powerless to stop. "We regret to inform you that we have not metal enough for Guns to carry us through the coming months," one of the partners informed the Cloverdale manager in late February. "We do hope you may now have good weather so that you may soon be in blast. There will be almost a revolution here when it is known that the work of casting heavy Guns ceases." [62] By March 20, the foundries had exhausted all gun metal at the works.[63] Not a single iron fieldpiece could be cast for the Army of Northern Virginia until Cloverdale resumed production.

In mid-April, the furnace finally got back into blast and the nearly frantic Tredegar management urged Glasgow to forward the metal immediately. "You have no idea what pressure is upon us for iron," they told their chief furnace agent.[64] A small lot of iron from the new blast arrived in Richmond on April 29, and the pressure eased considerably. But the respite was short-lived. A spring flood damaged the James River and Kanawha Canal during the first week in May and halted all traffic. The first large shipment of Cloverdale gun iron did not reach the Tredegar works until May 23.[65] The gun foundries had been without iron for two months.

When the metal finally arrived, the Tredegar facilities were in no condition to make full use of it. In the early morning hours of May 15, 1863, a fire originating in a woolen factory at the west end of the Tredegar roared through much of the Confederacy's most important industrial plant. The Crenshaw Woolen Factory went up like a torch and flames leaped from the top windows of the six-story structure almost before the Tredegar alarm bell rang through the still Richmond darkness. By the time firemen arrived at the origin of the blaze, a cascade of sparks had ignited the neighboring Tredegar locomotive and engine shops. The rolling mill was in operation at the time the blaze broke out and the workmen formed a bucket brigade in a frantic attempt to save some of the buildings. But flames quickly jumped from one structure to another and little could be done to arrest the

61. Glasgow to Anderson & Co., Feb. 3, 1863, ibid.
62. Anderson & Co. to Patton, Feb. 24, 1863, Tredegar Letterbooks.
63. Anderson & Co. to Patton, March 20, 1863, ibid.
64. Anderson & Co. to Glasgow, April 29, 1863, ibid.
65. Anderson & Co. to Glasgow, May 4, 1863, ibid.; Tredegar Pig Iron Receipt Book.

conflagration in the immediate vicinity of the woolen factory. Firemen drenched Tredegar buildings which had not caught fire and succeeded in saving a number of them before the blaze finally burned itself out.[66]

At dawn, the crestfallen senior partner walked through the smoldering ruins and assessed the damage. The fire, he quickly saw, had taken a heavy toll. Two older foundries, including the gun foundry where he had begun casting cannon in 1842, were badly damaged and the gun carriage works, the old blacksmith shop, the pattern shop, and a large section of the machine shops were completely destroyed. At the west end of the works, the blackened walls of the engine and locomotive shops stood in gaunt relief against the gray morning sky. As he turned to the gutted shell of his new gun mill, Anderson saw the most discouraging sight of all—the almost completed lathe for boring the 15-inch gun, now a mass of scorched and twisted metal. There was at least something to be thankful for, however, since a number of vital departments had come through the disaster unscathed. The fire had failed to reach the new gun foundry and blacksmith shop, the boiler shop, the rolling mills, and the ammunition, bronze, and car wheel foundries. At the end of his inspection, Anderson put on a brave face as he talked to reporters. Much of the irreplaceable machinery was salvageable and only a few days would be lost in the damaged departments, he predicted. He did not anticipate any delay in munitions production. Rebuilding would begin at once. At this news, the Richmond *Examiner* heaved a great sigh of relief. "What might, therefore, have been a serious national calamity, is a drawback which falls upon and is borne alone by private individuals." [67]

Anderson made good his promise to begin immediate reconstruction of the facilities producing vital military items. As soon as the ruins cooled sufficiently, workers began combing the wreckage for machines and tools which might be repaired and made useful. Other Richmond iron establishments offered jobs to Tredegar laborers but Anderson promised continuous employment to all his men and retained their services.[68] Publicly, the Tredegar management maintained an optimistic attitude toward the task ahead of them. Privately, they admitted that the prospect of reconstructing their plant in the face of shortages of labor, machines, and basic building materials was discouraging, to say the least. "Nevertheless we are going

66. Anderson & Co. to Glasgow, May 16, 1863, Tredegar Letterbooks. Spontaneous combustion apparently caused the fire; see Richmond *Examiner*, May 16, 1863.

67. Ibid.

68. Ibid., May 19, 1863.

ahead," they told a Virginia railroad official.[69] On July 4, the Richmond *Examiner* announced that several fire-damaged departments were resuming operations. That same day, Lee's battered army began its retreat from Gettysburg. The Tredegar fire and the defeat of the Army of Northern Virginia were not totally unrelated events.

V

In November 1863, Commander John M. Brooke, Chief of Ordnance and Hydrography, reported to the Secretary of the Navy that "in consequence of the difficulty of procuring iron during the past winter and the occurrence of a destructive fire just as the iron was obtained in the spring, the manufacture of guns was so far suspended that during an interval of five months none was made." [70] Brooke's statement was not literally true, but the production of iron cannon at the Tredegar was disappointingly small during the first six months of 1863. Only 134 pieces, iron and brass, were cast, compared with almost twice that number manufactured during the first half of 1862. (See Table 5, p. 111.)

Anderson and his men were able to complete only half of their assignment to modernize the field artillery of the Army of Northern Virginia. They almost completed the exchange of bronze ordnance prior to the invasion of Pennsylvania in June. The Tredegar foundries cast seventy-three Napoleons between January and June 1863 and replaced all of Lee's 6-pounder bronze guns before Gettysburg. But his artillerists still had a number of bronze 12-pounder howitzers which were useless at the most critical juncture of the three-day struggle. These howitzers lacked sufficient range to reach the Federal positions on Cemetery Ridge and could not participate in the bombardment preceding Pickett's charge on July 3. Anderson and Company's efforts to fill Lee's second artillery need had failed completely. The shortage of gun iron, followed by the May fire, had restricted Tredegar production of Parrott guns during the first six months of 1863 to only three 10-pounders and ten 20-pounders. The long-range Parrott rifles were precisely the type of ordnance needed at Gettysburg on that hot afternoon of July 3, as Porter Alexander, chief of Longstreet's artillery, noted.[71]

69. Anderson & Co. to Thomas Dodamead, May 20, 1863, Tredegar Letterbooks.

70. *O.R.N.*, Ser. II, 2, 550.

71. Tredegar Gun Foundry Book; Wise, p. 664; Fairfax Downey, *The Guns of Gettysburg* (New York, 1958), p. 207; E. P. Alexander, "Causes of the Confederate Defeat at Gettysburg," *Southern Historical Society Papers, 4* (1877), 106.

At Chancellorsville, where short-range fire on massed infantry had been required, the new Tredegar bronze Napoleons had met the tactical demands of the situation admirably. But at Gettysburg, long-range accuracy against Federal artillery positions was the primary requirement. The cannon that might have filled this need, the iron Parrotts, were not there in sufficient numbers to drive the enemy's guns off Cemetery Ridge. Several other factors were also involved in the poor performance of the Confederate ordnance at Gettysburg, including insufficient and faulty ammunition, unreliable fuses, bad positioning, and the failure to utilize all available field pieces. But the shortage of long-range rifled artillery was a major reason why the Confederate softening-up barrage just prior to Pickett's charge was, in the words of one Union artillery officer, "the biggest humbug of the season." [72] The Yankee gunners held their positions atop the ridge and broke the back of the final Confederate infantry assault with charge after charge of canister.[73]

Anderson, his partners, and their men had done their best to equip the batteries of the Army of Northern Virginia for their severest trial, but the Tredegar's best failed to equal the efforts of Northern foundries. Lack of gun iron and the May fire which virtually incapacitated the works for a month prior to Lee's invasion crippled Tredegar ordnance and ammunition production at the Confederacy's hour of greatest need. Gettysburg was as much a triumph of Northern manufacturers as it was a victory of Northern fighting men.

72. Capt. Charles A. Phillips, quoted in Naisawald, *Grape and Canister*, p. 420.

73. Wise, pp. 664–70, 692; Naisawald, pp. 417–35; Freeman, *3*, 149–61; Alexander, *Military Memoirs*, pp. 420–23.

10

Running the Yankee Blockade

I

Repairing the damage caused by the devastating May fire preoccupied the Tredegar management for several months. "Our loss has been very heavy and insurance but small," one of the partners wrote shortly after the blaze.[1] Anderson's first step was to repurchase the property where the conflagration originated to insure that no more fires would start there. The two lots which he had sold in 1854 for $16,500 he repurchased for $150,000 cash in late May 1863.[2] A particularly serious loss was the destruction of the company's entire stock of patterns. Not a gun or railroad wheel, or anything else for that matter, could be cast until new patterns were made. Each Southern railroad had its own wheel design, and over the years Anderson and Company had carefully built up a set of patterns containing models for almost every road. The Richmond firm advised any railroad that wanted wheels to send its own pattern.[3]

The crippling of the Tredegar machine shops was the most serious consequence of the fire. The blaze had gutted this vital department and the South lacked the machine tool facilities necessary to repair the destruction. Lathes, rifling machines, planers, and tools of all descriptions would either have to be scraped together from other establishments that could spare a machine or two or secured from abroad. The Tredegar owners immediately began canvassing both government and private shops seeking tools.[4]

The company concentrated most of its attention on foreign sources of

1. Anderson & Co. to Stoneburner, Belew & Co., May 17, 1863, Tredegar Letterbooks.

2. Richmond City Hustings Court, Deed Books No. 68A, pp. 205–10, and No. 79B, pp. 409–11, microfilm copy, VSL.

3. Anderson & Co. to Thomas Dodamead, May 20, 1863, Tredegar Letterbooks.

4. Anderson & Co. to Albert Johnson, May 23, 1863, to D. Moran, May 23, 1863, to Edward Denmead, June 2, 1863, to Hugh Rice, June 3, 1863, and to Capt. J. W. Archer, July 16, 1863, ibid.; entries for June 1863, Tredegar Receiving Book; Archer Account Book, VHS.

supply, however. Anderson and his partners had already sought to gain shipping privileges on government freighters a month prior to the fire in order to secure "various articles" that were "essential to enable us to continue to supply the wants of the Government in Iron and munitions of war." The Chief of Ordnance conditionally endorsed their request at that time and informed the War Department that "these applicants are large contractors & among the most meritorious to whom the privilege of shipping cotton might be conceded." But Gorgas recommended that government freight should continue to receive first priority as long as the War Department had cotton in Confederate ports ready for shipment. Secretary of War Seddon refused to approve Anderson's application in April on the grounds that needs of the army required all available steamer space.[5]

Immediately after the May fire, Anderson and Company reopened the subject. When both the War and Navy Departments offered to assist in the rebuilding and retooling of the works, Anderson replied that the government could best aid the Tredegar "by giving us ship room for two to three hundred bales of cotton and also for the tools and material[s] back . . . in its steamers."[6] He repeated the request later that month. The War Department again denied the application because its vessels were committed to transporting more vital government cargo.[7]

The Tredegar management now became irritated at what they considered an unwarranted denial of their just claims. "Our loss is indeed great but not irreparable & if the Government would regard us in the light in which we deserve to be remembered, & aid us in getting the tools abroad, we would soon be under way again," one of the partners wrote the superintendent of the Virginia and Tennessee Railroad. When the railroad official offered to assist the Tredegar in any way possible, the company replied that "we wish our Government would evince the same interest in getting our works in operation. While *on paper* they offer every facility, we get no assistance from them whatever. What can you suggest as the most probable chance of getting tools—the Government having declined to aid us."[8]

5. Anderson & Co. to Seddon, April 14, 1863, and endorsements, Letters Rec'd., Secretary of War, RG 109, NA; Seddon to Anderson & Co., April 20, 1863, Letters Sent, Secretary of War, ibid.

6. Anderson & Co. to Gorgas, May 16, 1863, and to R. D. Minor, May 16, 1863, Tredegar Letterbooks.

7. Anderson & Co. to Seddon, May 19, 1863, and to Mallory, May 29, 1863, ibid.

8. Anderson & Co. to Dodamead, May 23, June 1, 1863, ibid.

Anderson and Company did have some cause for complaint. A large lathe they had purchased in Raleigh was impressed by the government and turned over to Bellona foundry.[9] And during June, the War Department ignored the company's almost daily requests for details of carpenters, masons, and other skilled laborers needed to assist in reconstructing buildings.[10] But government shops turned some tools over to the works and made their facilities available to the Tredegar for reconditioning damaged machines.[11] By utilizing this aid, the Tredegar foundries were able to begin melting pig iron again by late May, and by the middle of the next month a good start had been made on rebuilding the boring mill.[12]

The chief reason for the Tredegar partners' irritation was the frustration of their plans to ship a considerable amount of cotton abroad, plans which they had formulated well before the May fire swept through their plant. They began large-scale cotton purchases in late March 1863, purchases which coincided with a sharp depreciation in the gold value of the Confederate dollar at Richmond banks.[13] On March 25, 1863, the company dispatched $10,000 in Confederate 6 per cent call loans to an agent in Mississippi and promised to forward an additional $10,000 shortly. "These amounts are to be invested in cotton at such points as you may consider for our mutual benefit always having regard to the fact that we would desire to have some of the cotton where it might be sent abroad without much delay, whenever vessels could be obtained," they instructed their purchasing agent. His commission was to be 25 per cent of the net profit realized by resale of the cotton.[14]

The Tredegar owners soon extended their search for cotton. During early April, they sought quotations on five hundred to one thousand bales from brokers in South Carolina, Georgia, and Alabama.[15] To facilitate

9. W. S. Downer to Gorgas, June 3, 1863, and endorsements, in "J. R. Anderson & Co.," Confederate Citizens File, RG 109, NA; Anderson & Co. to Downer, June 2, 1863, to Rice, June 15, 1863, and to Gorgas, June 20, 1863, Tredegar Letterbooks.

10. Anderson & Co. to Seddon, June 9, 10, 11, 12, 13, 17, 20, 1863, Letters Rec'd., Secretary of War, RG 109 NA; Anderson & Co. to John W. R. Moore, June 4, 1863, and to T. S. Rhett, June 20, 1863, Tredegar Letterbooks.

11. Anderson & Co. to Capt. J. H. Parker, May 30, 1863, and to J. M. Brooke, July 11, 1863, ibid.

12. Anderson & Co. to Gorgas, June 2, 1863, and to Brooke, June 19, 1863, ibid.

13. "Confederate Inflation Chart" *Official Publication No. 13,* Richmond Civil War Centennial Committee.

14. Anderson & Co. to W. Kenan Hill, March 25, 1863, Tredegar Letterbooks.

15. Anderson & Co. to Phillips, Fariss & Co., to Rufus Johnston, to S. Wyatt & Co., to Charles Rogers & Co., and to Reeves Battle & Co., all April 11, 1863, ibid.

this investment, Anderson and Company told railroad officials in the deep South to deposit remittances due the Tredegar in local banks.[16] Agents originally sent south to buy food were instructed to add cotton to their want lists.[17] Even after the Secretary of War refused to grant export space to the company in April and May, the partners continued to buy cotton. Coincident with these large purchases, the owners divested themselves of a considerable portion of their Confederate bonds. In June and July 1863, the company sold over $275,000 in government securities; by the end of July, the Tredegar management had purchased over four hundred bales of cotton and was negotiating for several hundred more.[18]

The problem was getting the cotton out of the Confederacy. After the War Department declined to permit Anderson and Company to ship on government steamers, the Tredegar owners decided to send the cotton abroad on their own vessel. In May and June 1863, the members of the firm subscribed a total of $100,000 in two new joint stock exporting companies organized by prominent Richmond commission merchants and businessmen.[19] Shortly after they had made these investments, the Tredegar partners saw a much better chance to ship their cotton to foreign ports and they quickly seized the opportunity. In late June, they learned that they could acquire an interest in a blockade-runner undergoing repairs at Wilmington. The *Merrimac,* a fast iron paddle-steamer originally built for opium smuggling along the China coast, had sustained engine damage and the War Department had sold the vessel to a group of Wilmington men. Anderson and Company acquired a quarter interest in the ship and its cargo of cotton for some $250,000 by promising to make the Tredegar facilities available for necessary repairs.[20] After a trip to Wilmington in early July to inspect the ship and talk to the owners, Anderson and Tanner hurried back to Richmond to rush the needed parts to comple-

16. Anderson & Co. to William Johnston, April 15, 25, 1863, to Campbell Wallace, April 17, 1863, to Baker, Lawles & Co., April 17, 1863, to H. T. Peake, April 15, 1863, and to Kirkwood & Knox, April 27, 1863, ibid.

17. Anderson & Co. to Atlee, April 17, 1863, ibid.

18. Entries for April–July 1863, Tredegar Journals; entries under "Confederate Bonds" and "Purchases of Cotton," Tredegar Ledgers; Anderson & Co. to Rogers & Co., June 24, 1863, and to Nathaniel Bass, June 24, 1863, Tredegar Letterbooks.

19. Entry for May 1863, Tredegar Journals; "Subscribers to the Blockade Scheme," June 4, 1863, list in Watson–Archer Papers, VHS; *Acts of the* [*Virginia*] *General Assembly, Called Session, 1863* (Richmond, 1863), pp. 37–38.

20. Anderson & Co. to Gorgas, June 26, 1863, and to Capt. Porter, June 29, 1863, Tredegar Letterbooks; entry for July 1863, Tredegar Journals. This vessel should not be confused with the ironclad *Merrimack.*

tion. Anderson, evidently forgetting about the tools for his burnt workshops, promptly negotiated a contract with the Ordnance Bureau for freighting arms out of Bermuda.[21]

When news of Lee's defeat at Gettysburg reached Richmond, the Tredegar management wired the Wilmington syndicate to "Hurry out our vessel . . . This is an anxious moment." [22] The ship sailed shortly after the urgent message from Richmond, but Union blockaders were waiting for the sleek vessel. The U.S. Steam Sloop *Iroquois* captured the *Merrimac* and its cargo of tobacco, turpentine, and 642 bales of cotton on July 24, 1863, forty miles off the coast of North Carolina, "She is reported to be very fast (16 to 18 knots), certainly looks it, and I am satisfied would not have been caught by us if she had been properly managed," reported the captain of the *Iroquois*.[23]

The Tredegar's initial venture into the risky business of blockade-running proved disastrous. The company's bookkeeper recorded an expense of $244,167 under "Stm[r] Merrimac" when he totaled the profit and loss figures for 1863.[24] The Richmond industrialists had some slight consolation in that none of their cotton purchased in April, May, and June was on board the vessel. The government had sold the *Merrimac*'s cargo along with the ship.[25] Anderson ordered the Tredegar's several hundred bales stored in South Carolina and Georgia until he could find another opportunity to get the cotton out.[26] He got a second chance, but not until the summer of 1864.

Anderson and his partners ostensibly wanted to ship cotton to England in order to purchase machinery, tools, Negro clothing, and other essential items.[27] But this was not their primary reason for running the blockade, as their subsequent course of action clearly demonstrated.

II

Despite this initial setback, Anderson and his partners continued to devote considerable time and effort to further cotton purchases and various

21. Anderson & Co. to Glasgow, July 3, 1863, and to John Dawson, July 17, 1863, Tredegar Letterbooks.

22. Anderson & Co. to S. T. Fremont, July 17, 1863, ibid.

23. *O.R.N.*, Ser. I, *9*, 131–33.

24. Tredegar Inventory Book.

25. *O.R.N.*, Ser. I, *9*, 133.

26. Entries for Aug., Sept., 1864, Tredegar Journals.

27. Anderson & Co. to William Johnston, April 15, 1863, to Wallace, April 17, 1863, and to Gorgas, June 26, 1863, Tredegar Letterbooks.

schemes for breaking through the Yankee blockade, including an abortive privateering venture chartered in October 1863 as the Virginia Volunteer Navy Company.[28] Anderson renewed his quest for export and import privileges in the spring of 1864, shortly after the government issued new commercial regulations. Under rules proposed by the War and Treasury Departments and approved by the President on March 5, 1864, all blockade-runners entering or leaving Southern ports were required to grant the Confederate government one half of their cargo space at a set freight rate.[29] Anderson, in his letter of April 30, 1864, asked the President to allocate government-controlled steamer space to his firm at the rate fixed for military cargo. To support this extraordinary request, the Tredegar head expressed his intention to rebuild vital portions of the works destroyed by fire the previous May, the locomotive shops in particular. "We think the keeping up [of] the Rail Roads, if the war continues, will depend on early preparations to build Locomotives," he added. Anderson also sought permission to send an agent abroad to negotiate the sale of Tredegar cotton and to purchase machinery and critical materials.[30]

The President met only part of Anderson's request. Davis was willing to permit the company to dispatch an agent to Europe and the War Department issued the necessary papers. Shipping on government vessels or using space reserved for military freight was quite another matter, however. The Chief Executive told Secretary of War Seddon to inform the company that it should seek its own transportation. The President did admit, however, that if Anderson could not accomplish his plans through ordinary private channels, "the matter is of such importance that further attention should be given to it." [31]

This partial rebuff failed to discourage the Tredegar senior partner. Anderson was well aware that he could still expect exceptional official consideration for any project promising aid to his works. With this in mind, he enlisted the aid of an influential politician, Congressman Eli M. Bruce of Kentucky, and the two men approached the Treasury Department in early July 1864 with an ambitious steamship project. The two partners proposed

28. *Acts of the [Virginia] General Assembly, Called Session, 1863*, p. 39; Anderson & Co. to M. J. Wicks, Dec. 12, 1863, Tredegar Letterbooks.

29. Richardson, ed., *Messages and Papers of the Confederacy, 1*, 417–20.

30. Anderson & Co. to the President of the Confederate States, April 30, 1864, Letters Rec'd., Secretary of War, RG 109, NA.

31. Endorsement of Davis, May 2, 1864, ibid.; J. A. Campbell to Anderson & Co., May 4, 1864, Letters Sent, Secretary of War, ibid.

to join with the government in establishing a line of blockade-runners, to ply between Southern ports and the British West Indies. The private investors and the government were each to put up one half of the cost of the vessels, and to share equally in the operating expenses and the cargo space. Anderson, Bruce, and any other private capitalists that might associate with them later would supervise and direct the operation of the line.[32]

After several weeks of negotiation, the Treasury Department accepted Anderson's proposal to establish a line of up to six steamers but attached a number of conditions. Although the contract stipulated that the object of the line was "to facilitate the introduction of supplies and materials" necessary to maintain and rebuild the Tredegar works, the new Secretary of the Treasury, George A. Trenholm, recognized the maximum profit and minimum risk potential of Anderson's proposition.[33] Trenholm's business experience eminently qualified him to appraise this contract. He had amassed a fortune, reputedly the largest in the Confederacy, through the operations of his fifty or so blockade-runners.[34] The Secretary was determined to see that the government received full value for its 50 per cent investment in the line. In order to insure that additional blockade-runners would be brought into service, he required Anderson and his associates to purchase new vessels, although this stipulation had not been in the original contract. The contract had, however, specifically limited Anderson's vessels to the underused Gulf ports.[35] After the closing of Mobile Bay in early August 1864, Trenholm sought to confine the fleet to Florida harbors, "but I think I will defeat him in this," Anderson predicted.[36]

Both these restrictions proved embarrassing to the private investors. The Tredegar owners had closed up their Mississippi cotton speculations in December 1863 and had confined their purchases to South Carolina and Georgia.[37] Getting cotton to Apalachicola or St. Marks and shipping supplies from these Florida west coast ports to Richmond would be almost impossible, given the condition of Southern railroads. Trenholm's order to use only new ships in the operation was even more disconcerting. In

32. Anderson to C. G. Memminger, July 2, 1864, Letters Rec'd., Secretary of War, ibid.

33. Anderson & Co. to G. A. Trenholm, Aug. 29, 1864, Tredegar Letterbooks.

34. Coulter, *Confederate States of America*, n. 27, p. 163.

35. Anderson to Trenholm, Aug. 29, 1864, and to Maj. B. F. Ficklin, Aug. 26, 1864, Tredegar Letterbooks.

36. Anderson to Ficklin, Aug. 26, 1864, ibid.

37. Anderson & Co. to W. K. Hill, Dec. 15, 1863, to George T. Rogers, Nov. 23, Dec. 12, 1863, and to C. V. Parrington, Dec. 24, 1863, ibid.

August, shortly after the signing of the contract, Anderson and his partners in the shipping venture had purchased a veteran blockade-runner, the iron steamer *Coquette,* from the Navy Department. Anderson's investment, a quarter interest in the vessel, amounted to £4,000, or approximately $345,000 in Confederate currency.[38] Trenholm then informed the Tredegar senior partner in late August that the *Coquette* would not qualify for the steamship line because she was not new. To make matters worse, the vessel was undergoing repairs at Wilmington, a port closed to Anderson's ships.[39]

Anderson worked hard to get these restrictions lifted, but was only partially successful. When he met with Trenholm during the last week in August, the Secretary informed him flatly that the Treasury would accept only new vessels in the proposed line. The government would demand half the cargo space of the *Coquette,* as was the case with all privately owned blockade-runners, but would not share in the cost of the vessel or in the outfitting and operating expenses.[40] Anderson's request for permission to use the Atlantic ports of the Confederacy got a more friendly hearing, however. He restated his case by letter on August 29 and pointed out the impossibility of restoring and maintaining "the present works with their vast dependencies of blast furnaces & collieries" without machinery and supplies from abroad. The only feasible ports for importing heavy equipment and materials were Charleston and Wilmington. If the government denied the line access to these harbors, "we have no means left of obtaining supplies," he concluded.[41] Trenholm saw the merit of this argument and gave Anderson and his partners permission to export and import through the two Atlantic port cities.

Once this permission was secured, the owners began feverishly to assemble a cargo and to prepare the *Coquette* for sea. Anderson telegraphed orders to various storage points in South Carolina and Georgia to rush the

38. Entry for Aug. 1864, Tredegar Journal. Anderson's partners included Congressman Bruce, one W. W. Finney, and B. F. Ficklin, a shipping agent at Wilmington. The *Coquette,* a two hundred horsepower, twin-screw iron steamer, was built in Scotland and had been purchased for the navy by Commander James D. Bullock in September 1863. After she had made a number of successful trips through the blockade, Secretary Mallory decided to sell the vessel because neglect of her machinery had so reduced her speed that he considered her a bad risk; see *Dictionary of American Naval Fighting Ships* (Washington, 1963), 2, 511.

39. Anderson to Ficklin, Aug. 26, 1864, Tredegar Letterbooks.

40. Ibid.

41. Anderson & Co. to Trenholm, Aug. 29, 1864, ibid.

Tredegar's bales to Wilmington and he dispatched substantial funds south for new purchases. The owners spent $80,000 to repair and outfit the vessel and by early September she was ready to sail.[42]

Although the Federal squadron off Wilmington knew the *Coquette* was repaired, loading cargo, and would soon be outward bound, the blockaders failed to apprehend her when she put to sea on a moonless night during the first week of September.[43] On the seventh, she steamed into Nassau harbor with a full cargo of cotton. She "formerly belonged to the Confederate Government, but [is] now owned by a Richmond company," the United States Consul at Nassau accurately reported.[44] "We have heard of the arrival at Nassau of the Steamer 'Coquette' by which we shipped some cotton consigned to your House," Anderson and Company joyfully informed their London factor on September 26. "On receipt of the cotton you will please sell it as you can most to our interest and place proceeds at our credit on your books." [45] The sale of this cargo in England inaugurated a sterling account for Anderson and Company that grew to handsome proportions by the time the war ended.

The *Coquette* delayed in Nassau only long enough to accumulate a return cargo—goods for sale on the Charleston market, not tools and machinery to rebuild the Tredegar locomotive works and other fire-ravaged departments. By early October, the vessel had slipped past Union blockaders guarding the South Carolina port and local newspapers carried announcements of the sale of her cargo. A yellow fever epidemic in Charleston delayed her departure, but on November 1 she sailed with another load of Tredegar cotton and arrived safely in Nassau six days later. The *Coquette* led a charmed life during the months when the Federal fleet was capturing every third vessel that attempted to run the blockade.[46]

The *Coquette*'s good fortune encouraged Anderson to press on with his plans for a full line of new steamers. In November, he began negotiating with the firm of Marshall Beach and Company in Wilmington for the pur-

42. Anderson & Co. to Rogers, Aug. 26, 29, 1864, to J. R. Bell, Sept. 14, 1864, and to George W. Adams, Sept. 15, 1864, Tredegar Letterbooks; entries for Aug., Sept., 1864, Tredegar Journals.

43. *O.R.N.*, Ser. I, *10*, 394, 427.

44. Ibid., p. 477.

45. Anderson & Co. to John K. Gilliat & Co., Sept. 26, 1864, Tredegar Letterbooks.

46. *O.R.N.*, Ser. I, *10*, 598, 601; Anderson & Co. to Glasgow, Oct. 10, 13, 1864, and to Gilliat & Co., Nov. 19, 1864, Tredegar Letterbooks; Frank L. Owsley, *King Cotton Diplomacy* (2d ed. rev. Chicago, 1959), p. 261.

chase in England of two to four new vessels. As an added inducement, Anderson originally offered the Wilmington parties a quarter interest in the line, but when they balked at this share, he upped their interest to three eighths and included the right to establish the shipping agency in the Confederate States. Anderson and his partners would retain control of the Liverpool end of the line.[47] While these discussions were continuing, Anderson sought alternative propositions from other Southern steamship interests. "The Government will make no more contracts of this kind, in our opinion—certainly none as favorable as ours, and we therefore consider it an opportunity to engage in the business that may not occur again," he wrote a Charleston firm in December.[48] The Tredegar senior partner even put out a tentative feeler to Germany to ascertain the prospects for acquiring vessels there and establishing direct communication with the Continent.[49]

After canvassing the market, Anderson decided that the Wilmington interests offered the best chance for ships. "We will close for three (3) steamers," he wired Beach and Company on January 9, 1865.[50] Six days later, before the deal could be completed, Fort Fisher fell and the firm had to make a hurried exit from Wilmington. By the time the Wilmington parties reestablished themselves in Columbia and reopened communication with Richmond, a month had elapsed. Anderson nevertheless reordered the vessels on February 14, but the evacuation of Charleston four days later killed the entire scheme.[51]

Meanwhile the *Coquette* continued her extraordinary career. Her luck had temporarily changed when she developed engine trouble, a persistent blockade-runner problem often brought on by burning naval stores in emergencies. After leaving Nassau in November 1864, she put in to Havana for repairs. By mid-January, her engines were overhauled and she was ready to attempt the port of Charleston again.[52]

Anderson, as usual, made every effort to assemble a full cargo of cotton for the vessel. By Christmas 1864, he had accumulated 280 bales at Charleston and had special agents combing South Carolina and Georgia

47. Anderson & Co. to Marshall Beach & Co., Nov. 11, Dec. 2, 1864, Tredegar Letterbooks.

48. Anderson & Co. to H. Cobia & Co., Dec. 12, 1864, ibid.

49. Anderson & Co. to J. Otto Ehbets, Dec. 12, 1864, ibid.

50. Anderson & Co. to Beach & Co., Jan. 9, 1865, ibid.

51. Anderson & Co. to Beach & Co., Feb. 14, 1865, ibid.

52. Anderson & Co. to Cobia & Co., Nov. 29, Dec. 7, 1864, and to Gilliat & Co., Jan. 13, 1865, ibid.

looking for up to 500 more.[53] When a fire destroyed over one hundred bales of Tredegar cotton at Charleston in late December, Anderson quickened his search for the precious fiber.[54] Union capture of Fort Fisher in mid-January only prompted the Tredegar head to urge his chief purchasing agent to act cautiously and attempt to get a better price.[55] This agent spent over $115,000 buying 184 bales at $1.50 per pound and Anderson and Company's total cotton purchases during the first three months of 1865 amounted to almost $375,000 in Confederate currency.[56]

When the *Coquette* miraculously made it back in to Charleston in late January 1865, Anderson and Company wired their agents there to "ship all cotton possible for us. Purchase some if necessary . . . Attend to sale inward cargo." [57] "We hope the vessel brought in a remunerative cargo," one of the partners wrote several days later.[58] Except for some wire rope needed for coal mining and perhaps some slave blankets, the ship again brought in only goods for public sale in Charleston.[59] Anticipating yet another round trip for the *Coquette*, the partners in Richmond sent their Charleston agents a personal want list that included twenty pieces of bleached shirting, twelve pieces of calico, ten dozen ladies' hose, and "one thousand best segars." [60] Tools and machinery were not on the list.

The *Coquette*, her holds bulging with cotton, made her last run through the blockade in late January. The government, unlike Anderson, had been unable to amass a full cargo in Charleston in time for the sailing so the private owners shared the extra freight space.[61] The ship made it to Nassau, discharged her cargo, and, because of a recurrence of engine trouble, was still there at the close of the war. She was seized by a Federal agent and brought into Baltimore in December 1865 before Anderson could regain control of the vessel.[62]

53. Anderson & Co. to Peake, Dec. 22, 1864, to Bell, Nov. 26, 1864, to James Sowers, Jan. 9, 14, 1865, and to William Johnston, Jan. 9, 12, 14, 1865, ibid.

54. Anderson & Co. to Peake, Dec. 29, 1864, and to Cobia & Co., Jan. 2, 10, 1865, ibid.

55. Anderson & Co. to Sowers, Jan. 17, 18, 1865, ibid.

56. Entry for March 1865, Tredegar Journals; entries under "Purchases of Cotton," Tredegar Ledgers.

57. Anderson & Co. to Cobia & Co., Jan. 26, 1865, Tredegar Letterbooks.

58. Anderson & Co. to Cobia & Co., Jan. 31, 1865, ibid.

59. Anderson & Co. to Tanner, Nov. 14, 1864, to Ficklin, Dec. 10, 1864, and to Cobia & Co., Feb. 1, 9, 1865, ibid.

60. Anderson & Co. to Cobia & Co., Jan. 25, 1865, ibid.

61. Anderson to Crum, Jan. 25, 1865, and to Ficklin, Nov. 2, 1866, ibid.

62. *Dictionary of American Naval Fighting Ships*, 2, 511.

The *Coquette* had more than accomplished her mission for Anderson and his partners, however. She had carried well over five hundred bales of Tredegar cotton to Nassau for transshipment to England.[63] But the prodigious expenditure of time, energy, and money (some $720,000 in Confederate currency for the purchase of cotton alone) which the Tredegar management devoted to this project did not result in stepped-up production at the Richmond works.[64] Only a minute amount of supplies returned through the blockade. If anything, the attention which Anderson, Tanner, and the other members of the firm lavished on this operation hindered the direction of manufacturing at the main plant. Blockade-running was a monumental diversion during the fall of 1864 and the first three months of 1865. Tanner was absent from Richmond from October 11 to November 24, 1864, supervising the acquisition of cotton and food supplies in South Carolina, Georgia, and Alabama and the loading of the *Coquette.* Anderson also went south in an attempt to set up the steamer line and he spent many long hours with Secretary Trenholm over details of the proposed operation.[65]

The efforts of Anderson and his associates resulted in the creation of a key resource, a sterling account in London. Indeed the growth of this account so concerned the Tredegar owners that they attempted some mild blackmail on Secretary of the Navy Mallory. Mallory had agreed to pay for some badly needed gunboat plates in 1864 with sterling exchange. Anderson and Company pressed for these funds in January 1865 and added that "Capt Brooke also directs the completion of some heavy ordnance—if you will include the value of these also in the [sterling] arrangement, it shall be fabricated at once." Mallory refused to be coerced and the company dropped the matter.[66] But the Tredegar funds accumulating in London provided small succor to the Confederate cause. The account remained virtually intact until after the war when it, more than any other means, enabled Anderson and his partners to retain control of the Tredegar works.[67]

63. Anderson & Co. to Gilliat & Co., Sept. 26, Nov. 19, 1864, Tredegar Letterbooks; entry for Sept. 1865, Tredegar Journals.

64. Entries under "Purchases of Cotton," Tredegar Ledgers.

65. Anderson & Co. to Glasgow, Oct. 10, 1864, to Peake, Nov. 25, 1864, to Crum, Aug. 23, 1864, to Trenholm, Aug. 29, Dec. 17, 1864, and Anderson to Ficklin, Aug. 26, 1864, Tredegar Letterbooks.

66. Anderson & Co. to Mallory, Jan. 17, 27, 1865, ibid.

67. When Anderson and his partners converted their sterling account to greenbacks after the war, they realized over $190,000; see below, p. 304.

In his correspondence and conversations with Confederate officials, Anderson steadfastly maintained that the Tredegar's cotton and shipping operations had a single purpose—increased production of military and railroad supplies. Access to foreign sources of supply was absolutely essential, he claimed, if he were to maintain his labor force and rebuild and retool vital portions of his works, the locomotive shops in particular. Such was his official position.

His actions reveal quite a different intention, however. The *Coquette*'s inbound cargo was limited almost exclusively to consumer goods intended for quick sale and returning a handsome profit. Anderson diverted none of his sterling exchange to the purchase of tools and machinery. The Tredegar's blockade-running was basically a profit-making venture, intended to transfer a sizable amount of the company's assets safely abroad. Anderson, putting first things first, was attempting to insure that the business he had devoted his life to would survive a possible Confederate collapse. The outcome of the war made his course prudent as well as profitable. But this enterprise hardly qualified as the high patriotism Anderson pretended it to be.

11

Prices and Profits

Of all the issues which the government and Anderson and Company debated during the war, the pricing of Tredegar products unquestionably prompted the most correspondence and produced the most antagonism. The Ordnance Department in particular fought long and hard to keep Tredegar prices down while the Richmond firm waged an equally arduous struggle for increases. Almost inevitably, these battles ended in an unstable compromise that satisfied neither side and tempted Anderson and his partners to channel more and more of their output into the hands of private consumers.

I

The government had strong reasons for wanting to hold down Tredegar rates. Since the company was the largest private supplier of cannon, munitions, and iron to the Confederate States, inflationary pressure on the budgets of the Army and Navy Ordnance Bureaus could be materially reduced if Tredegar prices were held in check, and both bureaus were extremely economy minded. The Tredegar's charges were doubly important because the firm set the pace for prices in the northern Confederacy. When the proprietors of a Lynchburg foundry supplying shot and shell to the government learned in the spring of 1862 that Anderson and Company was receiving higher prices for similar articles, they complained bitterly. "What we ask is to be placed upon an equal footing with Messrs. Anderson & Co. as long as we manufacture articles equal to those furnished by that concern," wrote the Lynchburg founders. The Secretary of War ordered a hike in the prices paid the protesting iron men and so it went.[1]

In April 1862, Captain Lardner Gibbon, the ordnance inspector at the Tredegar works, raised the first serious objections to Anderson and Com-

1. F. B. Deane, Jr., & Son to Randolph, April 19, Nov. 14, 1862, and Gorgas to Randolph, Oct. 1, 1862, Letters Rec'd., Secretary of War, RG 109, NA.

pany's prices. He considered the prices charged for munitions excessive and refused to certify the company's bills. Colonel Gorgas demanded that he approve the accounts so the Ordnance Department's requisitions could be settled at the Treasury, but Gibbon still declined. The Chief of Ordnance promptly relieved Gibbon of his duties at the Tredegar and transferred the officer to South Carolina. Before leaving Richmond, however, Gibbon felt compelled to present his case to the Secretary of War:

> There was no standard of prices in the Ordnance Bureau, and in many cases no agreements were made with contractors who charged what they pleased—This disorganized state of affairs necessarily produced confusion and after the accounts had been in the hands of Lt Col Gorgas and Captain Stansbury, I at a late date was required to take them up and certify to their correctness and justness. I found that many of them were neither correct nor just—and therefore explained to Col Gorgas the impracticability of my vouching for the truth of what I considered incorrect. Col Gorgas maintained that I had "no right to go behind the question" in that way.
>
> It appears on the files of the [Ordnance] office that the most unwarrantable prices have been paid for ordnance and ordnance stores which were unfit for the field and found their way there because a thorough system of inspection and proof was not allowed me by Col Gorgas.[2]

The Secretary of War promptly asked the Chief of Ordnance to explain these serious charges. "It is, I suppose, unnecessary to make a detailed report in reference to the complaints of Capt. L. Gibbon," Gorgas began a very detailed three-page letter. Gibbon's contention that there was no standard of prices for Tredegar products was untrue, Gorgas maintained. Contracts containing specific prices for heavy guns, shot, and shell had existed since May 1861. "It was the duty of Captain Gibbon, and he was directed, and urged, to establish prices for minor articles, in consultation with the business member of the firm of J. R. Anderson & Co. (Mr. Tanner)." The immediate cause of Gibbon's removal from duty was "his refusal to certify to the correctness of accounts which accrued after the lst of April 1862, under his immediate supervision, basing his refusal on the ground that he could not say that the prices charged were 'correct'—the contracts having been made and prices authorized by me and not by him-

2. Capt. Lardner Gibbon to Randolph, April 26, 1862, ibid.

self." "He was told that he 'could not go behind' my authority," Gorgas continued, "that whatever I approved or ordered would make the account 'correct.' " When Gibbon still refused to certify the Tredegar accounts, Gorgas relieved him of his duties rather than have him arrested and prefer charges against him.[3]

The matter did not close there, however. Gibbon had sent a copy of his letter to Davis and the President asked Gorgas to account for the complaint. The ordnance chief did not specifically answer the charges but replied with a personal attack on Gibbon. Gorgas had introduced him to the President and requested a commission for him in the summer of 1861. According to Gorgas, Davis remarked at the time that Gibbon was "a dull looking man." "Your judgement proved nearer the truth than my hopes," Gorgas wrote. "I did not, however, suspect that he would prove malicious as well as dull." "Your excellency will readily understand therefore that there were other reasons than those he alleges (in which there is only a grain of truth) to make me desire another officer in his place," concluded the chief of the Ordnance Bureau.[4] Gibbon reported for duty at Charleston and the subject was closed.[5] The incident remained on the President's mind, however, as events soon demonstrated.

One item that Gorgas failed to mention in his correspondence dealing with Gibbon's charges was the clause in Anderson and Company's contracts of October 1861 and April 1862 allowing periodic price increases to match higher labor and raw materials costs. This provision was of doubtful legality. The Confederate constitution stipulated that "Congress shall grant no extra compensation to any public contractor, officer, agent, or servant, after such contract shall have been made or such service rendered." [6] The War Department was well aware of the existence of this clear prohibition but chose to ignore it. R. G. H. Kean, Chief of the Bureau of War, told Secretary of War Randolph that a strict interpretation of this clause would "embarrass the Department almost fatally," and force renegotiation of contracts every time the currency fluctuated and contractors requested higher prices.[7] When the Secretaries of the War and Navy Departments and Anderson and Company drew up the September 22,

3. Gorgas to Randolph, June 5, 1862, ibid.

4. Gorgas to Davis, May 1, 1862, ibid.

5. *O.R.*, Ser. I, *14*, 566.

6. Article I, section 9, clause 10, in Richardson ed., *Messages and Papers of the Confederacy*, *1*, 44.

7. R. G. H. Kean to Randolph, Nov. 8, 1862, Letters Rec'd., Secretary of War, RG 109, NA.

1862, contract, they agreed on a clause allowing a 30 per cent increase in the price of all items furnished the government, a boost granted "in consequence of the increase in cost of labor and material." This new rate was to remain in force "until the fluctuations in the value of material and labor may justify a further change." If the price of labor and material fell to the levels of April 1862, the increase was to be abated.[8] At the time the September contract was signed, neither Randolph nor Mallory raised any objection to the 30 per cent increase or the provision allowing future price adjustments.

The Tredegar partners were thus completely unprepared for the government's violent reaction when they attempted to settle their bills on the basis provided for in the September agreement. In early November, Anderson and Company requested the Ordnance Department to grant the 30 per cent increase on all their bills since September 22, as authorized in their contract of that date. This was the first the Ordnance Department had heard of the new contract. Secretary of War George W. Randolph, a close friend of Anderson's, had not consulted the bureau most affected by the provisions of the agreement prior to signing the document! When Colonel Thomas S. Rhett, chief army ordnance inspector, examined the new contract, he took immediate issue with several specific articles and with the overall implications of the compact. "I cannot think that our Secretaries were aware of what they were actually doing," Rhett told Gorgas on November 8, 1862. The contract of April 1862 provided specific prices for heavy cannon, shot, shell, ordinary sizes of bar iron, and boiler and armor plate, but stated that "corresponding rates" were to be charged for articles not enumerated. "We have adhered to the prices of April '62 so far as they are fixed by the contract, but a construction has been placed upon 'corresponding rates' which makes it very objectionable, rather than advantageous," Rhett continued. " 'Corresponding rates,' I find, means really higher, & I might almost say, indefinitely higher prices than those fixed. Against this I have been contending ever since I came here. I found the officers in the Bureau dissatisfied with the prices they were charged & I believe justly so."

Rhett further stated that the government was already feeding large profits to the Tredegar. "These prices have been increasing pretty steadily, & I believe now yield a *profit* of from 30 to 50%. It is quite enough

8. Contract with the War and Navy Departments, Sept. 22, 1862, in "J. R. Anderson & Co.," Confederate Citizens File, ibid.

on a contract of $2,000,000 annually; by the last [September] contract their profits are from 60 to 80%." The government was unwittingly fostering the growth of an industrial behemoth in the name of defense, Rhett charged. "The continuance of this contract until the price of labor & material falls is perhaps the most objectionable feature in it. By this an immense monopoly is built up, Messrs. J. R. Anderson & Co. are furnished $500,000 wherewith to secure it, & it certainly will never be to their interest to reduce cost of materials & labor, so long as their profits are 60 to 80%." The ordnance inspector's closing paragraph was a warning of what might result from the growth of the Tredegar empire:

> To control the Iron interests of a country is to influence all other interests, add to this the Coal, & all mechanical operations are subject to the will of a Single Company. Since the commencement of the World, monopolies have been infamous, & I question if this one will furnish an exception. Had the Secretary of War known the views of yourself & myself on this subject, & had he discovered the indefinitiveness of the contract of April '62, I am quite sure he would at least have hesitated before authorizing an increase of 30% upon prices "at present paid;" he did not bear in mind that prices not fixed by the contract were of course keeping pace with the cost of labor &c.[9]

Gorgas forwarded this letter to the War Department with the earnest request that all contracts involving supplies for the Ordnance Bureau be submitted to his office for scrutiny regarding prices, especially agreements made jointly with the Navy Department. By the time the letter reached the desk of the Secretary of War, Randolph had resigned as a result of a dispute with the President over strategy in the west and the prerogatives of the office of Secretary of War. The interim Secretary, Gustavus W. Smith, sent the letter on to Davis for general instructions regarding future contracts. The President was stunned by the information Rhett had given. He replied angrily that the communication presented "a remarkable and objectionable case." "Contracts should be made by the bureau officers charged with supplying the several wants of the Dept. and specially informed on the matters involved," Davis ordered. "Exactness in all engagements can alone save the Govt. from loss and disappointment. Increase of rates on

9. Rhett to Gorgas, Nov. 8, 1862, Letters Rec'd., Secretary of War, ibid.

contracts is forbidden."[10] It was too late to do anything about the increase granted in the September contract. The government added 30 per cent to Anderson & Company's bills from October 1.[11] But the President specifically forbade any further hike in Tredegar prices.

Anderson and his partners stood in danger of losing one of the most attractive features of their contract and this was particularly irritating to the owners because the government was not adhering to its pledge to detail men and turn over iron to the works. The Tredegar management decided to press for an immediate reversal of the official policy regarding prices. Anderson lost an important ally when Randolph left the War Department. The new Secretary, James A. Seddon, although a Virginian, was not a close friend of the Tredegar senior partner. Seddon ignored Anderson's first attempts to reopen the subject of prices. Anderson wrote on December 8, less than a month after the final settlement of the September price increase, that the continuing advance of both labor and raw materials costs made further adjustments in Tredegar prices necessary. A similar communication was sent to Secretary of the Navy Mallory. When the company received no reply, Anderson requested personal interviews with both men.[12] These letters also went unanswered. Anderson and his partners finally decided to give Seddon a full account of the company's relations with the government in order to acquaint him with their problems and expectations. The ensuing document, eighteen pages long, summarized the history of the Tredegar's dealings with the Confederate States and presented grievances which Anderson and Company hoped the new Secretary would deal with.

After an opening statement outlining their unsuccessful efforts to secure adequate supplies of raw materials early in the war, the Tredegar owners reviewed the contract negotiations with the government that culminated in their move into pig iron and coal production. The loan of $500,000 had to be repaid when the contracts terminated in 1868. These properties, purchased with an inflated currency and worked nearly to exhaustion during the war, would then be worth only a fraction of their original cost, the partners pointed out. The company therefore had to accumulate a fund to settle the loan and this could be done only if they received an adequate

10. Endorsement of Davis, ibid.

11. Entries for Oct., Nov., 1862, Tredegar Foundry Sales Books and Tredegar Rolling Mill Sales Books; Anderson & Co. to W. S. Downer, Dec. 26, 1862, in "J. R. Anderson & Co.," Confederate Citizens File, RG 109, NA.

12. Anderson & Co. to Seddon and Mallory, Dec. 8, 16, 1862, Tredegar Letterbooks.

profit. Anderson and Company asserted, with only slight exaggeration, "that but for the efforts we have successfully used to manufacture Pig Iron & the contracts we have referred to for furnishing the Government with munitions, there would not now be iron to make a single gun."

The company stressed three points in their contracts which the government had to respect in the future if the works were to continue production: the army and navy had to turn over enough pig iron to the Tredegar to complement the company's own blasts; the Secretary of War had to detail needed men to the works; and prices had to be adjusted periodically. The Tredegar works had made extremely important contributions to the Confederate war machine and the owners wished to receive reasonable compensation for doing so. Prices charged the government and private customers were quite low, the Tredegar management claimed, considering what other manufacturers were demanding on the open market: "We have steadily sought to carry out in our sales to the community the same principle which has controlled our dealings with the Government, viz; to refer solely to cost in fixing our prices adding a reasonable profit thereto, as in times of peace." The company chose to sign the contracts binding the Tredegar to produce primarily for the government despite the tremendous profits available on the open market. "If we could have felt warranted in taking a different course by holding the large capacity of these Works free & unpledged so as to direct it to whatever branch of business would find least competition, & by demanding whatever price we could obtain, without reference to cost, we could soon have enriched ourselves," the partners continued. "We do not regret our decision & shall continue to labor in hopes of satisfying those who administer the Government, that we are rendering service to the country."

In the original draft of the letter, this sentence was followed by a further statement of attitude which was deleted from the final copy sent to the Secretary of War: "Whilst we claim for ourselves a higher motive than a mere desire to make money, we do not pretend to say that we propose to work for nothing." [13] Evidently the partners on reflection considered this too frank an expression of what they certainly believed was a legitimate and reasonable approach to their business.

After this long preface, encompassing fourteen pages of the letter, the Tredegar management reached the heart of the communication. They had carefully investigated the subject of their prices and had drawn up a de-

13. Anderson & Co. to Seddon, Dec. 23, 1862, ibid.

tailed schedule which they would present to the War and Navy Departments or to a board of examining officers, whichever the Secretaries preferred. If Seddon believed the Confederacy could better be served by government control of the Tredegar works, the owners stood ready to dispose of the entire Richmond plant, blast furnaces, and coal mines at a fair valuation. "But if we are to go on, it is essential that the Departments will continue to place us above the grade of speculating contractors, and regard us rather as agents of the Government." [14]

This letter had the effect desired by Anderson and Company. The forceful tone of the communication from the Tredegar owners reflected the partners' awareness of the strategic importance of their works. The War and Navy Departments laid aside the President's instructions to grant no further increases on contract prices. The new Secretary of War appointed a two-man board of officers to examine production costs and make price recommendations. Anderson and Company submitted an extremely detailed price list to this examining board on January 20, 1863, and forwarded a similar schedule to the Secretary of the Navy two days later.[15] The increases asked by the company would approximately double the prices granted in the April 1862 contract.

The examining officers conducted an extensive review of Tredegar operations, compiled data, and figured profits on various items. The findings of the board vindicated the company's position that increases were justified. Out of 109 separate items priced by Anderson and Company, the board scaled down only 42 and the reductions in every case were small. The navy was a little harder on the Tredegar, reducing the price on 26 of 49 items and usually by a greater margin than the army board. The company asked, for example, that they be paid $1,600 for double banding a 6.40-inch Brooke gun. The army reduced this price to $1,550 but the navy cut it to $1,509.[16]

The Tredegar partners were generally satisfied with the action of both the army and navy, with two very important exceptions. The company asked 16 cents per pound for iron cannon and 16 cents per pound for gunboat plates; the army and navy scaled the former down to 14 cents and

14. Anderson & Co. to Seddon, Dec. 23, 1863, Letters Rec'd., Secretary of War, RG 109, NA.

15. Anderson & Co. to Lt. Col. Saunders and Capt. S. Schooler, Constituting Board to Examine Accounts, Etc., Jan. 8, 1863, "List of Prices . . . ," Jan. 20, 1863, and Anderson & Co. to Mallory, Jan. 22, 1863, Tredegar Letterbooks.

16. Corrections on "List of Prices . . . ," Jan. 20, 22, 1863, ibid.

the navy cut the latter to 12½ cents. Anderson asked that the investigating officers reexamine closely these two items.[17] This was done and both prices were subsequently raised to the levels originally requested by the company, although the Tredegar senior partner had to appeal to the Secretary of the Navy before the Bureau of Ordnance and Hydrography would increase the price of armor plate.[18] "We have much trouble about getting such prices from the Government as will cover the increased cost of iron, but we hope they will yet see the propriety of it," Anderson told his chief furnace agent early in March.[19]

This dialogue between the government and its most important supplier of iron which opened in early December 1862 did not close until March 1863. The inevitable result of this slow and tedious bargaining was that by the time the prices had all finally been agreed upon, the advance in the cost of raw materials had again cut the Tredegar's profit margin. Although the final settlement of all prices in March, "by mutual concessions" according to one of the partners, made the charges retroactive to December 1, 1862, the Tredegar management was by no means satisfied.[20] At the end of June 1863, three months after the new price list received final approval, Anderson and Company requested another increase of 30 per cent.[21]

The fight began all over again. The examining board of officers was reconvened and Anderson and Company wrote another series of brusque letters. "Labour of all descriptions has advanced since the 1st January last full 33⅓ per cent & in the Rolling Mill Department, where we rely principally upon foreign labour, the advance has been fully 75 per cent," wrote the Tredegar management in July. "In materials, there is scarcely an article we purchase in open market which has not advanced from 50 to 200 per cent in the last 6 months, in consequence of the decreased supply in the Confederate States." "We believe the advance asked for necessary to enable us to continue our intensive operations and therefore respectfully request a favorable consideration of our application at the earliest moment consistent with your convenience." [22] The government subsequently granted a 24 per cent increase, 6 per cent less than the company requested.

17. Anderson & Co. to Gorgas, Feb. 9, 1863, and to George Minor, Feb. 11, 13, 1863, ibid.

18. Anderson & Co. to George Minor, Feb. 13, March 19, 24, 1863, to William R. Williamson, Feb. 20, 1863, and to Mallory, March 13, 1863, ibid.

19. Anderson to Glasgow, March 4, 1863, ibid.

20. Anderson & Co. to Gorgas, March 16, 1863, and to George Minor, March 24, 1863, ibid.

21. Anderson & Co. to Brooke and Gorgas, June 30, 1863, ibid.

22. Anderson & Co. to Brooke and Gorgas, July 27, 1863, ibid.

The Tredegar management accepted the settlement, but not for long. In October 1863, they asked for a further increase of 16 per cent because the government had jumped the wages of mechanics in the army and navy shops the previous August, thus forcing the Tredegar to make a similar increase, and had also increased the price paid other pig iron producers. Gorgas stated that the summer advance of 24 per cent more than covered the Tredegar's added expenses and recommended to the Secretary of War that no advance be made.[23] Gorgas' peremptory refusal prompted an angry reaction from Anderson: "We regret to say that for the last nine months, or more, there seems to have been wanting, on the part of some of the officers who have become connected with the Departments since our contracts were made, such an appreciation of the importance of our engagements with the Government, as we think is necessary to insure to us an official co-operation essential to our success." He requested a personal interview with the two Secretaries, "in order that we may lay before you the grievances of which we complain, the removal of which seems to us absolutely necessary to enable us to keep in operation another year." [24]

No response came from the War Department and the anger of the Tredegar owners increased. "The Government appears determined to keep iron below everything else on the market—It should be the highest considering the expense and trouble of making it," Tanner told another Virginia manufacturer.[25] Nothing but strong threats seemed to get results from the War Department so the Tredegar management again resorted to this expedient after waiting two months for a reply to their October requests.

> We have no reply as yet to our letter under date October 13th asking that an addition be made to our prices for increase in price of pig iron and of labor as per statement rendered thereon. We beg to say that this increase is necessary to enable us actually to discharge obligations we have come under for the Government. We had understood that it was a settled principle that we are to be allowed the value of pig iron with a reasonable percentage upon its cost in fixing the value of our productions. We think it incumbent on us to notify you formally that we cannot continue to operate any

23. Anderson & Co. to Seddon and Mallory, Oct. 13, 1863, and endorsements, Letters Rec'd., Secretary of War, RG 109, NA.

24. Anderson & Co. to Seddon, Oct. 31, 1863, ibid.

25. Anderson & Co. to Deane, Nov. 17, 1863, Tredegar Letterbooks.

> of the blast furnaces for the benefit of the Government upon any other principle.
>
> We have directed all our efforts since the beginning of war to keeping down the price of Iron, of all kinds, to a moderate standard, having for a basis such profit as would be reasonable and fair in time of peace.
>
> We have no hesitation in saying that the prices received from the Government for our work fall short of the cost and we therefore trust you will excuse us for asking that payment be made to us without delay of the amount yet due us upon work finished since 1st August last.[26]

This abrupt communication produced some scurrying in the War Department. Seddon ordered Gorgas to resummon the board of officers to review the prices allowed the Tredegar.[27] The Chief of Ordnance did so, but he also called the owners' bluff about abandoning their contract. He recommended that the entire subject of Tredegar prices be completely revised and that a new contract be drawn settling once and for all the subject of prices, military details, the allocation of government coal and iron to the works, and other matters at issue. The company agreed to submit the question of prices to the government commission which had already been appointed. "But we are unwilling to cancel the existing contract between the War & Navy Departments and ourselves for the reason that it fixes, after elaborate investigations, bases, on which we have undertaken large enterprises and incurred heavy expenditures and obligations." [28] As a result, Tredegar prices received a boost in January 1864 but no new settlement clarifying the company's relations with the government was formulated.

This January increase approximately doubled the charges allowed by the government for iron supplied by Anderson and Company. A smaller increase followed in March, but this hike was the final one in 1864. The last price advance granted by the Confederate government came in January 1865, when inflation was completely out of control. (See Figure 1.)

II

The government bureaus were very much concerned about the price they paid for articles but made no attempt to control the open market. As a re-

26. Anderson & Co. to Seddon, Dec. 12, 1863, ibid.

27. Anderson & Co. to Gorgas, Dec. 15, 1863, ibid.

28. Gorgas to Seddon, Jan. 15, 1864, and endorsements, Tredegar Contract Books.

Figure 1

Prices of Tredegar Products in Confederate Currency, March 1861 – April 1865
2.00
1.90
1.80
1.70
1.60
1.50
1.40
1.30
1.20
1.10
1.00
.90
.80
.70
.60
.50
.40
.30
.20
.10
0
Sources: Foundry Sales Book
Rolling Mill Sales Book
Key:
Price of R.R. wheels per pound
Price of standard size bar iron, private purchaser per pound
Price of standard size bar iron, government purchaser per pound
Price of cannon per pound
MAMJJASONDJFMAMJJASONDJFMAMJJASONDJFMAMJJASONDJFMA
1861
1862
1863
1864
1865

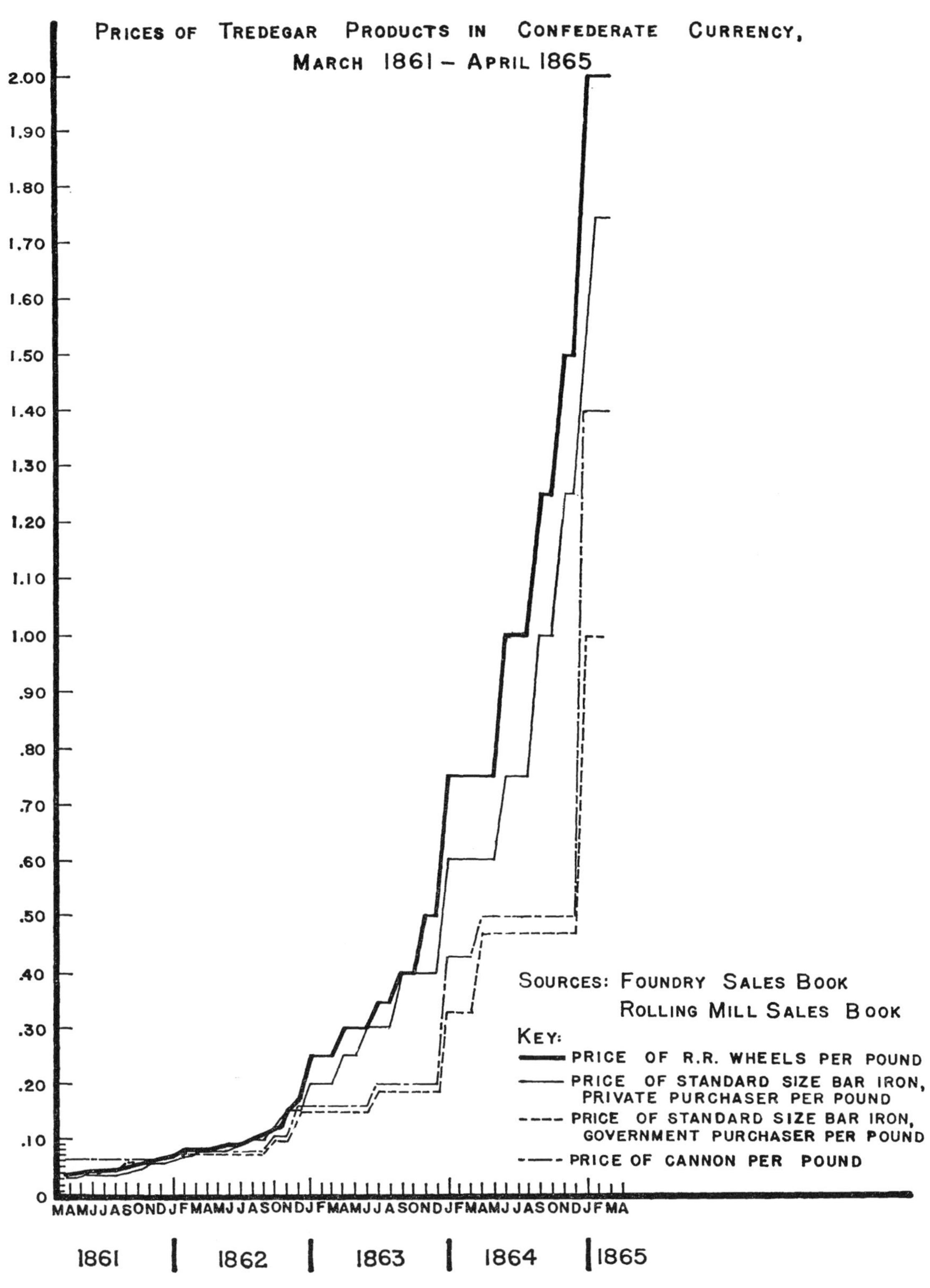

sult, the Tredegar could increase prices to railroads and other consumers almost at will. The price of bar iron to the government and private customers moved up together until the contract of April 1862 fixed the price paid by the military at 7½ cents per pound. (See Figure 1.) The open market rate on standard sizes of Tredegar bar iron continued to climb. In June 1863, railroads paid 30 cents per pound for iron that cost the government half that amount. This ratio was approximately maintained throughout the war. The existence of a government price for rolled iron appears to have had some dampening effect on the open market rate, however. Items which were not on army or navy purchase lists rose faster than articles bought by both public and private consumers. Railroad car wheels, for example, which began the war at approximately the same price as bar iron, rose in price considerably faster than rolled iron.

Although Anderson and Company could legally raise their open market rates at will, they were restrained in part by what the market would bear and by what other manufacturers charged for similar items. "We have struggled to keep down prices strange as it may seem," Anderson informed a complaining railroad superintendent in 1863.[29] But, like all other manufacturers in the Confederacy, they faced constantly inflating production costs, particularly in raw materials, and they sought to pass as much of this increase as possible on to the private consumer. When another Richmond foundry complained to the Navy Department about high Tredegar prices, Anderson and Company wrote that "if we are to supply every body at Government rates & in return pay *market* rates for what we consume, we could not long continue our operations." [30]

The Tredegar maintained communication with other iron manufacturers in the Confederacy and exchanged information on contracts and prices. Anderson asked a stockholder in the Shelby Iron Company of Alabama for detailed information on the terms of their government contract and prices. "It is important that as near as possible there should be uniform prices, although in Al[a] you have great advantages over us," wrote the Tredegar senior partner in 1863.[31] Anderson and Francis B. Deane, Jr., an original organizer of the Tredegar Iron Works who later established a foundry in Lynchburg, kept in close touch on price

29. Anderson & Co. to H. M. Drane, April 20, 1863, Tredegar Letterbooks.

30. Anderson & Co. to Brooke, July 11, 1863, ibid.

31. Anderson & Co. to Col. J. W. Lapsley, Feb. 21, 1863, ibid. See also Cappon, "Government and Private Industry," Univ. of Va. Studies, *1*, 185–86.

matters. "We think our prices ought to correspond, at least to some extent, with the prices we have to pay for articles consumed in our operations," Anderson and Company informed Deane in the fall of 1864. "Do you think we can increase rates beyond those we now stipulate? If so how far can we go."[32] The company jumped rates on railroad wheels and axles shortly after writing to Deane and informed him of the change.[33]

The Tredegar management increased prices to railroads and other private consumers as soon as they ascertained a rise in production costs. As a result, items on the open market earned a considerably greater profit than iron sold to the government. This higher return and the necessity of securing supplies from the lower South prompted the Tredegar owners to devote an increasing amount of their rolling mill production to the railroads during the last years of the war.[34]

III

Ordnance officers on several occasions expressed the view that Anderson and Company was earning enormous profits while the Tredegar owners lodged frequent and often bitter complaints that the prices paid by the government allowed them little or no profit margin. The truth lay between these two positions.

Part of the difficulty of assessing the accuracy of these two contentions arises from the government's imprecise definition of what constituted just profit. The conscription act of September 1862 set 75 per cent of the cost of production as the legal limit on profits.[35] Details would be denied producers earning a greater net return. The Ordnance Department considered this level excessive, however, and stipulated that profits on cannon and munitions should not exceed 30 per cent.[36] Other government bureaus followed the lead of the Ordnance Department and a profit level of 25 to 33⅓ per cent became the limit for most government contractors.[37] The conscription act of February 1864 made no mention of profits.[38]

The Tredegar's profit percentage on military items lay within these gen-

32. Anderson & Co. to Deane, Sept. 8, 1864, Tredegar Letterbooks.

33. Anderson & Co. to Deane, Nov. 11, 1864, ibid.

34. See below, pp. 271–72.

35. *O.R.*, Ser. IV, *2*, 161.

36. Schooler to Gorgas, Feb. 12, 1863, quoted in Anderson & Co. to George Minor, Feb. 13, 1863, Tredegar Letterbooks.

37. Ramsdell, "Control of Manufacturing," *Miss. Valley Hist. Review*, *8*, 237.

38. *O.R.*, Ser. IV, *3*, 178–81.

erous government limits. The first board of officers appointed in January 1863 to investigate the Tredegar's requests for price increases conducted an extensive examination of the company's ordnance production. This commission reported that if the army approved the tentative price set by Anderson and his partners for iron cannon, 16 cents per pound, the profit on a 10-inch columbiad would be 21.21 per cent of the cost of production. The board recommended acceptance of this price and Gorgas agreed to the recommendation.[39] Tanner told the chief of the Bureau of Ordnance and Hydrography in March 1863 that the price the company asked for gunboat plates, 16 cents per pound, would yield a net return of 17.71 per cent. "It is proper to state that when we determined to offer these plates at the price stated, we expected to make something more than 17.71 per cent on the cost of this work, but since our calculations were made there have been heavy advances in the values of labor, coal & other articles entering into the cost of iron," Tanner wrote.[40] The navy, with some reluctance, granted the price asked by Anderson and Company.

When the Tredegar had difficulty settling on new prices in early 1864, the partners took the extraordinary step of asking the government to name a profit level for their products: "We . . . suggest that you will name such percentage as you think will be reasonable for profit, as we have no doubt but that we should acquiesce in the views of the Departments and of the President on that point." [41] No evidence exists that the government ever set the actual net return on specific Tredegar items. The War and Navy Departments did succeed, however, in preventing Anderson and Company from earning exorbitant profits on government sales during the final two and one-half years of the war. The decisions of the boards of officers appointed to examine Tredegar requests for price increases were, in effect, binding on the company. The boards invariably scaled down some of the management's petitions and the Tredegar owners learned not to make excessive requests. The partners could appeal to the commissions to reinvestigate specific items and usually succeeded in obtaining a satisfactory settlement. As long as the government approved profits in the neighborhood of 20 to 25 per cent of the cost of production, however, Anderson and Company had little cause to complain. The profits allowed by the gov-

39. Schooler to Gorgas, Feb. 12, 1863, quoted in Anderson & Co. to George Minor, Feb. 13, 1863, Tredegar Letterbooks.

40. Tanner to George Minor, March 19, 1863, ibid.

41. Anderson & Co. to Seddon and Mallory, March 5, 1864, ibid.

ernment were not as great as those available on the open market but they certainly were substantial.

Tredegar profit and loss statements indicate that the company earned its best returns during the first two years of the war. On a capital investment amounting to $435,000 in 1860, Anderson and his partners

TABLE 8. Profits * of J. R. Anderson & Company, 1861–1865

	1861	*1862*	*1863*	*1864 to April 1865*
Rolling Mill	$175,455	$297,582	$694,667	$2,231,210
Foundry	322,777	397,545	6,624	2,326,404
Other	19,786	—	41,485	—
Total (Confederate currency)	$518,018	$695,127	$742,776	$4,557,614
Total (approximate gold valuation) **	$462,516	$331,013	$ 74,651	$ 147,974

* "Profits" is used here in the contemporary nineteenth-century sense and indicates net cash earnings on capital investment plus certain undistributed costs which do not appear in the company's books, principally depreciation. Depreciation was undoubtedly high during the war but was probably more than offset by the assets (coal mines, furnace properties, and new plant and equipment) acquired with government loans, loans which the company never repaid.

** These figures are only rough approximations, intended to indicate the company's net cash return in noninflationary terms. They result from dividing the net cash return for each year by the following average yearly value of $1.00 gold in Confederate treasury notes:

1861	$1.12
1862	2.10
1863	9.95
1864–65	30.80

These valuations were computed from gold purchases recorded in the Tredegar Journals and from "Confederate Inflation Chart," *Official Publication No. 13,* Richmond Civil War Centennial Committee. This publication gives the basic exchange value of gold in Confederate treasury notes at Richmond from May 1861 to May 1865, and is based primarily on bank quotations in Richmond newspapers.

Source: Profit and loss accounts in Tredegar Inventory Book.

earned a profit approaching 100 per cent in 1861 and 70 per cent in 1862.[42] (See Table 8.) In addition, the government loaned the Tredegar management $500,000 in 1862 to develop blast furnaces, collieries, and to expand the Richmond facilities. Anderson and Company was never required to repay any of this interest-free loan, which did not fall due until

42. The figure for capital investment is given in the manuscript returns, Census of Manufactures, 1860, Virginia, VSL.

1868. By 1863, when the government had developed the examining board as a fairly effective mechanism for restraining the price of military hardware, rising production costs, of raw materials in particular, set up a cost–price squeeze which reduced profits significantly. The disastrous May 1863 fire, continuing deterioration of plant and equipment, and an increasingly demoralized and always inadequate labor force created additional obstacles to profitable production during the last years of the war. But the company continued to make money, although on a less grandiose scale. The Tredegar owners did not intend to work for nothing, as they wrote in 1862, and their operations throughout the war gave ample evidence that they followed this dictum.[43]

Yet Anderson and his associates do not deserve to be dismissed merely as profiteering contractors. Their motives were more complex. Anderson neatly expressed the two elements which motivated much of the management's wartime activity in a letter to a prospective purchasing agent in 1863. If the man accepted Tredegar employment, "your work will . . . be one of patriotism as well as (I hope) of profit." [44]

The senior partner and the members of his firm shared a genuine zeal for the Confederate cause. When one of his young relatives died in battle in 1863, Anderson asked "how could a union ever be reconstructed over the graves of such heroes." [45] Even Grant's bloody push toward Richmond and the wasting siege of Petersburg in 1864 failed to snuff out Anderson's hopes for eventual victory. "We have now on the fortifications twenty-three hands and I learn that Genl. Lee has made a further requisition for teamsters. Whatever he requires however I will comply with, if it takes all the hands I have," he told his brother in October. "Here altho we have had the enemy pressing upon us our confidence that Genl. Lee with his noble Army will be able to hold the capital is still unabated," he continued. "The result as well as the fate of our beloved country is in the hands of an all wise and merciful God. My own faith in the final success of our cause is stronger as each year of the war rolls around." [46] These words would seem to be something more than an exercise in self-encouragement.

Sometimes, as in the case of the company's blockade-running, profit got the better of patriotism. As a businessman, Anderson knew that it was nec-

43. Anderson & Co. to Seddon, Dec. 23, 1862, Tredegar Letterbooks.

44. Anderson to W. H. Wilson, June 1, 1863, ibid.

45. Anderson to William A. Glasgow, June 30, 1863, Glasgow Papers, WLU.

46. Anderson to F. T. Anderson, Oct. 18, 1864, Anderson Papers, UVA.

essary to plan for any contingency. But as a Southerner, a Virginian, and a former Confederate officer, he still held the faith. Without a strong commitment to the cause of Southern independence plus the expectation that their labors would be amply rewarded, Anderson and his partners would have abandoned their struggle to stay in production. The absence of either of these factors would have considerably diminished the Tredegar's contribution to the Confederate war effort.

12

Labor: Details, Conscripts, and Aliens

The Tredegar management's struggle to acquire and hold an adequate skilled labor force during the war was a vexing and often frustrating battle. As an obstacle to production, only the ever-present lack of raw materials exceeded the constant shortage of workers. The deficiency of artisans brought on by overmobilization early in the war seemed mild in comparison with the company's labor problem in 1862. In that year, the acquisition of blast furnaces and coal mines more than doubled the Tredegar's need for workers. Anderson and Company's efforts to obtain skilled personnel initiated a correspondence with Confederate authorities on the subject of labor that lasted for the duration of the conflict. Unfortunately for Southern war production, this continuing exchange produced more ill-will than workers.

I

To put a furnace in blast and keep it in successful operation required the labor of approximately one hundred men. The isolated mountain furnaces acquired by the Tredegar in 1862 were virtually self-sufficient communities and demanded the presence of a wide range of both skilled and unskilled labor. Once the furnace machinery was put in order, extensive preparations were necessary before the making of iron could commence. Large quantities of wood had to be cut and converted to charcoal, ore and flux (usually limestone) had to be mined, and then all these materials had to be hauled to the furnace. If the property had been worked for a number of years, as was the case with most of the Tredegar stacks, teams and wagons were absolutely necessary to move the raw materials to the furnace site.

When adequate stocks of ore, flux, and charcoal had been accumulated, the blast began. The process of "blowing in" started by filling the furnace completely with charcoal. Cloverdale furnace, typical of the rough stone stacks that dotted the slopes of the Valley of Virginia, was thirty-seven feet high and nine feet across the egg-shaped bosh at the base. The charcoal was fired at the top and allowed to burn to the bottom of the bosh. This took several days. When the fire reached the base of the furnace, workmen refilled the stack with charcoal and the fire climbed back to the top. Laborers then fed charcoal, ore, and flux into the furnace, and bellows, actuated by a water wheel or steam engine, sent blasts of air through the bosh.

Once blown in, the furnace was worked day and night until the blast was completed. The founder supervised the feeding and tapping of the furnace. When, in his judgment, the iron was ready to be tapped, the molten metal was released from the furnace and taken down by runners into sand molds where the pigs hardened. Tapping usually occurred twice a day. In a good year, Cloverdale furnace could produce over one thousand tons of iron.[1] To insure such performance, Anderson and Company had to hold the workers already laboring at furnaces in blast and assemble a free and slave labor force at the dormant properties.

The Tredegar owners expected the labor clause of their April 1862 government contract to provide the bulk of their white furnace workers. The contract was clear on this point. The Secretary of War had promised to exempt or detail from military service such men as Anderson and Company "may consider indispensable to the faithful execution of this contract." [2] The equally important matter of details of artisans for the Tredegar works was also involved in the extended correspondence between Anderson and Company and the War Department in 1862 and early 1863.

It became evident soon after the signing of the April agreement that the Secretary of War had promised more help to meet the Tredegar's labor needs than he was willing or able to deliver. Less than three weeks after the signing of the contract, Anderson and Company requested Secretary of War Randolph to detail a total of nineteen blacksmiths and machinists from the army to the Tredegar works. Gorgas endorsed the request and forwarded the letter to the War Department. Randolph's reply doubtless amazed the Tredegar owners: "It has been found that so many of the detailed men abandon their work that details are only granted now in small numbers and in very special cases." Request for details denied.[3]

1. Bradford, "Ante-Bellum Charcoal Iron Industry," pp. 60–62; Lesley, *Iron Manufacturer's Guide*, p. 73.

2. Contract with the War and Navy Departments, April 29, 1862, in "J. R. Anderson & Co.," Confederate Citizens File, RG 109, NA.

3. Anderson & Co. to Randolph, May 19, 1862, and endorsements, Letters Rec'd., Secretary of War, ibid.

Just what did their contract mean, the Tredegar management wondered? Six days later they asked for the detail of only three men.[4] After waiting a month for some action at the War Department, Tanner bluntly told Randolph that his refusal to detail artisans would have serious consequences. "Your decision to detail no more men at present will delay us in complying with so much of our contract with the Army & Navy as requires the execution of certain work therein referred to, in as short a time as was expected when we made that contract," he wrote on June 30. "This work has been virtually suspended nearly two months in consequence of many of our men connecting themselves with the army & the withdrawal of a large number of state militia." A further complication had arisen when McClellan landed his forces at Fort Monroe in March and April and began his move toward Richmond. Many of the owners of slaves hired by the Tredegar demanded that their chattels be moved to a safer locale. "We are doing all we can with the men at our command & hope it may soon suit the public service to permit further details," concluded the Tredegar superintendent.[5]

This letter succeeded in securing the release of the three mechanics but grave labor deficiencies continued. During most of 1862, the Richmond plant was short of machinists, blacksmiths, strikers, pattern makers, file cutters, and carpenters.[6] The blast furnaces needed founders, teamsters, colliers, miners, blacksmiths, carpenters, wagon and harness makers, and the coal pits required miners. The demand for wagons and teamsters was especially critical at Anderson and Company's furnaces in the Shenandoah Valley. Federal control of the Manassas Gap Railroad forced the Tredegar to haul iron and blooms from the Columbia and Caroline furnaces in Shenandoah County to the Virginia Central Railroad at Staunton, a distance of over sixty miles.[7]

The company's subsequent attempts to secure the release of men in the ranks to labor at Tredegar furnaces, coal mines, or the Richmond plant met a stone wall of official resistance. The management tried to induce the

4. Anderson & Co. to Randolph, May 25, 1862, ibid.

5. Anderson & Co. to Randolph, June 30, 1862, ibid.

6. List of details in Archer Account Book, VHS; advertisements in Richmond *Dispatch*, April 3, May 30, 1862; Anderson & Co. to Gorgas, Dec. 12, 18, 1862, and to Seddon, March 5, 1863, Tredegar Letterbooks.

7. Advertisement in Richmond *Dispatch*, Nov. 3, 1862; Anderson & Co. to Seddon, Oct. 30, Nov. 25, 1862, Letters Rec'd., Secretary of War, RG 109, NA; Anderson & Co. to Seddon, Jan. 8, 1863, Tredegar Letterbooks.

War Department to alter its stand by limiting requests as far as possible to men not at the front lines and reported by military surgeons as unfit for active service.[8] This had no effect. Invariably the company's letters received virtually the same endorsement when they reached the desk of the Secretary of War: "Answer—that the condition of the army forbids the department to entertain any proposition to reduce its effective strength by details." [9] Numerically superior Federal forces faced Southern armies at all major engagements in the eastern theater in 1862, and the Army of Northern Virginia needed every man.

After the War Department had rejected repeated Tredegar requests for men from the ranks made in October, November, and December 1862, Anderson and Company asked that their case be presented to Lee personally. "Now whilst we appreciate the motives which have led to a refusal of our applications for details from the Army, we beg to remark that all the men we have unsuccessfully asked for, would probably not constitute more than a company & we respectfully suggest that a company of men employed in an Establishment of vast capacity upon arms & munitions of war, may be more effective than the same number of men in the field," the company informed the Secretary of War. "It is a military question we think worthy of reference to the General Commanding in the field." Seddon's notation on this letter consisted of one word: "File." [10] No action was taken on the request.

The Tredegar hoped that once the troops went into winter quarters, the War Department would release a few men.[11] But January brought no change in the government's policy. Anderson's temper was up when he sent a blunt letter to the Secretary of War on January 8, 1863. He asked for the detail of a disabled private and directed the attention of the Secretary of War to the last paragraph of the contract of April 29, 1862. "The important point to be settled is one which has doubtless escaped the attention of the Department," wrote the Tredegar senior partner with little attempt to hide his irritation. "Have we a right to the detail of this man under the

8. Anderson & Co. to G. W. Smith, Oct. 15, 1862, and to Seddon, Oct. 20, 30, Nov. 25, Dec. 1, 12, 1862, Letters Rec'd., Secretary of War, RG 109, NA; Anderson & Co. to Seddon, Dec. 4, 1862, and to Gorgas, Dec. 12, 18, 1862, Tredegar Letterbooks.

9. Anderson & Co. to Seddon, Nov. 25, 1862, and endorsement, Letters Rec'd., Secretary of War, RG 109, NA. See also Seddon to Anderson & Co., Dec. 13, 1862, Letters Sent, Secretary of War, ibid.

10. Anderson & Co. to Seddon, Dec. 23, 1862, and endorsement, Letters Rec'd., Secretary of War, ibid.

11. Anderson & Co. to Julia Wills, Dec. 5, 1862, Tredegar Letterbooks.

plain stipulations and covenants of our contract. If this stipulation is not to be observed it is impossible for us to 'execute' our contract." [12] The War Department could only reply that the requests of Anderson and Company for details had been forwarded to the commanding general but that Lee disapproved the applications.[13]

Despite these numerous rejections, the Tredegar management continued to seek details. In answer to Glasgow's urgent requests for some skilled furnace artisans, the Richmond partners replied that they were pressing the matter "with hopes of success." Their optimism was tempered, however, by past experience and a realization that "the War Department is a slowly moving machine." [14]

Finally, Anderson attempted to bypass this bureaucratic inefficiency in Richmond with a direct appeal to his friend Lee. "I am sure it will not surprise you that we have occasionally to ask you to let us have a few men to keep the wheels in motion," Anderson wrote on February 13, 1863. He asked specifically for two men to aid in the production of pig metal at the western furnaces: Lieutenant William Steptoe, a cavalry officer who had been brought up in the iron business by Anderson and who had been a partner in the Tredegar machine shop operations in the 1850s; and Private William L. Flaherty, an infantry soldier who had contracted typhoid fever and had been sent home to Botetourt County on sick leave. Anderson wanted Steptoe to manage Australia furnace, which was not producing well because of incompetent direction; the services of Private Flaherty were required because Flaherty's father, a skilled millwright needed to repair furnace machinery, refused to do the work unless his son was detailed to assist him. Anderson did not reveal the exact reason for Flaherty's detail in his letter to Lee. "I will be obliged to you, if you think it expedient, to let me have Mr. Steptoe and private Flaherty as they are so important," the Tredegar head concluded. "We shall have to ask for some more men hereafter, but I will promise that our applications shall be confined to such as are indispensable and I believe in the results you will find the country compensated well for the loss of the services of these men in the field." [15]

12. Anderson & Co. to Seddon, Jan. 8. 1863, ibid.

13. Seddon to Anderson & Co., Jan. 26, 1863, Letters Sent, Secretary of War, RG 109, NA.

14. Glasgow to Anderson & Co., Jan. 9, Feb. 7, 1863, Tredegar Furnace Letterbook; Anderson & Co. to Glasgow, Feb. 12, 1863, Tredegar Letterbooks.

15. Anderson & Co. to Lee, Feb. 13, 1863, ibid.; Glasgow to Anderson & Co., Feb. 7, 1863, Tredegar Furnace Letterbook.

Anderson thought Steptoe's presence at the furnace would result in the production of enough iron to cover two gunboats.[16]

Lee rejected Anderson's request. He was much too concerned about maintaining the strength of his army to counter the spring push of the greatly superior Federal forces camped at Fredericksburg to allow details. Lieutenant Steptoe remained with his regiment until wounded at Yellow Tavern in May 1864; Flaherty was finally detailed but not until October 1863, after the battles of Chancellorsville and Gettysburg.[17] Anderson failed completely in his initial attempts to change the attitude of Lee and the War Department on the crucial subject of details.

The company's inability to gain the release of soldiers with special skills impeded operations in several key areas in 1863. Tredegar coal mines were constantly shorthanded. "We have used every effort both in the United States and Europe to obtain coal miners without success and it will be impossible for us to meet the expectations of the Government in producing coal unless such hands can be obtained," one of the partners told the Secretary of War in mid-1863.[18] "I see no special act or skill necessary in such work and can't spare soldiers for such labor," Seddon replied to one of the company's frequent requests for miners.[19] The War Department rejected Anderson and Company's appeals for carpenters and bricklayers to assist in repairing the destruction of the May fire, for boat builders, for a saw mill superintendent needed to expedite work on gun carriage timber, and for skilled blast furnace personnel.[20]

When incompetent management put their Australia furnace out of blast in July 1863, the Tredegar owners enlisted the aid of the Chief of Ordnance in their quest for an experienced founder. "It is of the highest importance to us to increase the supply of iron to Messrs Anderson & Co., Contractors, & the detail is recommended," Gorgas advised the Secretary of War. Seddon as usual turned down the request and the furnace contin-

16. Anderson to Lee, March 2, 1863, Tredegar Letterbooks.

17. "Information Compiled from Confederate Muster Rolls," manuscript volumes, VSL, 8, 123; "Compiled Service Records . . . Virginia," *National Archives Microfilm Publications*, M-324, roll 452.

18. Anderson & Co. to Seddon, June 16, 1863, Tredegar Letterbooks.

19. Anderson & Co. to Seddon, April 25, 1863, and endorsement, Letters Rec'd., Secretary of War, RG 109, NA.

20. Anderson & Co. to Gorgas, March 12, 1863, to Seddon, July 25, 29, Sept. 25, Oct. 21, 1863, and endorsements, ibid.; Anderson & Co. to Seddon, June 9, 13, 17, July 23, 1863, and to G. Jordan, Jr., June 26, 1863, Tredegar Letterbooks.

ued to operate at a fraction of its productive capacity.[21] "They make strange decisions, but we have to submit patiently," the partners told their chief furnace agent after he complained about the War Department's policy.[22]

The frustration the Tredegar experienced in trying to secure skilled labor was shared by manufacturing plants throughout the Confederacy. Even the Selma foundry and rolling mill, the special pet of the Navy Department, was constantly crippled for want of artisans. Lieutenant Catesby ap R. Jones, the officer in charge at Selma, reported in September 1863 that "we will be ready to turn out work when we get mechanics that are promised us—thus far we have received none. . . . The Rolling Mill also drags for want of hands." Jones was fed up with trying to run the Alabama works without operatives, as he told a fellow officer: "What chance is there of getting service abroad—I am tired of this duty, where I have an immense establishment, from which much is expected, [but] the mechanics are not furnished." [23] The Tredegar had little hope of securing details if the navy could not get men to run the Selma plant.

The government's refusal to grant details to the Tredegar forced the company to seek other sources of manpower early in the war. An agent went to Maryland on the heels of the Army of Northern Virginia in the fall of 1862 to obtain skilled workers, but had no success. At the same time, Anderson and Company dispatched a man to Europe with instructions to hire almost every description of rolling mill and foundry labor for work at the Tredegar. Again, no new workers immigrated to Richmond.[24]

The Tredegar management found an unexpected source of labor in the city's overcrowded prisons. Union prisoners who took an oath of allegiance to the Confederate States were paroled and allowed to seek employment. To insure that they would not try to return to United States territory, Confederate authorities dispatched their names to the Federal government as deserters. In January 1863, Anderson and Company sent forty paroled prisoners to Glenwood furnace. When nearby chicken roosts were rifled

21. Anderson & Co. to Seddon, July 25, 29, 1863, and endorsements, Letters Rec'd., Secretary of War, RG 109, NA; Anderson & Co. to William Steptoe, Nov. 12, 1864, Tredegar Letterbooks; Tredegar Pig Iron Receipt Book.

22. Anderson & Co. to Glasgow, May 30, 1863, Tredegar Letterbooks.

23. Lt. Catesby ap R. Jones to R. D. Minor, Sept. 26, 1863, Minor Papers, VHS.

24. Anderson & Co. to Randolph, Nov. 4, 1862, Letters Rec'd., Secretary of War, RG 109, NA; Anderson & Co. to Amos P. Chamberlain & Co., March 9, 1863, and to Henry W. Moncure, July 18, 1863, Tredegar Letterbooks.

soon after their arrival, the good citizens of Rockbridge County protested vehemently against the presence of these men in their neighborhood. "In reference to the Yankee deserters—like you we have no favor to see a Yankee about us in any form," Anderson told a local citizen. They were working for the Confederate cause, however, and if they did satisfactory labor he would keep them employed. Restrictions were tightened and Glasgow was satisfied that they earned their keep, cutting timber for charcoal and driving wagons.[25] Parolees with iron working skills were kept at the Tredegar. Federal prisoners began working there early in 1863, and by the summer of 1864 Anderson and Company had hired over forty parolees for work at the Richmond plant. These men were paid the same wages at their Southern or foreign-born counterparts and constituted a valuable addition to the labor force.[26]

Although the War Department rebuffed the Tredegar management's efforts to acquire men in uniform, the owners could legally retain workers already at their blast furnaces. Legislation passed by Congress shortly after the April 1862 conscription law specifically exempted from the draft all persons "engaged in working iron mines, furnaces and foundries." [27] Subsequent Congressional action, taken in October 1862, revoked this blanket exemption, however, and required local enrolling officers to add the names of ironworkers between the ages of eighteen and forty-five to their draft lists. Upon approval of the Chief of Ordnance that the number of laborers was not excessive, conscript officers made out certificates detailing the workers back to their jobs for sixty days. Every two months, the company had to seek a renewal of the details from the local enrolling officer. Approximately three hundred workers were held at Tredegar furnaces under these regulations and they formed an important skilled nucleus around which the management built a dependable furnace labor force.[28]

These detail procedures also applied to three privately owned stacks

25. Anderson & Co. to Mrs. E. A. Waugh, Feb. 2, 1863, to Glasgow, Jan. 12, 22, 1863, to F. T. Anderson, Jan. 22, 1863, and to John Letcher, Jan. 26, 1863, ibid.; Glasgow to Anderson & Co., Jan. 26, 1863, Tredegar Letters re Furnaces; entry for Jan. 1863, Tredegar Journals.

26. Anderson & Co. to Gen. J. H. Winder, Jan. 8, 1863, and list of prisoners received, July 28, 1863, Tredegar Letterbooks; Provost Marshal I. H. Carrington to Capt. W. S. Winder, Aug. 8, Oct. 7, 1863, Letters Rec'd., Secretary of War, RG 109, NA; J. A. Campbell to J. H. Winder, Aug. 12, 1863, and to Carrington, Aug. 9, 1864, Letters Sent, Secretary of War, ibid.

27. *O.R.*, Ser. IV, *1*, 1081.

28. Ibid., *2*, 162, 167–68; Anderson & Co. to John T. Armstrong, March 17, 1863, to Glasgow, March 25, June 23, 1863, to M. A. Pender, March 31, 1863, to Stoneburner, Belew &

under contract to supply pig metal to Anderson and Company and it gave the Tredegar partners, who sought the details for this trio, considerable power over the operations of these furnaces.[29] "The Bureau of Conscription has frequently complained of the large number of hands detailed for your furnace and it will be quite a disappointment to them to know that only 150 tons of metal have been delivered to us in six months," one member of the firm bluntly informed a proprietor under contract to the Tredegar. He urged the furnace owner to "press on your operations so as to make amends for the small quantity delivered to this date." [30]

Anderson and Company managed to retain the bulk of their free blast furnace laborers until late 1864 by scrupulously attending to the renewal of their details. The owners in Richmond cautioned their furnace agents to stick to the letter of the Conscript Bureau's regulations and this warning paid off.[31] In February 1864, a local agent for the James River and Kanawah Canal Company in western Virginia complained to the Secretary of War that "Joseph R. Anderson has upwards of 300 able bodied men exempt to work at his different furnaces & is making a private fortune out of the Government." Seddon ordered the local enrolling officer to investigate and the latter reported after a "diligent inquiry" that all of the company's conscript workers were "regularly detailed & accounted for." [32]

Anticipating a more stringent official policy toward detailed conscripts in the coming year, the Tredegar's chief furnace superintendent advised the Richmond office in October 1863 that the company should attempt to replace as many conscripts as possible with slave labor. The management agreed and instructed Tredegar hiring agents to secure the maximum possible number of Negroes in the areas they combed. Severe competition among the hirers of large numbers of slaves in Virginia prevented this drive from reaching its goal and the company continued to employ several hundred conscripts at the furnaces during 1864. Only details and white non-conscripts worked the two Tredegar stacks in the northern Shenandoah

---

Co., July 23, 1863, to Crum, July 23, 1863, and to Col. Richard Morton, Nov. 4, 1864, Tredegar Letterbooks.

29. Anderson & Co. to Lewis, Crawford & Co., Jan. 15, June 2, 1863, to Graham & Son, March 19, June 2, 1863, and to Morton, Jan. 26, 1863, ibid. The three furnaces were Graham's, Mount Vernon, and Beauregard.

30. Anderson & Co. to Lewis, Crawford & Co., July 11, 1863, ibid.

31. Anderson & Co. to Glasgow, Dec. 15, 1863, ibid.

32. William Ridgeway to Seddon, Feb. 2, 1864, and endorsement of Capt. Jacob Bonde, April 28, 1864, Letters Rec'd., Secretary of War, RG 109, NA.

Valley because slave owners considered the region too vulnerable to enemy attack.[33]

Glasgow's forecast of a tighter government rein on Southern manpower was realized early in 1864. The conscription act of February 17 extended the limits of the draft to seventeen and fifty years of age and repealed all previous exemptions.[34] The Tredegar owners feared a wholesale removal of their free labor force, even though most of their Richmond workers were already serving in the Tredegar Battalion. They wrote Gorgas' office immediately and enclosed the names of 175 conscripts "whose services are absolutely necessary for the fulfillment of our contract with the Ordnance Department." [35] Their apprehensions were unfounded, however, as they learned when the general orders putting the new law into effect were published on March 1. Detail procedures remained virtually unchanged. Local enrolling officers could still grant sixty-day details to indispensable laborers of conscript age, if the applications had the approval of the appropriate government bureau chiefs.[36]

The new legislation did not affect details already at the various Tredegar facilities, but the manpower shortage which prompted the February revision of the draft laws made it impossible for the company to secure even the most urgently needed laborers from the army in 1864. In August, Anderson appealed personally to Lee in an attempt to solve the long-standing shortage of coal miners. The Tredegar head requested the detail of six experienced miners to insure his works an adequate supply of coal during the coming winter. He even promised to turn an equal number of less vital workers over to the Richmond conscript officer to replace those taken from the ranks. Lee refused to detail the men on the grounds that every available man in uniform was needed to repel Grant's assaults on his lines, and the Secretary of War disapproved of exchanging an experienced soldier for a raw draftee. Anderson was still seeking coal miners in January 1865.[37]

33. Glasgow to Anderson & Co., Oct. 31, 1863, Feb. 11, March 2, 1864, Tredegar Furnace Letterbook; Anderson & Co. to B. W. Moseley, Dec. 15, 1863, and to Maj. T. O. Chestney, Dec. 15, 1863, Tredegar Letterbooks; "Negroes and Rations at Catawba, 1863," manuscript Tredegar volume; "Monthly Report of Operations at Caroline Furnace," Jan. 31, 1864, Supplementary Tredegar Records. The two furnaces were the Caroline and the Shenandoah.

34. *O.R.*, Ser. IV, *3*, 178–81.

35. Anderson & Co. to Capt. R. K. Hudgins, Feb. 24, 1864, Tredegar Letterbooks.

36. *O.R.*, Ser. IV, *3*, 181.

37. Anderson & Co. to Lee, Aug. 24, 25, 1864, to I. M. St. John, Aug. 31, Sept. 7, 1864, to Joseph Marston, Sept. 16, 1864, and to Gen. J. L. Kemper, Jan. 26, 1865, Tredegar Letter-

Grant's pressure on the Confederate defenses of Richmond and Petersburg brought a sizable cut in the Tredegar's conscript labor force in the fall of 1864. The Adjutant and Inspector General's Office issued orders on October 20 calling up one fifth of all detailed artisans engaged in ordnance work, iron manufacture, and mining. The Niter and Mining Bureau informed Anderson and Company of this order immediately. On November 4, 1864, the management turned over to that bureau the names of ninety-two men, representing one fifth of the total number of conscripts employed by the company at Richmond and at the furnaces and mines. The government made no further draft on the details remaining with Anderson.[38] Those who served in the Tredegar Battalion had already seen ample duty in the Richmond trenches, however, and would see more before the war was over.

Both civil and military officials believed at the time that the system of exemption and detail was grossly abused and deprived the army of needed troops. A committee appointed by the Virginia House of Delegates to investigate exemptions and details in that state reported in October 1863 that "the evil is a great and growing one, and unless arrested, will be most disastrous in its consequences to the strength and efficiency of the army." The committee found widespread frauds and evasions of duty.[39] Modern scholarship has confirmed the findings of the Virginia legislators.[40]

Anderson and Company's experience indicates, however, that the approximately 100,000 Southern men of military age who managed to avoid field duty were not distributed among the economy where they could render most effective home service to the war effort. By November 1864, the entire free labor force at the most important ordnance and munitions establishment in the Confederacy had dropped from almost 1,000 workers in 1861 to between 400 and 500 men. Of that number, some 175 were Northern and foreign-born workers exempt from the draft. The conscript force at the Richmond works totaled no more than 275 men. During the

---

books; Anderson & Co. to Seddon, Nov. 16, 1864, and endorsements, Letters Rec'd., Secretary of War, RG 109, NA.

38. *O.R.*, Ser. IV, 3, 741; Anderson & Co. to John Bass, Oct. 23, 1864, to Morton, Nov. 4, 1864, to H. P. Tasker, Nov. 7, 1864, to Glasgow, Dec. 27, 1864, and to Kemper, Jan. 19, 1865, Tredegar Letterbooks.

39. *Journal of the [Virginia] House of Delegates, Called Session, 1863* (Richmond, 1863), pp. 52, 144–45.

40. See Albert B. Moore, *Conscription and Conflict in the Confederacy* (New York, 1924), pp. 76–80, 106, 111.

same period, the slave population at the Richmond plant had more than doubled. Approximately 200 conscripts and 550 slaves labored at the company's blast furnaces during late 1864 and another 250 workers, mostly slaves, mined coal at the Tredegar pits. An additional 58 Negroes and 9 white men manned a fleet of canal and smaller boats. By the end of 1864, Anderson and Company employed only some 400 to 500 details in a labor force totaling between 1,900 and 2,000 men.[41]

II

Throughout the war, the wages paid free Tredegar workers advanced much more slowly than either raw materials' costs or Anderson and Company's retail prices. In September 1861, following a brief strike at the works, the company increased the pay of skilled workers—first class blacksmiths, pattern makers, machinists, finishers, boiler makers, and top foundry laborers—from the prewar rate of $2.50 per day to $3.00. The next pay hike, delayed until July 1862, raised per diem wages to $4.00. The Tredegar provided a small increase to $4.50 in January 1863.[42] These advances did not begin to cover the rise in the cost of living in the Confederate capital, however. By the beginning of 1863, Tredegar wages were up only 80 per cent over antebellum levels while the general price index for the eastern Confederacy had risen to seven times the level of the first four months of 1861.[43]

When the wages offered by Anderson and Company failed to keep pace with those provided by the government facilities, these shops lured away a number of skilled Tredegar artisans.[44] "Our operations for your Department are now being interfered with to such an extent by the efforts of establishments being built elsewhere, especially at Selma, to draw off our hands that we beg to invoke your prompt and serious attention to the subject," the partners complained to the Secretary of the Navy in December 1862.[45] The numerous government establishments in Richmond consti-

41. Ledger of Details, 1864–65, RG 109, NA; Anderson & Co. to Lt. Col. R. Morton, Lt. A. M. de Bree, and Capt J. Wilcox Brown, Nov. 5, 1864, to Maj. B. F. Noland, Sept. 1, 1864, to Morton, Nov. 4, 1864, and "Statement Showing Number of Men . . . Employed . . . in Making & Transporting Pig Metal," Dec. 16, 1864, Tredegar Letterbooks.

42. Wage charges in Tredegar Foundry Sales Books; Anderson & Co. to J. Browne, Jan. 29, 1863, Tredegar Letterbooks.

43. Lerner, "Money, Prices, and Wages," *Journal of Political Economy, 63,* 22–24.

44. Anderson & Co. to Gorgas, Dec. 3, 1862, and to J. H. Winder, Dec. 9, 10, 1862, Tredegar Letterbooks.

45. Anderson & Co. to Mallory, Dec. 11, 1862, ibid.

tuted an equally serious threat. The Tredegar and the Confederate shops competed actively for the capital's limited number of artisans.[46] When called upon to share his laborers with another government plant, the officer in charge of the Richmond ordnance depot agreed to do so if necessary, but added "they have quite a number of hands of the kind asked for . . . at the Tredegar Works." [47]

After losing a number of workmen to various army and navy facilities, Anderson and his partners in January 1863 requested the Ordnance Bureau to arrange wage consultations between the superintendents of the local government shops and the owners of major private Richmond iron works. Only a general agreement on wages and a mutual pledge not to make unilateral advances could "prevent demoralization in our establishment," they claimed.[48] Their forecast proved correct. Before Gorgas acted on this petition, a group of Tredegar laborers, demanding the same compensation as that offered by the Confederate armory and the navy boiler shops, went on strike in mid-March. Anderson and Company informed the Chief of Ordnance at once and he promised an immediate review of his bureau's wage policies. As a result, Gorgas ordered all wages frozen at various ordnance establishments as of March 31, 1863, and instructed superintendents to make no changes in wage rates without referring first to him.[49] Anderson and his associates agreed to boost Tredegar pay levels up to the government standard and to follow the Ordnance Bureau's rates in the future.[50]

This agreement largely eliminated government pirating of Tredegar artisans for the duration of the war. Following the bureau's lead, Anderson and Company increased wages from the January 1863 level of $4.50 for skilled mechanics to $5.00 in late March and to $6.00 on August 1, 1863. When the company made the August raise, the partners attempted to pass along the added production cost to the government but Gorgas re-

46. Anderson & Co. to Maj. Smith Stansbury, Dec. 2, 1862, ibid.; advertisements in Richmond *Dispatch*, March 21, April 20, 1864.

47. W. S. Downer to Gorgas, April 4, 1863, Letters Sent, Richmond Arsenal (Ordnance Depot), RG 109, NA.

48. Anderson & Co. to Gorgas, Jan. 31, 1863, Tredegar Letterbooks.

49. Anderson & Co. to Gorgas, March 16, 25, 1863, ibid.; "List of men who 'struck' for wages at the Tredegar Works, March 14, 1863," Archer Account Book, VHS; Cappon, "Government and Private Industry," Univ. of Va. Studies, *1*, 186.

50. Anderson & Co. to Albert Johnson, June 4, 1863, Tredegar Letterbooks; Anderson & Co. to Seddon and Mallory, Oct. 13, 1863, Letters Rec'd., Secretary of War, RG 109, NA.

Ironworker James H. Wade and an unidentified African American worker in the Tredegar rolling mill. This was one of three photographs by Richmond's Huestis P. Cook related to Tredegar's Civil War history that appeared in the 17 October 1907 issue of *Iron Age,* an industry journal. Wade's father, Edward Wade, ran the rolling mill when it produced the iron plates for the CSS *Virginia (Merrimack).* The housings of the two-high mill, to James H. Wade's left and right, are from the Confederate period. African Americans worked in the rolling mills from the 1840s in skilled positions, and their numbers at Tredegar increased greatly during the Civil War due to the demands of wartime production.

Tredegar machinist George P. Perrini, with gun lathes used to finish Confederate cannon. Perrini began work at Tredegar in the 1850s and labored in the gun-boring and -turning operations during the Civil War. When this photograph by Huestis P. Cook appeared in *Iron Age* in 1907, the lathes were being used to turn rolls—seen in the foreground—for the rolling mills.

fused to allow an increase in Tredegar prices at that time. On Christmas Day, 1863, the management granted a 25 per cent pay boost which increased skilled wages to $7.50 per day. Final raises in August 1864 and January 1865 pushed the level to $10.00 but by early 1865, open market prices had reached astronomical levels and the Tredegar management had to feed all its workers, slave and free, at company expense.[51]

Government regulations concerning the pay of detailed conscripts acted as a partial brake on Tredegar wages until the fall of 1864. Congress in May 1863 limited the compensation of soldiers detailed to both government and private establishments to regular military pay plus rations or, in lieu of that, $3.00 per day.[52] Seddon pointed out in his report of April 1864 that a per diem wage of $3.00 was totally inadequate in the locales where most ordnance manufacturing went on. Foreigners performing the same work in the same establishments received three or four times the compensation paid conscripts, he noted, and the morale of the latter suffered accordingly. The Secretary strongly recommended that Congress make additional provisions for detailed men.[53] Congress acted on this advice in June 1864. The new regulations called for regular military pay, rations, and wages of $2.00 per day plus extra compensation for "extraordinary skill and superior workmanship." General orders putting this law into effect in August set the standard for extra pay allowed a first class mechanic at $6.00 per day and stated that wages paid details by private contractors "shall conform as nearly as possible to the wages received by similar classes in the employ of the government." [54]

Anderson and Company protested at once that these orders would send Tredegar wages soaring. Both public and private shops in Richmond then gave first class mechanics $7.50 per day. But with $2.00 base pay, $6.00 extra compensation, and a food and clothing ration worth over $7.00 per day, wages would total almost $16, an increase of better than 100 per cent. The partners agreed to comply with these orders but requested the government to hike Tredegar prices 30 per cent to cover the added expense. When the three-man military pricing board met in October, the

51. Anderson & Co. to Seddon and Mallory, Oct. 13, 1863, and endorsement, Oct. 16, 1863, ibid.; Anderson & Co. to Maj. E. B. Smith, March 14, 1864, and to F. B. Deane, Jr., Feb. 1, 1865, Tredegar Letterbooks; Tredegar Payroll.

52. Matthews, ed., *Public Laws*, 1st Cong., 3d Sess., p. 155; *O.R.*, Ser. IV, *3*, 3.

53. *Report of the Secretary of War, April 28, 1864* (Richmond, 1864).

54. *O.R.*, Ser. IV, *3*, 493, 591–92.

officers authorized only a 16 per cent price increase but the Tredegar owners "concluded it best to accept it." [55] War clerk Jones, perhaps after seeing some of this correspondence, noted acidly in early October that "at the Tredegar Works, and in the government workshops, the detailed soldier, if a *mechanic,* is paid in money and in rations (at the current prices) about $16 per day, or nearly $6000 per annum. A member of Congress receives $5500, a clerk $4000." [56]

Although skilled artisans may have fared better than legislators or government functionaries, skyrocketing inflation undoubtedly cut the real wages of industrial labor.[57] In October 1863, the superintendent of the Richmond armory favored moving his operations from Richmond and cited as his primary reason "the high price of all the necessities of life here and the continual appreciation of the same." Yet he reported in January of the following year that considering the difference in the value of currency, the labor required to manufacture a musket cost less in 1864 than in 1860.[58] Anderson and Company estimated in October 1863 that wages represented just over 31 per cent of the cost of Tredegar manufactured goods. A year later, the partners set labor's share of the cost of production at 25 per cent.[59]

Even the highest paid Tredegar operatives evidenced dissatisfaction with their lot. The fifty out of four hundred free workers paid by the piece—shot and shell molders, reamers, core makers, gun borers, gun band and trunion smiths, and chippers, for example—formed a privileged group among the Tredegar labor force.[60] One such artisan, a smith named John Yakel who turned out trunions and pintle plates for ordnance, earned $120 during a two-week period in November 1863 while the foreman of the smith shop made only $105. In March 1864, Confederate pickets caught Yakel, who was also a lieutenant in the Tredegar Battalion, trying to reach the Union lines. Because of his skills, authorities decided not to

55. Anderson & Co. to Seddon and Mallory, Sept. 6, 1864, to Capt. J. Wilcox Brown, Sept. 19, 1864, to Seddon, Oct. 1, 1864, to Mallory, Oct. 1, 1864, to Morton, de Bree, and Brown, Nov. 5, 1864, and to Deane, Nov. 19, 1864, Tredegar Letterbooks.

56. Jones, *Diary, 2,* 301.

57. Lerner, pp. 32–33.

58. Downer to Gorgas, Oct. 13, 1863, Jan. 6, 1864, Letters Sent, Richmond Arsenal (Ordnance Depot), RG 109, NA.

59. Anderson & Co. to the Secretaries of War and Navy, Oct. 13, 1863, Letters Rec'd., Secretary of War, ibid.; Anderson & Co. to Morton, de Bree, and Brown, Nov. 5, 1864, Tredegar Letterbooks.

60. Ibid.

court-martial him and returned him to his forge at the works.[61] Other reasons may well have prompted his attempted escape, but Yakel's wages, among the highest earned at the works, were insufficient to induce him to stay voluntarily.

If the owners had not begun selling provisions to their men at cost in the fall of 1862, a truly precipitous decline in real wages would have occurred. By 1864, the company had instituted regular disbursements of flour, beef, and pork as part of the biweekly payroll. Clerks deducted the value of the food at cost from the worker's cash earnings.[62] In February 1865, the company was issuing a monthly soldier's ration of ten pounds of bacon or thirty pounds of beef and thirty pounds of meal to each worker, in addition to his regular wages of $9.00 to $10.00 per day. "In addition we sell the men what we can spare," wrote one of the partners.[63] When Sherman's destruction of the Georgia railways forced the Tredegar onto the Richmond market extensively for the first time in January 1865, both the management and the workers realized the full significance of earlier provisioning operations in the lower South. The owners paid $65 to $80 locally for a bushel of corn but sold it to the workers for $30 a bushel.[64] If the company had depended on the local market for food and clothing throughout the war, both the laboring population and Tredegar production would have suffered materially.

III

With their real wages declining, large numbers of the Tredegar's foreign and Northern-born operatives sought to leave the Confederacy as early as 1862. In the fall of that year, Anderson and Company apparently made the mistake of attempting to use the conscription act as a tool to retain their services. On October 25, 1862, the Ordnance Bureau requested the Tredegar management to furnish a list of men of draft age employed on army work so that they might be enrolled by the local conscript officer and detailed back to the works. The roll made out by Anderson and Company for the foundry and machine shops and a similar list of rolling mill

61. Tredegar Payroll; Anderson & Co. to J. H. Winder, March 8, 1864, Tredegar Letterbooks; "Compiled Service Records . . . Virginia," roll 452.

62. Contract with Henry Hagans, Nov. 29, 1862, Tredegar Contract Books; Anderson & Co. to Peter Derbyshire, Dec. 20, 1862, Tredegar Letterbooks; entry for Feb. 1863, Tredegar Journals; Tredegar Payroll.

63. Anderson & Co. to Deane, Feb. 1, 1865, Tredegar Letterbooks.

64. Ibid.; Anderson & Co. to Glasgow, Jan. 24, 1865, ibid.

workers drawn up in December included names of many foreign-born operatives, some of whom had married local women but a number of whom had not. A schedule of all Tredegar workers subject to conscription compiled by the company in February 1863 listed 451 names and was even more inclusive.[65]

But in drawing up these lists, the Tredegar owners went beyond War Department regulations. The general orders which put the draft law of September 1862 into effect specifically stated that foreigners not domiciled in the Confederate States were exempt from conscription. The order defined domicile as residence in the Confederate States with intention to remain permanently. Long residence alone did not constitute domicile. "A person may acquire domicile in less than one year, and he may not acquire it in twenty years' residence," the orders read. The principal evidences of intention to remain in the South were listed as the statements of the persons involved, exercise of the rights of citizenship, marriage, and the acquisition of real estate, "but the intention may be gathered from other facts." [66]

When the commandant of conscription at Camp Lee was slow to act on the list furnished in October, Anderson and Company complained to Gorgas that many of their ordnance workers were leaving and that the management could do nothing to stop them since these men had not yet been enrolled. The company asked Gorgas' immediate attention to this matter.[67] The laborers took quite a different view of their military obligations, however. When military authorities ordered the Tredegar Battalion to turn out for inspection in mid-December, the commander of the battalion informed the Adjutant General's office that the men claimed total exemption from military duty and had discontinued drilling. Scarcely a company could be mustered.[68]

Conscript officers finally acted and enrolled the men listed by Anderson and Company but this action had the opposite effect from that intended by the Tredegar owners. The exodus increased rather than diminished because a number of the artisans listed by the management were technically

65. Capt. R. K. Hudgins to Anderson & Co., Oct. 25, 1862, Tredegar Order Book; "List of men employed at the Tredegar Rolling Mill subject to the Conscript Act," Dec. 1862, and "List of men employed at the Tredegar Iron Works between the ages of 18 and 45," Feb. 1863, Tredegar Letterbooks; "Men at work on ordnance for the Army," Oct. 27, 1862, Archer Account Book, VHS; manuscript population schedules, Henrico County, Va., 1860, in "Federal Population Censuses, 1840–1880."

66. *O. R.*, Ser. IV, 2, 164; Lonn, *Foreigners in the Confederacy*, pp. 386–90.

67. Anderson & Co. to Gorgas, Dec. 3, 1862, Tredegar Letterbooks.

68. *O.R.*, Ser. IV, 2, 240.

exempt. "Many of our hands are leaving us & we will be unable to continue our operations unless there be some mode of arresting this tide of emigration now becoming so fearful to our operations," the company complained to the provost marshal of Richmond in March 1863.[69] The next day one of the partners dispatched a similar communication to Colonel Gorgas: "We beg leave to report that many of the men, of foreign birth, employed at these works, are leaving to go beyond our lines, some of whom have been long engaged here, and have been regarded as entitled to conscription, but in most cases this may not be so." [70]

The Tredegar owners realized their mistake and sought to retreat from it, but only after large numbers of laborers were beyond Confederate lines. By July 1863, the Tredegar had barely enough puddlers left at the rolling mills to keep five furnaces lit while twice that number remained cold.[71] When the management attempted to guarantee some key foreign workers that they would not have to bear arms, Anderson and Company found that a state proclamation prevented them from granting an ironclad guarantee. The War Department informed the company that foreigners could be called out by the governor for local militia duty, even though these same men were exempt from regular army service.[72] All Tredegar artisans would have to fight when the time came.

IV

During the final two years of the war, Union movements against the Confederate capital frequently brought the Tredegar operatives into the Richmond fortifications. The 250 to 275 detailed conscripts and volunteers composing the Tredegar Battalion performed most of this military service. The battalion spent an inactive week in the trenches early in July 1863 while Federal forces undertook a series of diversionary maneuvers around Richmond during the Gettysburg campaign.[73] The Tredegar plant was just recovering from the May fire when the men left for the field. "It seems every difficulty now befalls us in our operations," one of the partners lamented.[74]

69. Anderson & Co. to J. H. Winder, March 6, 1863, Tredegar Letterbooks.

70. Anderson & Co. to Gorgas, March 7, 1863, ibid.

71. Anderson & Co. to Gorgas, July 9, 1863, ibid.

72. Anderson & Co. to Seddon, July 16, 20, 1863, ibid.; J. A. Campbell to Anderson & Co., July 17, 1863, Letters Sent, Secretary of War, RG 109, NA.

73. *O.R.*, Ser. I, *33*, 1301; Tredegar Payroll; Anderson & Co. to Morton, de Bree, and Brown, Nov. 5, 1864, and to Glasgow, July 3, 1863, Tredegar Letterbooks.

74. Anderson & Co. to H. M. Drane, July 11, 1863, ibid.

The Tredegar unit suffered its first battle losses when the workers saw action against Colonel Ulric Dahlgren's raiders in March 1864. The Tredegar Battalion and the other local defense units were ordered to Richmond's western defenses in order to check the picked cavalry force which was attempting to free Federal prisoners in the city. As dusk was falling on March 1, the inexperienced Tredegar infantrymen were surprised by Dahlgren's troopers. The first volley from the Yankees caught the battalion in an open field and inflicted a number of casualties. The mechanics returned a ragged fire until the cavalry charged and sent them into a disorderly retreat. Fortunately, the Armory Battalion had come up rapidly behind the Tredegar workers and under the skillful command of a veteran field officer, the artisans from the government shop checked Dahlgren's advance.[75]

Although his men had not performed well in their first encounter with the Federals, Anderson found some comfort in the final outcome of the raid. "The enemy have fared badly," he informed his brother three days after the attack. Confederate cavalry had ambushed Dahlgren and his men on the night of March 3 near King and Queen Court House and had killed the youthful Union commander and captured most of his men. When Anderson learned that documents had been found on Dahlgren's body calling on the raiders to burn Richmond and murder the President and his cabinet, he was aghast. "I have seen the papers taken on his body which will no doubt be published and will form one of the most remarkable incidents in this savage war upon us," he wrote.[76]

From March 1864 until the evacuation of Richmond, Tredegar workers saw almost regular military service. Grant's drive on Richmond forced Confederate authorities to call at least a portion of the battalion into the field during every month from May to December 1864. The bulk of the Tredegar's free laborers spent almost the entire month of October in the earthworks circling the city and production, especially of ammunition, dropped off sharply at the works.[77] Although foreign-born artisans were exempt from Confederate service, Governor William Smith of Virginia

75. Entries for March, July, 1864, Tredegar Journals, Tredegar Payroll; "War Time Story of Dahlgren's Raid," *Southern Historical Society Papers, 37* (1909), 200; Virgil Carrington Jones, *Eight Hours Before Richmond* (New York, 1957), pp. 75, 81–82.

76. Anderson to F. T. Anderson, March 4, 1864, Anderson Papers, UVA. The historian who has written the most detailed study of the raid believes the documents were in Dahlgren's handwriting; see Jones, *Eight Hours*, p. 174; Boatner, *Civil War Dictionary*, pp. 218–19.

77. "Compiled Service Records . . . Virginia," roll 452; entries for Dec. 1864, Tredegar Journals; Anderson & Co. to Gorgas, Oct. 1, 3, 1864, to Capt. J. Wilcox Brown, Oct. 20, 1864,

had called 8,000 aliens into militia service earlier in 1864 and these troops, including a number of Tredegar operatives, also participated regularly in the defense of the capital.[78]

During these extended periods of active duty, Tredegar mechanics in both the battalion and the militia deserted to the Federals in alarming numbers. In mid-October, Anderson advised recalling the men from the field as the only way to halt desertions. "Unless steps are promptly taken to arrest this evil we fear that we will be seriously crippled in our important operations for the Government," he warned the Ordnance Bureau.[79] The men remained in the trenches and the firm reported shortly after that the Tredegar's only skilled gun molder and a number of other highly important laborers had fled to the enemy.[80]

Gorgas, who was experiencing equally crippling losses from the government's ordnance shops, wanted to help but could do very little. Local defense troops were under the direct control of the War Department and, in the fall of 1864, the Secretary of War wanted every man who could shoulder a musket to take his place in the fortifications. The Ordnance Bureau chief did secure an order allowing one third of the city's able-bodied munitions workers to remain at their jobs at all times but he realized that this would neither halt the desertions nor maintain a satisfactory level of production. "This double duty will ruin our department unless it can be placed on some definite footing," he told a fellow ordnance officer in late October. "Mechanics will not work & soldier both. This idiosyncrasy I am trying to impress on the minds of those in authority, & by perseverance hope eventually to succeed." A total of 264 mechanics had fled from Richmond since May 1, a figure which "furnishes a strong, tho' somewhat rueful, argument in support of my views," he concluded.[81] When field officers

---

to Col. W. H. Stevens, Oct. 24, 1864, and to Gen. R. S. Ewell, Oct. 27, 1864, Tredegar Letterbooks; *O.R.*, Ser. I, *52*, pt. iii, 1178. The details working at the Tredegar furnaces were also summoned to Saltville in October to defend the vital works there; see Glasgow to Anderson & Co., Oct. 4, 1864, Tredegar Furnace Letterbook.

78. "Compiled Service Records . . . Virginia," roll 452; Lonn, p. 399; *O.R.*, Ser. IV, *3*, 670–71, 913.

79. Anderson & Co. to Gorgas, Oct. 15, 1864, Tredegar Letterbooks. See also: Anderson & Co. to J. H. Winder, March 8, 1864, ibid.; Anderson to G. A. Myers, Aug. 6, 1864, Letters Rec'd., Secretary of War, RG 109, NA; *O.R.N.*, Ser. II, *2*, 636–37.

80. Anderson & Co. to I. H. Carrington, Oct. 20, 1864, to Gen. G. W. C. Lee, Oct. 21, 1864, and to Gorgas, Oct. 27, 1864, Tredegar Letterbooks. For a list of Tredegar deserters, see "Compiled Service Records . . . Virginia," roll 452.

81. Gorgas to G. W. Rains, Oct. 30, 1864, Rains Papers, UNC.

informed General Richard S. Ewell, commander of the Department of Richmond, about these constant defections, Ewell quipped that as soon as enough reserves were brought up, the artisans "ought to be released and returned to their labor (such as are left)." [82] Military authorities sent the men back to their jobs during the first week of November and the desertions stopped.[83]

In December, the process began all over again. A call on Christmas eve requiring half the Tredegar Battalion to report to the trenches prompted Anderson to repeat his earlier warning about imminent desertions. Gorgas agreed that a number of these artisans would go over to the Federals at the first opportunity and he recommended the withdrawal of the battalion. Grant had so extended the Confederate line of defense, however, that Lee could not relieve the men immediately and the expected desertions followed. These losses finally convinced the War Department that the local defense troops should be used only in the gravest emergencies and the Tredegar operatives were not recalled to active service again until March 1865.[84]

The Tredegar works, like all other industrial establishments in the Confederacy, remained chronically short of skilled labor from 1862 on. "The want of expert workmen is felt in every workshop, public and private, some of which have had to discontinue operations, while others are employing only a third or a half of their productive capacity," the Secretary of the Navy informed President Davis in August 1862. "From the want of mechanics, contractors with this department for steam machinery, ordnance and ordnance stores, for lumber and iron, and the hulls of vessels fail to fulfill their engagements." [85] This description fitted the Tredegar works in 1862 and even larger gaps had appeared in Anderson's labor force by 1863. "The following workmen can find constant employment at about tenfold the prices paid in Europe," one of the partners told a Liverpool contact in July of that year: "30 Puddlers, 16 Heaters, five Rollers, 2 Hammermen and any number of Machinists, Blacksmiths and Pattern

82. *O.R.*, Ser. I, *52*, pt. iii, 1179.

83. Ibid., p. 1203; Anderson & Co. to Shay, Williamson & Co., Nov. 7, 1864, Tredegar Letterbooks.

84. Anderson & Co. to Capt. Gilwane, Dec. 24, 1864, ibid.; Jones, *Diary*, *2*, 370; *O.R.*, Ser. I, *52*, pt. iii, 1310–11; Anderson & Co. to Col. F. W. Sims, March 15, 1865, in "J. R. Anderson & Co.," Confederate Citizens File, RG 109, NA.

85. *O.R.N.*, Ser. II, *2*, 243.

Makers."[86] An acute lack of mechanics threatened production at every ordnance facility in the Confederacy in the final year and a half of the war.[87] "Heavy guns . . . are cast only at the Naval Foundry at Selma, and at the Tredegar Works," the chief of the Bureau of Ordnance and Hydrography reported in January 1865. "Neither of these foundries has ever been worked to its full capacity in consequence of the constant want of a sufficient number of skilled workmen, and an occasional scarcity of materials."[88]

The South never possessed the skilled labor force needed to maintain industrial production at the level demanded by the North's war of attrition. A more intelligent government detail policy, more restricted use of the Tredegar Battalion, and higher wages might have helped minimize the damage caused by an insufficient number of trained native-born artisans. But like so many other handicaps restricting Confederate manufacturing, this defect was congenital. Under wartime conditions, neither the government nor Anderson and Company could even begin to repair the damage resulting from a long-standing dependence on foreign and Northern-born labor.

86. Anderson & Co. to Henry W. Moncure, July 18, 1863, Tredegar Letterbooks.

87. *O.R.*, Ser. IV, *3*, 520–23, 734; Anderson & Co. to Brooke, March 11, 1864, Tredegar Letterbooks.

88. Brooke to Mallory, "Memorandum: Means of Supplying Munitions of War for the Navy," Jan. 4, 1865, Letters Sent, Office of Ordnance and Hydrography, RG 109, NA.

13

"We Must Have Hands"

Slaves played a growing role in all Tredegar operations as the military demands of the Confederacy reduced the number of free laborers available to private industry. In 1862, the Tredegar employed a total of 131 slaves. The following year, 226 Negro slaves worked at the Richmond plant and 500 to 600 more served the company's blast furnaces, coal mines, and fleet of boats. Slave labor continued to supplant free until, by 1864, Negroes held well over half of all Tredegar jobs.[1]

I

Negro slaves had traditionally formed a large segment of the labor force at Virginia's charcoal blast furnaces. They performed a wide variety of skilled and unskilled tasks, including mining ore, chopping wood, making charcoal, driving wagons, farming, cooking, boating, and acting as blacksmiths, carpenters, and general laborers. The primary job of the furnace hands was to accumulate enough "stock," iron ore, charcoal, and flux, to allow the furnace to be put into blast and to keep it in constant operation.[2] These tasks required considerable manpower. Anderson and Company indicated the scope of their needs in an advertisement placed in Virginia and North Carolina papers in late 1862 and early 1863: "Wanted—Five Hundred Hands—We wish to hire for the ensuing year five hundred able-bodied *Negro Men* to be employed by us at our Blast Furnaces, in Botetourt County, and at our Coal Mines, on James River, seventeen miles above this city." The advertisement stressed the safety of

1. City of Richmond, and Botetourt, Goochland, and Rockbridge Counties, Personal Property Tax Rolls, 1863, VSL; "Negroes and Rations at Catawba, 1863," manuscript Tredegar volume; "List of Negroes at Furnaces, 1863," in Tredegar Letters re Furnaces. Almost all of these slaves were hired by the year.

2. S. Sydney Bradford, "The Negro Ironworker in Ante Bellum Virginia," *Journal of Southern History*, *25* (1959), 197–99.

the company's mountain furnaces and promised good food and clothing for the hands.[3]

As the next step in securing furnace labor, the Tredegar owners sent hiring agents fanning out into eastern and southside Virginia and northern North Carolina.[4] Slave labor for the Valley furnaces had come primarily from counties east of the Blue Ridge Mountains before the war and the company found owners in these counties, now bordering battlefield regions, more than willing to rent their hands. Anderson had learned from past experience that Negroes hired in the city and sent to labor in the mountains did not work well away from their urban environment so he wanted to do as much hiring as possible in rural areas.[5] The company gave added incentive to their hiring agents by promising to employ them as overseers if they acquired thirty or more hands. The conscription laws provided exemption for one overseer for every twenty slaves.[6]

Anderson and his partners knew that without an adequate number of slaves their furnaces and coal pits would not provide the crucial raw materials so badly needed at their works. "It will be necessary that we use every effort to obtain hands," they told one of their furnace managers.[7] In their correspondence with agents and owners, the Tredegar partners stressed the distance of their properties from the Federal lines and the relative safety of hands working there. "We cannot undertake to insure against the negroes being taken by or running to the Yankees, while at the same time we think they are as little liable to run off in our service as from any other point, in this or the adjoining states," one of the partners told an agent. He claimed that "in the great excitement of the past year, none hired to us have gone to the enemy." [8] The company appealed to the patriotism as well as the self-interest of the owners. "We are supplying nearly all the cannon that is in the service and any aid that you can render us will be also

3. Richmond *Dispatch,* Nov. 22–Jan. 15, 1863. This advertisement was also inserted in the Richmond *Examiner,* the Richmond *Whig,* and a Wilmington, N.C., newspaper; see entries for May, Aug., 1863, Tredegar Journals.

4. Anderson & Co. to William Jordan, Nov. 27, 1862, to Benjamin Holladay, Nov. 28, 1862, to J. M. Poindexter, Dec. 4, 1862, to James R. Pulliam, Dec. 12, 1862, to James M. Fauntleroy, Dec. 16, 1862, to H. P. Tasker, Dec. 19, 1862, to P. B. Pritchard, Dec. 23, 1862, to P. O. Bolling, Dec. 24, 1862, to E. R. West, Dec. 26, 1862, and to Thomas Wright, Jan. 1, 1863, Tredegar Letterbooks.

5. Anderson & Co. to Stephen S. Lee, Dec. 1, 1860, ibid.

6. Anderson & Co. to Pulliam, Dec. 12, 1862, ibid.; *O.R.*, Ser. IV, *2,* 162.

7. Anderson & Co. to William T. Patton, Nov. 28, 1862, Tredegar Letterbooks.

8. Anderson & Co. to W. N. Sprotly, Dec. 9, 1862, ibid.

serving the interest of the Government," they told an important supplier of slaves.[9] The Tredegar owners were willing to purchase some men, especially blacksmiths and others possessing special skills, but preferred to hire the great majority of their laborers.[10]

Hiring for 1863 proceeded rapidly during the customary weeks in late December and early January. Because of the increasing cost of feeding and clothing hands, rents rose slowly. Ordinary laborers rented for $150 to $200 per year, carpenters and blacksmiths for $225 to $350—prices only slightly higher than prewar levels.[11] Early in January 1863, Glasgow informed the Richmond office that hiring agents had assembled enough men to serve the key Botetourt County furnaces for the year. Later that month, the Tredegar owners estimated that they had hired 750 Negroes. Although some difficulty was later encountered in securing hands to operate Glenwood furnace in Rockbridge County, acquired by the company after the traditional hiring season, this deficiency was corrected by the end of March. The company's furnaces were generally adequately manned with slave labor throughout 1863.[12]

Included in this furnace labor force were sixty-three Negro free and slave convicts, rented from the state in September 1862 for $125 each. These workers, sixty men and three women, were split between three of the Tredegar's furnaces. Like the residents of neighboring Rockbridge County who protested vigorously against the presence of paroled Federals at Glenwood furnace, the citizens of Botetourt County lodged vehement complaints with the governor when the convicts began working at Cloverdale and Grace furnaces. They charged the company with lax supervision of the convicts and complained of crimes committed by these slaves which culminated in the murder of a local citizen. The state investigated these accusations and found the Negroes housed in sturdy blockhouses and well guarded. The convict who committed the murder was hanged. The governor took no action to remove these slaves from Anderson and Company's control and the Tredegar secured more Negro prisoners as the year

9. Anderson & Co. to Samuel G. Staples, Dec. 6, 1862, ibid.

10. Anderson & Co. to Poindexter, Dec. 4, 1862, and to Glasgow, Dec. 13, 1862, ibid.

11. Anderson & Co. to William S. Fontaine, Jan. 8, 1863, ibid.; slave bond dated Dec. 31, 1863, Anderson Papers, UVA; Bradford, "Negro Ironworker," p. 196; "List of Negroes at Furnaces, 1863," in Tredegar Letters re Furnaces.

12. Glasgow to Anderson & Co., Jan. 11, 22, Feb. 7, 10, 1863, ibid.; Anderson & Co. to Glasgow, Jan. 13, 27, April 7, 1863, and to Lynch & Callander, March 28, 1863, Tredegar Letterbooks.

progressed. By the fall of 1863, the Tredegar owners had hired a total of 113 Negro convicts and they continued to use state prisoners at their furnaces throughout the war.[13]

The company had considerable difficulty hiring enough coal miners to work the Tredegar pits and had some trouble securing sufficient boat hands. They were still advertising for slaves for the Dover and Tuckahoe mines in June 1863.[14] Experienced slaves were needed to man the Tredegar's large canal boats and a fleet of smaller craft, used to float iron from the furnaces to Buchanan. This town was the terminus of the James River and Kanawha Canal and the company purchased an old lumber house and wharf there to serve as a storage and shipping point. From Buchanan, the fleet of nine canal boats, carrying an average of forty tons of iron per trip, transported the metal 195 miles to the Richmond plant in a week to ten days time. A white captain commanded each of the mule-drawn vessels and slaves composed the bulk of the four- to six-man crews. Of the forty-two Negroes serving as crewmen on the nine large boats, thirty-five were hired slaves. Boatmen ranked along with blacksmiths, carpenters, coal miners, and charcoal makers as an elite group among the slave population.[15]

Work had always been arduous for slaves at mountain blast furnaces and wartime scarcities of basic commodities made their condition even more unfortunate. Slaves had some choice about where they labored, especially if they possessed particular skills, and many hands were reluctant to go to the furnaces. Early in 1863, Anderson wrote the owner of a slave who had directed the manufacture of charcoal at Australia furnace and asked that the Negro be returned. "It is very important that Beverly shall return to the furnace at which he worked last year, & hope that he may be

13. "List of Negroes at Furnaces, 1863," in Tredegar Letters re Furnaces; entry for Aug. 9, 1862, Virginia Executive Journal, VSL; contract with Anderson & Co., Sept. 3, 1862, petition of citizens of Botetourt County, Aug. 12, 1862, Letcher to the General Assembly, Sept. 28, 1862, and report of James F. Pendleton to Letcher, Dec. 22, 1863, Virginia Executive Papers, VSL; "Annual Report of the Board of Directors of the Penitentiary Institution . . . September 30, 1863," Document 9, *Message of the [Virginia] Governor and Accompanying Documents, 1863* (Richmond, 1863), p. 19; entries for Dec. 1863, March, Dec., 1864, Tredegar Journals.

14. Richmond *Dispatch,* June 15, 1863.

15. Glasgow to Anderson & Co., May 14, Aug. [?], Oct. 23, Nov. 2, 1863, Tredegar Furnace Letterbook; Anderson & Co. to J. Wills, Nov. 29, 1862, and to J. H. Jamison, March 3, 1863, Tredegar Letterbooks; Glasgow to Anderson & Co., Jan. 9, 24, April 14, 1863, and "List of Hands employed on Canal Boats," in Tredegar Letters re Furnaces; Tredegar Pig Iron Receipt Book; advertisement in Richmond *Dispatch,* Sept. 17, 1862.

willing to do so, as no other arrangement has been made for a collier at that place & in the present condition of the country every ton of metal is important." "If Beverly does not wish to go to Australia please let us know," Anderson asked in conclusion. The slave agreed to work at the property for another year and a potentially severe production slowdown was averted.[16] One of the partners reported at the end of 1863 that the men hired for the Richmond plant were all anxious to return for another year, "and indeed the great trouble is that all the negroes in the Confederacy wish to come to the Tredegar Works." [17] If a slave expressed a strong desire to remain in Richmond and his owner supported his request, the company would allow the man to labor at the Tredegar.[18]

Anderson was not a rigorous disciplinarian. When one of his valuable Tredegar slaves expressed a wish to live and work in the mountains, he permitted him to move to Cloverdale furnace. The company had set up a shoemaking shop on the furnace property and the man wanted to work there. "The work will be lighter for him, a consideration he is justly entitled to by reason of his fidelity since I have owned him," wrote Anderson.[19] The management also tried to keep families together by placing the men at furnaces where land was cultivated. The wives cooked, did washing or farm labor, and the children helped on the farm. If a slave's wife did not accompany her husband to the mountains, the man was allowed to return home once a year in addition to the annual Christmas break. As a general rule, all hands were to be returned to their owners by December 24.[20] When Anderson learned that the family of a recently purchased blacksmith had remained in North Carolina, he wrote to ascertain the whereabouts of the wife and children. "We would be glad to keep the family together if we can and suggest that you will do us the favor to get their owner to send them here without delay and we will pay for them their value and keep them together." [21]

The exigencies of wartime production did not result in heavier tasks for the furnace slaves. Choppers, for example, were required to cut one and

16. Anderson & Co. to A. R. Blakey, Jan. 9, 1863, April 9, 1864, Angus R. Blakey Papers, DUL.

17. Anderson & Co. to David Anderson, Jr., Dec. 28, 1863, Tredegar Letterbooks.

18. Anderson & Co. to Alfred N. Bernard, Jan. 2, 1863, ibid.

19. Anderson & Co. to Patton, Dec. 1, 1862, ibid.

20. Anderson & Co. to Patton, Jan. 9, 1863, to Pender, March 25, Dec. 21, 1863, to C. T. Jones, Nov. 27, 1863, and to Glasgow, April 7, 1863, ibid.

21. Anderson & Co. to John H. Leary, Dec. 3, 1863, ibid.

one half cords of wood per day, the same demand that had existed in peacetime.[22] Discipline was probably less severe during the war years than had been the case during the antebellum period. An important reason for this was the Negro's recognition of the increased importance of his labor to his employer. The Tredegar owners saw this growing awareness and warned their chief furnace agent to issue instructions to all managers to be careful in their treatment of the slaves. "We think you had better recommend to all in charge as much modification in the management of the hands as may be compatible with our interests. Negroes expect much indulgence now, & whenever we can do so, it may be best to concede something as it may aid hereafter." [23] Slaves had always been able to earn extra money at the furnaces if they did labor over and above their required tasks, but during 1863 some slaves were given $1.00 at the end of each month if they worked and behaved well.[24]

If a Negro tried to escape from a furnace or coal mine, however, the lax discipline was liable to be promptly reversed. Slaves working at the coal pits made the most frequent attempts to leave. In April 1863, five hands ran away from the Tredegar's collieries in Goochland County. These men were evidently not trying to reach the Federal lines but were fleeing from underground labor at the mines. All headed for the home of their owner. Their master ordered them to be sent to a blast furnace and this appeared to satisfy the men.[25]

The following June, a number of Negroes escaped from the Botetourt County furnaces. The firm definitely believed these men were attempting to head north. The management was also growing increasingly concerned over the uncooperative attitude of the slaves at the Tredegar plant. "The demoralization among the negroes here and at our furnaces is a source of much disquietude to us who have contracts with the government for iron on the faithful compliance of which the fate of the country may depend," one of the partners wrote the owner of a group of escapees. "We are sure that here and at all of our furnaces, the negroes are humanely treated, well fed, and clothed as well as can be done at present and we know of no reason why they should run off except to get to the enemy. Re-

22. Bradford, "Ante-Bellum Charcoal Iron Industry," p. 121; Anderson & Co. to William H. Goodwin, Dec. 23, 1863, Tredegar Letterbooks.

23. Anderson & Co. to Glasgow, April 7, 1863, ibid.

24. Ibid.; Bradford, "Ante-Bellum Charcoal Iron Industry," p. 127.

25. Advertisement in Richmond *Dispatch*, April 7, 1863; Anderson & Co. to Pender, May 6, 1863, Tredegar Letterbooks.

cently several have been captured nearly within the enemy lines," he continued. The partner suggested that the cases be fully investigated by the owner, "& if they have left without any just cause, they be corrected properly and placed at work." [26] Another group of slaves left the furnaces at the same time and again headed for free territory. "There appears to be almost a stampede among your hands," the Richmond office wrote the Tredegar's furnace agent.[27] The apprehension, punishment, and return to work of these men temporarily discouraged other slaves from attempting to escape from the secluded mountain furnaces.

Shortages of food, clothing, shoes, and blankets increased the plight of the slave population at the various Tredegar facilities. When Beverly, the collier at Australia furnace, complained to his owner in 1864 about the failure of the furnace manager to provide blankets and clothes, John Tanner explained that "it has been impossible to obtain negro blankets for the past two years & we have therefore commuted with the owners or slaves for money in lieu thereof." [28] Such scarcities undoubtedly had an important influence on a slave's decision to flee. Inadequate supplies also contributed to the spread of sickness and disease among the furnace hands. Several furnace slaves died of pneumonia in March 1863 and Glasgow reported that same month that a number of Negroes had been unable to work for weeks because of a lack of warm clothing and shoes. Six Negro convicts were returned to the state penitentiary the following June as permanently diseased and smallpox broke out at two furnaces in 1864.[29]

II

The Confederate Engineer Bureau's demand for slave labor to build military defenses in Virginia cut into the Tredegar's work force periodically throughout the war. The Virginia General Assembly in March and October 1862 gave the governor authority to call slaves into Confederate service for sixty days, whenever fortifications needed labor. These acts

26. Anderson & Co. to R. C. Dabney, June 24, 1863, ibid.

27. Anderson & Co. to Benjamin Holladay, June 23, 1863, and to Glasgow, June 25, 1863, ibid.

28. Anderson & Co. to Blakey, April 9, 1864, Blakey Papers, DUL.

29. Anderson & Co. to W. W. Forbes, April 8, 1863, Tredegar Letterbooks; Glasgow to Anderson & Co., March 11, 1863, and "List of Negroes at Furnaces, 1863," in Tredegar Letters re Furnaces; Glasgow to Anderson & Co., March 23, 1863, Tredegar Furnace Letterbook; entry for June 29, 1863, Virginia Executive Journal, VSL.

made no provision for exemptions.[30] As a result, calls made in January and March 1863 took a number of Tredegar slaves, including furnace and coal pit hands and a much-needed Negro tanner. Anderson's protests had no effect and the slaves served out their sixty-day terms.[31]

The impressment of one key free Negro laborer in the summer of 1863 produced a minor crisis in Tredegar operations. The Engineer Bureau and the governor had recommended in January 1863 that the Virginia legislators modify the laws to permit specific exemption of slaves employed in mining and manufacturing. The assembly ignored this advice when it rewrote the impressment legislation in March but did allow Confederate authorities to detail impressed Negroes back to their former employer if the public necessity demanded.[32] Shortly after this act became law, Anderson sought official exemption for all the Tredegar slaves from both Governor Letcher and Secretary of War Seddon. Both men refused his request, Seddon on the grounds that he had no such authority.[33] Then in June, William Brackens, a free Negro in charge of the Tredegar's small boat fleet, was arrested and sent to the Richmond fortifications. The Tredegar management spent over a month trying to obtain his final release and even enlisted the aid of the Secretary of the Navy. Gun iron and pig intended for gunboat plates piled up on the banks of small streams in western Virginia while Brackens, the only Tredegar boatman who could direct the navigation of these creeks, was wielding a shovel on the Richmond earthworks. The Engineer Bureau finally detailed him in July and he performed his vital duties for the company for the remainder of the war.[34]

In 1864, the Confederate government at long last provided exemptions for some of the Tredegar's Negro hands. The Adjutant and Inspector General issued orders in October 1863 instructing the Engineer Bureau to in-

30. *Acts of the [Virginia] General Assembly, Called Session, 1862* (Richmond, 1862), pp. 6–8.

31. Glasgow to Anderson & Co., Jan. 1, 11, 24, 1863, Tredegar Furnace Letterbook; Anderson & Co. to Glasgow, Jan. 14, 1863, to Col. J. F. Gilmer, March 3, 1863, and to Dr. R. M. Anderson, March 7, 1863, Tredegar Letterbooks.

32. Letcher to the General Assembly, Jan. 26, 1863, Virginia Executive Papers, VSL; *[Virginia] Senate Journal, Extra Session, 1862–63* (Richmond, 1863), p. 224; *O.R.*, Ser. IV, 2, 428.

33. Anderson & Co. to Letcher, March 26, 1863, Tredegar Letterbooks; Anderson & Co. to Seddon, March 28, 1863, and endorsement, Letters Rec'd., Secretary of War, RG 109, NA.

34. Anderson & Co. to Col. W. H. Stevens, June 2, 1863, to Glasgow, May 30, June 2, 15, July 9, 1863, to Gilmer, June 9, 1863, to Mallory, June 15, 1863, and to John W. Langhorne, Jan. 12, Feb. 10, 1865, Tredegar Letterbooks; Glasgow to Anderson & Co., June 3, 1863, Tredegar Furnace Letterbook; Glasgow to Anderson & Co., June 5, 1863, Tredegar Letters re Furnaces.

sure that slave impressments did not interrupt important industrial undertakings.[35] When Anderson and Company applied for exemptions for the furnace slaves the following March, the bureau agreed. But the Tredegar owners failed to include their coal pit force in this request and an enrolling officer stripped the Tuckahoe mines near Richmond of many Negro hands in January 1865.[36] Compared with the other obstacles to Tredegar production, however, the slave draft constituted a minor harassment.

III

The management's decision, made late in 1863, to dispense with as many furnace conscripts as possible during the coming year prompted a determined effort to hire additional slave labor. The Tredegar began advertising in Virginia, Georgia, and Alabama papers in November for one thousand Negroes. Anderson and Company assured owners that ample supplies of provisions and clothing had been secured and promised to keep slaves well fed and clothed at all times. "Our furnaces and other works are located in healthy sections of the country, remote from the enemy's line," the advertisement emphasized. The Tredegar owners also offered to hire entire families and place the women and children on farms at the husband's work site.[37]

"It is of infinite importance that we obtain hands for our Blast furnaces and Coal pits, now so important to the Confederacy in her struggle," the Tredegar partners told their hiring agents. "We must have the labour or the work of making iron must stop." [38] They urged the hirers to use every possible method to acquire hands. Stress the importance to refugees of safekeeping and care for their chattels, offer highest market rates, see owners dissatisfied with previous employers, point out the expense of maintaining slaves, the management instructed.[39] Buoyed by a recent offer of 330 slaves from two parties in the Carolinas, Anderson and Company pre-

35. *O.R.*, Ser. IV, 2, 897.

36. Anderson & Co. to Stevens, March 1, 15, 1864, to William A. Glasgow, Oct. 26, 1864, and to Gen. J. L. Kemper, Feb. 7, 1865, Tredegar Letterbooks.

37. Advertisement in Richmond *Examiner*, Nov. 14, 1863, with instructions to the Augusta, Ga., *Constitutionalist*, the Atlanta *Intelligencer*, and the Montgomery, Ala., *Mail* to copy.

38. Anderson & Co. to E. R. Pullen, Dec. 23, 1863, and to William A. Bibb, Dec. 24, 1863, Tredegar Letterbooks.

39. Anderson & Co. to John T. Shanks, Nov. 24, 1863, to D. Anderson, Dec. 18, 1863, to C. V. Carrington, Dec. 26, 1863, to J. D. Hill, Dec. 5, 1863, and to W. W. Forbes, Dec. 19, 1863, ibid.

dicted early in December that hiring would proceed rapidly and on good terms.[40] Although they anticipated some difficulty acquiring coal miners, the Tredegar owners thought good hands would rent for $225 to $300, figures not much higher than the previous year. They believed that the skyrocketing cost of feeding and clothing slaves would induce owners to make an ample number available and would keep the price at a moderate level.[41]

Price-raising competition from large slave employers soon curbed this optimism, however. During the first two weeks of December, Anderson and Company corresponded with the major Virginia employers—the canal company, the railroads, and the works at Saltville—and all parties agreed on a maximum price of $300.[42] Individual agents overbid this almost immediately, however, and the hire for ordinary laborers rose quickly to $350 and then to $400. The Tredegar management had originally limited its agents to $300 but now instructed them to bid with the highest.[43] The Secretary of War finally ended this competition in late December by setting a maximum price of $350 and threatening to impress hands for government use if owners asked more. But by the time the Secretary acted, Anderson and Company had lost a number of slaves to other parties.[44]

A Federal cavalry raid through Virginia's blast furnace country at the peak of the hiring season further dimmed the company's chances for assembling an adequate slave force. Union troopers led by Brigadier General W. W. Averell penetrated deep into the Virginia Alleghenies in mid-December. His men reached Salem on the 16th and destroyed large stores of provisions, a few bridges, and some track of the vital Virginia and Tennessee Railroad before retiring unmolested into West Virginia.[45] This foray had an immediate effect on Tredegar hiring. A North Carolina owner who had earlier promised the company a large number of slaves now declined to deliver his men.[46]

40. Anderson & Co. to Glasgow, Dec. 4, 1863, ibid.

41. Anderson & Co. to John N. Wynn, Nov. 16, 1863, to Shanks, Nov. 17, 1863, to John Jones, Nov. 26, 1863, and to Forbes, Nov. 26, 1863, ibid.

42. Anderson & Co. to Glasgow, Dec. 4, 1863, to Stuart, Buchanan & Co., Dec. 10, 1863, and to Forbes, Dec. 11, 1863, ibid.

43. Anderson & Co. to Forbes, Dec. 19, 1863, to Nathaniel Bass, Dec. 23, 1863, and to J. D. Brooks, Dec. 28, 29, 1863, ibid.

44. Anderson & Co. to Patton, Dec. 29, 1863, to Forbes, Dec. 11, 19, 1863, and to Brooks, Dec. 28, 1863, ibid.

45. Freeman, *Lee's Lieutenants, 3*, 325–26.

46. Anderson & Co. to Morgan, Dec. 23, 1863, Tredegar Letterbooks.

The partners labored mightily to turn this raid into an advantage. "With regard to the recent raid in a portion of Botetourt [County] you can say that such was the position of our furnaces that we did not lose one dollars worth of property nor did the enemy get to one of our furnaces," they told a hiring agent. "Still matters were so arranged that had they ventured in, we think we could have saved every negro." [47] "We have not lost a negro this year by going to the Yankees and the recent raid of Averell demonstrated the security of our property against such raids," the company informed a worried slave owner on Christmas eve, 1863.[48]

This line of reasoning failed to convince a number of masters, as Anderson and Company admitted privately to the Niter and Mining Bureau.[49] A January Tredegar advertisement for eight hundred hands revealed a distinct concern about declining hiring prospects: "Should parties prefer to hire their negroes and receive *Bar Iron* or *Nails,* which in view of the scarcity of those articles, may be important to planters and others, we are willing to hire on that basis." [50] The company was still seeking hands in late January and now promised, "when required," to guarantee against capture by the enemy.[51] Although Anderson and his partners eventually managed to acquire some six hundred furnace and boat hands, hiring difficulties forced the Tredegar owners to abandon their plans to dispense with all except the most essential conscript furnace workers. Glasgow reported in March that Grace furnace, a key producer of gun metal, had to retain its details to fill out its labor force.[52]

By the end of 1864, Anderson could hardly repeat his previous year's boast that not a single slave had fled to the Yankees. In June 1864, Hunter's cavalry carried off a large number of Negroes from Cloverdale, Grace, and Mount Torry furnaces. Sheridan's movements in the Valley during the fall of 1864 gave slave owners and the Tredegar management numerous anxious moments, but none of his devastating Shenandoah raids reached the company's stacks. Negroes continued to escape from Tredegar

47. Anderson & Co. to Forbes, Dec. 24, 1863, ibid.

48. Anderson & Co. to John S. Kemper, Dec. 24, 1863, ibid.

49. Anderson & Co. to Col. Richard Morton, Dec. 26, 1863, ibid.

50. Richmond *Examiner,* Jan. 4, 1864.

51. Richmond *Dispatch,* Jan. 28, 1864.

52. "Statement Showing Number of Men . . . Employed . . . in Making & Transporting Pig Metal," Dec. 16, 1864, Tredegar Letterbooks; Glasgow to Anderson & Co., March 2, 1864, Tredegar Furnace Letterbook.

facilities in small numbers, however.[53] In December, Anderson gave a bleak summary of the year's difficulties with slave labor: "This has been a rather disastrous year for the hirers and owners of slaves, so many having run off to the Yankees, a large portion from within the fortifications of this city." [54]

Although the partners anticipated difficulty hiring Negroes for 1865 because of the Federal raids, Anderson and Company inaugurated a search for hands after the government promised provisioning aid in December 1864. The company ran its usual advertisment in December and January, but promised only that slaves would be "well cared for and amply provided with good food and clothing." The advertisement offered neither payment in iron nor a guarantee against loss.[55] A number of North Carolina slave owners had responded in January 1864 to the previous year's offer to pay rents in iron and wanted to make a similar arrangement for 1865, but the Tredegar owners claimed transportation difficulties now made this plan unfeasible.[56]

When Anderson and his associates experienced difficulty securing slaves for cash rents, they again were forced to offer bars and nails. A more stringent government policy toward details for overseers, a rapidly depreciating currency, and slave owners' fears of new Union raids all handicapped their hiring efforts.[57] By January, they were promising $400 for ordinary hands, payable in iron at $1.25 per pound for nails. They later upped the rate to $500 for furnace and coal pit hands but continued to pay only $400 for slaves employed at the works in Richmond, a reflection of widespread confidence in Lee's ability to hold the Confederate capital. Teamsters brought $650, boatmen $1000, and a blacksmith's owner received $1200 in the form of seven 100-pound kegs of nails, one of the highest rents paid for any Tredegar slave.[58]

53. Anderson & Co. to James Whitfield, Oct. 12, 1864, and to Anne F. Mansfield, Sept. 16, 1864, Tredegar Letterbooks.

54. Anderson & Co. to Forbes, Dec. 16, 1864, ibid.

55. Richmond *Examiner*, Jan. 4, 1865.

56. Anderson & Co. to Whitfield, Dec. 20, 26, 1864, Tredegar Letterbooks; entry for Sept. 1864, Tredegar Rolling Mill Sales Books.

57. Glasgow to Capt. Gordon, Dec. 10, 1864, Tredegar Furnace Letterbook; Anderson & Co. to J. M. Shelton, Dec. 20, 1864, and to Gen. J. S. Preston, Jan. 31, 1865, Tredegar Letterbooks.

58. Anderson & Co. to Dr. S. Maupin, Jan. 5, 1865, to Dr. J. S. Davis, Jan. 24, 1865, to A. S. Jackson, Jan. 10, 1865, to John S. Kemper, Jan. 16, 1865, to William M. Gruder, Feb 10, 1865, and to Forbes, Jan. 9, 16, 1865, ibid.

Even after offering these high rates, the company continued to have trouble gathering labor. Glasgow informed Richmond in mid-January that agents had acquired sufficient boat hands and enough furnace slaves to man two stacks. Two other furnace managers had not yet reported, but one blast furnace the company planned to operate in 1865 had only a fraction of its laborers.[59] The company canvassed Petersburg in early February for one hundred hands and reported later that month that a Tredegar coal mine had only one fourth of the personnel needed to produce at its full potential.[60] By the middle of February, the Tredegar had secured sufficient labor to keep four furnaces in blast, to push repairs at three burnt stacks, and to operate two coal mines and the Richmond plant at considerably less than full capacity.[61] All these facilities continued to function until Richmond fell early in April.

IV

The Tredegar plant became increasingly dependent on skilled slave labor during the South's final two years of futile bloodshed. In November 1864, the main works employed about six hundred men, of whom two hundred were Negroes.[62] A majority of the slaves at the Richmond plant still worked in the rolling mills but they also entered departments previously manned almost exclusively by free white labor. Ten or eleven Negroes labored in the machine shops in 1863 and 1864, the first time slaves had worked there. During the same period, twenty-five or thirty slaves worked in the foundry, and a Negro engineer was placed in charge of a steam engine when a white laborer quit the job because the owners refused to raise his wages. Fifty-two slaves, including blacksmiths, strikers, and helpers, twelve free Negroes, and twenty-seven whites comprised the smith shop force in February 1864.[63]

Slaves performed many skilled and sometimes highly important and sensitive tasks. Blacksmith Ed Taylor, one of twenty-three skilled slaves

59. Glasgow to Anderson & Co., Jan. 13, 14, 1865, Tredegar Furnace Letterbook.

60. Anderson & Co. to Editor, Petersburg *Express*, Jan. 30, 1865, and to J. L. Kemper, Feb. 7, 1865, Tredegar Letterbooks.

61. Glasgow to A. C. Garnett, March 27, 1865, Tredegar Furnace Letterbook.

62. Anderson & Co. to Morton, de Bree, and Brown, Nov. 5, 1864, Tredegar Letterbooks. Union intelligence incorrectly estimated in October 1864 that the Tredegar rolling mills alone employed three hundred slaves; see *O.R.*, Ser. II, *52*, pt. iii, 291.

63. Tredegar Payroll; entries for Jan., Oct., 1863, Tredegar Journals; "Hands hired for Smith shops in 1863," Feb. 12, 1863, Tredegar Letterbooks; Archer Account Book, VHS.

belonging to Anderson, hammered out the iron bands used to strengthen Tredegar Parrott and Brooke guns. The company paid Anderson $1000 rent for Taylor in 1863, five times the hire of an ordinary laborer. He was required to work twenty-four days of the month for the company but in 1863, for any day he labored over that amount he earned $6.00 plus $3.00 for each band—the same wages paid first class white smiths. In January 1864, when he shared in a general Tredegar pay raise that boosted his wages to $7.50 per day and $6.00 per band, Taylor earned $127.50 in overtime. Skilled slave grinders and core makers also assisted munitions production at the works.[64]

Most slaves, like Taylor, took advantage of the overtime wages available to them. In the two-week period from February 22 to March 5, 1864, forty-six of the fifty-two smith shop slaves earned money for themselves. The company allowed these men to take beef, pork, and flour rations for part or all of their overtime pay, if they desired.[65]

The rising cost of food, clothing, and other essentials made the slave an increasingly expensive laborer. When one owner requested an increase in the rent paid for his slave because the Tredegar had increased wages, the company refused. "Taking his provisions into consideration, his pay exceeds that of any white man in the shop with him," they replied.[66] But expensive or not, if the Tredegar owners expected to maintain production at all, they had no choice but to hire large numbers of Negroes and provide them with adequate food, clothing, and care.

Anderson and Company's wartime experience clearly reveals the important role of the Negro in sustaining Confederate military production, and the Tredegar was not an isolated case. The chief of the Niter and Mining Bureau reported in September 1864 that government-controlled blast furnace and mining operations employed 4,301 Negroes and 2,518 whites; the naval ordnance works at Selma had a labor force of 310 slaves and 90 free workers in the closing months of the conflict.[67] Without large numbers of Negro laborers, it is difficult to see how Anderson and his associates could have maintained their industrial empire through four years of

64. Tredegar Payroll; entries for Dec. 1862, Dec. 1863, Tredegar Journals. Anderson had reduced his personal slave force to fifteen workers by 1864; see entry for Dec. 1864, Tredegar Journals.

65. Tredegar Payroll.

66. Anderson & Co. to D. Grigg, April 7, 1863, Tredegar Letterbooks.

67. *O.R.*, Ser. IV, 3, 696; Bell I. Wiley, *Southern Negroes, 1861–1865* (New Haven, 1938), pp. 112–13.

war. They held key jobs in practically every phase of the company's operations, from the mining of iron ore and coal to the final banding of Tredegar cannon. Industrial slave labor was certainly one of the Confederacy's indispensable economic resources.

14

Declining Output

Beginning as early as 1862, increasingly acute shortages of raw materials and skilled labor cut Tredegar output sharply. Anderson and Company's operational difficulties had an important impact on both the efficiency of the railroads and the South's military effort. But as the war deepened in 1863 and 1864, the army and the navy suffered most from the inadequacies of Tredegar production.

I

Immediately after the completion of the *Merrimack* in early 1862, the Tredegar rolling mills started manufacturing the iron plates for the C.S.S. *Richmond*, also on the ways at the Gosport Navy Yard. When Confederate forces evacuated Norfolk in May, the uncompleted hulk of the *Richmond* was towed up the James and construction recommenced at the navy yard in Richmond. The navy also began work on two other vessels at Richmond, the *Fredericksburg* and the *Virginia II*. Anderson and Company had responsibility for providing the plates, spikes, engines, shafts, and armament for these three vessels.

Since each ship would require approximately one thousand tons of armor, the Tredegar works faced a major challenge. The Navy Department was particularly anxious to complete these three ironclads because the destruction of the *Merrimack* removed the Confederacy's most powerful warship from Virginia waters. The rolling of the plates for the *Richmond*, begun in April, was not completed until November 1862.[1] The job took almost twice as long as the *Merrimack* simply because the Tredegar could not get enough iron.

Production of armor for the other two vessels dragged on interminably.

1. Entries for April–Nov. 1862, Tredegar Rolling Mill Sales Books; entries for July–Nov. 1862, Tredegar Foundry Sales Books; *O.R.N.*, Ser. I, 5, 117; *Dictionary of American Naval Fighting Ships*, 2, 561–62.

The naval designer even shortened the casement of the *Virginia II* to conserve metal but this action failed to hasten her completion.[2] Jones, the War Department diarist, noted acidly in November 1862 that "J. R. Anderson & Co. (having drawn $500,000 recently on the contract) have failed to furnish armor for the gunboats—the excuse being that iron could not be had for their rolling mills." [3] "We have considerable orders from your two shops for bar iron, which cannot be executed for want of materials, and we can make no progress with the plate for Gun Boats for the same reason," the Tredegar management informed the Bureau of Ordnance and Hydrography in December 1862.[4]

To help alleviate the acute shortage of iron, the government established a three-man military iron commission in January 1863 to look into the possibility of removing the trackage of nonessential lines.[5] The iron commissioners requested Anderson and Company in February to furnish a list of railroads that might yield iron for rolling armor plate. The Tredegar senior partner was reluctant to give his views on this subject. "As our intercourse with the Ex. officers of these several Roads has been of long duration and knowing how sensitive they are in relation to interference with their respective interests, we desire to be understood as not volunteering to supply this information, but furnish it on the application of Heads of Departments," Anderson wrote the commissioners.[6] The board made its report in late March and agents soon began stripping rails from nonstrategic roads.[7]

By that time, the iron shortage at the Tredegar was extremely critical. Secretary of the Navy Mallory complained of the slow delivery of armor on March 25, 1863, and got an immediate reply from the Tredegar management. "We cannot make more iron for want of the material. We have used every effort in our power to obtain it—have spared no expense or labor and we assure you that we convert it into iron as fast as we receive it." The partners also voiced an old complaint. "The Department of War and of the Navy, convenanted that so much of the pig iron contracted for by the Government as we should find necessary to fulfill our contract should be turned over to us. We have formally applied for it, but with the

2. Ibid., p. 579.
3. Jones, *Diary, 2,* 195.
4. Anderson & Co. to George Minor, Dec. 6, 1862, Tredegar Letterbooks.
5. *O.R.*, Ser. IV, *2,* 365–66, 393.
6. Anderson & Co. to I. M. St. John, March 5, 1863, Tredegar Letterbooks.
7. Black, *Railroads of the Confederacy,* pp. 205–08.

exception of insignificant lots, our application has been disregarded." "We have iron to run six puddling furnaces instead of twenty and these have been stopped much for want of coal," they concluded.[8]

Private customers did not suffer from this iron shortage as acutely as the navy, however. On the last day of March, the company informed the Navy Department that the manufacture of gunboat plates would cease completely on April 1 because the works had exhausted all materials.[9] Yet during that same month of March, the Tredegar rolling mills produced 188 long tons of iron for private consumers, mostly railroads, and for the maintenance of the Tredegar works. Only 58 long tons of iron were delivered to the government.[10] This production for railroads and other nonmilitary customers was accomplished despite what the Tredegar management referred to as "high pressure" from the Navy Department and an "unprecedented" demand for armor plate.[11] If the government supplied the pig metal, Anderson and Company would roll it into armor plate. But if the Niter and Mining Bureau could not provide iron, then the Richmond industrialists would allocate their pig as they saw fit and the navy would have to wait its turn. As a result, the *Fredericksburg* was not finally completed until late 1863 and the *Virginia II* was not commissioned until March 1864, eighteen months after work began on the ship. The navy also pressed the Tredegar, with the same mixed success, for plates for the *Albemarle,* under construction on the Roanoke River in North Carolina. Another ironclad on the ways at the Richmond Navy Yard in 1863 never received her sheathing of Tredegar armor.[12]

II

Southern railroads were in great need of all types of iron supplies by 1862. Railway executives lobbied hard for government support for the iron industry in 1862 and legislation was subsequently passed which financed the Tredegar expansion. The railroads discovered, however, that

8. Anderson & Co. to Mallory, March 25, 1863, Tredegar Letterbooks.

9. Anderson & Co. to Mallory, March 31, 1863, ibid.

10. Tredegar Rolling Mill Sales Books.

11. Anderson & Co. to A. L. Maxwell, March 31, 1863, and to L. J. Fleming, April 9, 1863, Tredegar Letterbooks.

12. Chief Engineer M. Quinn to Anderson & Co., May 9, 1864, and John H. Parker to Anderson & Co., May 20, 1864, Brock Papers, HL; Anderson & Co. to Mallory, March 8, 10, 1864, Tredegar Letterbooks; entries for March, April, 1864, Tredegar Rolling Mill Sales Books; *O.R.N.*, Ser. II, *1*, 253, 271, *2*, 528, 531–32; John G. Barrett, *The Civil War in North Carolina* (Chapel Hill, 1963), p. 214.

aid given iron manufacturers did not result in any increase in the production of rail supplies. In 1862 and 1863, just the opposite occurred. (See Table 6, p. 130.)

At the invitation of the Secretary of War, a group of railway executives met in Richmond in April 1863 to tackle the problem of increasing the efficiency of the railroads. High on the list of resolutions signed by a number of presidents and submitted to the convention was a call for more iron: "For the maintenance of the railroads the greatest and most urgent need exists for iron rails, wheels and axles, tires, springs, and locomotives, with materials for their repairs." The convention eventually adopted resolutions calling on the government to release the Atlanta rolling mill entirely for private use and see that the Armory mill at the Tredegar works was equipped to reroll rails. Thus "a considerable portion" of the rails needed could be supplied quickly without importation or the erection of new facilities.[13]

P. V. Daniel, Jr., president of the Richmond, Fredericksburg, and Potomac, scoffed at the suggestion that the Atlanta and Tredegar mills could supply the almost 50,000 tons of rails needed annually in the Confederacy. Both mills were engrossed in government work and even if they were made available for railroad production, they possessed a combined capacity of less than 20,000 tons of rails per year. Daniel particularly cautioned against placing the government and the railroads "at the mercy of one or two factories whose pecuniary interests will prompt them to promise and perhaps attempt far more than they can accomplish, if thereby they only succeed in keeping down completion of other factories or sources of supply." "After extorting for their productions any price they may choose to exact," the owners of the Tredegar and Atlanta mills would still have made no contribution toward increasing the manufacturing capacity of the Confederacy. "On this point past experience has furnished many most important lessons," warned Daniel.[14] But like it or not, Southern railroads had no alternative but to appeal to the Tredegar for iron.

The Navy Department refused to surrender the use of the two largest rolling mills in the South, but the government became increasingly aware in 1863 of the growing plight of the railroads. The Davis administration

13. *O.R.*, Ser. IV, *2*, 499–505.

14. Ibid., pp. 511–13.

took a tentative step toward creating some order out of the chaotic Southern railroad situation in November 1862 by appointing a superintendent of government rail transportation. The office had limited powers but the first appointee, William M. Wadley, was an extemely capable and energetic railroader. Wadley, who acted as a trouble shooter for some of the largest roads in the South before the war, recognized the acute shortage of material facing all Confederate railroads and he was determined to take action to correct this deficiency.[15]

One of his first moves was to approach the Tredegar management. When Wadley asked for a memorandum on what might be done to increase the manufacture of railroad iron, wheels in particular, Anderson submitted a detailed reply to the Secretary of War in January 1863. Anderson believed that the maintenance of the railroads was "of an importance to the defence of the country, next to putting arms in the hands of our troops, feeding & clothing them—& essential even to accomplish these objects." The Tredegar had undertaken to put nine pig iron furnaces into blast. If the company could obtain and retain a sufficient furnace labor force and secure wagon transportation for pig made at three furnaces in the Shenandoah Valley, enough metal could be secured to supply the quota of wheels Wadley wished the Tredegar to make, 2,500 tons. Wadley also wanted 100 tons of locomotive tires; Anderson termed this a "trifle." Bar iron could be rolled for railroads in such quantities as the government wished, as long as the government supplied the pig metal. The Tredegar expected in the neighborhood of 16,000 tons of pig from the government in 1863. If the Niter and Mining Bureau turned over this metal to the works, if forty wagons and teams were furnished to haul iron out of the Shenandoah Valley, and if the War Department allowed conscripts now at the furnaces to remain and detailed an additional two hundred men to the furnaces and the Richmond plant, "I pledge myself to you, Sir, that the part of the service, proposed by Col. Wadley's report, to be assigned to this establishment, will with blessing of Providence be performed," Anderson concluded.[16]

These were large "ifs" indeed. The entire 1863 production of every blast furnace in the South would not total 16,000 tons. Lee's attitude toward details in 1863 precluded the release of twenty men, much less two hundred. The War Department took no action on Anderson's proposals.

15. Black, pp. 107–10.

16. Anderson to Seddon, Jan. 31, 1863, Tredegar Letterbooks.

And Wadley left public service in April 1863 after Congress, under puzzling circumstances, refused to approve his appointment.[17]

Colonel Frederick W. Sims, Wadley's successor as chief of military rail transportation, did not contact Anderson and Company about large-scale production of railroad iron until the spring of 1864. He came to the works in March of that year with an order for 225 freight cars. Anderson and Company responded to his request with terms similar to those presented fifteen months before. The cars would require 800 tons of iron and 15,000 pounds of brass; the Tredegar would supply three fourths of the iron but all the brass would have to come from the Railroad Bureau. Government wagons would be required to haul metal from the Valley furnaces to Staunton. The company would also need the detail of some two dozen men, including molders, blacksmiths, finishers, rolling mill hands, "and such other men and material as we may find necessary as the work progresses." Because the fire the previous May had destroyed the Tredegar carpenter shop, the woodwork would have to be done elsewhere.[18]

Lee was then in desperate need of food and forage for his soldiers and draft animals and he reluctantly reversed his policy on details. "In the present instance, if mechanics cannot otherwise be had, they must be sent from the army, as the work to be done is essential to its existence." Lee had the names of a number of blacksmiths, carpenters, molders, finishers, puddlers, and rollers, "who can be had as soon as required." [19]

The Tredegar went to work on the irons, trucks, wheels, and axles in April and made the first deliveries that month. The actual construction of the cars took place at Raleigh, under the direct supervision of the Railroad Bureau. The works continued production of the car irons up until the end of the war and furnished the basic material for almost 150 freight cars. Total Tredegar sales to the Railroad Bureau amounted to $850,000 in 1864 and 1865. The contract was on the usual cost-plus basis and the profit allowed was probably in the neighborhood of 25 per cent.[20]

Sales to individual railroad companies accounted for a much larger percentage of Tredegar production than the purchases of the government Railroad Bureau. Foundry and rolling mill sales to private railroads amounted to $2,721,287 in 1864, while the bureau bought only $456,111

17. Black, pp. 122–23.

18. Anderson & Co. to Col. F. W. Sims, March 15, 1864, Tredegar Letterbooks.

19. *O.R.*, Ser. I, *33*, 1294–95.

20. Entries for June 1864–March 1865, Tredegar Foundry Sales Books; entries under "C.S. R.R. Bureau," Tredegar Ledgers; Black, p. 236.

worth of iron. The same pattern prevailed in the first three months of 1865, with $1,069,270 in Tredegar iron going to specific railroads and $394,428 to the government rail agency.[21]

During the final two and a half years of war, two factors lay behind the Tredegar owners' increasing neglect of the government's demands for rolling mill products, including gunboat armor, and their stepped-up deliveries to Southern railroads. The company earned a greater profit on sales to private customers, of course, but equally important was the Tredegar's need for transportation for provisions from the south and for cotton to Wilmington and Charleston. "By rendering us this aid, you will place us under obligations to supply your road whatever you may order from us in your line," one of the partners told the superintendent of the Richmond and Petersburg Railroad in 1863 in a typical letter.[22] The railroads also controlled the South's main supplies of scrap iron, a major raw materials item for the Tredegar rolling mills. The Richmond industrialists consequently delivered the major part of their production of railroad iron to those lines which were on the main supply routes to their operations or had sizable stores of scrap iron which could be exchanged for bar iron, wheels and axles, or spikes. The roads involved in transporting food from the lower South had first call on Tredegar products. "Our works have been placed at your disposal for the maintenance of your Road, although doing

TABLE 9. Tredegar Foundry and Rolling Mill Sales, 1861–1865 (in Confederate currency)

	Confederate States	*Railroads*	*Total Sales* **
April–December 1861	$ 560,201 *	$ 112,867	$1,139,943
1862	1,169,149	201,122	1,822,665
1863	1,871,506	848,373	3,675,472
1864	3,597,409	2,721,286	9,336,269
January–March 1865	2,233,242	1,069,270	3,269,360

* This figure does not include sales to individual states, which amounted to $265,947 in 1861.

** Rolling mill products consumed in Tredegar foundry operations were recorded in the Rolling Mill Sales Books, and vice-versa.

Sources: Tredegar Rolling Mill Sales Books; Tredegar Foundry Sales Books; Tredegar Ledgers.

21. Figures compiled from Tredegar Ledgers.

22. Anderson & Co. to C. O. Sanford, Jan. 19, 1863, Tredegar Letterbooks. See also Anderson & Co. to Maj. J. W. Goodman, Aug. 25, 1864, and to J. M. Selkirk, Jan. 9, 1865, ibid.

this we are compelled to suspend the execution of orders under our contract with the Government which press heavily upon us," the Tredegar owners informed the president of the Virginia and Tennessee Railroad in November 1863.[23]

The result of this deliberate policy was an increase in the production of railroad iron, but often at the expense of government orders. Although total rolling mill production was declining, sales to the railroads jumped sharply in late 1863 and 1864 as the Tredegar line of supply extended deeper into the South. (See Table 9.) This was not necessarily a misallocation of Southern resources. Railroads were a vital cog in the Confederate war machine and needed much more aid than they received. The Tredegar supply routes did not, however, always coincide with the logistical needs of the Army of Northern Virginia. The two most important rail lines feeding Lee's troops in the fall and winter of 1864 were the Richmond and Danville and the Southside Railroad.[24] Yet six other Southern roads, four of which were outside Virginia, received more Tredegar iron than did the Richmond and Danville, and the Southside ranked eighteenth on the list of Tredegar rail customers in 1864. (See Table 10.) The chief beneficiaries of the Tredegar's increased private production were the Virginia Central, which hauled pig iron produced at the company's furnaces in the Shenandoah Valley, and the roads in North Carolina, South Carolina, and Georgia that formed the main trunk line tapping the rich agricultural region of southwestern Georgia. These iron deliveries served the purposes of Anderson and Company but not always those of the government.

The failure of the Davis administration to institute close control over rail transportation and the supply of railroad iron was a major blunder. When the government finally took action to provide for increased production of railroad materials and establish effective direction over rail movements, the chances of a Southern military victory were nonexistent. The Railroad Bureau never attempted to direct the allocation of rail supplies and did not place large orders with the South's largest iron works until the spring of 1864. The War Department took no action to put a rail mill into production until the latter part of 1864 and that effort, when made, was ineffective. Congress did not enact legislation providing for full military control of Confederate railways until February 1865.[25]

Rails were among the most critically needed items in the South during

23. Anderson & Co. to R. D. Owen, Nov. 19, 1863, ibid.

24. Johnston, *Virginia Railroads*, pp. 227–29.

25. Black, p. 280.

the war, yet the Tredegar mills failed to roll a single rail. A combination of mistakes and timidity prevented Anderson and Company from even attempting to reactivate their rail mill before the twilight months of the Confederacy.

TABLE 10. Tredegar Sales to Railroads, 1864 (in excess of $25,000, Confederate currency)

Virginia Central	$378,048
Charlotte & South Carolina	289,019
North Carolina	262,947
South Carolina	261,940
Virginia & Tennessee	254,965
Wilmington & Manchester	203,953
Richmond & Danville	149,467
North Eastern	125,905
Piedmont	125,102
Petersburg	115,842
Wilmington & Weldon	96,834
South Western	91,642
Georgia Central	59,725
Muscogee	48,947
Mobile & Ohio	48,158
Greenville & Columbia	44,688
Montgomery & West Point	44,599
Southside	44,050
Richmond & Petersburg	42,988
Georgia R.R. & Banking Co.	41,258
Macon & Western	25,831

Source: Tredegar Ledgers.

The Armory rolling mill, which had produced several thousand tons of rails during the mid-fifties, had been converted into a rail chair and merchant bar mill before the outbreak of the war. Under the terms of the Tredegar's 1862 contracts with the War and Navy Departments, this mill was to be completely rebuilt and enlarged into a plant capable of rolling the heaviest descriptions of armor and boiler plate. Work commenced on the project in the fall of 1862, but after a year's labor and the expenditure of over $70,000, the new mill was not yet completed. The company halted construction completely in November 1863 because there was no prospect of getting enough pig or scrap iron to keep it employed.[26] In January

26. Entries under "Armory Extension," Tredegar Ledgers; Anderson & Co. to Gorgas, Dec. 8, 1863, in "J. R. Anderson & Co.," Confederate Citizens File, RG 109, NA.

1863, the Tredegar management received an inquiry from the Richmond and Danville about rerolling rails. Forty-seven miles of that extremely important road were laid with flat bar rails on wooden stringers and this flimsy track deteriorated quickly under heavily laden military trains.[27] No such work could be done, however, because the mill with the equipment for performing the job was torn down and in the process of reconstruction.

The government made no attempt to reconvert the Armory mill to rail production until the Confederate cause was almost hopeless, and Anderson and Company refused to risk the capital to activate the mill without government support. The Engineer Department questioned the Tredegar owners about rerolling rails in July 1864 but did not pursue the matter.[28] The Niter and Mining Bureau reopened the subject in November and Anderson replied that he thought the rail mill could be placed in operation in four months' time if the bureau appropriated $150,000 to the project. This the bureau agreed to do.[29]

The Tredegar management then set out to put the mill in operating condition. The company had not rolled rails for ten years, however, and Anderson sought to hasten the renovation by getting help from the other large Southern rolling mill. He requested detailed information on the machinery of the Atlanta rail mill from Secretary of the Treasury Trenholm, who had purchased the equipment and moved it to Columbia, South Carolina, prior to Sherman's capture of the Georgia city. Trenholm was agreeable but his agent at Columbia refused to furnish the plans because the information would create a potential rival in the production of rails. After haggling with the recalcitrant superintendent at Columbia for two months, Anderson decided to go ahead on his own. By this time it was the first of February 1865; the rail mill was still unfinished at the close of the conflict.[30] Not a single new rail was rolled in the entire Confederacy during the war.[31]

This incident was all too typical of the inadequate response of both the

27. Anderson & Co. to Charles G. Talcott, Jan. 31, 1863, Tredegar Letterbooks; Johnston, p. 10.

28. Col. A. L. Rives to Anderson & Co., July 3, 1864, Letters Sent, Engineer Department, RG 109, NA.

29. Anderson & Co. to Richard Morton, Nov. 7, 1864, Tredegar Letterbooks.

30. Anderson & Co. to Tanner, Nov. 14, 1864, to R. A. Talley, Nov. 26, 1864, Feb. 1, 1865, to Trenholm, Dec. 14, 1864, Feb. 3, 1865, and to T. Alphonse Jackson, Jan. 12, 21, 1865, ibid.; entry for Feb. 1865, Tredegar Journals.

31. Black, pp. 124, 152; Johnston, n. 26, p. 258.

Confederate government and private entrepreneurs to industrial problems which did not directly involve ordnance and munitions production. A confusion of bureaucratic voices, resulting in delayed and incorrect decisions, the unwillingness of capitalists to make large investments without government aid, and petty business jealousy all combined to deprive the South of what would have been an invaluable manufacturing asset. Unfortunately for the Confederate cause, this pattern was the norm rather than the exception. In a final and futile gesture, the Confederate Congress passed a resolution on February 18, 1865, authorizing the President to ascertain if liberal encouragement from the government could stimulate the domestic manufacture of railroad iron.[32]

III

The head of the Bureau of Ordnance and Hydrography was confident in November 1863 that the fire of the previous spring would not permanently damage Tredegar ordnance operations. Although a shortage of gun metal and the May blaze had prevented Anderson's foundry from casting heavy cannon for several months, "these works are again in operation," Brooke reported to the Secretary of the Navy, "and with the facilities afforded by . . . the completion of a new foundry and boring mill, the number of guns provided in an equal interval will be double what it was before the fire." New Tredegar ordnance "will be generally of greater power and caliber," he added.[33]

Anderson and Company's subsequent performance failed to justify Brooke's optimism. At the same time this officer was forecasting more, bigger, and better guns, the Tredegar owners were giving a discouraging report to the army on the progress of preparations for manufacturing much-needed heavy ordnance, including the huge 15-inch gun. The company had promised in April 1862 to complete this weapon within four months' time.[34] On November 20, 1863, Anderson informed Captain J. Wilcox Brown of the Ordnance Bureau that although the furnaces and pits for casting the gun had long been completed, neither the pattern, the flasks, nor the boring lathe was ready. The fire had severely damaged the new lathe specially built for the 15-inch cannon and workmen were still repair-

32. Charles W. Ramsdell, ed., *Laws and Joint Resolutions of the Last Session of the Confederate Congress* . . . (Durham, 1941), pp. 45–46.

33. *O.R.N.*, Ser. II, *2*, 550.

34. Contract with the War and Navy Departments, April 29, 1862, in "J. R. Anderson & Co.,' Confederate Citizens File, RG 109, NA.

ing this tool. Tredegar patternmaking facilities, completely consumed in the blaze, remained crippled and Anderson urged Brown to have the pattern for the gun made elsewhere while Tredegar artisans worked on the flask patterns. "With this aid and the help of five or six of our old hands now in the employment of the Government we think we could cast the first Gun in January and get it on the lathe as soon as cast," the senior partner predicted. He hoped Tredegar founders could begin casting 12-inch guns, also desired by the army, in late December.[35]

The army and the navy were still looking for work to begin on these weapons in March 1864. "I feel very sensibly the importance of getting on faster at the Foundry," Anderson wrote the Ordnance Bureaus on March 15. "But too much we fear is expected of the establishment, considering its capacity." Labor problems had seriously impeded Tredegar operations. "If we could have had, for six months past, 12 good finishers more, our capacity for work would be far different now," he pointed out. "And it is undoubtedly true that the hands we have, many of them, do not work with much spirit, which is discouraging." Anderson promised nevertheless to do all in his power to expedite work on the weapons.[36]

The Tredegar's inability to cast by the Rodman hollow core process was still the basic obstacle preventing the manufacture of very large caliber guns. At the outset of the war, Tredegar facilities, using the solid casting method, could produce guns of up to 10-inch caliber. But Southern harbor defenses required larger and more powerful weapons to challenge heavily armored Federal monitors. Using the new furnace built during the war, Tredegar foundrymen cast an 11-inch Brooke gun in December 1863, but it was July 1864 before this solid piece and a companion cast in February were bored, triple banded, and dispatched to the Charleston defenses.[37] With the Tredegar works producing at this pace, Union fleets would soon control every port in the Confederacy.

Anderson realized his earlier mistake in rejecting the Rodman method and he made a futile attempt to repair the damage. By October 1864, workmen had completed preparations for casting a 12-inch gun around a hollow core. The summoning of the Tredegar Battalion to the trenches delayed the casting, but on November 14, 1864, gun founders poured 41,000 pounds of molten iron into a specially designed flask, with water circulat-

35. Anderson & Co. to J. Wilcox Brown, Nov. 20, 1863, Tredegar Letterbooks.

36. Anderson & Co. to Brown, March 15, 1864, and to Brooke, March 15, 1864, ibid.

37. Tredegar Gun Foundry Book; Tredegar Foundry Sales Books.

ing through the core to cool the casting. When experiments revealed the remarkable strength of this piece, the Tredegar cast another 12-inch Rodman gun in February 1865. Tools needed to finish these weapons were not ready before the end of the war and neither of the big guns ever saw service.[38] The successful casting of these weapons, a remarkable technical achievement in wartime, came much too late to aid the Confederate cause. The 15-inch guns, first ordered by the Ordnance Bureau during the opening weeks of the war, never got beyond the draftsman's board. Anderson's refusal to accept the Rodman technique in 1859 had a profound impact on the production of heavy ordnance in the Confederacy.

Although Anderson and Company failed to meet the ordnance bureaus' requests for the heaviest descriptions of cannon, the Tredegar works manufactured a wide range of siege and seacoast artillery during the final two years of the war. Casting of ordnance resumed at the plant on May 28, 1863, two weeks after the fire. The extensive damage suffered by the gun mill prevented Tredegar artisans from boring or rifling heavy cannon for several months and during the interim, the company's carry-log crew carted large caliber guns to the naval ordnance works in Richmond for finishing.[39] Between May 1863 and March 1865, Anderson and Company delivered to the government almost 150 siege and seacoast guns and mortars, primarily 10-inch columbiads, 7-inch Brooke rifles, 8-inch siege guns, and 8-inch columbiads—certainly a creditable performance considering the numerous production problems. Most of these heavy pieces went to river and harbor defenses at Wilmington, Charleston, Mobile, and Savannah, and to the Richmond fortifications.[40] The Tredegar also armed the Richmond-built ironclads *Fredericksburg* and *Virginia II* with 6.40- and 7-inch Brookes and 10-inch smooth bore banded guns in May 1864.[41] Torpedoes built by Anderson and Company provided additional defense for key Confederate ports and rivers in 1863 and 1864.[42]

Charleston received special attention from the War Department and the

38. Gorgas, "Notes on the Ordnance Department," *Southern Hist. Soc. Papers, 12,* 94; Anderson & Co. to Brown, Jan. 10, 1865, Tredegar Letterbooks; entries for March 1865, Tredegar Foundry Sales Books; Tredegar Gun Foundry Book.

39. Tredegar Foundry Sales Books; Tredegar Gun Foundry Book.

40. Tredegar Foundry Sales Books.

41. "Ordnance Report of Stmr. 'Virginia,' James River Squadron," May 26, 1864, Minor Papers, VHS; entries for May 1864, Tredegar Foundry Sales Books.

42. Entries for Feb., March, June, 1863, ibid.; Anderson & Co. to Lt. J. Pembroke Jones, Nov. 12, Dec. 29, 1864, Tredegar Letterbooks; bill of Anderson for "Submarine Battery," Nov. 18, 1864, in "J. R. Anderson & Co.," Confederate Citizens File, RG 109, NA.

Tredegar works. The port was of great strategic importance to the South but this was not the only reason for this exceptional consideration. The chairman of the powerful House Committee on Military Affairs, William Porcher Miles, was a Charlestonian and he put constant pressure on the Secretary of War to strengthen the city's defenses with heavy Tredegar guns.[43] The Richmond firm dispatched a large number of cannon to Charleston but General Beauregard, back at the scene of his greatest glory, was never satisfied with either the quantity or the quality of the artillery he received.[44] Some of his heavy rifled pieces burst and Beauregard repeated the complaints voiced earlier by D. H. Hill about bad gun metal and unsafe ordnance.[45] Gorgas categorically denied Beauregard's accusations. "The bursting of the heavy rifled guns is not sufficiently explained by the character of the metal, as General Beauregard supposes," wrote the ordnance chief. "The cast-iron of these guns was entirely satisfactory, and their premature destruction is due to the constant heavy charges with which they have been fired." [46] The Tredegar partners were, in fact, highly pleased with the overall performance of their weapons at Charleston. On April 7, 1863, Confederate gunners at Fort Sumter repulsed a long anticipated attack of Federal monitors, sinking the *Keokuk* and severely damaging several other Union craft. Tredegar 7-inch Brooke guns, equipped with armor-piercing bolts, played a key role in the Confederate triumph.[47] "The news from Charleston is highly encouraging and the success there is due to the heavy Guns we have lately made for Beauregard," wrote one of the partners shortly after the battle.[48]

Tredegar gun founders directed most of their attention to field artillery during the final years of the war. (See Table 5, p. 111.) From the time casting began again after the fire in May 1863 until March 1865, Anderson's skilled workmen cast 162 siege and seacoast weapons as against 254 pieces of field artillery.[49] The great majority of the latter were 12-pounder bronze and iron Napoleons. The Confederacy had not possessed the quantities of copper needed for large-scale production of Napoleons since 1862. Lee had supplied the raw materials in 1863 in the form of ob-

43. *O.R.*, Ser. I, *53* (Supplement), 287.
44. *Battles and Leaders*, *4*, 4.
45. *O.R.*, Ser. I, *28*, pt. ii, 365.
46. Ibid., p. 388.
47. *Battles and Leaders*, *4*, 37–40; *O.R.N.*, Ser. II, *2*, 418.
48. Anderson & Co. to Gorgas, April 10, 1863, Tredegar Letterbooks
49. Tredegar Gun Foundry Book.

solete bronze cannon, but by the end of that year the Tredegar had completed the recasting of these weapons. Anderson and Company then developed an iron 12-pounder, banded at the breech for additional strength. Founders cast the first experimental pieces in January 1864 and the new model passed proof firings in March.[50] By the spring, the gun had proven itself in the field and the Ordnance Bureau ordered the Tredegar to give the manufacture of iron Napoleons preference over all other cannon.[51] The Richmond firm cast 120 of these excellent field pieces before the end of the war.[52]

Equipping the Army of Northern Virginia for trench warfare constituted a major task for the Tredegar in the summer of 1864. In May and early June, the Tredegar began strengthening the Richmond defenses at Chafin's and Drewry's Bluffs and at Chester with heavy ordnance.[53] Even before Grant invested Petersburg in mid-June, Confederate ordnance officers requested Anderson's works to begin rapid manufacture of weapons needed for siege operations. On May 4, the Ordnance Bureau ordered twenty light coehorn trench mortars and beds and two weeks later doubled the requisition. Anderson and Company delivered the first six on May 16, and turned thirty-six more over to the department in June and July.[54] Once the siege of Petersburg began, the Tredegar rushed 30-pounder Parrotts, 8- and 10-inch columbiads, and 8-inch siege mortars and guns to the vital rail center south of the James.[55]

Anderson and Company also increased the output of artillery projectiles to meet the demands of Lee's army. An Ordnance Bureau requisition on May 26 asked for 10,000 rounds of various caliber shot and shell and advised Anderson that "there is great need of all these projectiles & I trust you will appreciate the importance of accumulating supplies of them as soon as possible."[56] Although stores of pig iron were dangerously low, the works delivered over 5,500 rounds of mortar ammunition and additional quantities of other projectiles to the forces defending Richmond and

50. Ibid.; entries for Feb., March, 1864, Tredegar Foundry Sales Books.

51. Brown to Anderson & Co., May 31, 1864, Brock Papers, HL.

52. Tredegar Gun Foundry Book.

53. R. K. Hudgins to Anderson & Co., May 26, 1864, Brock Papers, HL; entries for May, June, 1864, Tredegar Foundry Sales Books.

54. Brown to Anderson & Co., May 4, 26, 1864, Brock Papers, HL; entries for May–July 1864, Tredegar Foundry Sales Books.

55. Entries for June–Aug. 1864, ibid.

56. Brown to Anderson & Co., May 26, 1864, Brock Papers, HL. See also W. N. Smith to Anderson & Co., May 27, 1864, and W. Leroy Broun to Anderson & Co., Aug. 7, 1864, ibid.

Petersburg during the summer months.[57] When production fell off sharply during October because the Tredegar Battalion was in the field, the Ordnance Bureau hurriedly secured the release of key mechanics to prevent a severe shortage of artillery ammunition.[58]

By 1864, Anderson and Company turned out a baffling range of ammunition for the Confederacy's motley collection of artillery. A February 1861 Tredegar price list enumerated nine different types of projectiles the works could manufacture; a similar breakdown drawn up in January 1863 listed thirty-seven separate items.[59] Different army and navy specifications for similar projectiles further perplexed the firm's ammunition production. For example, the windage—the difference between the diameter of the bore and that of the projectile—in a navy Brooke gun was 15/100 of an inch; in the army Brooke this difference was 10/100 of an inch. "Permit us to suggest that it would save much time—increase the quantity of work done and avoid, or prevent, confusion and, perhaps, many mistakes if the Navy & Army Ordnance Bureaux could agree on the same windage," Anderson suggested to Brooke in 1864.[60] The ammunition requirements of the many types of foreign-built and captured weapons employed by Southern artillerists compounded this confusion.

Destruction of Anderson and Company's best gun iron furnaces by Hunter's cavalry in June 1864 seriously limited the Tredegar's contribution to the defense of Richmond and Petersburg. In June, before stocks of Cloverdale and Grace gun metal began to give out, founders cast thirty-three pieces of ordnance; during July and August, they cast a total of only twenty-one and were forced to use unreliable brands of iron.[61] Both army and navy ordnance officers reported during the late summer that the loss of these two stacks would have a very damaging effect on the manufacture of cannon and mortars in the Confederacy.[62] Tredegar ordnance production bore out this prediction. From a total of 128 weapons cast during the first six months of 1864, output dropped off to 85 pieces during the last half of

57. Tredegar Foundry Sales Books.

58. Anderson & Co. to Gorgas, Oct. 1, 3, 1864, to Brown, Oct. 20, 1864, and to W. H. Stevens, Oct. 24, 1864, Tredegar Letterbooks.

59. "Weight, calibre & price per lb. of cannon, shot & shell at Tredegar Works," Feb. 4, 1861, and "List of prices proposed to be charged by J. R. Anderson & Co.," Jan. 20, 22, 1863, Tredegar Letterbooks. See also Berkeley R. Lewis, *Notes on Ammunition of the American Civil War* (Washington, 1959).

60. Anderson & Co. to Brooke, March 15, 1864, Tredegar Letterbooks.

61. Tredegar Gun Foundry Book.

62. *O.R.*, Ser. I, *62*, pt. ii, 1164, Ser. IV, *3*, 521.

that year and, most serious of all, these guns were of highly questionable quality.[63]

IV

A strain of war-weariness began to creep into the correspondence of the Tredegar owners in 1863. In June of that year, one of the partners voiced "our ardent prayer for the termination of this unholy war." [64] When the Army of Northern Virginia carried the war into Pennsylvania later that month, however, their spirits rose. "Today we have the U. States papers to 17th which tell us that their whole country is in a panic at the approach of Genl. Lee's army," Anderson wrote on the day before the battle of Gettysburg began. "What an army his is and such officers [,] indeed such an army the world has never seen." Anderson admitted that he was "very much concerned for the situation in Miss.," but he hoped for the best.[65] News of Lee's defeat and the fall of Vicksburg abruptly changed his mood to one of despair. "We are all sad today at the news from Genl. Lee's army," wrote a member of the firm on July 9. "It is sad indeed but we will not enter upon details." [66] But two days later, word that the Army of Northern Virginia had retreated intact to the Potomac lifted much of the gloom in the Tredegar offices. "We have never faltered in our faith in the strength and safety of Genl. Lee's Army," they informed their chief furnace agent.[67]

When Grant launched his drive on Richmond the next spring, Anderson and his associates expressed continued confidence in Lee and in the Confederate cause. "We feel as strong as ever in the defenses of Richmond and generally I think our affairs have never looked more promising since the war began," Anderson told his brother on the day following Lincoln's reelection. "It may last a long time and our people may be called on to endure much and make great sacrifices. But of the final result," he continued, "the establishment of our Independence, I have not now and never have entertained any doubt." [68] Occasionally the optimism was qualified, as in a message conveyed to a Tredegar correspondent in October that "the news from all quarters is as favorable to our cause as we have any reason

63. Tredegar Gun Foundry Book; *O.R.*, Ser. I, *46*, pt. iii, 1009–10.

64. Anderson & Co. to D. & H. Riker, June 6, 1863, Tredegar Letterbooks.

65. Anderson to William A. Glasgow, June 30, 1863, Glasgow Papers, WLU.

66. Anderson & Co. to F. T. Glasgow, July 9, 1863, Tredegar Letterbooks.

67. Anderson & Co. to Glasgow, July 11, 1863, ibid.

68. Anderson to F. T. Anderson, Nov. 9, 1864, Anderson Papers, UVA.

to expect." [69] A tone of defiance was more common, however. "Grant will make as glorious a failure over the capture of Richmond as his illustrious (?) predecessors have done," young William Tanner predicted later in October.[70]

Anderson's professed faith in the ultimate triumph of Southern arms was not matched by a confidence in the Tredegar's ability to make money in 1865. On December 21, John Tanner told Glasgow that "military matters wear a grave aspect, although we have nothing very definite." [71] That same day, the senior partner outlined to the Ordnance Department the difficulties facing Tredegar operations during the coming year. In addition to inadequate provisions, insufficient labor, and shortages of pig iron and coal, "there remains the question of funds," Anderson wrote. "We have, as you are aware, been operating largely for the Government on a depreciating currency. This is a sufficient explanation for the fact that instead of realizing a reasonable profit upon our operations for the Department, we have lost very heavily (several hundred thousand dollars, probably) during the current year." [72] Worse still, the government had not paid its bills and the company was in desperate need of cash. The Niter and Mining Bureau owed the firm $300,000 for the rebuilding of the blast furnaces and the conversion of the Armory rolling mill to rail production; the Ordnance Department had not settled its account since October 4; the navy and the Railroad Bureau were also heavily in arrears. "The want of this money embarrasses us much in meeting the heavy engagements attendant upon this period of the year and makes it necessary that some better financial arrangement shall be adopted before entering upon the arduous labors of another year and we respectfully invite your attention to this subject," he informed the Ordnance Department.

The government held the panacea for the Tredegar's many ills, Anderson told the bureau. Earlier in December, the problems of provisioning and acquiring slaves for the coming year had prompted the Tredegar head to suggest that the government take over his blast furnaces in 1865. He now thought "that the Government had better operate not only the blast furnaces but this establishment, also, on its own account." He offered to meet with ordnance officials at any time to discuss this subject. "We feel it

69. Anderson & Co. to D. A. James, Oct. 4, 1864, Tredegar Letterbooks.

70. Anderson & Co. to Sam Tate, Oct. 12, 1864, ibid.

71. Anderson & Co. to Glasgow, Dec. 21, 1864, ibid.

72. Tredegar profits were down but Anderson's claim that he had lost money was unfounded; see Table 8.

our duty to announce to the Bureau that we will not be able to supply the wants of the Department without important changes—willing as we are still to do all in our power," Anderson concluded.[73]

Discussions opened with both Gorgas and Brooke during the week following the dispatch of this communication. The two ordnance chiefs requested Anderson to state his proposition in writing and he did so on December 30. The government should purchase at fair market value both finished and unfinished work underway at the Richmond plant, the raw materials and supplies then on hand, all Tredegar buildings and tools (except the spike and nail machines), and all the company's boats, mules, and wagons. Both the government and Anderson and Company would appoint appraisers and these two were to call in a third party if disagreements arose. The company would retain ownership of the coal mines, blast furnaces, and the land on which the Tredegar works stood. The government would rent the furnaces and the Richmond property for the duration of the war and take over the slave labor hired for these facilities. Anderson and his associates would continue to operate the coal mines under their exclusive jurisdiction. Finally, the Tredegar management was "willing to conduct the whole operations as agents of the Govt. under direction of the Ordnance Bureaux on such terms as may be agreed upon." [74]

Negotiations continued into the first week of January, but Anderson and the chiefs of the Ordnance Departments and the Niter and Mining Bureau failed to reach an agreement. The Tredegar senior partner then revealed what was probably the major reason behind his earlier proposition to turn the works over to the government. On January 6, he consented to continue operations at the various Tredegar facilities, provided the government would allow higher Tredegar prices. "We claim that we are entitled to a reasonable profit upon the productions of these works & that in adjusting the prices thereof, pig iron produced by us, should be assumed either at its market value, or at its cost, with a reasonable profit added." Anderson demanded a new system to determine the prices of Tredegar products. "We claim that the prices shall be adjusted not by one of the parties as hitherto, but by mutual agreement, and we respectfully suggest that you select an officer & we a member of our firm, who shall fix the prices monthly or quarterly." The company was unilaterally raising its prices to the Confed-

73. Anderson & Co. to Brown, Dec. 21, 1864, Tredegar Letterbooks. See also Anderson & Co. to Gorgas, Dec. 6, 1864, to Brooke, Jan. 25, 1865, and to Sims, Feb. 10, 1865, ibid.

74. Anderson & Co. to Gorgas and Brooke, Dec. 30, 1864, ibid.

erate States as of January 1, 1865, he informed the Secretaries of the War and Navy Departments, and rates would remain at these new levels until changed by joint consent.[75]

Anderson's action failed to relieve his company's financial distress. Seddon and Mallory agreed to appoint a military commission to discuss pricing with the Tredegar management, but this was small comfort when 1864 Tredegar bills on the government totaling over $1,000,000 remained unpaid as of February 1, 1865.[76] "Our heavy operations must terminate in disaster unless we obtain speedy relief," Anderson informed Brooke in late January.[77] The company lacked money to meet the next payroll and he warned that all work would stop if the men remained unpaid.[78] When an appeal to the Tredegar's large railroad customers for funds went totally unanswered, Anderson had to borrow $100,000 from a Richmond bank to cover the first February payroll.[79] The Treasury finally authorized a requisition for $150,000 to cover the Ordnance Department's back bills in mid-February. But this relief was further reduced when the bureau's paymaster insisted on settling one fourth of the account in virtually unmarketable government bonds.[80] By the first week of March, the government had settled about $650,000 of its Tredegar bills, but the Confederate States still owed Anderson and Company almost $900,000 at the end of the war.[81]

V

Following a two-week shutdown for repairs, the Tredegar works went back into operation in mid-January 1865.[82] A severe shortage of pig iron crippled production from the outset. "We are entirely out of all metal from your furnaces," the management informed Glasgow on the twelfth. A

75. Anderson & Co. to the Secretaries of War and Navy, Jan. 6, 1865, ibid. See also Anderson & Co. to St. John, Jan. 6, 10, 1865, ibid.

76. Anderson & Co. to Deane, Jan. 31, Feb. 1, 1865, to Mallory, Feb. 1, 1865, to Gorgas, Feb. 1, 13, 1865, to St. John, Feb. 1, 1865, to Trenholm, Feb. 1, 1865, and to Sims, Feb. 10, 1865, ibid.

77. Anderson & Co. to Brooke, Jan. 25, 1865, ibid.

78. Anderson & Co. to Sims, Feb. 10, 1865, and to W. S. Watkins, Feb. 10, 1865, ibid.

79. Anderson & Co. to C. Bouknight, Feb. 2, 1865, to S. D. Wallace, Feb. 2, 1865, to Henry M. Williamson, Feb. 4, 1865, to J. Emery, Feb. 7, 1865, and to Gorgas, Feb. 13, 1865, ibid.; entries for March 1865, Tredegar Journals.

80. Anderson & Co. to Gorgas, Feb. 13, 1865, Tredegar Letterbooks.

81. Entries for March, Sept., 1865, Tredegar Journals; *O.R.*, Ser. I, *46*, pt. ii, 1287–89.

82. Anderson & Co. to John T. Armstrong, Jan. 16, 1865, Tredegar Letterbooks; Tredegar Gun Foundry Book.

month later, the Tredegar owners repeated this message and urged their furnace agent to get some metal to Richmond as quickly as possible.[83] In early February, the Niter and Mining Bureau further heightened the critical situation at the works. Officers of that bureau impressed three hundred tons of pig iron, produced by a furnace under contract to Anderson and Company, awaiting shipment at Staunton. Despite Anderson's heated protest to the Secretary of War, this iron remained in official hands.[84]

Ordnance and munitions production proceeded at an extremely slow pace. To prepare Fort Fisher for an anticipated duel with Federal monitors, the Bureau of Ordnance and Hydrography sent the Tredegar a rush order for two hundred armor-piercing wrought iron bolts on December 7, 1864; the company gave the navy twenty-three in January.[85] The Tredegar delivered sixteen pieces of field artillery, a number of light coehorn mortars, and twenty-one siege and seacoast weapons during the first three months of 1865. Founders had cast most of these pieces in 1864, some as far back as April. The gun mill finished only two of the thirty-five cannon cast in January, February, and March.[86] By the end of March, the shortage of iron had brought the works to a complete stop. President Davis told Lee on April 1 that he would try to keep the Tredegar in operation, "though it must be on a reduced scale." [87] The next day, Lee replied that his forces could no longer hold the capital.

When government bureaus began preparing in late February for a possible evacuation, Anderson's concern over the fate of his works mounted. In March, he sought assurances from the War Department that the government would not put the torch to the Tredegar works. "It is presumed that it will not be considered proper that our forces should destroy them," he hopefully suggested to the new Secretary of War, John C. Breckinridge. The North had an abundance of ordnance manufacturing plants, he argued, and would neither need nor employ his facilities. When Breckinridge asked Mallory for his opinion, the Secretary of the Navy voted for destruction. Gorgas supported Anderson's argument, however, and his opinion seems to have weighed most heavily with the Secretary of War.

83. Anderson & Co. to Glasgow, Jan. 12, Feb. 11, 1865, Tredegar Letterbooks.

84. Anderson & Co. to Charles Crum, Feb. 9, 10, 1865, and to John C. Breckinridge, Feb. 11, 1865, ibid.

85. Brooke to Anderson & Co., Dec. 7, 1864, Letters Sent, Office of Ordnance and Hydrography, RG 109, NA; Tredegar Foundry Sales Books.

86. Ibid.; Tredegar Gun Foundry Book.

87. *O.R.*, Ser. I, *46*, pt. iii, 1370.

Much to the relief of Anderson and his partners, Breckinridge issued no orders to burn the Tredegar.[88]

When the government began moving out of Richmond on the afternoon of April 2, Anderson took added precautions to insure the safety of his plant. Loyal members of the Tredegar Battalion answered his call for aid, loaded their muskets, and took up positions around the works. This action saved the Tredegar. Looting broke out as Confederate troops tramped south across the James, and in the moonless early morning hours of April 3 a rampaging mob seized control of the warehouse district. Their ranks swollen by convicts who had broken loose en masse from the nearby penitentiary, looters spread the flames originally put to government depots and tobacco storehouses. Countermanding Gorgas' order not to destroy any ordnance facilities, this motley crowd set fire to the Confederate arsenal, causing an explosion that shattered practically every window at the Tredegar and sent shells crashing through the roofs of Anderson's buildings. The arsonists then moved toward the nearby Tredegar plant to finish off their night's handiwork. The resistance of Anderson and his men blunted the thrust of the mob, however, and it broke and retreated back toward the center of town.[89]

The Tredegar works survived and soon stood ready to assist in the rebuilding of the shattered South.

VI

Looking back over the Tredegar's wartime experience, we can find answers to a number of long-standing questions about the industrial economy of the Confederacy. In what condition was Southern manufacturing at the outset of the war? What obstacles arose to impede production and which were the most important? How serious were labor shortages and how effective were the efforts to repair them? What attitude did manufacturers take toward their profits and what levels did these profits reach? What was the nature of the government's relationship with private industry? How did industrial output influence the outcome of land and naval engagements? Admittedly, the history of one firm will not provide the last word on these and

88. Ibid., pt. ii, 1287–89.

89. Bill, *Beleaguered City*, pp. 269–73; Vandiver, *Gorgas*, pp. 266–67; Jones, *Diary, 2*, 465–68; William M. E. Rachal, "The Burning of Richmond," *Virginia Cavalcade, 1* (Spring 1952), 23–28; Rembert W. Patrick, *The Fall of Richmond* (Baton Rouge, 1960), p. 50; W. Asbury Christian, *Richmond, Her Past and Present* (Richmond, 1912), pp. 262–63. Confederate troops did not attempt to burn the Tredegar works, as several of the above authors suggest.

other questions concerning the South's war industries. Yet the preeminent position of the Tredegar Iron Works among Southern manufacturing establishments makes the story of this company particularly significant to the student seeking to unravel the complex and often obscure economic history of the Confederate South.

The war quickly revealed the strengths and more numerous weaknesses of the South's industrial economy. James Ford Rhodes was incorrect when he wrote that "the Confederacy was but a farm, dependent on Europe and the North for everything but bread and meat, and before the war for much of those." [90] Although the South was a predominantly agricultural region, heavy manufacturing had made important antebellum beginnings in Virginia, Tennessee, Georgia, Alabama, and several other states. Underdeveloped domestic sources of raw materials, not a total lack of manufacturing facilities, was the South's fatal industrial weakness. Foundries and rolling mills which had grown dramatically during the 1850s were starved for iron, copper, lead, coal, and a host of other strategic items. Inadequate transportation and the government's failure to control the railroads until the war was virtually over prevented plants from drawing on distant sources of supply and compounded the plight of the war industries.

Secession also revealed the full extent of the South's dependence on skilled Northern workers. The Confederacy's industrial labor force was inadequate at the start of the war and early overmobilization, followed by an unsympathetic official attitude toward exemption and detail, prevented key plants from assembling and holding sufficient numbers of trained artisans. Negro slaves, although performing monumental service for Confederate industry, could not fill all the gaps left by the departure of expert gun molders, cannon riflers, pattern makers, and the like.

Both labor and raw materials shortages cut the Tredegar's wartime production but of the two, insufficient supplies of critical materials, pig iron in particular, had the most significant impact. Output at the Richmond plant peaked in the spring of 1862 but, even at its height, production did not begin to approach full potential. Pig iron produced by the company's furnaces, supplemented by smaller tonnages from the Niter and Mining Bureau's stacks, enabled the Tredegar works to operate at no more than one third of plant capacity during the four years of conflict.

A close relationship often existed between Tredegar production and mil-

90. James Ford Rhodes, *History of the United States from the Compromise of 1850 . . . to . . . 1877* (7 vols. New York, 1892–1906), *3*, 387.

itary success or failure. On the rare occasions when sufficient materials were at hand, Anderson and Company accomplished some notable feats. The rolling of the *Merrimack's* armor and the recasting of Lee's bronze ordnance prior to Chancellorsville were dramatic achievements that had a direct and positive bearing on the military fortunes of the Confederacy. More often than not, however, performance fell short of expectation. Faulty Tredegar cannon, resulting primarily from unreliable gun iron, had a devastating effect on the morale and performance of Confederate gunners at Port Royal, Yorktown, Fort Fisher, and other key engagements. The failure of Anderson's foundries to cast sufficient numbers of iron field pieces, especially prior to Gettysburg, the inability to produce the heaviest descriptions of ordnance, limited output of artillery projectiles, and delayed deliveries of gunboat armor and machinery contributed significantly to the South's defeat.

As the war deepened and the Tredegar's responsibilities and difficulties grew, production for the government declined even further. Iron was the primary resource Anderson and his associates possessed that could maintain the private quartermaster system needed to support a labor force numbering as high as 2,500 free and slave workers, including their dependents. Hard-pressed Southern railroads agreed to transport stores to Richmond and cotton to the coast but demanded payment in the products of the Tredegar mills and foundries. This, plus the higher profit available on the uncontrolled open market, meant a diversion of precious iron supplies from public to private use, often to railroads that did not form part of the vital lifeline to the Army of Northern Virginia. Such iron as the Tredegar supplied the railways still did not come close to meeting their demands and the works built no locomotives after 1860.[91] Anderson and Company's failure to roll a single rail during the war was a major reason why "the railroad system of the Confederacy could be maintained only by destroying its own substance." [92]

Anderson's wartime activities indicate that Southern businessmen shared many of the basic preoccupations of their counterparts in the North, including a desire to make money.[93] The Tredegar owners attempted both to meet the needs of the Confederate government and to real-

91. By contrast, Northern manufacturers were delivering a locomotive a day to the Federal government in April 1864; see Nevins, *War Becomes Revolution*, p. 461.

92. Black, *Railroads of the Confederacy*, p. 200 (italics deleted).

93. For an account of the wartime career of another like-minded Southern businessman, see Edwin B. Coddington, "The Activities and Attitudes of a Confederate Business Man: Gazaway B. Lamar," *Journal of Southern History*, 9, (1943), 3–36.

ize a profit on their operations, to help the Southern cause and at the same time help themselves. Frequently they were able to do both. During 1861 and 1862, Tredegar war production reached its highest point and the company's profits climbed to record levels. By 1863, however, a growing cost–price squeeze on military items and mounting fears concerning the course of the war prompted Anderson and Company to launch two new and highly speculative ventures. The Tredegar's cotton and blockade-running activities were clearly attempts to place a sizable portion of the company's assets beyond the reach of both Southern inflation and the Northern invaders. Anderson still made every effort to keep Tredegar output at the highest possible levels during the last two years of the war. But it was comforting to know that he had an insurance policy, in the form of a sterling account in London, against a possible Confederate financial or military collapse.

The relationship between the Confederate government and private industry is another shadowy aspect of Civil War history which the Tredegar's experience illuminates. The Davis administration began the war with a strong laissez-faire attitude toward all phases of manufacturing which did not directly concern the production of arms and ammunition. In less than a year, however, the Tredegar's inability to secure adequate quantities of pig iron forced the government to modify this policy. Under legislation passed in April 1862, the War and Navy Departments extended large loans to Anderson and Company to enable the Richmond firm to produce its own iron and coal. Anderson and his associates then proceeded to organize what one historian has called "one of the earliest far-reaching . . . vertical combinations in the American iron industry." [94] But after advancing capital to underwrite the cost of expansion, the government proved unwilling to offer private manufacturers the assistance they needed to maintain these growing operations.

Indeed as the tools of official control over industry began to take shape in 1862, the Tredegar management often found civil and military officials offered more hindrance than help. Government contracts with furnace owners placed much of the South's deficient pig iron production under the authority of the War and Navy Departments and then the Niter and Mining Bureau, but the Tredegar received very little of this metal. The power to draft and detail gave the War Department control over the South's free labor supply, but the Secretary of War and generals in the field refused to detail needed workers. Military boards set prices on items purchased by

94. Redlich, *American Business Leaders, I*, 85.

the government and held profits to levels the company considered unsatisfactory. The Tredegar owners needed far more official cooperation than they ever received, particularly in securing details of skilled mechanics and in acquiring pig iron and provisions. Some problems Confederate officials admittedly could do little about—the underdeveloped raw materials base of the Southern economy, for example. But the government's largely negative approach to the problems facing private manufacturers was still a major reason why Southern industrial production did not reach higher levels. Thrown largely on its own resources, the company faced a constant struggle just to stay in operation.

TABLE 11. Number of Cannon Produced by J. R. Anderson & Company and Three Northern Establishments, 1861–1865

Establishment	*1861*	*1862*	*1863*	*1864*	*January–March 1865*	*Total*
J. R. Anderson & Co.	214	351	286	213	35	1,099
Cyrus Alger & Co., Boston, Mass.	110	222	272	132	19	755
Charles Knap, Pittsburgh, Pa.	166	245	263	160	108	942
R. P. Parrott, Cold Spring, New York	380	316	310	534	89	1,557

Sources: Archer Account Book, VHS; Tredegar Gun Foundry Book; U.S. Congress, House of Representatives, *Executive Documents*, Document No. 99, 40th Cong., 2d sess. (Washington, 1868), pp. 706–14, 805–13, 864–912.

Yet the deficiencies of Tredegar production, glaring though they were, should not be permitted to overshadow the impressive showing the company made despite staggering problems and shortages. Although total Northern ordnance production—some eight thousand pieces—far outstripped that of the Confederacy, R. P. Parrott's foundry was the only one of the three Northern establishments in competition with Anderson in 1859 to outproduce the Richmond works during the war.[95] (See Table 11.) Anderson and Company performed monumental service for the Confederate armies and, more than any other single industrial concern, helped the South sustain four years of war. Given the handicaps to their production, the Richmond industrialists could not have done much more than they did.

95. The figure for Northern ordnance production is given in Nevins, *War Becomes Revolution*, p. 467.

15

Pardon and Restoration

Anderson wasted no time in attempting to make his peace with the Union. He had good reason to sound the themes of reconciliation and restoration during the months following the fall of Richmond. Under the terms of the confiscation act of 1862, his property was clearly liable to Federal seizure and sale.[1] Union troops occupied the works immediately after the evacuation and gave every indication that they intended to remain until the government and the courts decided the fate of the Tredegar.[2]

I

Anderson was among a group of prominent Richmonders who ascended the steps of the Davis mansion to seek an interview with Lincoln when the President visited the former Confederate capital on April 4. Lincoln talked with Anderson, John A. Campbell, the Confederate assistant secretary of war, and several other local citizens and from these discussions emerged a tentative plan to bring a quick end to the fighting in Virginia.[3]

When Campbell again conferred with Lincoln on April 5, the President had prepared a memorandum embodying several ideas discussed the previous day. If the South continued to resist, he would insist on making

1. J. G. Randall, *Constitutional Problems Under Lincoln* (reprint ed. Urbana, 1955), pp. 278–79.

2. *O.R.*, Ser. I, *46*, pt. iii, 1007.

3. Thomas T. Graves, a military aide present at the mansion, reported later that "Judge Campbell, General Anderson (Confederates), and others called and asked for an interview with the President. It was granted, and took place in the parlor with closed doors"; see *Battles and Leaders, 4,* 728. Campbell claimed that only General Godfrey Weitzel, the head of the occupation forces in Richmond, was present during his interview with Lincoln on April 4; see Campbell to Horace Greeley, April 26, 1865, and to James Speed, Aug. 31, 1865, *Southern Historical Society Papers, 42* (1917), 61, 67. See also John A. Campbell, *Reminiscences and Documents Relating to the Civil War During the Year 1865* (Baltimore, 1887), p. 39, and J. G. Randall, *Lincoln the President* (4 vols. New York, 1945–55; volume 4 completed by Richard N. Current), *4*, 347.

confiscated property bear at least the additional cost of prosecuting the war. But, he went on, "confiscations . . . will be remitted to the people of any state which shall now promptly, and in good faith, withdraw its troops and other support, from further resistance to the government." [4] Campbell thought the Virginia legislature, if permitted to assemble, would take the state out of the Confederacy and remove Virginia troops from Lee's command. Lincoln, hoping to avoid a final bloody contest between Grant's forces and the Army of Northern Virginia, gave Campbell permission to attempt to summon the General Assembly and carry out this course of action.[5] "I do not think it very probable that anything will come of this," the President wrote Grant the next day. "From your recent dispatches it seems that you are pretty effectively withdrawing the Virginia troops from opposition to the government." [6]

Campbell acted quickly following his meetings with Lincoln. On April 7 and 8, he held a series of discussions with Anderson, several local newspaper editors, the handful of state legislators remaining in Richmond, and a number of other local leaders in order to organize the movement to recall the assembly. This group named Anderson chairman of a citizens' committee which was to issue the call to the legislature. Campbell than addressed a letter to Anderson outlining the contents of Lincoln's memorandum and recommending immediate legislative action to restore Federal authority in Virginia and disband the army. Anderson replied in writing that his group intended to convey Lincoln's proposals to both state and Confederate authorities through General Lee and would do so as soon as Federal military officers granted permission.[7]

When Campbell and Anderson and his committee held an interview with Union authorities in Richmond on the morning of April 8, the Federal officers objected to several features of their proposed plan of action. Charles A. Dana, Lincoln's assistant secretary of war, informed Anderson at once that "his paper could not be received, nor his proposition entertained, for the reason that it involved a recognition of Confederate authorities and also because General Lee's intervention had now become entirely superflu-

4. Basler, *Lincoln, 8,* 386–87. The best account of the discussion of April 5 is in Randall and Current, *4,* 353–55.

5. Basler, *Lincoln, 8,* 388–89; *O.R.*, Ser. I, *46,* pt. iii, 575. Campbell claimed the suggestion to recall the Virginia assembly originated with Lincoln; see Campbell, *Reminiscences*, p. 42.

6. Basler, *Lincoln, 8,* 388.

7. *O.R.*, Ser. I, *46,* pt. iii, 619, 656–67; Richmond *Whig*, April 7, 8, 1865; Jones, *Diary, 2,* 473.

ous." They could "call a convention of prominent citizens of the State, with a view to the restoration of the authority of the Union" and Dana authorized the military commander in Richmond, General Godfrey Weitzel, to issue passes allowing Anderson and his committee unrestricted travel in Virginia. Weitzel also agreed to provide transportation, if necessary. But the Federal authorities would promise nothing more and Dana very carefully avoided any commitment that might imply legal recognition of the Confederate state legislature. The assistant secretary ignored Campbell's suggestion that the technique for ending the war in Virginia be extended to South Carolina and other Southern states. Secretary of War Stanton had ordered his assistant to Richmond to keep a close rein on Campbell's activities and Dana was doing an excellent job.[8]

Lee's surrender at Appomattox on April 9 cut most, but not all, of the ground from under the Richmond movement. On April 11, the day the call to resummon the legislature went out over the signatures of Anderson and his associates, Lincoln discussed the plan with the cabinet. He quickly discovered that his advisers, Stanton in particular, were solidly against it. Although a major reason for recalling the assembly had disappeared with the capitulation of Lee's forces, the President still believed the meeting of the legislature might be advisable. To restore law and order and prevent guerilla warfare, "prominent Virginians who had the confidence of the people" should "come together and turn themselves and their neighbors into good Union men." But he refused to act on such an important question without the support of his cabinet. On April 12, he wired the commander in Richmond to withdraw permission for the legislature to assemble.[9]

The Southerners never succeeded in reopening this approach to peace. A telegram advising Lincoln that Campbell and former Confederate Secretary of State R. M. T. Hunter desired permission to come to Washington arrived in the capital on the evening of April 14, shortly after the President and Mrs. Lincoln had left for Ford's Theater.[10]

8. *O.R.*, Ser. I, *46*, pt. iii, 655, 657; Benjamin P. Thomas and Harold M. Hyman, *Stanton, The Life and Times of Lincoln's Secretary of War* (New York, 1962), p. 353.

9. Richmond *Whig*, April 11, 12, 1865; Basler, *Lincoln, 8*, 406–07; Randall and Current, *4*, 357–59; Thomas and Hyman, pp. 355–56. For a highly critical account of Lincoln's actions toward Virginia, see William M. Robinson, Jr., *Justice in Grey* (Cambridge, Mass., 1941), pp. 591–93.

10. Randall and Current, *4*, 359.

II

The end of the fighting in Virginia only strengthened the motives which had prompted Anderson to take a prominent part in the movement to reassemble the legislature. Dana wrote Stanton on the day following Lee's surrender that among Richmonders "there is no sentiment but submission to the power of the nation, and a returning hope that their individual property may escape confiscation. The greatest rebels seem most keenly alive to this consideration," he continued, "and men like General Anderson, the proprietor of the Tredegar Works, are most zealous in efforts to produce a thorough pacification and save their possessions." [11] Anderson had been so certain his peace efforts would prevent the seizure of the Tredegar that four days after the Confederate evacuation, he and his associates had discussed resuming operations at both the Richmond plant and the company's coal pits.[12] But Lincoln's assassination abruptly shattered their hopes. Although Anderson and his partners took the Lincoln amnesty oath, pledging future allegiance to the United States, later in April, the Federal guard remained around their plant and the works continued to stand idle.[13]

The Tredegar owners found an unexpected source of support in the new Union commander in Richmond, Major General Henry W. Halleck. Halleck told the Ordnance Bureau in April that he thought the works should be put in operation to repair captured artillery before the government shipped the cannon north. This would give employment to Tredegar mechanics and take them and their families off relief. The Chief of Ordnance ordered an examination of the plant but the inspecting officer advised that the cost of transporting materials to Richmond and the unsettled labor conditions there would make operations both expensive and difficult.[14] A military order for irons to repair a local bridge over the James put the rolling mill back into limited production in May but after the company filled this

11. *O.R.*, Ser. I, *46*, pt. iii, 683–84.

12. William M. E. Rachal, ed., "The Occupation of Richmond, April 1865; The Memorandum of Events of Colonel Christopher Q. Tompkins," *Virginia Magazine of History and Biography*, *73* (1965), 193.

13. Anderson & Co. to Charles Marshall, March 15, 1866, Tredegar Letterbooks; oath of John F. Tanner, April 25, 1866, Office of the Adjutant General, Amnesty Papers, Virginia, RG 94, NA. Hereafter cited as Amnesty Papers.

14. *O.R.*, Ser. I, *46*, pt. iii, 917, 1007–10.

requisition the next month, blue-coated soldiers again closed the works.[15]

Anderson did not let up in his efforts to secure the return of his property. He disavowed any lingering loyalty to the pro-Confederate state government by appearing at a reception on May 19 given by newly arrived Governor Francis H. Pierpoint, the leader of the Unionist Alexandria administration during the war. "There was quite a commingling of ladies and gentlemen from the North and South . . . apparently animated by a fraternal feeling," the Richmond *Whig* commented approvingly following the evening's festivities.[16]

The Tredegar senior partner very soon had need of the support of Pierpoint and any other parties who could command a hearing in the White House. Andrew Johnson's amnesty proclamation of May 29, 1865, contained three clauses that excluded Anderson from the general pardon: he was a West Point graduate; he had been a general officer in the Confederate army; and he owned taxable property worth over $20,000. All persons falling into the excepted classes had to petition the President for a special pardon.[17]

Anderson quickly launched a new campaign to secure the removal of his disabilities. After taking the oath required in Johnson's proclamation on June 6, he enlisted the aid of a prominent Richmond attorney, William H. Macfarland, and drafted a carefully worded petition.[18] In the document forwarded to the White House later in June, Anderson presented the best possible construction of his activities during the war. He had served in the army only from September 1861 to July 1862 and, after resigning, had held no other military or civil posts under the "insurgent confederacy." Anderson glossed over some of the more embarrassing aspects of his wartime career. His contention that he "had no agency of any kind in bringing about the hostilities with the United States, or the secession of the state of Virginia" was hardly an accurate description of his activities or his attitudes prior to the war. He stressed the role he had played in attempting to end the fighting in Virginia and referred the President to Dana and Weitzel for confirmation of these activities.

15. Ibid., p. 1265; Tredegar Foundry Sales Books.

16. Richmond *Whig*, May 20, 1865.

17. James D. Richardson, ed., *Messages and Papers of the Presidents* (11 vols. Washington, 1897–1909), *5*, 3508–10.

18. Oath of J. R. Anderson, June 6, 1865, Amnesty Papers, RG 94, NA; Anderson to Mosley & Speed, Nov. 6, 1865, Tredegar Letterbooks.

He then proceeded to outline the history of the Tredegar works during the past four years. Evidently he neglected to check his sales books before drawing up this petition because he claimed that military production for the Confederacy had amounted to about one third of total Tredegar output. Only "by consenting to execute such orders of the Confederate authorities could your petitioner and his partners have retained control of the property in question," Anderson wrote, "for any refusal of theirs to comply with such orders would undoubtedly have led the Confederate authorities to take the establishment at once into their own hands, and work it exclusively for their own purposes."

In conclusion, the Tredegar head stressed the importance of restoring the works to himself and his partners. Federal occupation of the plant deprived hundreds of mechanics of the means of earning a living and rendered them completely dependent on government charity. The continued idleness of the works also hindered the rebuilding of Virginia's railroads and farms. In asking to be restored to his rights of property and citizenship, Anderson assured the President of "the perfect good faith and sincerity with which he has returned to his allegiance to the Union." Tanner, Robert Archer, and Robert S. Archer appended a briefer but similar solicitation to the senior partner's petition.[19]

Anderson did not trust his case solely to this document, however. He obtained the endorsements of a number of persons, ranging in influence from the governor of the state to the proprietor of a small iron works near the Tredegar. Governor Pierpoint claimed no knowledge of the facts in the petition but told the President that the Tredegar owners "all have the reputation of energetic sincere men." On the pragmatic grounds that "it is energy in building up the country we need here," the governor recommended their pardon.[20] Anderson successfully solicited the aid of three prominent Georgians passing through Richmond on the way to Washington, attorney John W. Duncan, former circuit judge Osborne A. Lochrane, and Atlanta railroader and financier Richard Peters.[21] He retained Charles L. Mosley of Lynchburg, a leading Virginia lawyer who knew the President personally, to present his petition.[22] And Asa Snyder, the owner of a stove

19. Petition of J. R. Anderson to Andrew Johnson, and of John F. Tanner, Robert Archer, and Robert S. Archer, June [?], 1865, Amnesty Papers, RG 94, NA.

20. Gov. Francis H. Pierpoint to Johnson, June 12, 1865, ibid.

21. John W. Duncan, O. A. Lochrane, and Richard Peters to Johnson, June 19, 1865, ibid.

22. Endorsement of C. L. Mosley, ibid.; Anderson & Co. to Mosley & Speed, Nov. 6, 1865, Tredegar Letterbooks.

foundry adjacent to Anderson's works, described to the former tailor who now occupied the White House how over the years the Tredegar owner had helped him and other Richmond mechanics and artisans organize and sustain small businesses.[23] Anderson hoped the influence of these men would counterbalance Northern opinion, expressed editorially in the New York *Herald* in late June, that he and other large Richmond manufacturers were "personally and justly obnoxious and amenable to punishment." [24]

Anderson undoubtedly showed his petition to General Halleck, because the general wrote Stanton a detailed letter on June 8 in which he repeated many of the arguments used by the Tredegar senior partner. The management claimed that manufacturing for the Confederacy "was a matter of necessity and compulsion, the company having been notified that it must execute all orders of the Confederate authorities or that that government would seize upon the works and use them exclusively for its own purposes, as was done in many other cases." He added that he was unable to decide on the truth of these allegations. The works, still closed and under military guard, could give employment to hundreds of laborers and materially aid in the reconstruction of Southern railroads. Halleck therefore proposed that, after ordnance officers had removed all cannon and munitions, the guards be removed and the works put back into operation.

The general suggested three ways in which production might be resumed: the government could return the Tredegar to the owners; agents appointed by Federal authorities could run the plant on government account until the courts decided the fate of the works; or the Treasury could take over the establishment as abandoned rebel property marked for confiscation. Since he found serious objections to the second and third alternatives, the burden of Halleck's argument was a strong recommendation to restore the plant to Anderson and his partners. His advice, like Governor Pierpoint's, was based on a knowledge of the practical needs of the South and the Tredegar's ability, if well managed, to meet many of those needs.[25]

The Secretary of War was not willing to let Anderson and Company off quite so easily, however. In early July, Stanton followed Halleck's third proposal and ordered the military authorities in Richmond to surrender

23. Asa Snyder to Johnson, June 22, 1865, Amnesty Papers, RG 94, NA.

24. New York *Herald,* June 20, 1865, quoted in part in Jonathan F. Dorris, *Pardon and Amnesty under Lincoln and Johnson* (Chapel Hill, 1953), pp. 222–23.

25. *O.R.*, Ser. I, *46,* pt. iii, 1264–65.

the Tredegar property to agents of the Treasury Department. The local military commander informed the owners of this action on July 6.[26] Anderson quickly discovered the significance of this transfer. On July 19, the United States district attorney in Richmond filed suit to confiscate the works and all other property owned by Anderson and his associates in the city, including their residences.[27] News received in late July that Federal confiscation threatened their holdings in western Virginia only added to their distress.[28]

The confiscation suits were not scheduled for trial until November but Anderson began reorganizing his amnesty campaign immediately after Federal marshals attached his property. His first move was to secure a petition signed by the presidents of the major Virginia railroads stating that they were "greatly in want of the aid of the Tredegar Iron Works" and asking the President to restore the plant to Anderson and Company.[29] The senior partner then enlisted the support of a Pittsburgh firm that licensed the spike machines used at the Tredegar works. This company claimed royalties for all the spikes made during the war and stood to lose a considerable sum if the government confiscated Anderson and Company's assets. After several members of the Pennsylvania company visited Richmond during late June or early July, Anderson wrote them a letter obviously intended for President Johnson's perusal. "I was originally opposed to secession and thought all differences between north and south ought to have been settled amicably within the union," Anderson claimed. Yet, he continued, "I would consider it dishonorable to ignore the fact that I went with my state, sympathized in the cause of the south and aided it to the extent of my ability." After reciting the basic facts presented in his petition to the President, Anderson concluded by describing his strained financial circumstances. The threat to the Tredegar works, the seizure and sale during the war of several thousand acres of his land in Maryland, the loss of his slaves, and unpaid bills on the Confederate government left him in a "shat-

26. Anderson, Tanner, R. Archer, and R. S. Archer to Gen. J. W. Turner, July 3, 1865, and endorsement of Turner, July 6, 1865, in "Letters, Clippings, etc., Involving the Tredegar Company."

27. John Underwood, U.S. Marshal, to Anderson, R. S. Archer, J. Tanner, and W. E. Tanner, July 26, 1865, ibid.; U.S. District Court, Richmond, "Order Book A, Confiscation, etc., July 19, 1865–May 27, 1869," VSL.

28. M. Strickler to R. S. Archer, July 21, 1865, Watson-Archer Papers, VHS.

29. William H. Macfarland, P. V. Daniel, Jr., Charles Ellis, J. Garrett, John F. Fry, Thomas H. Ellis, and Thomas Dodamead to Johnson, July 6, 1865, copy in "Letters, Clippings, etc., Involving the Tredegar Company."

tered condition." "Nevertheless with a strong constitution and a will not accustomed to succumb to trifling obstacles, I should feel no lack of confidence in the future of myself, or the people of this state if we could be relieved of our disability," Anderson concluded. He added in a postscript that "as to my status & feelings toward the union and every body in it, white or black, you are fully informed by our free conversations which you are authorized to use." [30]

The Pittsburgh parties forwarded the letter on to the President at once along with their unqualified endorsement. They also credited Anderson with remarkable clairvoyance during the war. He had resigned his commission in July 1862, eighteen months before Lincoln's first amnesty proclamation, "with the intent and expectation of being relieved by the Presidential Proclamation of Amnesty," they assured Johnson.[31]

On the same day the Pennsylvania firm was writing the White House, Senator Orville H. Browning of Illinois was in Johnson's office seeking pardons for a number of Richmond manufacturers. The Senator did not get very far. The President "was not yet satisfied of the propriety of pardoning that class of men ($20,000 men) and would leave them, for the present, where the law and their rebellion placed them," Browning noted in his diary. Johnson "thought new men had better go there and do the manufacturing" and he believed "they were still rebels at heart, and only anxious to make money that they might give more trouble." [32] Anderson's renewed drive for a pardon obviously did not find the Chief Executive in a very receptive mood.

The anxiety of Anderson and his partners mounted as the summer passed and no word came from Washington. By the middle of September, Anderson could wait no longer and he decided to present his case personally to the President. He asked for and received a letter of introduction from Governor Pierpoint which was easily the most persuasive document presented to the Chief Executive in support of his pardon. The Tredegar head was "a man of great energy and has done much to develop the mechanical and manufacturing interest of the state," the governor wrote. "He had the force of character to engage in manufacturing pursuits in the state when labor among the first circles was not very honorable."

30. Anderson & Co. to Dilworth, Porter & Co., July 15, 1865, Amnesty Papers, RG 94, NA.

31. Dilworth, Porter & Co. to Johnson, July 20, 1865, ibid.

32. Theodore C. Pease and James G. Randall, eds., *The Diary of Orville Hickman Browning, 1850–1881* (2 vols. Springfield, Ill., 1927–33), *2*, 38. Anderson's name was not among the businessmen specifically mentioned by Browning.

> I have thought much about this case, and it strikes me under the circumstances, it is not policy to strike down men of great energy in developing the country. It is such we now want. The petty amt of his property is of no consideration in a national point of view when compared with the great benefit he may render the state. Perhaps I have a false estimate of this class of men; if I have it is because they are so scarce. I would not give one of them for as many politicians as will fill an acre field. It is on this ground I ask for his pardon.

Pierpoint noted in closing that Anderson had "thrown his whole influence since I arrived here in favor of state and federal government and has I have no doubt acted sincerely and his influence has been potent for good." [33]

As soon as he obtained this letter, Anderson headed for Washington. He chose an opportune moment to approach the President. Johnson, holding previously to the view that persons in the excepted categories "should sue for pardon, and so realize the enormity of their crime," had issued very few pardons during his first months in office.[34] The inevitable result was an ever-growing mountain of petitions, a swarm of pardon-seekers around the White House, and an increasing demand, even from his supporters, for a coherent policy. This log jam broke in the fall and Anderson was there to take advantage of the President's new disposition. Johnson had sufficiently satiated his desire to humble the Southern aristocrats. Their petitions and obsequious performances provided the tangible evidence of repentance the President seemed to crave.[35] Anderson met with the Chief Executive on four separate occasions and witnessed his interviews with a number of other petitioners.[36] During these sessions, the Tredegar owner undoubtedly made it clear that he was a thoroughly reconstructed rebel. On September 21, he held his final interview with Johnson and emerged from the President's office with a small white card reading "Joseph R. Anderson of Virginia" on one side and "Issue pardon this case, Andrew Johnson, Pres" on the other.[37] The President granted amnesty to Tanner and the Archers the following day.[38]

33. Pierpoint to Johnson, Sept. 16, 1865, Amnesty Papers, RG 94, NA.

34. Quoted in Eric L. McKitrick, *Andrew Johnson and Reconstruction* (Chicago, 1960), p. 146.

35. Ibid., pp. 146–49; Dorris, pp. 138–43, 225–27.

36. Anderson to F. T. Anderson, Sept. 25, 1865, Anderson Papers, DUL.

37. Amnesty Papers, RG 94, NA.

38. Notations dated Sept. 22, 1865, on petitions of Tanner, R. Archer, and R. S. Archer, ibid.

"I went to Washington and made personal application to the President and brought my pardon home with me," Anderson wrote his brother exultantly on September 25. His admiration for Johnson was unbounded. "He is kind in his manners, calm and business like and I believe firm in maintaining what he believes right. More than that," Anderson continued, "he is our sole defense . . . against the assaults of an unscrupulous and savage party at the North who it seems would annihilate us if they could. I am satisfied they will be disappointed and that the President will triumph." [39] The Tredegar senior partner had made his peace with the Union and in the process had found a national political leader he could endorse with enthusiasm. His pro-Johnson sympathies would soon aid materially in his quest for Northern capital.

The Presidential pardons ended all threat of government confiscation of the works. When the cases came up for trial on November 14, 1865, the court dismissed all the suits against Anderson and his associates.[40] The seizure of the *Coquette*, the removal of ordnance remaining at the works at the end of the war, and one hundred tons of pig iron confiscated by Federal agents in the Shenandoah Valley were the only losses the South's largest munitions makers incurred at the hands of the victors.[41] And they lost the metal seized in western Virginia only because Secretary of War Stanton, commenting that he would "rather suspend their pardons, and send them to the Penitentiary," refused to halt the sale.[42] Through repurchase and the settling of his prewar Northern debts, Anderson eventually reclaimed most of the Maryland land his creditors had attached in 1862.[43]

The Tredegar owners deserve neither praise nor censure for their conduct during the summer of 1865. True, Anderson had asked in 1863 how the Union could ever be reconstructed over the graves of Confederate heroes.[44] But in seeking amnesty and in presenting their case in the most favorable light, he and his partners did no more than many other ex-Confederates were doing during the tense weeks following the end of the war. "Our citizens are much exercised at this time by not being permitted to

39. Anderson to F. T. Anderson, Sept. 25, 1865, Anderson Papers, DUL.

40. U.S. District Court, Richmond, "Judgment Docket, Confiscation, 1865–1867," VSL.

41. Anderson & Co. to Watterson & Crawford, Feb. 26, 1866, and to Charles Marshall, March 12, 1866, Tredegar Letterbooks; Robert Carse, *Blockade: The Civil War at Sea* (New York, 1958), pp. 250–51.

42. Pease and Randall, *Browning, 2,* 53.

43. Anderson to William E. Dodge, Jan. 22, 27, April 7, June 2, Nov. 9, 1866, and to Marshall, March 26, June 2, 1866, Tredegar Letterbooks; P. Hamill to Anderson, July 27, 1866, Anderson Papers, VSL.

44. Anderson to William A. Glasgow, June 30, 1863, Glasgow Papers, WLU.

carry on any kind of business without taking the oath of allegiance," a Richmonder noted shortly after the Federal occupation began. "Nearly all of them have come to the conclusion to take it, as they must do that, or see their families starve." [45] Anderson doubtless shared this attitude. His primary goal was to salvage his life's work, the Tredegar, and maintain this source of support for himself and his family. To accomplish this end, he helped organize the movement to restore Virginia to the Union in April 1865 and later told the government something less than the full truth about his wartime activities—a fact that did not go unnoticed in Richmond.[46] But Lee called at the Anderson home in Richmond on several occasions during late 1865 and early 1866, an indication that he did not consider dishonorable Anderson's attempts to withdraw the Virginia regiments from his command and remove the state from the Confederacy.[47] And during the period prior to his pardon, the Tredegar owner did not confine himself solely to statements concerning his property and his disabilities. "How much we have to be thankful for, that our sons are spared to us alive at the end of such a destructive war," he wrote his brother in July 1865. "If necessary I would willingly have resigned everything in the way of worldly goods, to have secured so great a blessing." [48]

45. Margaret K. Ellis to Powhatan Ellis, Jr., May 1, 1865, Munford-Ellis Papers, DUL. See also Dorris, p. 245.

46. Walthall, *Hidden Things Brought to Light*, p. 23.

47. Douglas Southall Freeman, *R. E. Lee* (4 vols. New York, 1934–35), *4*, 341; Anderson to F. T. Anderson, Jan. 13, 1866, Anderson Papers, UVA.

48. Anderson to F. T. Anderson, July 21, 1865, ibid.

16

Back to Business

I

When Anderson and his partners assessed the needs of their business following the restoration, they kept returning to one key item—capital. Customers were available, if the company could extend credit; skilled workers were at hand, if payrolls could be met; raw materials were abundant, if the Tredegar could pay for them; furnaces could again be relined with top quality firebrick and worn machinery replaced with the most up-to-date tools, if the Richmond industrialists could come up with the necessary funds. In addition, prewar Northern creditors demanded satisfaction of debts sequestrated in 1862.

Because the works had suffered no extensive damage during the period of the Confederate evacuation and Federal occupation, the Tredegar was physically prepared to begin limited production almost immediately. Wartime depreciation of plant and equipment did necessitate considerable renovation, as indicated in the report of the Union ordnance officer who inspected the works at Halleck's request in April 1865. The buildings destroyed in the May 1863 fire had never been rebuilt and the remaining facilities were in varying states of disrepair, he noted. Machines, tools, and belting in all departments were much worn and every furnace needed a new lining of firebrick. The rolling mills were in the best condition, the carpentry and patternmaking shops in the worst. A partially enclosed dirt floor shed had housed these latter operations since the blaze. The two blacksmith shops, containing a total of thirty-five forges, and the boiler shop were both in good order. The foundries and machine shops, expanded with Confederate loans during the war, required conversion to peacetime production but were still intact; Tredegar furnaces could now melt 155,000 pounds of iron per day, an amount more than double prewar capacity. "With the exception of the gun foundries, the works are well adapted to the manufacture of iron and iron parts for the repair of railroads, cars, agricultural implements, and machines, and for general iron work," the inspecting officer concluded his report.[1] The Tredegar owners gave much the same analysis to a Southern railroad superintendent in December: "We have suffered immensely by the War, but still have the ability to do much for our old customers." [2]

Only one source of fluid capital survived the war and was available to assist in the reconstruction of the works—the sterling account in London. In late 1865 and early 1866, the Richmond industrialists realized over $190,000 in greenbacks on the sale of their cotton.[3] These funds were of inestimable importance to the Tredegar owners. Without this money, they would not have been able to take even the first steps toward putting their works back into production.

Aside from the London account, the partners had little to show for their past four years of constant operation except a bundle of promissory notes. When the company attempted to collect some of the money owed them by Southern railroads, most railway officials replied by asking for further credit to enable them to buy needed iron. The handful of roads that did agree to settle their prewar debts refused to pay more than 50 per cent of the amount due the Tredegar.[4] Richmond's banks offered very limited assistance and that came only at "ruinous rates," as Anderson called them, of 1¼ to 1½ per cent per month.[5] "Like you we find difficulty in obtaining the necessary funds to conduct our operations, but hope that the clouds that now overhang us may soon be dispelled," one of the partners told a South Carolina rail official early in 1866.[6]

While he was waiting for the proceeds of his cotton sales, Anderson relieved some of the financial pressure on his firm by arranging for short-term credit in the North. The New York mercantile house of Fowle and Company agreed in November 1865 to market Tredegar iron and al-

1. *O.R.*, Ser. I, *46*, pt. iii, 1007–10.

2. Anderson & Co. to E. B. Walker, Dec. 9, 1865, Tredegar Letterbooks.

3. Anderson & Co. to J. K. Gilliat & Co., Nov. 7, 1865, Feb. 16, July 14, 30, 1866, ibid.; entries for Sept., Nov., 1865, and Dec. 1866, Tredegar Journals.

4. Entry for Sept. 1865, ibid.; Anderson & Co. to William Mahone, Oct. 21, Nov. 10, Dec. 20, 1865, to J. Emery, Oct. 24, Nov. 20, 1865, to A. L. Maxwell, Nov. 23, 1865, to Edward Denmead, Nov. 24, Dec. 18, 20, 1865, and "Paper taken by J. F. Tanner," July 31, 1866, Tredegar Letterbooks; Anderson to F. T. Anderson, Nov. 24, 1866, Anderson Papers, UVA.

5. Anderson to F. T. Anderson, Dec. 1, 1866, ibid.; Anderson & Co. to John M. Robinson, Dec. 20, 1865, Tredegar Letterbooks.

6. Anderson & Co. to C. Bouknight, Jan. 16, 1866, ibid.

lowed Anderson and Company to draw on them for $30,000 for two to three months.[7] These funds helped relieve a tight money situation in Richmond, brought on when local banks called in all their loans at the end of 1865, but the New York drafts were due in forty-five to sixty days.[8] This technique offered only a temporary solution to the Tredegar's credit needs.

"The close of the war stripped me of nearly all my available means and I am now depending upon the sale of real estate to provide means for paying old debts at the North and for current business wants," Anderson wrote in November 1865.[9] He hoped to convert the company's six blast furnaces and two coal properties, acquired with loans from the Confederate government during the war, into cash and then plow these funds back into the business. In November, the partners placed their furnaces in the hands of a real estate dealer with offices in Richmond and New York and authorized their agent at the Tuckahoe pits to seek a purchaser for that property.[10] After his pardon, Anderson went to New York to handle personally the disposition of the Dover coal mines, his most valuable holding aside from the actual Tredegar plant.

The sale of the Dover property to a syndicate of prominent New York and Boston financiers brought one of the first large infusions of Northern capital into the South following the Civil War.[11] Anderson started his search for a buyer at the top of the American industrial world. He first called on Peter Cooper and Abram Hewitt but the two pioneering Northern ironmasters considered Anderson's price too high—$150,000 for a half

7. Anderson & Co. to Fowle & Co., Nov. 28, Dec. 8, 18, 1865, Jan. 20, Feb. 16, March 13, 1866, ibid.; entry for Dec. 1865, Tredegar Journals.

8. Anderson & Co. to Robinson, Dec. 20, 1865, and Anderson to F. T. Anderson, Dec. 22, 1865, Tredegar Letterbooks; entry for Dec. 1865, Tredegar Journals.

9. Anderson & Co. to Samuel J. Harrison, Nov. 30, 1865, Tredegar Letterbooks.

10. Anderson & Co. to Watkins James, Nov. 22, 1865, to Atkinson, Ten Eyck & Co., Nov. 22, 1865, and to J. J. Werth, Dec. 1, 1865, ibid. Prices asked were:

Catawba furnace	$60,000
Cloverdale "	60,000
Grace "	40,000
Rebecca "	40,000
Mount Torry "	40,000
Australia "	30,000
Tuckahoe mines	65,000

See memoranda dated Nov. 21, 1865, and Jan. 23, 1866, Tredegar Contract Books.

11. John Hope Franklin, *Reconstruction: After the Civil War* (Chicago, 1961), p. 10.

interest in the mines.[12] His luck changed when he approached William H. Aspinwall shortly after his discussions with Cooper and Hewitt. Aspinwall, a prominent New York merchant who had made a fortune in the China and California trades, agreed to buy a 40 per cent interest in the Dover property for $80,000, contingent upon an examination of the land by an engineer of his choosing. When the mining engineer, former Union General Charles P. Stone, gave a favorable report on the Dover, the deal went through.[13]

A group of New England capitalists also participated in the Dover purchase. Nathaniel Thayer, Boston merchant, financier, and one of the wealthiest men in New England, led this contingent of investors, which also included Joel Parker, a prominent jurist and Harvard law professor, and John Carter Brown, the Providence bibliophile. These men subscribed $100,000 in Dover Company stock in February and March 1866, following the organization of the company under a charter granted by the Virginia assembly in January.[14] In all, Anderson and his partners realized $180,000 on the sale of the property and retained 2,000 of the 10,000 shares of capital stock valued at $25 per share.[15]

"Since my property has been restored to me I have devoted myself assiduously to efforts to sell so much of it as may be necessary to pay all the debts of myself and [my] firm," Anderson told a close friend in April

12. Anderson to Anderson & Co., Oct. 15, 1865, Brock Papers, HL.

13. Ibid.; Anderson & Co. to C. Q. Tompkins, Nov. 15, 1865, to William H. Aspinwall, Jan. 20, 1866, and to Charles Scranton, Sept. 25, 1866, Tredegar Letterbooks; entries for Dec. 1865, Jan., June, 1866, Tredegar Journals; memoranda dated March 28, April 12, 1866, Tredegar Contract Books; *D.A.B.*, *1*, 396–97, *18*, 72.

14. Anderson & Co. to W. L. Jenkins, Feb. 13, 1866, and to Anderson, March 16, 1866, Tredegar Letterbooks; entries for March, June, 1866, Tredegar Journals; memoranda dated March 16, 28, April 12, 1866, Tredegar Contract Books; *D.A.B.*, *3*, 136–37, *14*, 230–31, *18*, 409–10; *Acts of the [Virginia] General Assembly, 1865–66* (Richmond, 1866), pp. 357–58.

15. Memorandum dated April 12, 1866, Tredegar Contract Books. Although the sale of this property brought Anderson and Company desperately needed capital, the Dover enterprise itself was a financial failure. The Northern investors were originally attracted by a chemical analysis indicating that Dover coal would produce illuminating gas. This analysis turned out to be incorrect and the coal therefore could not be marketed at a premium in Eastern cities, as the investors had anticipated. Fire, water, bad tunnel construction, and excessive impurities in the coal plagued operations at Dover almost from the outset. The directors tried to ward off bankruptcy by purchasing the nearby Westham furnace, manufacturing coke from their coal, and producing pig iron but this venture only plunged the company deeper into debt. In 1870, the entire operation was shut down. See President's Reports, Feb. 12, June 28, 1869, Feb. 9, 1870, and Anderson to Joel Parker, Dec. 29, 1868, and Allan Campbell to Parker, Feb. 28, 1870, Dover Company Records, UVA.

1866. "So far I have had such success that we have been able to liquidate much the larger portion of our indebtedness. It is necessary however to sell more of my property here to accomplish my object fully," he added, and he thought prospects for further sales bright.[16] The Tredegar senior partner overestimated the marketability of his remaining holdings, however. In July 1867, he reported that the Tuckahoe coal pits and all six of the company's blast furnaces remained unsold. Anderson ascribed his inability to sell these assets "to the continuation of the unsettled political condition of the country" but in the case of the furnaces, the antiquated charcoal production techniques were a more serious obstacle to sale.[17]

Anderson was much too prudent a businessman to rely completely on the sale of these properties for his capital needs. He and his partners secured corporate privileges from the legislature in February 1866 and, the next month, Anderson asked the Northern capitalists who were behind the Dover project if they would like to extend their investments to include the Tredegar works. Thayer and another Boston financier, railroad builder John Murray Forbes, expressed an immediate interest in Anderson's proposal, as did Aspinwall of New York. But their support hinged on one key consideration—the reestablishment of the Tredegar as a major government contractor.[18]

As long as Stanton remained in charge of the War Department, Anderson was hardly *persona grata* in Washington. To remove this obstacle, the potential Northern investors suggested that Gustavus V. Fox, who was preparing to resign his post as assistant secretary of the navy, be offered the presidency of the proposed Tredegar corporation. Anderson agreed and called on Fox in Washington during the first week of April 1866. Fox knew the excellent reputation of the company's Cloverdale pig iron and Admiral John A. Dahlgren, the ordnance inventor, had told him "that the Tredegar Works, and the iron mines with them are . . . the most valuable of any similar ones in the country." Fox also expressed the opinion that the Tredegar would receive government contracts as quickly as any Northern establishment. But he thought the salary Anderson mentioned, $10,000 per year, inadequate and he did not want to leave Washington.[19]

16. Anderson & Co. to Francis Thomas, April 3, 1866, Tredegar Letterbooks.

17. Anderson to S. B. Barcroft, July 18, 1867, ibid.

18. *Acts of the [Virginia] General Assembly, 1865–66,* pp, 356–57; Anderson & Co. to Anderson, March 16, 1866, and Anderson to Aspinwall, April 7, 11, 1866, Tredegar Letterbooks.

19. Gustavus V. Fox to Thayer, April 6, 1866, copy, Anderson Papers, VSL; *D.A.B., 6,* 569.

Anderson returned to Richmond impressed by Fox but discouraged about the prospect of his accepting the presidency.[20] On the tenth, however, Fox wrote the Tredegar senior partner that if Aspinwall, Thayer, and Forbes all came into the company, if he could continue to reside in Washington, and if his salary were increased, he would weigh the offer very carefully.[21] After consulting with the Northern capitalists, Anderson replied that they were prepared to offer him a percentage of the profits plus an annual salary of $10,000, which together would total approximately $20,000 yearly. He had no objections to Fox remaining in the capital. Aspinwall, Thayer, and Forbes were each planning to take one fifth of the capital stock of the corporation, he would hold one fifth, and the remaining share would quickly be subscribed elsewhere, Anderson concluded.[22]

Fox's letter sent Anderson's hopes soaring but an unfavorable report by two engineers sent by Aspinwall to inspect the works destroyed any chance for an immediate organization of the corporation. Anderson argued that his superintendents did not share the adverse opinion of the two inspectors concerning the layout and equipment of the Tredegar works. "These are questions upon which practical men . . . often differ," he told Aspinwall, but all to no avail. The Northern investors backed out and Fox went with them.[23]

After the Northern financiers turned down Anderson's offer, the Richmond industrialists turned to the South in their search for fresh capital and wider markets. "It is our purpose to offer the Rail Roads inducements to take stock with us in the whole property, we reserving one-half," Tanner wrote Sam Tate, the president of the Memphis and Charleston Railroad, in July. "We have offers at the North for such an arrangement but it is much more in accordance with our taste and we think for the interest of the Southern Roads that an arrangement with them should be made." [24] With capital supplied by the railroad companies, Anderson and his partners proposed to rebuild their locomotive works, equip their rolling mills for rail production, and supply every iron need of the roads. "*In union is our strength,*" Anderson told the president of the Wilmington and Weldon

20. Anderson to Aspinwall, April 7, 1866, Tredegar Letterbooks.

21. Fox to Anderson, April 10, 1866, copy, ibid.

22. Anderson to Fox, April 25, 1866, ibid. See also Anderson to Aspinwall, April 11, 1866, to Thayer, April 11, 1866, and to Tanner, April 11, 16, 1866, ibid.

23. Anderson to Aspinwall, May 5, 1866, and to Sam Tate, July 28, 1866, ibid.

24. Anderson & Co. to Tate, July 28, 1866, ibid.

Railroad. "If we put our shoulders together I assure you we can make this enterprise the most brilliant that has ever been undertaken in the South." [25] The Tredegar owners saw more than capital in an organization that included the principal Southern lines, as Tanner frankly admitted. "There is more work to be done now than we may reasonably expect again & once in possession of it it will be difficult to divert it to the other channels." [26]

When Tanner toured several Southern states in August, he found much interest in the scheme but little ready capital. Most railway officials preferred to purchase their supplies on the open market by competitive bidding. The Tredegar partners tried to persuade William M. Wadley, the former Confederate rail superintendent, to take a position with the firm and push the reorganization but he declined. Tanner returned to Richmond with best wishes but no firm commitments of support. This Southern plan, like its Northern predecessor, never materialized.[27]

"We are still conducting our large business with an inadequate capital & absolutely no banking facilities—and this at a time when more than ever our correspondents require accommodation," Anderson wrote in September 1866.[28] Conditions had not changed by the end of the year. "I don't see how we are to transact business since we have lost the aid of the old Banks. We cannot borrow money from one of the present Banks now on paper having 60 days to run—indeed on any paper however good or short," the Tredegar head told his brother in December. "It is quite obvious therefore that people cant do business now in Va. without capital of their own" [29] This need for fluid capital was the primary factor behind the dissolution of the Tredegar partnership and the organization of a joint stock enterprise early the next year.

Their recent experiences had convinced Anderson and his partners that the best chance for injecting new money into their business lay in an appeal to Northern capitalists *after* the reorganization of their company. This approach had two advantages: it would permit the kind of investment the Tredegar owners seemed most likely to attract—limited subscriptions

25. Anderson & Co. to R. R. Bridges, Aug. 11, 1866, ibid.

26. Anderson & Co. to Tate, Sept. 25, 1866, ibid.

27. Anderson & Co. to W. J. Magrath, Aug. 1, Sept. 24, 1866, to Charles T. Pollard, Aug. 1, 1866, to Tanner, Aug. 8, 1866, to William M. Wadley, Oct. 20, 1866, and to the President & Directors of the Central Railroad, Oct. 31, 1866, ibid.

28. Anderson & Co. to Dilworth, Porter & Co., Sept. 14, 1866, ibid.

29. Anderson to F. T. Anderson, Dec. 1, 1866, Anderson Papers, UVA.

from a fairly large number of individuals; and once the corporation was organized and in successful operation, Northern confidence in the future of the company should increase. The owners now entertained no illusions about massive aid nor did they hatch any additional schemes for recapturing their former share of government ordnance contracts or cornering the Southern railroad market. On February 27, 1867, Anderson and his son Archer, John Tanner, and Robert and Robert S. Archer organized the Tredegar Company in Richmond. The legislature had amended their charter six days before to permit the inclusion of the Armory rolling mill, built on property leased from the state, in the corporation.[30] They capitalized the company at $1,000,000—10,000 shares of $100 each. Anderson accepted 6,950 shares at par for his portion of the assets of the company, the Archers received 1,500, Tanner and Archer Anderson 500 each, and other members of the Archer and Anderson families took the remaining stock. Anderson assumed the presidency of the corporation, Tanner took the vice-president's position, and Archer Anderson, the Archers, and William H. Aspinwall filled out the board of directors. The election of Aspinwall to a seat on the board was perhaps wishful thinking on the part of Anderson and his Richmond associates. The New York financier resigned from his position the next month, however.[31]

Anderson now realized his hope of securing outside capital. In his annual report the following year, he noted that Northern businessmen had subscribed $75,000 in Tredegar stock and he confidently expected more sales.[32] The list of stockholders included Thayer, Aspinwall, and William E. Dodge. Other names prominent in Northern financial and industrial circles were entered on the company's stock ledger between 1868 and 1873. John F. Winslow, the Troy, New York, iron manufacturer who urged Lincoln to order the *Monitor* and then rolled the plates and built the machinery for the vessel, was the largest Northern investor. During the three years ending in 1871, he subscribed over $100,000 in the stock of the works that had produced the *Merrimack's* armor. A. A. Low, New York merchant and a backer of the first Atlantic cable and the Chesapeake and Ohio Railroad, took over $50,000 in Tredegar stock during this same period. When the

30. *Acts of the [Virginia] General Assembly, 1865–66*, pp. 662–63.

31. Tredegar Corporate Minutes, 1867–1930, pp. 1–17, 19; Richmond City Hustings Court, Deed Book No. 84A, pp. 250–53, microfilm copy, VSL.

32. Tredegar Corporate Minutes, 1867–1930, pp. 27–28.

depression of 1873 struck, Northern capitalists had invested a total of $373,000 in the Richmond company.[33] But in the case of the Tredegar works, Northern money did not mean Northern control. Anderson and his associates in Richmond held approximately two thirds of the company's stock and made the major corporate decisions. Only two Northerners served on the board of directors during the nineteenth century.[34]

The Northern financiers who invested over half a million dollars in the Dover mines and the Tredegar works in the years immediately after the war were, almost without exception, Conservative Republicans. Most of them had adopted virtually identical positions toward secession and the war—strong advocates of compromise with the South after the election of 1860, but firm Union men and supporters of Lincoln following the firing on Fort Sumter.[35] They did not agree on all the economic issues facing America during and after the conflict. The New York City investors, predominantly men of merchant backgrounds, favored a low tariff and hard money while those Tredegar subscribers already engaged in heavy manufacturing were largely protectionists and soft money advocates.[36] All these men were united, however, in favor of a lenient postwar policy toward the South. They expressed this attitude by openly supporting Andrew Johnson in his battle with the Radicals in late 1865 and 1866 and by demanding, in subsequent years, that Radical Reconstruction be terminated.[37] Their public positions on key Reconstruction issues offer little support to the thesis that Radical Republicans were "the political agents of

33. Tredegar Stock Ledger, 1867–1944; Irene D. Neu, *Erastus Corning, Merchant and Financier, 1794–1872* (Ithaca, N.Y., 1960), pp. 39–43, 49, 52–55, 75; Paul H. Buck, *The Road to Reunion* (Boston, 1937), pp. 180–81; *D.A.B., 11,* 444–45, *20,* 399–400.

34. List of directors of the Tredegar Company, 1867–1947, in "Guide to the Tredegar Company Records," typescript, VSL.

35. Foner, *Business and Slavery,* pp. 248–49, 251, 256–57, 298, 308; Allan Nevins and Milton H. Thomas, eds., *The Diary of George Templeton Strong* (4 vols. New York, 1952), *4,* 548; *D.A.B., 14,* 230–31, *20,* 399–400.

36. Foner, p. 262; George R. Woolfolk, *The Cotton Regency; Northern Merchants and Reconstruction* (New York, 1958), p. 26; Stanley Coben, "Northeastern Business and Radical Reconstruction: A Re-examination," *Mississippi Valley Historical Review, 47* (1959), 73, 76–77, 81–82; Robert P. Sharkey, *Money, Class, and Party; An Economic Study of Civil War and Reconstruction,* The Johns Hopkins University Studies in Historical and Political Science, 77 (1959), 149, 285; Irwin Unger, *The Greenback Era; A Social and Political History of American Finance, 1865–1879* (Princeton, 1964), pp. 48–49, 54–59, 148, 240–41.

37. New York *Herald,* Feb. 22, 23, Aug. 30, 1866; Coben, pp. 87–88; Sharkey, pp. 272–75; *D.A.B., 14,* 230–31.

the masters of capital," who promised "to make easy the road of Northern economic penetration and exploitation in the South." [38]

Anderson met the conciliatory attitudes of the Northern investors more than half way. A month after his pardon, he tersely expressed the attitude that would dominate his future course of action. "The war is over," he wrote a New York businessman; "my efforts have been devoted and are being devoted to a restoration of amity between the people of all the states." [39] Anderson shared the pro-Johnson outlook of his new business associates but he refused to let his enthusiasm for the President divert him from his primary goal—the rebuilding of his business. When news of sweeping Radical Congressional victories in Pennsylvania, Ohio, Indiana, and Iowa reached Richmond in October 1866, Anderson remained calm. "Today we *know*, as we *expected* for some time, that the Northern elections are not going favorably to those who sympathize with us," he wrote a disgruntled Virginia conservative. "But we do not anticipate the extreme results you seem to apprehend and do not intend to let these things affect our nerves, or disturb us in the even tenor of our business ways." [40] Even the advent of military reconstruction failed to discourage the Tredegar president, as he indicated to his London cotton broker in March 1867:

> Business of all kinds is still retarded and enterprise paralysed in the Southern Country, by the unsettled political status of the Southern States. It is our impression, however that these states will reorganize their governments in accordance with the recent acts of Congress, notwithstanding the fact that these acts are universally, in the South, regarded as directly in conflict with the plainest provisions of the Constitution of the United States. But anxiety to put an end to strife, we think, will prevail with our people and we trust they may not be disappointed in the hoped for results of these measures.[41]

38. William B. Hesseltine, *Confederate Leaders in the New South* (Baton Rouge, 1950), p. 136. This is part of the "Beale thesis," set forth in Howard K. Beale, *The Critical Year; A Study of Andrew Johnson and Reconstruction* (New York, 1930), particularly Chapter X. For an excellent critique of this point of view, see Sharkey, pp. 290–311. Unger challenges Sharkey's emphasis on the primacy of economic motivation but shares a number of his conclusions; see his "Business Men and Specie Resumption," *Political Science Quarterly*, *74* (1959), 69, and *The Greenback Era*, p. 7. Sharkey discusses the question of motivation in his review of *The Greenback Era* in the *Journal of American History*, *52* (1965), 380–83.

39. Anderson to George D. Fowle, Nov. 20, 1865, Tredegar Letterbooks.

40. Anderson & Co. to Col. J. M. McCue, Oct. 12, 1866, ibid.

41. Anderson & Co. to Gilliat & Co., March 14, 1867, ibid.

Anderson, like so many other business leaders in the postwar South, worked quietly and consistently for a restoration of sectional harmony. He concentrated his activities in the economic sphere rather than the political arena, but his efforts were no less effective because they were unspectacular.

II

Anderson's willingness to retain large numbers of his former slave workers enabled him to resume operations quickly in 1865 and take advantage of the market for iron provided by Southern railroads. Shortly after Anderson's pardon, William E. Dodge, the Northern copper and iron developer who had purchased large tracts of Anderson's Maryland lands during the war, had accused the Tredegar head of refusing to hire either Negroes or Unionists. In reply, Anderson gave a clear statement of his views on Negro labor: "I have given employment and promise its continuance, to every colored man whilst he remains diligent and attentive and resisted successfully all effort on the part of white men to deprive them of their employment." General Halleck could confirm this statement, he added. "And as to the employment of Union men I have never at any time before, during or since the war, had the slightest regard to politics in giving employment to men." [42]

An incident which occurred in the summer of 1866 demonstrated that Anderson adhered to this policy even after all possibility of Federal confiscation of his works had passed. The superintendent of the Tredegar rolling mill recruited a number of heaters and rollers in Philadelphia in August of that year but the Northerners had some misgivings about coming to the Richmond mill. "We have heard it rumored that these men would not work with colored men," Anderson wrote to Philadelphia immediately after learning of their predilection for segregated employment. "We write now to say that we dont want any men to come here who object to working with a colored man. We Southern men regard Negroes as an inferior race, but we make no distinction of color in employing men and pay all the same wages as all have to live." [43]

His refusal to hire the Northern workers triggered a reaction in his rolling mill superintendent, Henry McCarty. Evidently McCarty objected to Anderson's action and told the owner so in plain terms. The Tredegar head

42. Anderson & Co. to Fowle & Co., Nov. 20, 1865, ibid.

43. Anderson to John H. Bradley, Aug. 11, 1866, ibid.

promptly offered his superintendent the option of either immediate dismissal plus one month's wages or notice that his services would terminate in three months. Anderson also informed him that "my action was not communicated to any negro." [44] McCarty left the Tredegar and the company asked Negro heaters seeking employment in Chattanooga to fill the jobs in the Richmond rolling mill.[45]

As long as Anderson paid the same wages and gave equal opportunity to white and Negro workers, the former slaves would probably not have been overly concerned had they known that the Tredegar senior partner considered their race "inferior." They labored at the works in large numbers after the war, primarily in the rolling mills. Probably some 300 of the 650 workers at the Tredegar in 1870 were Negroes.[46] When Anderson died in 1892, the local Negro newspaper mourned the passing of a man who "was too great to know any prejudice, either on account of race or colour." The paper also quoted a reply Anderson reportedly gave to those who urged him to dismiss his Negro laborers: "Some of these men have been with me ever since I entered business and I shall never turn my back on them." [47]

Wages for skilled workers at the Richmond plant fell almost to the prewar level of $2.50 per day. Anderson paid first class machinists, molders, and blacksmiths $2.50 to $2.75 and pattern makers $3.00 per day in late 1865. Rollers received $2.88 per ton if they paid their own helpers or $1.30 per ton if the company paid the work gang; skilled rollers could earn $150 to $175 per month. Prior to the war, the Tredegar owners had been forced to offer substantially higher wages than their Northern competitors in order to attract skilled labor. In 1865 and 1866, however, Tredegar workers were paid the same wages as artisans with similar skills received north of the Potomac.[48] In addition to their wages, Anderson offered his men a voluntary health plan. The company appointed a physi-

44. Anderson & Co. to Henry McCarty, Aug. 13, 1866, ibid. See also agreement with McCarty, Sept. 11, 1865, Tredegar Contract Books.

45. Anderson & Co. to Gen. G. W. Smith, Aug. 31, 1866, Tredegar Letterbooks; agreement with David Eynon, Nov. 6, 1866, Tredegar Contract Books.

46. Manuscript returns, Census of Manufactures, 1870, Virginia, VSL; Bruce, *Virginia Iron Manufacture*, p. 237.

47. Richmond *Planet*, Sept. 1892, quoted ibid., p. 258.

48. Anderson & Co. to T. Alphonse Jackson, Nov. 8, 1865, to John Round, Sept. 26, 1866, and to J. M. Read and G. W. Derr, Sept. 26, 1866, Tredegar Letterbooks; "History of Wages in the United States from Colonial Times to 1928," *Bulletin of the United States Bureau of Labor Statistics*, No. 499 (Washington, 1929), pp. 276, 311, 319.

cian to call at the works daily and attend to the needs of the laborers and their families. Bills for his services and medicines were paid out of a medical fund, built up by assessing those workers who wished to join the plan 1 per cent of their monthly pay.[49]

Anderson's virtual immunity from strikes failed to outlast the war. The company's molders walked off their jobs in September just as they were rushing through a major railroad bridge order promised for October 1. After the men stayed out for several weeks, Anderson had to meet their demands. "You will doubtless have learned in your business that since the war it is almost impossible to rely on mens [sic] doing as before the war, altho you may pay them their own price & comply with all the unreasonable demands they may make," one of the partners complained to the railroad official whose order had been held up.[50] Southern workers could no longer be threatened with slave labor and the Tredegar operatives gave early evidence that they intended to take advantage of their position.

III

After the war, Tredegar sales quickly fell into the antebellum pattern. Southern railroad officials and bridge builders whose names were very familiar around the Tredegar offices provided the orders that carried the company financially during the immediate postwar period. The mills and foundries turned out iron bridges for railroads in Virginia, North and South Carolina, Georgia, and Tennessee and delivered thousands of kegs of spikes to Southern roads in late 1865 and 1866. By the fall of 1866, Tredegar spike machines were manufacturing one hundred kegs of spikes daily. The newly rebuilt mills began rolling high-quality rail chairs in the summer of 1866 and the car wheel foundry, reconverted from ammunition production, commenced large-scale manufacture at the same time.[51] Although the owners did not immediately undertake to adapt their gun foundries and boring mills to peaceful uses and a lack of capital prevented them from rebuilding their engine department, one of the partners

49. Notice re Dr. David S. Watson, Oct. 4, 1866, Tredegar Letterbooks; Tredegar Corporate Minutes, 1867–1930, p. 24.

50. Anderson & Co. to W. J. Ross, Sept. 28, 1866, Tredegar Letterbooks; contract with Jones & Westlake, July 24, 1866, Tredegar Contract Books.

51. Anderson & Co. to Tanner, Aug. 6, 1866, and to Col. A. Terry, Sept. 29, 1866, Tredegar Letterbooks; agreements for 1865–66, Tredegar Contract Books; entries for 1865–66, Tredegar Rolling Mill Sales Books and Tredegar Foundry Sales Books.

commented in May 1866 that "we were never better satisfied with our facilities for doing work or the quality of our manufactures." [52]

In 1867, Anderson made one final attempt to rebuild his ordnance business. John M. Brooke, Catesby ap R. Jones, and Richard D. Minor, three officers who had helped build the Confederate Bureau of Ordnance and Hydrography, formed a partnership in November 1866 to act as agents for foreign countries seeking ordnance and munitions in the United States. When this trio had difficulty securing orders and began to run short of funds, Minor suggested that Brooke give up his professorship at the Virginia Military Institute and accept a position with Anderson's firm. The Tredegar head offered the job but Brooke and Jones believed such an association might restrict their ability to bid competitively and Brooke therefore declined the position. The three ex-Confederates were never able to make their venture a paying proposition and they broke up their partnership in 1869.[53] Anderson did not receive a single order from this group. The Tredegar's total ordnance production during the postwar years amounted to a single brass 12-pounder howitzer, cast for the Maryland oyster patrol in 1868.[54]

The company managed to complete one project begun during the war with Confederate aid. In the summer of 1866, workers finished the conversion of the Armory rolling mill into a rail manufacturing facility. Soon after, Anderson contracted to roll the rails and manufacture the spikes and tram plates for the Richmond street railway. Production began the next month and the company completed the order, totaling over four hundred tons of rails, early in 1867.[55] In 1868, Anderson received a major contract to supply the Chesapeake and Ohio Railroad with the rails and bridgework for the entire line.[56] "We are full of work and have orders to employ the Rail Mill *for three years*," Anderson reported with obvious pleasure to a Northern stockholder in 1869.[57] These orders required a

52. Anderson & Co. to E. W. Cole, May 2, 1866, and to William Gordon, July 14, 1866, Tredegar Letterbooks. For a detailed description of Tredegar equipment as of Jan. 1, 1867, see Richmond City Hustings Court, Deed Book No. 84A, pp. 253–58, City Hall, Richmond, Va.

53. Jones to Minor, Nov. 10, 1866, Brooke to Minor, May 1, 13, June 10, July 5, 31, 1867, July 31, 1869, Minor to Anderson, May 10, 1867, Anderson to Minor, May 18, 1867, and Jones to Minor, June 11, 25, Aug. 20, 1867, Feb. 28, 1868, Aug. 17, 1869, Minor Papers, VHS.

54. Entry for Sept. 1868, Tredegar Foundry Sales Books.

55. Contracts dated Aug. 13, Sept. 11, 1866, Tredegar Contract Books; entries for June, Sept., Dec., 1866, Jan., Feb., 1867, Tredegar Foundry Sales Books; Anderson & Co. to Maj. R. H. Temple, Sept. 20, 1866, Tredegar Letterbooks.

56. Williams, *Maury*, p. 647.

57. Anderson to Joel Parker, Nov. 25, 1869, Dover Company Records, UVA.

further heavy capital investment in the Tredegar's rolling mill facilities during the late 1860s.[58]

To secure orders in the South, Anderson offered to meet the prices of any and all competitors.[59] Rates were competitive with those of Northern manufacturers but were considerably above prewar levels. The price of ordinary sizes of bar iron had jumped from 3 cents a pound to 5½ cents per pound and spikes had risen from 3¾ cents to 6½ cents per pound.[60] One of the partners expressed the hope in June 1866 that new tariff duties would give iron prices an additional boost.[61] During the immediate post-war period, the company often took jobs at prices near cost. "These are close figures and leave but little profit for the manufacturers," a member of the firm told a Georgia customer in May 1866. But he accepted the order because "we are anxious to supply all the wants of the South in our line." [62] The next month, Anderson arranged with a number of Southern railroads for a through freight rate for Tredegar products of 2½ cents per ton per mile. This rate, he believed, gave him an advantage over all other competitors in the Southern market. It unquestionably eased the pressure on the Tredegar's profit margin.[63]

The Tredegar owners, after flirting with the idea of attempting to manufacture their own pig iron, also returned to their former sources of raw materials. During the months following the restoration of the works to Anderson and Company, Tredegar canal boats floated the considerable amount of metal still at the furnaces to Richmond and several stacks went back into blast. But in less than a year, the partners began closing down their furnace operations and resumed large-scale purchases of cheaper Northern anthracite pig iron. The Dover and Tuckahoe pits supplied the company with coal.[64]

58. Tredegar Corporate Minutes, 1867–1930, p. 27.

59. Anderson & Co. to R. M. Dunlop, Oct. 26, 1865, to S. L. Fremont, Dec. 9, 1865, July 26, 1866, to Atkinson & Shepperson, Feb. 1, 1866, to Col. R. C. McCalla, Aug. 21, 1866, and to W. J. Ross, Aug. 29, 1866, Tredegar Letterbooks.

60. Tredegar Rolling Mill Sales Books.

61. Anderson & Co. to Offutt & McAnerney, June 1, 1866, Tredegar Letterbooks.

62. Anderson & Co. to T. E. Timmons, May 1, 1866, ibid.

63. Anderson & Co. to R. D. Owen, June 6, 1866, to J. W. Goodman, June 19, 1866, and to William Johnston, Oct. 13, 1866, ibid.

64. Anderson & Co. to Glasgow, Oct. 17, 18, 30, 1865, April 29, May 18, 1866, to William T. Patton, Oct. 24, 30, Dec. 29, 1865, Jan. 31, Feb. 7, 22, March 2, April 9, 21, 1866, and to

IV

The Tredegar made a swift and highly profitable transition back to peacetime production. Despite several slack months during early 1866, Anderson and his associates netted a handsome return on their first eighteen months of operation following the close of the war. "In our business . . . the demand continues brisk—particularly from our railroads, which, though torn up again & again during the war, are still, for the most part, financially sound and can look forward to a promising future," Archer Anderson wrote in the summer of 1866.[65] Foundry and rolling mill sales from July 1865 through December 1866 totaled $933,552 and profits amounted to $108,971.[66]

Six years of expansion and unparalleled prosperity followed the organization of the Tredegar Company early in 1867. The directors sank $75,000 into the construction of new trains of rolls for the rail and chair mills in 1867 and authorized the expenditure of an additional $25,000 on a puddle mill the next year. A completely equipped railroad car shop rose at the charred site of the old locomotive works, and in 1872 the directors were considering further new construction, including a horseshoe mill.[67] By 1873, the Tredegar had more than twice its prewar capacity in every department and employment had climbed to over one thousand men, a figure exceeding the highest antebellum total.[68]

In a prospectus drawn up in 1866 to publicize the proposed Tredegar corporation, Anderson estimated that his foundries and rolling mills could return an annual profit of $400,000.[69] Six years later, he proved that this prediction was not entirely the fantasy of an overzealous promoter. In

---

Charles Jackson, Jr., June 20, 1866, ibid.; entries for March, June, Dec., 1866, Tredegar Journals.

65. Anderson & Co. to Gilliat & Co., Aug. 25, 1866, Tredegar Letterbooks.

66. Tredegar Inventory Book.

67. Tredegar Corporate Minutes, 1867–1930, pp. 27–29, 31, 49. The car shop had a productive capacity of 2,000 freight cars per year; see *Richmond City Directory, 1873–74* (Richmond, 1873), p. xii.

68. Ibid., pp. xii–xiii. The rolling mill department, for example, in 1860 had 11 heating furnaces, 18 puddling furnaces, and 5 trains of rolls, capable of producing between 12,000 and 14,000 tons of iron per year; in 1873, these figures had jumped to 20 heating furnaces, 25 puddling furnaces, and 5 trains of rolls and a three-high forge train, with an annual productive capacity of 30,000 tons.

69. "Corporate Holdings, 1866," manuscript Tredegar volume, p. 15.

1867, the company earned a profit of $136,515 and declared a 10 per cent dividend. The capital stock continued to earn a 10 per cent return during the next three years and on January 11, 1873, the directors voted a 12 per cent dividend out of the previous year's profits of $417,699.[70]

There was one catch to these phenomenal profits of 1872, however. The dividend was payable in New York and Oswego Midland Railroad second mortgage bonds at 80 per cent of par. The Tredegar Company had the misfortune in 1871 and 1872 to contract to supply the iron work for 1670 box cars for that ill-fated line, described by one railroad historian as "the most ambitious and, in some respects, the most tragic of all the publicly subsidized lines" of New York.[71] This contract and similar agreements with the Chesapeake and Ohio, the New Jersey Midland, and the Montclair Railroad proved disastrous for the Richmond corporation. During the depression following the panic of 1873, all of these lines went bankrupt, paced by the New York and Oswego Midland in September 1873, four months after its opening.[72]

The failure of these roads threw the Tredegar into receivership in 1876, following an unsuccessful attempt by the company to float a $1,200,000 bond issue. Anderson acted as the receiver until September 1879, when the board announced the successful funding of the company's debt through the issue of $1,000,000 in 4 per cent twenty-year bonds.[73]

"While the panic of 1873 brought utter ruin upon many of the Iron Masters of this Country . . . it is some consolation to us that we have our works left," Anderson told the stockholders in 1880.[74] Yet in many ways, the Tredegar works never recovered from the depression. Iron gave way to steel in the 1870s and 1880s but the Tredegar Company, shackled with a sizable debt, lacked the capital needed to make this transition. Richmond soon yielded its position as the industrial capital of the South to the richly endowed Birmingham area. Before Anderson died in 1892, he had rebuilt his enterprise into a profitable operation, but the works now produced primarily for the local market. The depression of 1873, not the Civil War, stunted the growth of the South's largest industrial plant.

70. Tredegar Corporate Minutes, 1867–1930, pp. 25, 33, 39, 41, 52.

71. Ibid., pp. 47, 50; Harry H. Pierce, *Railroads of New York: A Study of Government Aid, 1826–1875* (Cambridge, Mass., 1953), pp. 84–85.

72. Tredegar Corporate Minutes, 1867–1930, pp. 54–57; Pierce, p. 85.

73. Tredegar Corporate Minutes, 1867–1930, pp. 54, 56, 57, 63, 72, 74.

74. Ibid., p. 73.

The Tredegar Company is still in existence, operating a small rolling mill at a new site in Chesterfield County, near Richmond. The old plant, although gutted by fire in 1952, remains impressive evidence that the industrial economy of the South once revolved around a few acres of land in the capital of the Confederacy.

Appendix

Types of Ordnance Cast at the Tredegar Iron Works, 1861-1865

I. *Field Artillery*

A. *Smoothbores*

	Bore diameter (inches)	Material
U.S. models of 1841–44		
6-pdr. gun	3.67	bronze; iron
12-pdr. gun	4.62	bronze
12-pdr. howitzer	4.62	bronze; iron
24-pdr. howitzer	5.82	bronze; iron
12-pdr. mountain howitzer	4.62	bronze
U.S. model 1857		
12-pdr. Napoleon	4.62	bronze
12-pdr. Napoleon, banded	4.62	iron
B. *Rifles*		
4-pdr.	3.35	iron
6-pdr.	3.00	bronze; iron
6-pdr., banded	3.00	iron
3-inch ordnance rifle	3.00	wrought iron
10-pdr. Parrott	3.00	iron
20-pdr. Parrott	3.67	"
12-pdr. James	3.67	"
24-pdr. James	4.62	"
Mountain rifle	2.25	bronze

II. *Siege and Garrison Artillery*

	Bore diameter (inches)	Material
18-pdr. gun	5.30	iron
24-pdr. gun	5.82	"
24-pdr. gun, rifled	4.62	"
30-pdr. Parrott	4.20	"
8-inch gun, banded	8.00	"
8-inch howitzer	8.00	"
8-inch howitzer, rifled	4.62	"
8-inch mortar	8.00	"
12-pdr. coehorn mortar	4.62	"
24-pdr. coehorn mortar	5.82	"

III. *Seacoast Artillery*

A. *Smoothbores*

	Bore diameter (inches)	Material
32-pdr. gun	6.40	iron
42-pdr. gun	7.00	"
8-inch columbiad	8.00	"
10-inch columbiad	10.00	"
8-inch mortar	8.00	"
10-inch mortar	10.00	"

B. *Rifles*

	Bore diameter (inches)	Material
8-inch columbiad	5.82	iron
10-inch columbiad	6.40	"
32-pdr. gun, rifled	6.40	"
7-inch Army Brooke rifle	7.00	"
8-inch Army Brooke rifle	8.00	"

IV. *Naval Ordnance*

A. *Smoothbores*

	Bore diameter (inches)	Material
12-pdr. howitzer	4.62	bronze
24-pdr. howitzer	5.82	"
32-pdr. gun	6.40	iron
9-inch Dahlgren gun	9.00	"
10-inch gun, banded	10.00	"
11-inch gun, banded	11.00	"

B. *Rifles*

	Bore diameter (inches)	Material
6-pdr.		iron (?)
12-pdr.		bronze
32-pdr. gun, rifled	6.40	iron
6.40-inch Brooke	6.40	"
7-inch Brooke	7.00	"
8-inch Brooke	8.00	"

Bibliographical Essay

Manuscript Collections

The Tredegar Company Records, housed at the Virginia State Library in Richmond, were the major source for this study. These records, covering the history of the company from 1837 to 1952, contain a total of 1,118 volumes and approximately 557,400 separate items. In size, scope, and completeness, the Tredegar papers dwarf all other collections of Confederate business manuscripts.

Twenty-four letterbooks containing some 15,000 letterpress copies of correspondence sent by J. R. Anderson and Company are probably the most important Tredegar manuscripts dealing with the years 1859–67. These letterbooks were read in their entirety. Several gaps exist, the most serious running from December 1861 to November 1862, but these volumes still provide an almost complete account of the company's manifold activities during the Civil War era. Unfortunately, incoming correspondence is not full until 1872.

Production and sales can be closely traced through the following volumes: Contract Books, 1859–65, 1865–66; Order Book, 1861–62; Gun Foundry Book, 1861–65; Foundry Sales Books, 1854–60, 1860–67, 1865–72; and Rolling Mill Sales Books, 1858–65, 1865–66. These records give complete details of Tredegar output and make it possible to determine the prices, allocation, and often the destination of Tredegar products.

Financial records are virtually intact and include the complete Journals, Ledgers, and Cash Books. An Inventory Book, 1860–70, contains the company's annual profit and loss statements and gives details of production costs.

Records dealing with labor, furnaces, and coal mining are more fragmentary but nevertheless yield abundant information about these phases of the Tredegar operation. A Payroll Ledger, 1863–64, breaks down the free and slave labor force in the foundry, gun mill, machine, finishing, boiler, patternmaking, blacksmith, and carpentry departments and gives both free wage rates and overtime compensation for slaves. Volumes entitled "Letters to J. R. Anderson & Co., 1863, re: Furnaces" (Tredegar Letters re Furnaces), and "Negroes and Rations at Catawba, 1863," and a letterpress copybook kept by chief furnace agent Francis T. Glasgow, July 7, 1856–December 17, 1866 (Tredegar Furnace Letterbook), contain much of the company's incoming furnace correspondence, list free and slave labor at the various stacks, and give some production figures. The latter information is completely summarized in a Pig Iron Receipt Book, 1861–64, which reveals the full extent of the company's pig metal and coal deficiencies.

Other records providing information on Tredegar activities during the period under investigation include two scrapbooks, "Letters, Clippings, etc., Involving the Tredegar Company," and "Deeds, Agreements, etc., Involving the Tredegar Company," and a detailed prospectus on the new Tredegar corporation entitled "Corporate Holdings, 1866." The Corporate Minutes, 1867–1930, and a Stock Ledger, 1867–1944, give a concise summary of the company's history following its incorporation and specify the amount of Northern capital flowing south to the

Tredegar works. An amorphous group of odds and ends listed as Miscellaneous Unbound Records did not repay the time spent in investigation. Among a small group of 105 supplementary items added to the Tredegar Records in 1963 (Supplementary Tredegar Records) are several valuable letters on ordnance profits. A separate collection of Anderson Family Papers at the Virginia State Library is extremely thin on the antebellum and Civil War periods.

Other State Library holdings containing material relevant to this study include the Robert E. Lee–Jefferson Davis Correspondence, 1862–65, the Virginia Executive Papers, the manuscript Census of Manufactures, Virginia, for 1850, 1860, and 1870, microfilm copies of the Richmond City Hustings Court Deed Books, the records of the United States District Court at Richmond, the Richmond City Council Minute Books, and the Personal Property Tax Rolls for Richmond and the various counties in which Tredegar operations were conducted.

Kenneth W. Munden and Henry P. Beers, *Guide to Federal Archives Relating to the Civil War* (Washington, 1962), is a superb directory to the Civil War records of the United States government, now housed primarily at the National Archives. At this writing, the companion volume, *Guide to the Archives of the Government of the Confederate States of America,* is still being compiled. Until it is published, Elizabeth Bethel, *Preliminary Inventory of the War Department Collection of Confederate Records* (Record Group 109) (Washington, 1957), remains the best guide to the National Archives' rich collection of Confederate manuscripts.

Extensive National Archives material pertaining to prewar Tredegar ordnance production for the Federal government is found in the Records of the Office, Chief of Ordnance, Record Group 156, and Records of the Bureau of Ordnance (U.S.N.), Record Group 74. Especially valuable are Letters Sent, Ordnance Office, Letters from the War Department, Ordnance Office, and Statement of Contracts, Ordnance Department, in Record Group 156, and Letters to Foundries, Letters Received from Foundries, Reports from and Inspections at Foundries, and Record of Contracts ("Contract Ledger A"), in Record Group 74.

Record Group 109, the War Department Collection of Confederate Records, provides a wealth of information on Confederate economic activity, including the Tredegar's operations. Correspondence contained in Letters Received, Secretary of War, often fills in key gaps resulting from missing volumes in the Tredegar Letterbooks. This is particularly true for 1862. The War Department's replies to Anderson and Company's queries and complaints are found in Letters Sent, Secretary of War. This correspondence and additional material (especially the company's government contracts) contained in the Confederate Citizens File under "Joseph R. Anderson & Company" reveal in detail the relationship between the government and the South's largest manufacturer.

Other collections in Record Group 109 found to contain Tredegar material include Letters and Telegrams Sent, Engineer Department, Letters and Telegrams Sent, Quartermaster Department, and Letters and Telegrams Sent, Army of Northern Virginia, 1862–1864. The Field and Staff Officers File ("Carded" Records Showing Military Service, 1861–65), contains correspondence dealing with J. R. Anderson's military service.

The Confederates evidently destroyed most of the Ordnance Department, Niter and Mining Bureau, and Navy Department archives following the evacuation of Richmond but fragmentary survivals, now in Record Group 109, throw some light on the Tredegar's wartime activities. These include the records of the Richmond Arsenal (Ordnance Depot), particularly Letters Sent, 1862–65, and Letters Received, 1864–65, and Office of Ordnance and Hydrography, Letters Sent, 1864–65. The slim collection of Niter and Mining Bureau materials, consisting of one box of reports and miscellaneous papers, contained nothing of value. In the Naval Records Collection, Record Group 45, Subject File, Confederate States Navy, Boxes 117, 118, 130, 523, and 524, are scattered letters and bills of sale and lading concerning Tredegar naval production.

Finally, in the National Archives, Record Group 94, Records of the Adjutant General's Office, contains two collections of material significant for this study: details of the Tredegar owner's early life and education are revealed in his West Point application papers, filed under Joseph Reid Anderson, 121–1832, in Military Academy Applications; the Amnesty Papers, Virginia, have the pardon applications of Anderson and his partners, supporting correspondence, and a record of Presidential action.

In addition to the Virginia State Library's holdings, there are two important collections of Anderson manuscripts: the Anderson Family Papers, University of Virginia Library, and the Francis T. Anderson Papers, Duke University Library. The J. R. Anderson letters in these collections, written primarily to his brother Francis, reveal personal opinions and attitudes which rarely emerge in his business correspondence. The Robert A. Brock Papers at the Huntington Library have ninety pieces of largely routine Anderson correspondence, most of which deal with the Civil War years. A small collection of Glasgow Family Papers at the Washington and Lee University Library contains several important Anderson letters. As far as I can ascertain, materials for a biography of Anderson do not exist outside of these rather fragmentary survivals and the generally impersonal Tredegar Records.

Collections in several Southern depositories offer some significant Tredegar information. The Account Book, 1861–63, of Edward R. Archer, the Tredegar foundry superintendent, is in the Virginia Historical Society, Richmond. This small but important volume fills in gaps existing in the Tredegar Gun Foundry Book for 1861. The papers of Confederate officers who dealt with Anderson and Company during the war provide insight into the way the military viewed the firm's operations. Particularly helpful were the manuscripts of William Nelson Pendleton, Lee's Chief of Artillery. The Pendleton Papers are deposited in the Southern Historical Collection at the University of North Carolina Library and in the Duke University Library. Other Confederate manuscripts in the Southern Historical Collection which proved useful were the papers of Edward Porter Alexander, John Mercer Brooke, W. LeRoy Broun, and George Washington Rains. The Dover Company Records, chronicling the misfortunes of the Northern-backed corporation which attempted to operate the Dover coal mines after the war, are in the University of Virginia Library.

Government Publications and Official Documents

For any study dealing with the Civil War, the *War of the Rebellion: A Compilation of the Official Records of the Union and Confederate Armies* (128 vols. Washington, 1880–1901), and the *Official Records of the Union and Confederate Navies in the War of the Rebellion* (31 vols. Washington, 1894–1927), are indispensable collections. Particularly valuable for information on the economic history of the Confederacy are Series IV of the *O.R.* and Series II of the *O.R.N.* Volume two of *The Dictionary of American Naval Fighting Ships* (Washington, 1963), updates and considerably amplifies the information on Confederate vessels given in *O.R.N.*, Ser. II, *1.* Illuminating comparative data on Federal ordnance production is contained in two Congressional publications: *Report of the Joint Committee on the Conduct of the War, 1865,* 39th Cong. 2d sess. (3 vols. Washington, 1865), *2,* and House of Representatives, *Executive Documents,* Document No. 99, 40 Cong., 2d sess. (Washington, 1868). Muster rolls revealing the Tredegar Battalion's military service are found in "Compiled Service Records of Confederate Soldiers who Served in Organizations from the State of Virginia," *National Archives Microfilm Publications,* No. 324 (Washington, 1961).

Three census volumes furnish a detailed picture of the industrial position of the South vis-à-vis the North in the decades surrounding the Civil War: J. D. B. DeBow, *Compendium of the Seventh Census of the United States* (Washington, 1854), *Eighth Census of the United States, Manufactures* (Washington, 1865), and *Ninth Census of the United States,* vol. 3, *Wealth and Industry* (Washington, 1872). *The United States on the Eve of the Civil War* (Washington, 1964), conveniently summarizes some descriptive and statistical data from the 1860 census. Manuscript schedules for Henrico County, Virginia, in "Federal Population Censuses, 1840–1880," *National Archives Microfilm Publications,* No. 55–7 (Washington, 1955), show the Tredegar's dependence on Northern and foreign-born labor and list the slaves owned personally by Anderson and his associates.

Among publications dealing with the official actions of the Confederate government, the *Journal of the Congress of the Confederate States of America,* Sen. Doc. No. 234, 58th Cong. 2d sess. (7 vols. Washington, 1904–05), and the *Proceedings of the . . . Confederate Congress,* published as *Southern Historical Society Papers, 44–52* (1923–59), provide information on Congressional attitudes toward industry and economic problems. The legislative results are given in James M. Matthews, ed., *Statutes at Large of the Provisional Government of the Confederate States of America . . .* (Richmond, 1864), Matthews, ed., *Public Laws of the Confederate States of America . . .* (5 vols. Richmond, 1862–64), and Charles W. Ramsdell, ed., *Laws and Joint Resolutions of the Last Session of the Confederate Congress . . .* (Durham, 1941). James D. Richardson, ed., *Messages and Papers of the Confederacy* (2 vols. Nashville, 1905), includes Presidential messages, vetoes, and other executive actions touching on economic matters.

Virginia state publications provide additional information on the Tredegar. *Documents of the House of Delegates (Extra Session) January–April, 1861,* Documents No. 1, 30 (Richmond, 1861), and *Documents of the Convention, 1861,*

Documents 31, 40, 43 (Richmond, 1861), cover Anderson and Company's contract to outfit the State Armory. The *Journals of the House of Delegates* for 1852, 1853–54, and 1857–58, trace Anderson's legislative career. Legislation dealing with the Tredegar can be found in *Acts of the General Assembly* for 1837, 1838, 1859–60, and 1865–66. The *Calendar of Virginia State Papers, 1652–1869* (11 vols. Richmond, 1875–93), *11*, also contains some important correspondence between the company and the state.

Memoirs and Diaries

Unfortunately, none of the Tredegar owners ever, to my knowledge, wrote any account of the company's wartime experiences. Among the memoirs and diaries found useful for this study were Thomas Cooper De Leon, *Four Years in Rebel Capitals* (Mobile, 1892), E. P. Alexander, *Military Memoirs of a Confederate* (New York, 1907), Daniel Harvey Hill, *Bethel to Sharpsburg* (2 vols. Raleigh, 1926), Susan P. Lee, ed., *The Memoirs of William Nelson Pendleton* (Philadelphia, 1893), and C. G. Chamberlayne, ed., *Ham Chamberlayne—Virginian* (Richmond, 1932). John B. Jones, *A Rebel War Clerk's Diary*, Howard Swiggett, ed. (2 vols. New York, 1935), contains numerous references to Anderson and the Tredegar works but must be used cautiously because the author evidently made additions after the war. Frank Vandiver, ed., *The Civil War Diary of General Josiah Gorgas* (University, Ala., 1947), and Robert G. H. Kean, *Inside the Confederate Government*, Edward Younger, ed. (New York, 1957), proved disappointing.

Clarence C. Buel and Robert U. Johnson, eds., *Battles and Leaders of the Civil War* (4 vols. New York, 1887), contains recollections of principles on both sides involved in key engagements. The *Southern Historical Society Papers*, published at Richmond between 1876 and 1959, are a rich mine of Confederate memoirs. Articles especially relevant to the Tredegar's history include Josiah Gorgas, "Notes on the Ordnance Department of the Confederate Government," *12* (1884), 67–94; W. LeRoy Broun, "The Red Artillery; Confederate Ordnance During the War," *26* (1898), 365–76; and J. W. Mallet, "Work of the Ordnance Bureau of the War Department of the Confederate States, 1861–5," *37* (1909), 1–20.

Newspapers and Periodicals

Newspapers are an extremely valuable source of information on the economic life of the Confederate South. The four Richmond dailies that published regularly during this period, the *Dispatch*, the *Enquirer*, the *Examiner*, and the *Whig*, all contain Tredegar advertisements and news stories and articles concerning the works. *DeBow's Review*, the leading Southern economic, industrial, and business journal during the Civil War era, is strangely silent on the Tredegar. *DeBow's* does, however, record Anderson's activities as a delegate to the Southern commercial conventions before the war.

General Histories, Monographs, and Articles

Mary Elizabeth Massey, "The Confederate States of America: The Homefront," in Arthur S. Link and Rembert W. Patrick, eds., *Writing Southern History; Essays in*

Historiography in Honor of Fletcher M. Green (Baton Rouge, 1965), is an excellent guide to the scholarly literature dealing with economic and social conditions behind the lines. There is no adequate study of the Southern economy during the war. The standard work on Confederate economic conditions, John C. Schwab, *The Confederate States of America; A Financial and Industrial History of the South During the Civil War* (New York, 1901), is considerably fuller on finances than on industry. A far more penetrating examination of the South's wartime economy is Charles W. Ramsdell, *Behind the Lines in the Southern Confederacy* (Baton Rouge, 1944). Ramsdell concludes that "the greatest single weakness of the Confederacy . . . was in . . . [the] matter of finances," but also gives close and insightful treatment to Confederate industrial affairs. William Garrott Brown, *The Lower South in American History* (New York, 1902), calls "the industrial backwardness of the South . . . the most serious of its disadvantages," but devotes most of his chapter on Confederate economic problems to financial difficulties. Good but brief discussions of Southern war resources are found in Charles H. Wesley, *The Collapse of the Confederacy* (Washington, 1937), and Charles P. Roland, *The Confederacy* (Chicago, 1960). The two best general histories of the Confederate South, E. Merton Coulter, *The Confederate States of America, 1861–1865* (Baton Rouge, 1950), and Clement Eaton, *A History of the Southern Confederacy* (New York, 1954), offer more detailed general introductions to the Southern industrial background. *Southern Economic History*, vols. 5 and 6 in Julian A. C. Chandler, et al., eds., *The South in the Building of the Nation* (12 vols. Richmond, 1909), is very thin on the Confederacy. An excellent collection of scholarly articles on economic developments in both the North and the South during the war is Ralph Andreano, ed., *The Economic Impact of the Civil War* (Cambridge, Mass., 1962). Albert D. Kirwan, ed., *The Confederacy* (New York, 1959), is a superb compilation of documentary material dealing with the Confederate homefront.

A thorough history of the Southern iron industry during the nineteenth century is badly needed. The best study of the American iron industry during this period, Peter Temin, *Iron and Steel in Nineteenth-Century America* (Cambridge, Mass., 1964), takes only an occasional glance at developments south of the Potomac. Victor S. Clark, *History of Manufactures in the United States* (3 vols. New York, 1929), is excellent on postwar industrial growth in the South but is weak on antebellum and wartime industrialization. The historical section in H. H. Clapham, et al., *The Iron and Steel Industries of the South* (University, Ala., 1953), is very brief. At present, the history of Southern heavy manufacturing during the antebellum period can be only partially pieced together from a number of monographs and articles. Lester J. Cappon, "History of the Southern Iron Industry to the Close of the Civil War" (unpublished Ph.D. dissertation, Harvard University, 1928) is a good general introduction to the subject. Two articles drawn from this study, "Trend of the Southern Iron Industry Under the Plantation System," *Journal of Economic and Business History, 2* (1930), 353–81, and "Iron-Making—A Forgotten Industry of North Carolina," *North Carolina Historical Review, 9* (1932), 331–48, concentrate on the prewar blast furnace industry in Virginia,

Kentucky, Tennessee, and North Carolina. Samuel S. Bradford, "The Ante-Bellum Charcoal Iron Industry of Virginia" (unpublished Ph.D. dissertation, Columbia University, 1958), and his article, "The Negro Ironworker in Ante Bellum Virginia," *Journal of Southern History, 25* (1959), 194–206, provide a detailed account of the manufacture of charcoal pig iron in the Old Dominion. Ethel M. Armes, *The Story of Coal and Iron in Alabama* (Birmingham, 1910), and two articles by Ernest M. Lander, Jr., in the *Journal of Southern History,* "The Iron Industry in Ante-Bellum South Carolina," *20* (1954), 337–55, and "Charleston: Manufacturing Center of the Old South," *26* (1960), 330–51, trace the development of the iron and manufacturing resources in two other Southern states. A valuable listing of American iron establishments on the eve of the Civil War is J. P. Lesley, *The Iron Manufacturer's Guide to the Furnaces, Forges, and Rolling Mills of the United States* (New York, 1859). Volume one of Fritz Redlich, *History of American Business Leaders: A Series of Studies* (2 vols. Ann Arbor, Mich., 1940), takes a detailed look at the entrepreneurs who organized the iron industry in both the North and the South. The economic, social, and political problems facing antebellum Southern manufacturers are discussed in several illuminating chapters of Eugene D. Genovese, *The Political Economy of Slavery* (New York, 1965).

Kathleen Bruce, *Virginia Iron Manufacture in the Slave Era* (New York, 1930), is the only work of any substance dealing with Anderson and the Tredegar works during the antebellum and Civil War years. Her "Economic Factors in the Manufacture of Confederate Ordnance," *Army Ordnance, 6* (1925–26), 166–73, summarizes many of the points elaborated in the longer study. Anne Hobson Freeman, "A Cool Head in a Warm Climate," *Virginia Cavalcade, 12* (Winter 1962–63), 10–14, gives some information on Anderson's earlier life.

Among studies dealing with Confederate industry, Frank E. Vandiver, *Ploughshares into Swords: Josiah Gorgas and Confederate Ordnance* (Austin, Texas, 1952), is a superb account of the manifold activities of Gorgas and his department but gives little attention to the role of private manufacturers. Naval ordnance production and ship construction are well covered in William N. Still, Jr., "The Construction and Fitting Out of Ironclad Vessels-of-War Within the Confederacy" (unpublished Ph.D. dissertation, University of Alabama, 1964), in two articles by the same author, "Selma and the Confederate States Navy," *Alabama Review, 15* (1962), 19–37, and "Facilities for the Construction of War Vessels in the Confederacy," *Journal of Southern History, 31* (1965), 285–304, and in Ralph W. Donnelly, "The Charlotte, North Carolina, Navy Yard, C.S.N.," *Civil War History, 5* (1959), 72–79. Frank E. Vandiver, "The Shelby Iron Company in the Civil War: A Study of a Confederate Industry," *Alabama Review, 1* (1948), 12–26, 111–27, 203–17, and Joyce Jackson, "History of the Shelby Iron Company, 1862–1868" (unpublished M.A. thesis, University of Alabama, 1948), offer the opportunity to compare the Tredegar's experiences with those of a smaller manufacturing plant in the iron-rich Alabama region. Unfortunately, the two histories of the Confederate capital during the war, Alfred H. Bill, *The Beleaguered City; Richmond, 1861–1865* (New York, 1946), and Clifford Dowdey, *Experiment in Rebellion* (New York,

1946), contain only superficial accounts of Richmond's industrial life. Diffee W. Standard, *Columbus, Georgia, in the Confederacy; The Social and Industrial Life of the Chattahoochee River Port* (New York, 1954), Florence F. Corley, *Confederate City: Augusta, Georgia, 1860–1865* (Columbia, S.C., 1960), and George W. Rains, *History of the Confederate Powder Works* (Newburgh, N.Y., 1882), trace the economic history of two important manufacturing centers in Georgia. William A. Albaugh, III, and Edward N. Simmons, *Confederate Arms* (Harrisburg, Pa., 1957), has a valuable appendix listing Southern ordnance and arms manufacturers. The history of Confederate railroading receives excellent coverage in Robert C. Black, III, *The Railroads of the Confederacy* (Chapel Hill, 1952), George E. Turner, *Victory Rode the Rails: The Strategic Place of the Railroads in the Civil War* (Indianapolis, 1953), and Angus James Johnston, II, *Virginia Railroads in the Civil War* (Chapel Hill, 1961).

Much remains to be done concerning the relationship between the Confederate government and private enterprise. By far the ablest and most suggestive study on this subject is Lester J. Cappon, "Government and Private Industry in the Southern Confederacy," in *Humanistic Studies in Honor of John Calvin Metcalf,* University of Virginia Studies, *1* (1941), 151–89. Also pertinent are two articles by Charles W. Ramsdell, "The Control of Manufacturing by the Confederate Government," *Mississippi Valley Historical Review, 8* (1921–22), 231–49, and "The Confederate Government and the Railroads," *American Historical Review, 22* (1917), 794–810. Wilfred B. Yearns, *The Confederate Congress* (Athens, Ga., 1960), contains an illuminating chapter on the government's management of economic affairs and Richard C. Todd, *Confederate Finance* (Athens, Ga., 1954), is an excellent study of a difficult subject.

The broad problem of whether the Civil War retarded American industrial growth lies outside the purview of a study of this scope. The Tredegar's wartime expansion and rapid peacetime rehabilitation would seem to indicate, however, that the statistical affirmative given by Thomas C. Cochran to the question "Did the Civil War Retard Industrialization?" *Mississippi Valley Historical Review, 48* (1961–62), 197–210, needs closer examination. For criticisms of Cochran's approach, see Stephen Salsbury, "The Effect of the Civil War on American Industrial Development," in Andreano, ed., *The Economic Impact of the American Civil War,* and Pershing Vartanian, "The Cochran Thesis: A Critique in Statistical Analysis," *Journal of American History, 51* (1964), 77–89. Scholars participating in a recent conference on the economic impact of the Civil War tended to support the position that the war did not have a decisive influence one way or the other on American industrial growth; see David T. Gilchrist and W. David Lewis, eds., *Economic Change in the Civil War Era* (Greenville, Del., 1965).

Index

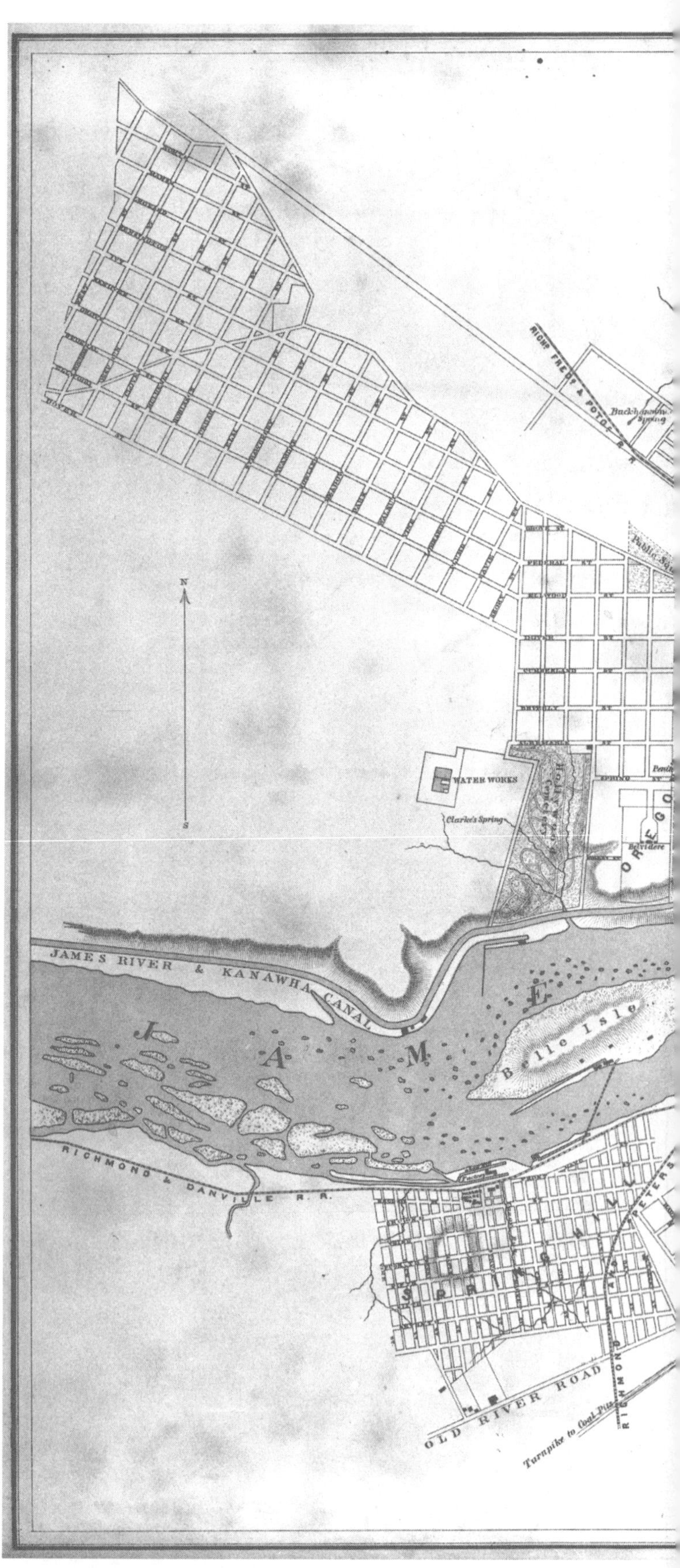

The City of Richmond in 1864. The Tredegar (misspelled "Tredigar") works are located between the James River and the Kanawha Canal, just northeast of Belle Isle.